PRAISE FOR TED BARRIS'S BESTSELLING BOOKS

Dam Busters: Canadian Airmen and the Secret Raid against Nazi Germany

"Ted Barris has written an exceptional tribute to one of the most audacious, and perhaps until now, underappreciated combat actions of the Second World War. The RAF Bomber Command raid by 617 Squadron was a marvel of technological ingenuity and a supreme test of human resolve, courage, and determination. Canadian airmen factored proudly and significantly in this daring attack. Exceptionally well-researched and balanced between the technological challenges and the stellar courage and innovativeness of the participants, this book is a definite must-read. Highly recommended."
—LIEUTENANT-COLONEL (RET'D) DAVID L. BASHOW, OMM, CD, author of *No Prouder Place: Canadians and the Bomber Command Experience, 1939–1945*; editor-in-chief of the *Canadian Military Journal*; and associate professor of history at the Royal Military College of Canada

Juno: Canadians at D-Day, June 6, 1944

"A compelling tale that never loses either the pace of the remarkable story or the broad sweep of the larger picture of the invasion. *Juno* is a remarkable book that should be required reading in every Canadian school." —*National Post*

"A book that's as full of tension as any novel. Even, one might say, as any Hollywood war movie. Read this book. More importantly, make your kids read this book." —*Edmonton Journal*

"His crisp writing style paints a poignant word picture. This is history from the sharp end. Barris's strength is in highlighting the stories of individuals. It is an effective means to present the experience of battle."
—*International Journal*, Canadian Institute of International Affairs

ABOUT THE AUTHOR

TED BARRIS is an award-winning journalist, author, and broadcaster. He regularly writes in the national media and has hosted many CBC Radio network programs and shows on TV Ontario. His eighteen best-selling non-fiction books include *Juno, Behind the Glory, Deadlock in Korea, Victory at Vimy,* and *Breaking the Silence.* His book *The Great Escape: A Canadian Story* won the 2014 Libris Non-Fiction Book of the Year Award. In 2018, the RCAF Association awarded *Dam Busters* the NORAD Trophy for "significant and unequalled contribution to Air Force traditions, history, and heritage." His latest book, *Rush to Danger: Medics in the Line of Fire*, will be published in August 2019.

ALSO BY TED BARRIS

MILITARY HISTORY

Behind the Glory: Canada's Role in the Allied Air War

Days of Victory: Canadians Remember, 1939–1945

(with Alex Barris, 1st edition, 1995)

Deadlock in Korea: Canadians at War, 1950–1953

Canada and Korea: Perspectives 2000 (contributor)

Juno: Canadians at D-Day, June 6, 1944

Days of Victory: Canadians Remember, 1939–1945

(sixtieth anniversary edition, 2005)

Victory at Vimy: Canada Comes of Age, April 9–12, 1917

Breaking the Silence: Veterans' Untold Stories
from the Great War to Afghanistan

The Great Escape: A Canadian Story

OTHER NON-FICTION

Fire Canoe: Prairie Steamboat Days Revisited

Rodeo Cowboys: The Last Heroes

Positive Power: The Story of the Edmonton Oilers Hockey Club

Spirit of the West: The Beginnings, The Land, The Life

Playing Overtime: A Celebration of Oldtimers' Hockey

Carved in Granite: 125 Years of Granite Club History

Making Music: Profiles from a Century of Canadian Music

(with Alex Barris)

101 *Things Canadians Should Know about Canada* (contributor)

DAM
BUSTERS

Canadian Airmen and the Secret Raid against Nazi Germany

TED BARRIS

HARPER
PERENNIAL

Published by Harper Perennial, an imprint of HarperCollins Publishers Ltd

First published by Patrick Crean Editions, an imprint of
HarperCollins Publishers Ltd, in a hardcover edition: 2018
This Harper Perennial trade paperback edition: 2019

HarperCollins books may be purchased for educational, business,
or sales promotional use through our Special Markets Department.

HarperCollins Publishers Ltd
Bay Adelaide Centre, East Tower
22 Adelaide Street West, 41st Floor
Toronto, Ontario, Canada
M5H 4E3

www.harpercollins.ca

Library and Archives Canada Cataloguing in Publication
information is available upon request.

*Maps and diagrams created by Lightfoot Art & Design Inc.
Photo inserts by Gordon Robertson.*

ISBN 978-1-4434-5545-9

Printed and bound in the United States
LSC/H 9 8 7 6 5 4 3 2

For those who served in the British Commonwealth Air Training Plan. They gave an air force a way to turn the tide, and a people a reason to hope.

CONTENTS

HE WAS YOUNG—STILL IN HIS TEENS—A LITTLE bit nervous but overall terribly excited by the moment. He peered out the mid-upper gunner's turret at a vast expanse of water spreading toward the shoreline a few kilometres distant. It was loud, very loud, inside the Lancaster, the four huge Rolls-Royce Merlin engines pounding away with a rhythm that made it virtually impossible to hear anything else. He scanned the sky, looking for anything sharing the space, but there was nothing. The plane and its occupants were alone, dancing past the clouds, aloft in the most famous Allied bomber of all time.

But this wasn't the English Channel he was flying over and that wasn't the enemy coast ahead. In fact, it was Lake Ontario on a beautiful summer's day, dotted with sailboats enjoying the peace of the world we live in today. And in the distance was the CN Tower, pointing skyward from the middle of Canada's largest city. For my son, William Stanley Mansbridge, this was a day to remember. This flight was the result of a night in 2015 when Will had seen his name drawn from hundreds of others during a fundraiser for the Canadian Warplane Heritage Museum in Hamilton, Ontario. The big prize was a flight in one of only two Lancasters anywhere in the world still capable of navigating the skies. One belongs to the Royal Air Force in Britain, the other to the good people at the CWHM who, thanks to donors, keep the grand old aircraft airworthy and flying throughout the warm months of the year.

Will's grandfather knew the Lancaster, knew it intimately. He had not only seen the enemy coast ahead, he had also seen the enemy. Seen it close up and many times during two tours and more than fifty missions over Europe. W/C Stanley Mansbridge was a navigator and bomb aimer with RAF No. 49 Squadron, No. 5 Group, based at Scampton, England. He was much decorated, including with a Distinguished Flying Cross for his part in the famous raid on Peenemünde in August 1943, where the Nazis were developing the V-1 rocket. The raid didn't end the V-1 story, but it did delay the rocket's introduction as a weapon of war by at least six months, a critical period that may have changed the course of the war.

Like so many veterans of that conflict, my father rarely talked about it. He'd seen too much horror and lost too many friends—many reached the point where making friends was something they found just too emotional to do. But as he got older and I got older, he felt an obligation to pass on some of his experiences. He didn't talk about himself and his exploits but he did talk about others. And one of those was another RAF wing commander, Guy Gibson, who led perhaps the most famous bombing mission of the war—the dam busters raid. Gibson, was the commanding officer of 617 Squadron, 5 Group, and, like my father, was also based at RAF Scampton. Most of those guys were in their twenties, risking their lives most nights while flying the skies in Lancasters with airframes so thin they seem comparable to today's beer cans. Inside it was freezing cold and cramped, and the seven-man crew shared space with thousands of pounds of high explosives. In downtimes, they'd hit the mess at Scampton with other squadrons and at times, not surprisingly, those became moments of youthful excess. Stanley Mansbridge remembered Guy Gibson at the bar and around the billiards table. He recalled a brash, handsome, extremely self-confident fellow who loved the camaraderie and cared deeply about his fellow flyers. He was known to handwrite personal comments about fallen colleagues at the bottom of formal letters sent out by the Air Ministry to grieving parents.

My father talked about Gibson with extreme admiration. I'll always remember him sitting in his living room chair, trying to explain to me how Gibson had won his Victoria Cross. He'd hold his hands out and use his palms to show how Gibson guided his Lancaster on bombing run after bombing run over the Ruhr dams, protecting his fellow Lancaster mates as they dropped their "bouncing" bombs. These sorties took incredible courage and my father would get emotional each time he told the story.

But he told me something else about Gibson: he said when Gibson handpicked the crews that would train for the raid, he had a particular affection for the courage and skill of Canadian flyers, and as a result, many made the cut. I didn't know that. And I've rarely heard much discussion about it. In the pages ahead, that all changes. My friend Ted Barris is a terrific chronicler of great Canadian accomplishments in our military past, accomplishments often forgotten by history. In *Dam Busters*, Ted ensures that we remember.

A final note about Will, me, and our hero, Stanley Mansbridge. Stanley passed in 2005. We will always miss him. When I flew in the Lancaster as part of a CBC documentary crew a few years ago, I took with me his DFC and held it close to my heart. When Will flew in the Lancaster, he took his memories of his grandfather along too. Three generations of Mansbridges have now flown in a Lancaster—a privilege we will cherish forever.

Peter Mansbridge, OC
Stratford, Ontario
April 2018

ABOUT A YEAR AGO, I TRAVELLED FROM MY HOME in eastern Canada to the foothills of the Rocky Mountains. There, in the town of Rocky Mountain House, Alberta, I met Air Force veteran Fred Sutherland. Yes, everybody told me, "He's the last surviving Canadian Dam Buster." But when I entered the modest Sutherland home, both Fred and his wife, Margaret (who has since passed), welcomed me warmly. Fred was front gunner in the Lancaster whose bouncing bomb delivered the final underwater concussion that breached the Eder Dam in Germany early on the morning of May 17, 1943. During the several days I visited and listened to his recollections, Fred answered every one of my questions about his role in the dams raid. He spoke articulately and dis-passionately, and he rather surprised me with his attitude to the whole dams raid.

"Sure it was important. We had to win that war at all cost," he said. "But I never really talk about it to anybody. I don't go to remembrance events. I do it quietly, privately."

He has every right to feel that way. The statistical impact of that night left a deep impression on every man who flew the operation; of the nineteen Lancasters and 133 aircrew who left RAF No. 617 Squadron base at Scampton for the Ruhr Valley attack on May 16, eight aircraft were lost, fifty-three men killed, and three taken prisoner. But Fred Sutherland's reticence stayed with me. Military historians recording that event have, quite appropriately, given most of their attention to Barnes Wallis, the designer of the unique bouncing bomb, and to Wing Commander Guy Gibson, squadron leader on this unprecedented Second World War bombing operation. Just as appropriate are the commemorations every five or ten years, when news magazines publish features, when museums roll out displays and artifacts connected to the raid, when air forces stage flypasts and remembrance events, and when documentary TV channels rerun the original 1955 black-and-white movie *The Dam Busters*, based on Paul Brickhill's book of the same name.

Since Brickhill's book was published in 1951 and the movie released by Associated British Picture Corporation four years later, the bookshelves of libraries, museums, and aviation buffs have filled with works, some of them memoir, about Operation Chastise. Perhaps the most famous, Guy Gibson's account, *Enemy Coast Ahead*, was published twice—originally in 1946 and then as an "uncensored" edition in 2010.* Detailed profiles of other Dam Busters have followed regularly. In 2008, writer and editor Charles Foster released *Breaking*

---

* If there are gaps in the accounts by authors Brickhill and Gibson, it's because the secrecy of the war and its immediate aftermath limited the content of their books; Gibson had to take into account wartime censorship, and Brickhill couldn't be explicit about the Wallis bombs since they remained on the Secret List until 1962.

the Dams: The Story of the Dambuster David Maltby and His Crew, while the same year Arthur G. Thorning published *The Dambuster Who Cracked the Dam: The Story of Melvin "Dinghy" Young*. A series of books taking a wider view of the dams raid began to appear in 1990, with the publication of military historian John Sweetman's *The Dambusters Raid*, followed, in 1994, by *The Dam Busters*, written by military aviation historian Jonathan Falconer. A 2001 book, *The Dams Raid Through the Lens*, by Helmuth Euler, emphasized the German perspective in the aftermath of the raid.

In 2009, military obituary writer and popular historian Max Arthur released *Dambusters: A Landmark Oral History*. The same year, Professor Richard Morris completed 16/17 *May 1943 Operation Chastise: The Raid on the German Dams*; then, in 2012, acclaimed author and journalist James Holland released his work, *Dam Busters: The Race to Smash the Dams, 1943*. In 2013, co-authors Robert Owen, Steve Darlow, Sean Feast, and Arthur Thorning took a closer look at the airmen lost during the op in *Dam Busters: Failed to Return*, while RAF veteran and writer Clive Rowley covered the sixtieth anniversary of the raid in *Dambusters: The Most Daring Raid in the RAF's History*. Most recently, in 2014, celebrated dams raid bomb aimer George "Johnny" Johnson released his memoir, *The Last British Dambuster*.

All well and good. But a closer look at the canon of Dam Buster literature released over the seventy-five years since the raid has revealed, at least to me, a history with substantial pieces missing.

Where, for example, has the account of Flight Sergeant Ken Brown gone? Originally from Moose Jaw, Saskatchewan, streamed from fighter aircraft to bombers, and only half a dozen operations into his wartime bombing career, Brown was transferred to 617 Squadron for the unspecified raid. He and his bomber crew attacked the Sorpe Dam, which "most of the crew really felt . . . was a one-way ticket." Or, for that matter, where are the stories of the two other Canadians aboard Brown's Lancaster—gunner Grant McDonald, from British Columbia, and fellow Saskatchewan bomb aimer Stefan Oancia, who won the Distinguished Flying Medal for his service in the Sorpe attack? And though he was lost on the historic raid that night, why has the contribution of pilot Lewis Burpee, from Ottawa, been generally overlooked?

And while Wing Commander Gibson applauded him for successfully guiding "the whole squadron to the dams," what has happened to the fuller story of Harlo Taerum, the Canadian navigator aboard 617's lead Lancaster? Motivated by the Nazi invasion of his parents' Norwegian homeland, a graduate at the top of his observers' class, highly experienced at long-distance and low-level navigation, Taerum was handpicked by Gibson for the dams raid but seems lost in the shadow of his skipper. What about other Canadian navigators on Operation Chastise, such as Revie Walker and Don MacLean? The former, born in the Crowsnest Pass area of Alberta, had a complete operational tour behind him (and, incidentally, a Distinguished Flying Cross) when his pilot, Flight Lieutenant David Shannon, invited him to be on the mystery mission. And MacLean, a former teacher from Toronto and eventually a Bomber Command navigator, developed a system of memorizing landmarks just outside the route to the dams, in order to keep his Lancaster, piloted by American RCAF

Flight Lieutenant Joe McCarthy, on course all the way to the Sorpe and back.

And what about the personal accounts of Canadian aircrew Ken Earnshaw and John Fraser? Another former teacher from farm country in central Alberta, and trained as bomber navigator, Earnshaw joined bomb aimer Fraser, from British Columbia, when they crewed up with Flight Lieutenant John Hopgood for the raid. Part of the wave attacking the Möhne, Hopgood's Lancaster followed Guy Gibson's initial low-level run against the dam, and consequently took heavier anti-aircraft fire on its pass. Climbing away from the dam, the Lancaster exploded, but not before Fraser managed to bail out; he learned of the impact of the raid only much later, while imprisoned at German POW camps in occupied Europe. And why haven't the lives of boyhood pals Abram Garshowitz and Frank Garbas—who both enlisted in Hamilton, Ontario, and wound up together aboard the same dams raid Lancaster—been told? As wireless radio operator and gunner, respectively, theirs was a story of the vitality and vulnerability of young warriors, captured in letters and photographs home—sometimes illegally—and then summed up in a piece of graffiti chalked onto one of the famous bouncing bombs: "Never has so much been expected of so few."

Why have the experiences of the two Canadian Dam Buster flight engineers, Bill Radcliffe and Charles Brennan, apparently escaped detection? Brennan, from Calgary, was so proficient as a technician in the air that Bomber Command took him among its best to train others; he then volunteered to complete his combat tour with his former pilot, Hopgood. Meanwhile, Radcliffe, a graduate of a technical school in BC, moved from ground crew mechanic at conversion units to 617 Squadron flight engineer with RCAF pilot McCarthy. They flew the dams raid together, and in so doing Radcliffe initiated a ritual for the Squadron that "protected" it throughout his tour of duty.

Given the perilous, seven-hour sortie at treetop level that the dams raid required, whose perspectives could be more compelling than those airmen working in the Lancasters' front and rear gunnery turrets? Harvey Glinz left a retail job in his hometown of Winnipeg, Manitoba, to join the Air Force. He led his air gunnery class in 1942 and was proficient enough to guide other gunners training for the secret operation; he flew in the front turret of the second wave of bombers. Dave Rodger left work with Algoma Steel in northern Ontario to train as a gunner. By the time of the attack on May 16–17, 1943, he was an officer and positioned in the rear turret of Flight Lieutenant McCarthy's Lancaster. Meanwhile, gunners Harry O'Brien and Fred Sutherland, also from the Canadian Prairies, had endured the worst luck—weathering several crashes leading up to the dams raid. But then Sutherland, in the front turret of Flight Lieutenant Les Knight's Lancaster, and O'Brien, in the rear, both witnessed the spectacular breaching of the Eder Dam from front-row seats. If that wasn't harrowing enough, they would both endure a crash in a subsequent combat operation that would lead to hair-raising experiences as evaders in occupied Holland, Belgium, and France.

And what of the training and techniques that made any or all of this momentous raid possible? Would it surprise you to learn that the fundamentals had come from Canada? And how does history view the raid—a success or a failure? In the aftermath, what happened to the aircrew who'd learned so much from the experience? How did the pressure, the risk, and the results of the raid—both positive and negative—affect its firsthand witnesses? And, ultimately, what ensured that the accounts of Operation Chastise and the Dam Busters themselves survived the decades that followed? Why is their legacy—with so few of the dams raid participants still with us—a thriving and yet litigious phenomenon three-quarters of a century later?

Aside from historian Dave Birrell's 2012 book *Big Joe McCarthy: The RCAF's American Dambuster*, which included accounts from three Canadians who served with McCarthy on the Sorpe Dam attack, the role that Canadian aircrew played in this pivotal 617 Squadron operation remains largely unreported. So, following my visit with Canadian Dam Buster Fred Sutherland, I concluded that a retelling of the Dam Busters' story, but one that featured the experiences of Canadians— who comprised nearly a quarter of the 617 Squadron aircrew assigned to the dams raid—was fitting and necessary.

FOR MUCH OF THE THREAD OF THE STORY, I HAVE sought out and where possible gained permission to cite some of the works already mentioned. But, in addition to their permission, I have enjoyed correspondence with and received valuable guidance from British authors Jonathan Falconer, James Holland, Steve Darlow, Charles Foster, Clive Rowley, and Robert Owen, the official historian of RAF 617 Squadron. In Canada, both directly and indirectly, fellow authors Carl Christie, Murray Peden, David Bashow, Chris Hadfield, Dave Birrell, Mike Filey, Susan Raby-Dunne, Elinor Florence, Mort Lightstone, and Jonathan Vance have assisted my research with their reliable historical publications. Above and beyond the call, however, three fellow journalists and authors deserve special thanks: Peter Jennings for his keen sense of storytelling; Ellin Bessner for the passion we share to honour the service of veteran servicemen and women in Canada; and Malcolm Kelly, not only for encouraging me to write this story in the first place, but also for preventing my publishing those forest-for-the-trees oversights.

Since all of the Canadians who served on the raid, save Fred Sutherland, have passed, I have relied heavily on immediate family members of the Canadian Dam Busters for firsthand research. Without exception, all have readily given me access to correspondence, journals, flight logs, telegrams, contemporary news clippings, recordings, and rare photographs collected or composed by the Dam Busters themselves. Both Bill and Jim MacLean supplied personal papers, photos, and interview recollections of their father, Don MacLean. Likewise, the details of Ken Brown's long Air Force career became more vivid via the memories and memorabilia supplied by his wife, Beryl, and sons Brock and Terry. The same generosity that delivered Revie Walker's uniform to the Nanton museum was afforded me by his wife, Doreen, son John, and daughter-in-law Amy. And my direct contact with Fred Sutherland was followed by additional flight data and photographic material via his children—Joan Norris, Tom Sutherland, and Jim Sutherland.

Elsewhere among family contacts, I wish to thank Don Lightbody for his assistance in compiling the story of his uncle, Floyd Wile, and likewise Joel Joy and the Canadian Letters and Images Project, sponsored by Vancouver Island University, at Nanaimo, BC, for providing access to the letters of Vincent MacCausland. Insights into the peace and wartime life of Dave Rodger came readily from his wife, Nell, and their daughters Sheila, Andrea, and Carolyn, but as important were the skill and dedication of fellow broadcaster J'Lyn Nye, who took time away from her holiday to interview Rodger family members for me in Sault Ste. Marie to help lift Dave's story off the page. At the eleventh hour, I met the daughter of air gunner Jimmy McDowell; I am grateful to Marilyn McDowell, who cast a different light on the home-front experience when the dams raid took away a beloved father. And when he opened a treasure trove of letters and photographs during our interview in Ottawa, Lewis Burpee Jr. helped us both understand Lewis Burpee Sr., the pilot, the husband, the hero, the father. The blood families of the Dam Busters from Canada care as passionately as anyone about the legacy of their ancestors' accounts of the raid, perhaps none greater than those who felt compelled to fight to preserve it. For reasons that will become clear in the book, in the years following the raid, the artifacts and literature left by Dam Busters John Fraser, Ken Earnshaw, and Abram Garshowitz were threatened. Only the work of their descendants has prevented the permanent loss of that history—Jim Heather acting on behalf of his uncle, Ken Earnshaw; Hartley Garshowitz on behalf of his uncle, Abram Garshowitz; and Shere Fraser and her husband, Joe McCarthy Jr., bringing the theft of John Fraser's logbook to court in Britain. Their labour of love continues.

The search through more traditional channels—archives, libraries, museums—was assisted by individuals who care as much about relating this story as I do. At the Canadian War Museum, Carol Reid and Dr. Jeff Noakes and their library staff helped track down relevant photographs, as did Sebastian Wainwright at the Imperial War Museum in Britain. I also received photographic assistance and guidance from Steve and Mark Postlethwaite, as well as Sue Wong at Canadian Press in Toronto. I acknowledge support from aviation periodical editors Dean Black at *Airforce* magazine in Canada and Chris Gilson and Steve Beebee at *FlyPast* in the United Kingdom.

Ultimately, the two best archival resources for the dams raid story proved to be the Canadian Warplane Heritage Museum in Hamilton, Ontario, and the Bomber Command Museum of Canada (BCMC) in Nanton, Alberta. At the former, I wish to thank Al Mickeloff and Bill McBride especially for their wholehearted endorsement of this work. At the latter, Bob Evans, Dan Fox, Rob Pedersen, Karl Kjarsgaard, and Dana Zielke provided valuable assistance from the start. But the BCMC gave my Dam Buster story something even more powerful; that's because Dave Birrell, a founding director of the museum, believes to his marrow that giving Canadian military aviation stories a human face almost supersedes the need to save the artifacts of war. His obsession to research and broadcast this history matches my own.

I have long shared a fascination for wartime stories with broadcast colleague and journalist Peter Mansbridge. When he agreed to compose a foreword to this book, I sensed that both his personal connection to military aviation and his professional one would give readers exactly the right entrée to this story. As well, two artists—Gordon Robertson, who designed the book jacket and photo sections, and John Lightfoot, who created the maps and diagrams—have offered their special touch to this project. Further, at HarperCollins Canada, I wish to thank production and editorial staff Noelle Zitzer and Natalie Meditsky, as well as freelance editor Linda Pruessen and publicity staff Colleen Simpson and Melissa Nowakowski, for their dedication to this project. None of what follows, however, none of the Canadian Dam Busters' story could have made it this far without publisher/editor Patrick Crean supporting the idea from the beginning. His belief in such storytelling inspired my meeting with Fred Sutherland. And the rest is history as Patrick and I believe it should be told.

When I'd completed this book, I turned to another friend to do a read-through. Robert Middleton agreed. In 1942, at nineteen, Bob had enlisted in the RCAF, first as a pilot trainee but then redirected to observer school. Bob received his navigator's brevet in 1943. In the UK he crewed up with pilot Don Rombough and navigated aboard all manner of bombers, eventually moving to Lancasters in 1944. He flew a full tour of operations, mostly against targets in the Ruhr River area (a.k.a. "Happy Valley") between September 1944 and February 1945. Bob's encyclopedic knowledge of wartime navigation—from both experience and self-directed research—gave my manuscript its final wings test. I thank him for his thorough reading and his devotion to the memory of his Air Force comrades.

As anyone with experience in military aviation would say, nothing gets airborne without backup on the ground. I want to thank my faithful interview transcriber, Kate Paddison. I've had support second to none on this project from friends, including Lindy Oughtred, Steve Cogan, Phil Alves, Rob Hart, Mike Parry, Tom Taylor, Shelley Macbeth, Lisha Van

Nieuwenhove, Elaine DeBlicquy, Brian Evans, Don Mason, Garry Balsdon, Dave and Mary Ross, Stuart and Barbara Blower, G.B. Henderson, and Brenda Righetti. But I especially thank my family—my sister, Kate; my sister-in-law, Pat; my wife, Jayne; our daughters Quenby and Whitney, sons-in-law J.D. and Ian, and their children, particularly granddaughter Layne and grandson Coen, who've regularly asked over the past year, "How's the book coming?"

I can now say, with my thanks, "It's done!"

Ted Barris
Uxbridge, Ontario
April 2018

AIR MINISTRY AND AIRMEN

AIR MINISTRY, AIR DESIGN, AND AIR FORCE

AIR MINISTRY

Air Vice-Marshal Norman H. Bottomley
Assistant Chief of the Air Staff (Operations)

Air Vice-Marshal Frank Inglis
Assistant Chief of the Air Staff (Intelligence)

Air Chief Marshal Sir Charles Portal
Chief of the Air Staff

Wing Commander Fred Winterbotham
Head of Air Intelligence, MI6

MINISTRY OF AIRCRAFT PRODUCTION

Air Vice-Marshal Francis Linnell
Controller of Research and Development

Benjamin Lockspeiser
Deputy Director of Scientific Research

Dr. David R. Pye
Director of Scientific Research

Norbert Rowe
Director of Technical Development

Sir Henry Tizard
Chief Scientific Advisor

MINISTRY OF HOME SECURITY

A.R. Collins
Scientist, Concrete Section at Road Research Laboratory

PRIME MINISTER'S OFFICE

William Maxwell Aitken (Lord Beaverbrook)
Minister of Aircraft Production

Sir Maurice Hankey
Industrial Intelligence in Foreign Countries Committee

Prof. Frederick A. Lindemann (Lord Cherwell)
Scientific Advisor to the Prime Minister

RAF BOMBER COMMAND

Air Vice-Marshal Ralph A. Cochrane
Air Officer Commanding No. 5 Group

Air Vice-Marshal W. Sholto Douglas
Air Officer Commanding-in-Chief

Air Marshal Sir Arthur Harris
Commander-in-Chief

Air Vice-Marshal Arthur W. Tedder
Deputy Air Officer Commanding-in-Chief

Marshal Hugh Montague "Boom" Trenchard
Marshal

A.V. ROE

Roy Chadwick
Chief Designer

VICKERS

Sir Charles Craven
Chairman

Rex K. Pierson
Chief Designer

Captain "Mutt" Summers
Chief Test Pilot

Barnes Wallis
Assistant Chief Designer

AT 617 SQUADRON, SCAMPTON

F/L C.C. "Capable" Capel
Station Engineering Officer

F/L Harry Humphries
Founder Adjutant

Sgt. Hugh Munro RCAF
Radar Specialist

F/Sgt. George "Chiefy" Powell
Chief Administrator

F/L Henry "Doc" Watson
Armament Officer

Group Captain Charles Whitworth
Station Commander

RAF 617 SQUADRON AIRCRAFT AND CREWS ON OPERATION CHASTISE

Sequence: Lancaster bomber call sign; pilot, flight engineer, navigator, wireless radio operator, bomb aimer, front gunner, rear gunner. Aircrew RAF unless otherwise indicated (i.e., Royal Canadian Air Force, Royal Australian Air Force, Royal New Zealand Air Force)

FIRST WAVE

AJ-*G*-*George*
W/C Guy Gibson
Sgt. John Pulford
P/O Torger "Harlo" Taerum RCAF
F/L Robert "Hutch" Hutchison RAAF
P/O Fred "Spam" Spafford RAAF
P/O George Deering RCAF
F/L Richard Trevor-Roper

AJ-*M*-*Mother*
F/L John Hopgood
Sgt. Charlie Brennan (Canadian)
F/O Ken Earnshaw RCAF
Sgt. John "Minchie" Minchin
P/O John Fraser RCAF
P/O George Gregory
P/O Tony Burcher RAAF

AJ-*P*-*Popsie*
F/L Harold "Mick" Martin RAAF
P/O Ivan Whittaker
F/L Jack Leggo RAAF
F/O Len Chambers RNZAF
F/L Bob Hay RAAF
P/O Bert Foxlee RAAF
F/Sgt. Tammy Simpson RAAF

AJ-*A*-*Apple*
S/L Melvin "Dinghy" Young
Sgt. David Horsfall
F/Sgt. Charles Roberts

Sgt. Lawrence Nichols
F/O Vincent MacCausland RCAF
Sgt. Gordon Yeo
Sgt. Wilfred Ibbotson

AJ-*J-Johnny*
F/L David Maltby
Sgt. Bill Hatton
Sgt. Vivian Nicholson
Sgt. Anthony Stone
P/O Jack Fort
F/S Victor Hill
Sgt. Harold Simmonds

AJ-*L-Leather*
F/L David Shannon RAAF
Sgt. Bob Henderson
F/O Daniel Revie Walker RCAF
F/O Brian Goodale
F/Sgt. Len Sumpter
Sgt. Brian Jagger
P/O Jack Buckley

AJ-*Z-Zebra*
S/L Henry Maudslay
Sgt. Jack Marriott
F/O Robert Urquhart RCAF
W/O2 Alden Cottam RCAF
P/O John Fuller
F/O William Tytherleigh
Sgt. Norman Burrows

AJ-*N-Nuts*
F/L Les Knight RAAF
Sgt. Raymond Grayston
F/O Harold "Sidney" Hobday
P/O Robert Kellow RAAF
F/O Edward Cuthbert "Johnny" Johnson
Sgt. Fred "Doc" Sutherland RCAF
Sgt. Henry "Harry" O'Brien RCAF

AJ-*B-Baker*
F/L Bill Astell
Sgt. John Kinnear
P/O Floyd Wile RCAF
WO2 Abram "Albert" Garshowitz RCAF
F/O Donald Hopkinson
F/Sgt. Frank Garbas RCAF
Sgt. Richard "Dick" Bolitho

SECOND WAVE

AJ-*T-Tommy*
F/L Joe McCarthy RCAF
Sgt. Bill Radcliffe RCAF
F/Sgt. Don MacLean RCAF
Sgt. Len Eaton
Sgt. George Leonard "Johnny" Johnson
Sgt. Ronald Batson
F/O Dave Rodger RCAF

AJ-*E-Easy*
F/L Norman Barlow RAAF
P/O Leslie Whillis
F/O Philip Burgess
F/O Charles Williams RAAF
P/O Alan Gillespie
F/O Harvey Glinz RCAF
Sgt. Jack Liddell

AJ-*K-King*
P/O Vernon Byers RCAF
Sgt. Alastair Taylor
F/O James Warner
Sgt. John Wilkinson
P/O Neville Whitaker
Sgt. Charles Jarvie
Sgt. Jimmy McDowell RCAF

AJ-*H-Harry*
P/O Geoff Rice
Sgt. Edward Smith
F/O Richard Macfarlane

Sgt. Chester Gowrie RCAF
W/O John Thrasher RCAF
Sgt. Bill Maynard
Sgt. Stephen Burns

AJ-*W-Willie*
F/L Les Munro RNZAF
Sgt. Frank Appleby
F/O Grant "Jock" Rumbles
Sgt. Percy Pigeon RCAF
Sgt. James Clay
Sgt. Bill Howarth
F/Sgt. Harvey Weeks RCAF

THIRD WAVE

AJ-*Y-York*
F/Sgt. Cyril Anderson
Sgt. Robert Paterson
Sgt. John Nugent
Sgt. Douglas Bickle
Sgt. Gilbert "Jimmy" Green
Sgt. Eric Ewan
Sgt. Arthur Buck

AJ-*F-Freddie*
F/Sgt. Ken Brown RCAF
Sgt. Harry Basil Feneron
Sgt. Dudley Heal
Sgt. Herbert "Hewie" Hewstone
F/Sgt. Stefan Oancia RCAF
Sgt. Daniel Allatson
F/S Grant McDonald RCAF

AJ-*O-Orange*
P/O Bill Townsend
Sgt. Dennis Powell
P/O Lance Howard RAAF
F/Sgt. George Chalmers
Sgt. Charles Franklin
Sgt. Douglas Webb
Sgt. Ray Wilkinson

AJ-*S-Sugar*
P/O Lewis Burpee RCAF
Sgt. Guy "Johnny" Pegler
Sgt. Tom Jaye
P/O Sam Weller
WO2 Jimmy Arthur RCAF
Sgt. William "Ginger" Long
WO2 Gordon Brady RCAF

AJ-*C-Charlie*
P/O Warner "Bill" Ottley
Sgt. Ron Marsden
F/O Jack Barrett
Sgt. Jack Guterman
F/Sgt. Tommy Johnston
Sgt. Harry Strange
F/Sgt. Fred Tees

DAM BUSTERS

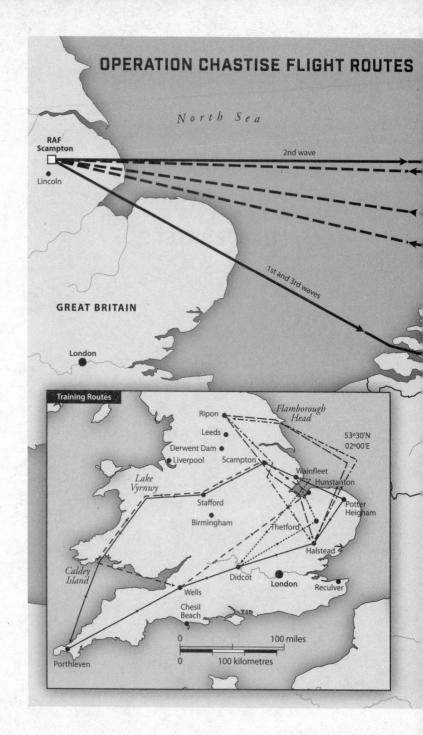

OPERATION CHASTISE FLIGHT ROUTES

North Sea

RAF Scampton

Lincoln

2nd wave

1st and 3rd waves

GREAT BRITAIN

London

Training Routes

Flamborough Head

Ripon

Leeds

Derwent Dam

Liverpool

Scampton

Wainfleet

Hunstanton

53°30'N
02°00'E

Lake Vyrnwy

Stafford

Birmingham

Thetford

Potter Heigham

Halstead

Caldey Island

Wells

Didcot

London

Reculver

Chesil Beach

Porthleven

0   100 miles

0   100 kilometres

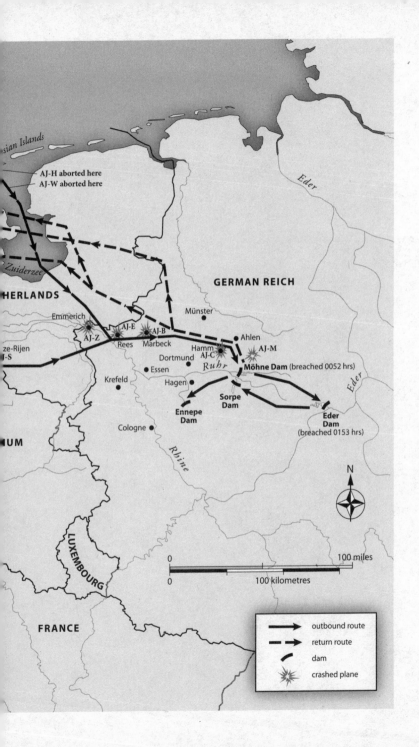

AJ-H aborted here
AJ-W aborted here

GERMAN REICH

HERLANDS

Emmerich

AJ-Z

ze-Rijen
J-S

Rees

AJ-E

AJ-B

Marbeck

Münster

Ahlen

AJ-M

Hamm

AJ-C

Dortmund

Ruhr

Möhne Dam (breached 0052 hrs)

Essen

Krefeld

Hagen

**Sorpe
Dam**

**Ennepe
Dam**

Cologne

Rhine

**Eder
Dam**
(breached 0153 hrs)

Eder

N

LUXEMBOURG

FRANCE

Prussian Islands

Zuiderzee

Eder

0   100 miles

0   100 kilometres

UM

outbound route

return route

dam

crashed plane

CHAPTER ONE

"HAPPY VALLEY"

NOBODY EVER FIGURED HIS NUMBER WAS UP. Not even on a first op. As daunting as a first combat operation over enemy airspace might seem, it couldn't unnerve Jimmy Arthur. It wouldn't. As long as he stayed focused on his job as a bomb aimer in the nose of his Lancaster bomber, everything would be okay, he kept telling himself. It didn't hurt, either, that he was joining a combat-experienced crew. Warrant Officer (W/O) Arthur, from Toronto, would be flying this winter night with Lewis Burpee, a sergeant pilot who had thirty-one bombing operations under his belt, and who was a fellow Canadian, from Ottawa. So too was one of the air gunners, Gordon Brady; he hailed from Ponoka, Alberta, in western Canada. With so much experience and two countrymen in the crew around him, Arthur hoped his first trip to war might be an easy one. Either way, he wouldn't actually learn what the target was until the late-afternoon briefing.

On this early March day in 1943, aircrews began trickling into the briefing room at Royal Air Force (RAF) Syerston aerodrome, in east-central England, at about 4:30 p.m., before their evening meal. The young men of RAF No. 106 Squadron, many of them perhaps nineteen or twenty, were outfitted in their roll-necked pullovers and battledress. They smoked cigarettes or sipped tea or coffee. And they tended to gather with their own crewmen along benches, or leaning against the side walls of the room, waiting for a crew roll call. Also waiting, a few war correspondents with pens and pads at the ready stood off to the side. As usual, the small stage at the far end of the room featured a set of curtains covering aerial maps of that night's target. They would remain drawn until the squadron's commanding officer (CO) and the lead navigation officer arrived. A lot of speculation about the op generally preceded the briefing. But when the CO, Group Captain (G/C) Edward Bussell finally arrived, all the chatter died down.

At the briefing that afternoon, Jimmy Arthur sat with his new crewmates. In addition to Canadians Burpee and Brady, there were flight engineer Sergeant (Sgt.) Johnny Pegler, navigator Sgt. Tommy Jaye, wireless operator Pilot Officer (P/O) Sam Weller, and the Lancaster's other gunner, Sgt. William "Ginger" Long. WO Arthur would be replacing a bomb aimer who'd just completed his tour of duty with Burpee's crew. Arthur had gone on one test flight with them to get acquainted. That was all. But the next order of business was the ritual of the reveal, as the CO nodded to his adjutant to open the drapes in front of the target map.

"Gentlemen, the target for tonight is Essen," Bussell announced.

"Christ. It's Happy Valley," one of the experienced bomber crewmen said, so his voice could be heard above the din of general reaction.

When Arthur needed a further explanation, one of his Lancaster crewmates provided it: "He's talking about the *Ruhr* Valley."

The wall chart showed a magnified map of western Germany. The turnip-shaped blotch of red,[1] about a foot long and nearly as wide, showed the length and breadth of the Ruhr River Valley, its industrial cities and massive hydroelectric generating dams and reservoirs. Red circles on the map marked areas expected to throw up heavy enemy flak en route. And the belt of searchlights surrounding the valley appeared as a continuous blue border framing the blotch. A red ribbon showed the route to the target over the North Sea and the Zuiderzee and inland to Essen.

In the seconds that followed the announcement, WO Arthur dealt with the realizations that came with being assigned to a first combat op. He experienced the mental recognition that tonight he'd be aiming bombs at an actual enemy target, not a practice one back home at No. 1 Bombing and Gunnery School in Jarvis, Ontario. In the final moments of tonight's bombing run, he'd be the one determining where the Lancaster's bomb load would fall. But as well, he felt the physical response, the butterflies in the stomach, or worse, that came with knowing he was about to embark on his first trip into hostile airspace. Arthur looked around at the faces of those who knew what the announcement meant.

* * *

JAMES LAMB ARTHUR WAS BORN IN TORONTO ON JULY 3, 1917, the second of four children of an Anglican clergyman in the city. Jim did well in mathematics, and after graduating from high school he got a job at the Bank of Toronto. Father and both sons had the opportunity to learn to fly early on, so when the war broke out, Jim first applied for pilot training; by May 1942, however, the Air Force had streamed him into observer training. After graduating from No. 1 Air Navigation School at Rivers, Manitoba, he was shipped overseas through the Bournemouth personnel reception centre, to advanced flying, operational training, and then a heavy conversion unit (HCU) destined for service on Lancasters as a bomb aimer. He was assigned to Lewis Burpee's crew in February 1943. This would be WO Arthur's first combat operation with 106 Squadron.

Bussell continued the briefing by informing the aircrews they'd fly this sortie as part of a stream of 442 bombers attacking Essen. "The bomb load will be one 4,000-pounder and sixteen cans of incendiaries," he said, and added that crews would bomb the target from an altitude of 19,000 feet. "Don't get out of this height band or you'll run into other aircraft."[2]

Essen, a city about three miles in diameter, lay twelve miles east of the Rhine, wedged between two rivers—the Ruhr and the Lippe. From the air, bomber crews would find the city extremely difficult to locate at night. The river intersection might help, but German defensive strategists had drained a large adjacent lake, called Baldeney See, to remove a convenient locator for Allied navigators and bomb aimers making a timed run-up to the target.[3] The city, with a population of about 670,000 and a density of 125 people per acre, consisted almost entirely of factories and workers' accommodation. Krupp industries, the plant manufacturing flak, bombs, torpedo tubes, armour plating, armoured cars, tractors, and other war hardware for the Nazi war effort, presented the largest target. Nearby, on the outskirts of the city, sat Goldschmidt AG chemical and metal works, as well as large hydrogenation plants producing aviation fuel from tar. Making an air attack tougher than usual, industrial chimney smoke tended to obscure the entire region day and night. To help mitigate the poor visibility, however, Pathfinders—Mosquito fighter aircraft—would fly ahead of the bomber stream to mark the targets with flares.

Bussell turned over the briefing to the lead navigation officer, who outlined the Pathfinder approach. "At zero hour minus three and a third minutes, Pathfinders will sky-mark the lane to the objective with red TI (target indicating) markers, which change to green after 120 seconds," he said.[4]

To assist them, Pathfinder Mosquitos would have Oboe, a blind-bombing targeting system through which a pair of radio transmitters on the ground in England sent signals received and retransmitted by a transponder in the Mosquito aircraft, guiding them with greater precision to the target. For the Essen raid, the Pathfinders would mark a point on enemy territory exactly fifteen miles short of the aiming point. Passing over the flares at a ground speed of 240 miles per hour (mph), the bombers would therefore take about three to four minutes to arrive at the targets, also marked by Pathfinder flares dropped just moments earlier.

"The TIs will go down right on the factory roofs," the navigation officer promised. "The sky above the city will also be marked with green flares in case the TIs are obscured by fog or smoke."[5] He handed the briefing back to the CO.

Bussell pointed out that ten Mosquitos would lay the TIs, and then the Main Force would attack in three waves— Halifaxes first, Wellingtons and Stirlings second, and third, the Lancasters of 106 Squadron. Two-thirds of the bomb tonnage would be incendiary. The remaining third—high-capacity explosives called "Cookies"—would be fused for long delay.

"You are to take no evasive action," Bussell added as a matter of course, "but keep straight on past the targets. No straggling. And don't forget to twist your tails a bit so that you can see those fighters coming up from below."

From as early as the spring of 1942, the concentrations of industrial plants along the Ruhr had become obvious targets for Allied bombing; as much as 10 percent of the year's strategic bombing was directed against those Ruhr Valley targets.[6] In that year, during the so-called obliteration raids, Bomber Command had focused attacks on the centres of Lübeck and Rostock, virtually razing them in the process. Allied bombers had staged the first 1,000-bomber raid against the industrial city of Cologne in May 1942, but the industrial centres of Mainz and Karlsruhe also received special attention from bomber ops. By the end of the year, 380 acres of Düsseldorf had been destroyed, along with 260 acres of Münster and 60 percent of Emden.

In response, Hitler had bolstered the SS presence in the region to eliminate even the slightest flagging of morale around the war plants. As well, because production in the Ruhr supplied so much of the German war effort, by 1943 the entire valley and all approaches to it had witnessed a ramping up of anti-aircraft guns, searchlights, and night-fighter airstrips. And with as many as nineteen power plants situated along the Ruhr, including the large hydroelectric Möhne, Eder, and Sorpe Dams, German engineers laid netted iron in the adjacent reservoirs to protect the dam walls from potential torpedo attack. But the commander-in-chief of Bomber Command would not be deterred.

"At long last," Arthur Harris wrote in his diary in March 1943, "we were ready and equipped . . . to undertake with real hope of success the task which had been given to me—the task of destroying the main cities of the Ruhr."[7]

Trips to the Ruhr had only one redeeming aspect for the bomber crews: they were generally shorter than those going deeper into enemy airspace, perhaps five hours instead of seven or eight. Otherwise, "Happy Valley" was among the most heavily defended industrial areas of Europe, with hundreds of flak batteries and walls of searchlights establishing a ground deterrent and the *Nachtjagdgeschwadern* (night-fighter groups) of Messerschmitt Bf 110 and Junkers Ju 88 aircraft prowling the skies. The Luftwaffe night fighters generally exhibited greater speed and agility than the Lancaster bombers; they also employed a lethal system of interception, known as *Himmelbett*, whereby ground controllers used mobile *Würzburg* radar sets—one trained on the fighter, the other on the bomber—to stalk their quarry.[8]

"A piece of cake," one RAF pilot said in jest about the ops against the Ruhr, admitting that the remark was so much whistling past the graveyard.[9]

Finally, the CO reminded all aircrews to empty their pockets of letters and other personal items, to bury their parachutes if forced to bail out, and to recite only "name, rank, and number" if captured. He finished with the requisite

"Good luck, chaps." As if to punctuate the end of the briefing narrative, all the chairs and benches scraped across the briefing room floor as dozens of aircrews rose to go about their pre-operation rituals.

Bomb aimer Jimmy Arthur's baptism of fire, his first combat op, would coincide with Bomber Command's latest sustained salvos against Nazi Germany's industrial might in the Ruhr Valley. With 106 Squadron's attack on Essen, on March 12, 1943, Jimmy Arthur and the rest of Lewis Burpee's crew would join the opening week of the Battle of the Ruhr, heralded by a British Air Ministry official "as one of the decisive battles of history."[10] Historic or not, for WO Arthur and his comrades, the late afternoon had become the pregnant pause between briefing and combat op, between knowing the target and taking off. Most didn't like this period; there was nothing anybody could do but wait. Even the late-afternoon meal was uncomfortably quiet, with airmen eating their precious eggs and bacon mechanically.[11] Some sat and listened to the radio in the mess or played billiards. Others took the time to write letters to loved ones. But most stared or paced and waited for the clock to indicate it was time to don their flying clothes.

All day long the Syerston flight line had been alive with preparation. Bowsers pumped thousands of gallons of petrol into bomber fuel tanks. Trucks delivered oxygen cylinders for the breathing apparatus the crew would need during the high-altitude sortie. Aero-mechanics scoured engine, instrument, and hydraulic systems for faults, and completed repairs. Along the perimeter track, tractors towed strings of bomb trolleys, dispersing the assigned 4,000-pound Cookies and incendiaries for loading into the Lancaster bomb bays.

Meanwhile, air gunners went through the ritual of stripping and cleaning their machine guns while armourers delivered belts of ammunition, which the front, mid-upper, and rear turret gun positions would require to defend the bomber against German fighter aircraft during the operation. Dozens of ground and aircrew moved around each aircraft like drones working in a hive—each focused on a task, none bothered by the other.

At Lewis Burpee's Lancaster ZN-H, just before climbing aboard, the crew members told new man Jimmy Arthur they'd flown previous ops to Essen, one as recently as the week before. Indeed, they had been to Happy Valley a number of times: they'd bombed Duisburg twice, Düsseldorf twice, and Essen on three previous occasions. Guy "Johnny" Pegler, Burpee's flight engineer from the UK, had flown twenty-five ops with his skipper; Tom Jaye, also from the UK, had served as Burpee's navigator on sixteen trips; and fellow Brit Sam Weller had worked ten ops as Burpee's wireless operator. British mid-upper gunner Ginger Long had flown twenty-one trips with Burpee, and rear gunner Gordie Brady had served with Burpee from his very first op for 106 Squadron.

Brady's parents had emigrated from the United States to Ponoka, Alberta, during the Great War. Born in 1916, Gordon finished school in the 1930s and then worked in a drugstore. Early in the war, he worked as a field ambulance driver. By 1941, he'd joined the Royal Canadian Air Force (RCAF) and trained as a wireless radio operator at Calgary, going overseas to serve in the RAF as a gunner in February 1942. He crewed up with Burpee in June of that year and flew every wartime op with him; Brady had earned a promotion to warrant officer in February 1943, just before his skipper, Flight Sergeant (F/Sgt.) Burpee, was recommended for a Distinguished Flying Medal (DFM).*

Crew chemistry was vital aboard any military aircraft, for survival and sanity. Burpee's bomber crew had gelled well in the short months of their first tour; one day, as Burpee signed and sealed a letter to a loved one, Brady insisted his skipper reopen the envelope to add a postscript "Hello" from him.[12] A photograph taken on January 18, 1943, following their fifteenth op, a raid on Berlin, shows the crew of Lancaster ZN-H arm in arm like brothers—although F/Sgt. Burpee is sombre-faced, perhaps feeling the weight of his responsibility to get his crew to target and back safely. Burpee disliked the strict protocol that often separated Air Force officers (Arthur, Brady, and Weller) from sergeants (Pegler, Jaye, Long, and himself), even on the same crew. So, to buck the protocol and promote esprit de corps, Burpee frequently gathered his crew away from the station to socialize.

"[Lewis] couldn't go drinking with some of his crew," a family member said, "because officers and NCOs [non-commissioned officers] were forced to go to different messes."[13]

Born in Ottawa in 1918, Lewis Johnstone Burpee grew up the eldest son of Lewis Arthur Burpee, vice president of Ogilvy's, a higher-end department store in Canada's capital city. Lewis Jr. excelled in athletics and academics, earning a

---

* The Distinguished Flying Medal (DFM), awarded only to a non-commissioned officer (NCO) member of an aircrew, was highly prized and revered; despite the fact that 70 percent of Bomber Command crews were NCOs, only 6,638 DFMs were awarded. By contrast, 20,000 Distinguished Flying Crosses (DFCs) were awarded to Bomber Command officers.

degree in English, history, and politics from Queen's University in Kingston, while also serving with the army militia in the Canadian Officers' Training Corps. He enlisted on December 17, 1940, a year to the day after the creation of the British Commonwealth Air Training Plan (BCATP), Canada's largest financial and employment contribution to the war effort;* nine months later he'd received his pilot's wings and embarked for England. Outwardly calm and reserved, in a bomber cockpit F/Sgt. Burpee exhibited intelligence, capability, and a natural ability to lead. In mid-1942, he'd completed courses converting him from twin-engine light bombers to the four-engine heavies, including the A.V. Roe Lancaster; Burpee also caught the eye of RAF brass, who considered his skills strong enough to be considered for the Pathfinder Force—advanced bomber crews.

The twenty-four-year-old Burpee had also fallen in love with Lillian Westwood, whose family had lost a home in Greenwich to the Blitz, and whose wish to study performance art at Oxford was displaced by her country's need for workers in the home service. As the RAF moved Lewis from one bomber station to another, Lillian did her best to follow. They exchanged countless letters as he pressed the Air Force to find and register their wedding certificate, while trying to find her accommodation.

"Hoping to see you in Lincoln on Saturday," he wrote to her in October 1942. "I don't know how much flying we'll

---

* In December 1939, Canada, Australia, New Zealand, and the UK agreed to establish the British Commonwealth Air Training Plan (training of military aircrew) in Canada; it would cost the Canadian government nearly $2 billion and employ 104,000 Canadians at 230 training sites from coast to coast, while training nearly a quarter of a million qualified aircrew in five years.

be doing in the next two or three days, but I imagine meal times would be the best bet to put a call through to the switchboard. . . . There's lots more I want to say, my darling, but it's time to get down to the flight. Your loving husband, Lewis."[14]

By the winter of 1942–43, the couple had found a flat near his air base, F/Sgt. Burpee had accumulated thirty-one combat operations with the RAF's crack 106 Squadron, and he was up for a Distinguished Flying Medal.

"Flight Sergeant Burpee has shown coolness and courage," the citation of merit stated, "and has performed his duties conscientiously and efficiently."

The skipper of Lancaster ZN-H would need all of that courage and efficiency to successfully complete the crew's thirty-second combat operation, to bomb the Krupp factories at Essen in the Ruhr Valley. At dusk on March 12, Burpee hustled his crew aboard the lorry for transport to their bomber. En route he scanned the pages of a YMCA pocket pad on which he had a checklist of what each man would need, from flight gear to chewing gum. When he was sure every item was accounted for, he directed his six crewmates up the short ladder and through a door on the starboard side of the bomber. Since they would be working in unheated sections of the Lanc, mid-upper gunner Long and rear gunner Brady were dressed in flying gear that included an electrically heated inner suit, gloves, and boot liners.[15] Brady turned left along the fuselage, sliding over the tailplane spar and entering his rear turret feet first. Meanwhile, Long pulled down a moveable step to climb into the mid-upper turret and secured himself into a drop seat there. There wasn't room for either man to wear or hold his parachute in his gun position, so the chutes were stowed nearby.

Once inside the crew door, the rest of Burpee's aircrew moved to the right, up the bomb-bay steps, and closed an armoured bulkhead door behind them. Clambering over the main wing spar, they entered the heated portion of the fuselage; though they didn't have to wear heated suits, temperatures at high altitude could hover just above freezing for the whole trip. And with no pressurization in the aircraft, everybody wore oxygen masks with intercom microphones attached.*

First to settle into his position on the port side forward of the crew door was wireless operator Weller; in front of him, navigator Jaye sat in a curtained-off area that allowed him to use some light on his maps and nav table. Farther ahead, on the flight deck, Burpee's pilot seat took up the space on the left; to the right was a moveable seat for flight engineer Pegler. Bomb aimer Arthur moved past them both down a narrow passageway into the nose, where he would spend the entire trip in a prone position—his bomb sight directly in front of him and the bomb release controls at his right hand. When called for, Arthur could stand and immediately be at the controls of the front turret guns above him. Presently, with his crew in place, Burpee called on Pegler for start-up, first the port outer engine, then the port inner, the starboard inner, and finally the starboard outer. This gave life to the Lanc's hydraulics, allowing Long and Brady to test their turret rotation and

---

* On a similar high-altitude sortie in the same month, March 1943, the pilot of a Lancaster from RAF No. 44 Squadron couldn't raise his rear-turret gunner, Grant McDonald (from Grand Forks, British Columbia), on the bomber's intercom. When the wireless operator checked on McDonald, the airman was unconscious; condensation in his breathing apparatus had frozen solid, cutting off his oxygen supply. Despite days of severe headaches afterward, F/Sgt. McDonald went on to serve with a fellow Canadian, pilot Ken Brown, on the dams raid of May 16–17, 1943.

gun-laying controls. Eventually, Burpee taxied ZN-H from the dispersal pad into a lineup on the perimeter track for takeoff.

One by one, each fully loaded 68,000-pound bomber accelerated across Syerston's grass airstrip, getting airborne just before reaching the hedges surrounding the airfield, and rose into a darkening sky. Once up to about 6,000 feet, Burpee throttled back ZN-H's four Merlin engines to cruising revolutions and waited for the rest of "A" Flight to rise and join him in a left-hand circuit above Syerston. That's when F/Sgt. Burpee completed an intercom check with each crewman— mid-upper and rear gunners, flight engineer, wireless radio operator, navigator, and bomb aimer.

"Okay, sir," Arthur said, even though as a warrant officer he outranked his sergeant pilot skipper.

Each flight of bombers, with navigation lights now turned off, began the sixty-mile flight over the North Sea to the rendezvous spot off the enemy coast—occupied Holland. It was zero hour minus sixty minutes when the bomber stream formed up before entering enemy airspace. Burpee called for a double-check to ensure all lights inside and outside the aircraft were doused. Gunners Brady and Long cocked their weapons. Meanwhile, bomb aimer Arthur completed his final task before entering enemy territory: he fused the bombs by turning an electro-mechanical switch on a fusing panel inside the Lancaster, in effect making the payload "live."[16] Now in complete darkness, the bomber force seemed like "a glass brick, two miles across, twenty miles long, 8,000 feet thick, filled with hundreds of Lancasters,"[17] a wave of the most lethal firepower Bomber Command could unleash on a target. Before long, the bombers attracted the attention of German coastal batteries, and the first bursts of flak stabbed up at the night sky ahead of them. Registering the locations of the flak bursts, Burpee began to weave, changing altitude, course, and speed in order to evade the next bursts. It was tricky work. On the one hand, he needed to avoid a mid-air collision with another bomber in the dark; on the other, he had to remain unpredictable, since German anti-aircraft batteries had sufficient experience to estimate symmetrical movements if the searchlights caught a bomber in their sweeps.

As the bomber passed the coastline and edged ever closer to that turnip-shaped blotch of red the aircrew had seen on the briefing map back at Syerston, the reality of the Ruhr became ever clearer to W/O Arthur, isolated in the bomb aimer's blister in the nose of the Lancaster. Perhaps twenty minutes from Essen itself, W/O Arthur saw them.

"Scores of searchlights," he reported.[18]

In particular, two great cones of light straddled their intended path into Happy Valley. It would be up to the skipper and the navigator to thread the Lancaster past the belt of lights without being coned—caught in a convergence of searchlights. The glaring beams could quickly and devastatingly disorient a pilot.

"For long seconds on end, the dazzling glare would render a pilot helpless," pilots said, "making it almost impossible for him to see his instruments and maintain any sense of equilibrium."[19]

At the same time, amid the blinding lights, the bomber pilot had to evade the streams of heavy shells racing up from the ground and exploding around the aircraft. Burpee had flown with five different navigators, once he'd gone operational in October 1942, but throughout his most recent sixteen ops, he'd settled on Tommy Jaye. The coal miner's son from Durham, England, had been trained as an observer at a flying school run by Pan American Airways in Miami, Florida. He'd been to the Ruhr Valley a handful of times—Essen twice before—and knew what to expect.

"A forty-mile-long corridor of exploding shells" had to be considered, "and the danger of collision with four hundred . . . aircraft going through the aiming point in twenty minutes."[20]

Burpee's crew knew, at least, that by the time the Lancasters reached the aiming point, just minutes from the target, the Halifaxes, Wellingtons, and Stirlings would already have passed through the lights and the most dangerous anti-aircraft fire and would have begun the bombing run. As well, all the 106 Squadron Lancasters would be flying at the same altitude—19,000 feet—and all in the same direction. But the sky was still alive with red stars, all of them angry explosions, all of them crackling louder by the second. Every airman knew he was running the gauntlet, the acrid smell of cordite in his nostrils or stinging his eyes, and the beams of searchlights ricocheting wildly inside the fuselage, casting demonic shadows on everything. Gunner Brady looked through his rear-viewing blister in time to see a bomber coned by a number of searchlights, flak bursting around it. The pilot pushed the stricken craft into a dive, left, then right, attempting to escape, but in vain. Its starboard wing dropped and the aircraft fell earthward, trailing smoke and fire.

"Bastards!" one of the crew blurted out.

Finally the explosions faded momentarily, and Burpee's Lancaster was past searchlights and anti-aircraft bursts. Dead ahead were the welcome carpets of red and green light—the TI markers laid down by the RAF Pathfinders—right on time, and right in line with their route to the targets. The Mosquitos had done their job perfectly.

Burpee gave Arthur his warning for the bombing run.

"Bomb doors open, sir," Arthur reported. "I can see the target."

The skipper waited for last-second course adjustments from Arthur and responded according to his directions to make sure the load went down accurately.

"Left, left . . . Steady . . ." Then a light appeared on Arthur's controls that allowed him to make a final intercom call to his pilot: "Bombs gone!"

ZN-H responded predictably, buoying upward in response to the sudden reduction in weight. Burpee made sure to finish the run over the target for about three minutes, and then quickly banked port to 290 degrees for the route home. Behind them, the muffled explosions of their 4,000-pound high-capacity bomb and sixteen incendiaries added to the light show from the ground. From his astro-dome, mid-upper gunner Long could see the scene behind the tailplane. A volcano of flame flashed upward, followed by black smoke billowing everywhere. But even as his Lancaster made its quick exit, the battle still raged over Essen.

On three of Burpee's previous trips to Happy Valley, his aircraft had been hit by flak and night-fighter cannon fire; the attacks knocked out his wireless radio on one trip and Brady's rear turret on another. Twice the damage sustained forced Burpee to make an emergency landing at an alternative airfield on the return flight, but the combined skill of his aircrew and its good fortune left nobody injured and the Lancaster intact. So it was on March 12, 1943: Jimmy Arthur's first trip with Burpee's crew went exactly the way he'd hoped—relatively uneventfully. They had deftly dodged the searchlights and flak all the way there and back. They had dropped their payload on the target identification flares as ordered. It had been only a five-hour sortie, and rookie Arthur had experienced his share of first-op anxiety. But unlike dozens of other crews in this first week of the air offensive against the Ruhr Valley, the crew of Lancaster ZN-H made it home safely. That same night, eight other Lancasters, seven Halifaxes, six Wellingtons, and two Stirlings and their crews—5 percent of the force—had not.

Photographic reconnaissance after the March 12 raid showed that the Main Force of bombers had passed right across the massive Krupp factory, west of Essen, and had delivered 30 percent more damage than the sortie on March 5–6. The factory's locomotive shops had burned to the ground. In addition, five hundred houses used to accommodate factory workers had been destroyed.[21] The Battle of the Ruhr marked Bomber Command's first concerted initiative to concentrate on one target area—the industrial cities of the Ruhr River Valley—with significant results. Put another way, such positive operations reports represented the first body blows delivered in the enemy's corner of the ring. And war-weary Britons and their allies needed every morale boost their warriors could provide. The Battle of the Ruhr would last for four months—from March to July 1943—and would include forty-three major Bomber Command operations against the heart of Germany's war-production plants. The battle would test the machinery, talent, and fortitude of all involved, most critically the bomber crews, such as the one W/O Jimmy Arthur had joined for the first time during the March 12 raid against Essen.

"That is how it is done, by young men with guts, by science and by skill," wrote one Ruhr Valley veteran. "This was the beginning, the end of three years' hard experiment. The bomber could at last hit hard. It could choose tactical or strategical targets. It didn't mind which. Both were allergic to bombs."[22]

JUST AFTER 1 A.M. ON MARCH 13, 1943, LEWIS BURPEE brought his bomber and its crew safely down at Syerston airfield, completing his thirty-second combat operation and advancing the Battle of the Ruhr through another significant night. There was a requisite debriefing with an intelligence officer about the effectiveness of the bombing run, the impact of the German defences, and observations of anything out of the ordinary. All of his crewmen then sat down to a hearty breakfast and a tot of rum, if they wanted it. Finally, they retired to the barracks huts for a well-deserved sleep. When the skipper of ZN-H awoke later that same day, he had paperwork to complete. Even though it was just mid-month, Burpee was asked to add up his service time, now just over 635 hours in the air, and enter the totals in his pilot's log.

Then, as protocol required, he submitted the log to his senior officers for review and verification. First, the officer commanding Burpee's "A" Flight checked the Air Force–blue ledger of Burpee's service. Next, the wing commander (W/C) of 106 Squadron looked it over and signed off on it too. Both Burpee's flight commander and wing commander had flown their own Lancasters to most of those same targets on the Ruhr with him. The Wingco took great pride in the crews of his outfit, including the twenty-five-year-old RCAF sergeant pilot from Ottawa; he'd signed Burpee's pilot's log every month since October 1942, each time acknowledging the young Canadian's capability in the cockpit, each time noting the effectiveness of his operational sorties, and each time assessing his ability as a leader of men. Indeed, earlier that winter, the wing commander had endorsed Burpee's recommendation for the DFM.

As noteworthy as Lewis Burpee's just-completed first tour of duty and the DFM seemed, his wing commander had distinguished himself as a bomber pilot almost like no other. Guy Gibson, twenty-five years old (like Burpee), had flown not just one tour of duty but a combination of 174 fighter and bomber combat operations. Eventually ranked among its most celebrated citizens, Guy Gibson did not see Britain until the age of four, in 1922, when his family moved from India. He fell in love with flying while at boarding school in the early 1930s, but was refused entry to the Air Force on his first application. By 1937, however, he'd graduated from RAF flight school, had a short service commission, and was posted to Scotland. On the first day of the Second World War, he flew his first combat operation against German shipping. By September 1940 he'd completed one tour at RAF No. 83 Squadron in Bomber Command and earned a Distinguished Flying Cross (DFC). Arthur Harris, then the officer commanding No. 5 Group, described the young flight lieutenant (F/L) as "the most full-out fighting pilot" in his command. During his second tour, at RAF No. 29 Squadron in Fighter Command through 1941, F/L Gibson earned a handful of kills and another DFC, but was shot down in April.

"I'd just come back from shooting down [a Heinkel He 111] and was very pleased with myself coming in to land," Gibson later described. "And a ruddy . . . Junkers 88 dived out of the sun and smacked me down in front of all the boys."[23]

With no time or altitude to bail out, Gibson crashed into trees right on his home aerodrome, but remarkably suffered no injuries. He underwent further training and scored among the highest flying and gunnery ratings in his course, and then became a flight instructor for a short time. But he got restless and sought a return to active service when Harris, now air officer commanding-in-chief of Bomber Command, promoted Gibson to wing commander at 106 Squadron, flying the new four-engine Lancasters. He completed three more full tours through 1942 and early 1943. He earned a colourful if sometimes overzealous reputation, pushing his crews aggressively against more difficult targets. Some aircrew he rubbed the wrong way nicknamed him "The Boy Emperor," but while Gibson expected supreme effort from his squadron, he readily shared the high risk of ever more dangerous combat operations, including the attack against the German battleships *Gneisenau* and *Scharnhorst* as well as the bombing run against the electric transformer station at Le Creusot, France. In November 1942, he was awarded the Distinguished Service Order (DSO). In January 1943, Gibson agreed to take British Broadcasting Corporation (BBC) journalist Richard Dimbleby aboard his Lancaster on a night bombing raid to Berlin; the resulting broadcast shed new light on the bomber crews' Herculean efforts to turn the tide in the war and give Britons hope of eventual victory.

"I understand their hardship now," Dimbleby reported. "And I am proud to have seen the stars with them."[24]

In the new year, Bomber Command's focus shifted to large German centres of industry and population. Commander-in-Chief Arthur Harris called it his "main offensive," a concentration of the bomber force's growing strength against major targets until they were destroyed. Harris considered Berlin a top priority; to destroy it, he calculated, would put Germany out of the war. But he recognized that Bomber Command wasn't quite up to that task yet. Earlier in the war, Wellington, Whitley, and Hampden bombers had struggled with bomb loads too small, distances to the target too great, and German defences too overpowering to inflict serious damage on Berlin. As evidenced by the raids early in March, Harris chose to first test the striking power of his bomber force in a pitched battle against Germany's major war-production centres, along with its power plants, dams, and reservoirs—hence the Battle of the Ruhr River Valley. And W/C Gibson, who'd been up for an additional citation, was emerging as one of Harris's rising stars.

"Any Captain who completes 172 sorties in outstanding manner," Harris wrote in his approval of Gibson's second Distinguished Service Order decoration, "is worth two DSOs, if not a VC [Victoria Cross]."[25]

As high a priority as citations of merit were to the Bomber Command brass, the processing of Air Force awards, such as Gibson's second DSO and Burpee's DFM, took place way over the bomber pilots' heads. The war that aircrews waged existed in briefing rooms, crew trucks, cockpits, and post-op paperwork. At the end of the first week of the Battle of the Ruhr, F/Sgt. Burpee had his pilot's log to update on the March 12–13 Essen trip. And, as it turned out, WC Gibson was recovering from a rough trip he'd completed the night before, a sortie to Stuttgart on March 11–12. On that op, the outer port engine of his Lancaster had suddenly lost power. Nevertheless, Gibson managed to drop his bomb load, at a dangerously low altitude, and then pilot his crippled bomber past German night fighters and coastal defences and home to Syerston station. He rose from his sleep the next morning feeling the effects of five tours of duty and countless near misses, and craving some rest.

"After a year of this sort of thing," he wrote, "I was getting a bit weary."[26]

Gibson had planned a quiet escape with his wife, Eve, in Cornwall. But it was not to be. Instead, he'd been awoken at his officer's barracks at Syerston and told that Air Vice-Marshal (AVM) Ralph Cochrane, the air officer commanding (AOC) No. 5 Group of Bomber Command, wanted to see him at St. Vincents, in group headquarters. Grudgingly, Gibson drove his Humber to St. Vincents in Grantham, expecting that his CO was about to post him to a new station. Not so. Cochrane asked if he would relocate to group headquarters and write a guidebook for novice bomber pilots. He returned to Syerston to say goodbye to his comrades at 106 Squadron. He partied into the night and rose on March 14 to pack for his new posting. But Cochrane wanted to see him again. Back in his CO's office at St. Vincents, Gibson received word that a second DSO would be awarded him. That had barely sunk in when Cochrane changed the subject.

"How would you like the idea of doing one more trip?" the CO said.[27]

Gibson's immediate thought was of more night fighters and flak, but he finally spoke. "What kind of a trip, sir?"

"A pretty important one, perhaps one of the most devastating of all time," Cochrane suggested. "Do you want to do it?"

Gibson agreed. But the other shoe didn't drop until three days later. Back in Cochrane's office, Gibson met G/C Charles Whitworth, who offered him a cigarette, told him to sit down, and began to explain. "This is no ordinary sortie."[28]

The thought of an attack on German naval vessels crossed Gibson's mind.

"The training for the raid is of such importance," Whitworth went on, "that the commander-in-chief has decided that a special squadron is to be formed for the job."

Gibson absorbed every word Whitworth and Cochrane had to say, but there was little intelligence offered as to the target, the nature of the attack, or the timing—except that the attack couldn't take place for two months. Gibson's superior officers emphasized urgency, efficiency, training, and strict discipline but gave him no specifics. Their meeting was over almost as quickly as it had been convened. For a moment, Gibson stood there wondering where his flight gear was. Then his thoughts turned to contemplating his future, and the futures of those he would choose to join him. Whitworth wanted the best crews Gibson could find. Naturally, he first considered the aircrew with whom he'd been flying at 106 Squadron, including Australian Dave Shannon, fellow Briton John Hopgood, and the Canadian, Lewis Burpee.

The now-decorated Burpee, like Gibson, had taken the short leave available after the Essen sortie and returned to Newark, Nottinghamshire, and Elmhurst, where he and his wife of seven months, Lillian, had rented a flat. But Gibson was soon in touch. He congratulated the sergeant pilot on his

DFM and explained he needed experienced crews for a special operation. Was Burpee up for it? Burpee agreed to volunteer but wanted to get a commitment from his crew first. Within the week, Burpee's Lancaster crew, including his newly christened bomb aimer Jimmy Arthur, had agreed to join a mystery squadron that had not yet been assigned a number or name. They and twenty other aircrews—some 147 Commonwealth airmen from Britain, Australia, Canada, and New Zealand, and one from the United States—agreed to train and operate in total secrecy for almost two months. Although they didn't yet know it, these men would soon spearhead a pivotal operation in the Battle of the Ruhr, unleashing a powerful new weapon against the Ruhr River dams and becoming known in military aviation history as Bomber Command's famous "Dam Busters."

CHAPTER TWO

AN EARTHQUAKE BOMB

It was March 24, 1943, about a week after Guy Gibson agreed to take on the top-secret operation, when the not quite twenty-five-year-old bomber pilot met military aircraft designer Barnes Wallis, fifty-five, for the first time. For the purposes of maintaining wartime secrecy in his journal, W/C Gibson used caricatures to identify the men connected with his new assignment. That morning, instead of beginning a well-deserved leave with his wife, Eve, in Cornwall, Gibson was whisked away in a car, put on a train to Weybridge, southwest of London, and met by a man he simply referred to as "Mutt" (it was chief test pilot Mutt Summers from Vickers, the British engineering company), who drove the two to a Georgian-style country home at the former Burhill Golf Club. There, clearing several security checks, Mutt led Gibson along corridors, down dark stairs, through an iron door, and into an underground laboratory, where he met a man he described as bespectacled, neither young nor old, but earnest, hard-working.

Gibson called him "Jeff" in his journal.* Then he recounted his conversation with the man—Vickers scientist Barnes Wallis.

"I'm glad you've come," Wallis began. "I don't suppose you know what for."[1]

"No idea," Gibson said.

The fair-haired scientist raised his eyebrows and asked, "Do you mean to say you don't know the target?"

"Not the faintest idea."

Momentarily, the discussion diverted from the issue at hand into the protocol of it all. Gibson tried to explain the secrecy imposed around his visit. Wallis waved a paper in the air with a short list of names of those allowed to hear what he was about to say. And Summers called the whole charade silly. After a few awkward moments, Gibson went silent and Wallis, choosing his words very carefully, started to explain. He said that enemy territory housed certain objectives that were vulnerable military targets—things such as viaducts, submarine pens, and large ships, for example. The difficulty, he pointed out, was that attacking them required a high-performance aircraft, a uniquely designed bomb or mine, and deadly accuracy. He noted that the arrival of the Lancaster bomber had reduced the delivery problem. But beyond that, the attack would have to occur at a low level, below three hundred feet, which increased the risk that the explosion would damage or destroy the Lancaster delivering the bomb. Drop the weapon from higher than the prescribed altitude,

---

* Augustus *Mutt* and Jim *Jeffries* were fictional characters created by American cartoonist Henry Conway "Bud" Fisher for his newspaper comic strip, which debuted in the *San Francisco Chronicle* in 1907; the phrase "Mutt and Jeff" was allusively used in conversation to describe a pair of affable losers—Mutt being the tall one and Jeff the short one.

he said, and accuracy diminishes. It was a vicious circle. He alluded to additional snags in the scenario: "the danger of flak at that level and balloons, and the difficulty of flying over water at low level."[2]

"Over water?" Gibson said.

"Yes, over water at night or early morning, when the water will be as flat as a millpond, backed up with a lot of haze or fog all around," Wallis said.

It was Gibson's nature to think ahead, so he deduced the target was the German battleship *Tirpitz*, moored in a Norwegian fjord, or perhaps the U-boat pens along the coasts of Germany and France. But before he could say anything, Wallis had turned off the lab lights, cuing the start of a motion-picture projector. The three men watched a title, *Most Secret Trial Number One*, flash on the movie screen. The scene cut to a Wellington bomber diving toward the surface of a body of water, then levelling out at about two hundred feet. Gibson watched in amazement as a large object fell from the bomber to the water and began bouncing across the surface. Gibson didn't know it at the time, but Mutt and Jeff were the pilot and bomb aimer aboard that Wellington in the film, and the location was a secret test range over the Fleet, a narrow, seven-mile-long lagoon just inland from Chesil Beach on the south coast of England, near the Isle of Portland. *Most Secret Trial Number One* had been shot fifteen weeks earlier, on December 4, 1942.

"That's my special mine to overcome our difficulties, and it does work," Wallis said emphatically.[3]

Gibson asked if the trials had gone beyond the prototype stage. Wallis said he'd been told that A.V. Roe, the aircraft manufacturer, had crews working around the clock to outfit a Lancaster with special calipers to carry a bomb four times the size of the one depicted in the motion-picture film. But now Wallis wanted answers from Gibson on the more pressing issues of delivery of his secret bouncing bomb. Could Gibson and his aircrews bring a bomber out of a 2,000-foot dive, level off at 150 feet above smooth water at an air speed of 240 miles per hour, and drop a bomb on target?

Gibson considered the loaded question and suggested it would be tough, but worth trying. Then, just as quickly as he'd arrived at the old Burhill Golf Club grounds, Gibson was escorted from Wallis's laboratory and transported back to the reality of assembling a new squadron of Lancasters and their crews to make a low-level attack over water with a mysterious bouncing explosive device against an unknown target at night.

FAR FROM THE "JEFF" CARICATURE GIBSON HAD USED in his journal, but not without an animated personality, Barnes Wallis was quite remote, driven by analytical thinking whether in his home or at work. According to both his family and his co-workers, he was painstaking and unstinting in whatever project he faced.[4] In his prime, he was both demanding of himself and stubborn in his faith in any idea he believed could succeed. He was also realistic enough, as a scientist working inside a corporate bureaucracy but with a non-conformist perspective, to choose his battles carefully. He understood systems and the people within those systems. He recognized the need to find allies for any new project. It was a matter of patience and persistence, and he had plenty of both.

Born in 1887, the second son of four children, Barnes and his older brother, John, had designated a corner of their home in London as a workshop where they made paper structures for their sister Annie; Barnes had already decided to become an engineer. At seventeen, he left grammar school to take a job with Thames Engineering Works. Next, an apprenticeship with the shipbuilding firm J. Samuel White on the Isle of Wight helped him attain his marine engineering papers. In 1913, Wallis took a position with Vickers working in its aviation department, but at the outbreak of the Great War, when the Admiralty cut back its airship production, Wallis lost his job. He tried to enlist, but failed because of his bad eyesight. No problem. When he tried a second time and was asked to strip for the physical, he did so next to the eye chart and memorized it well enough to be accepted as a sub-lieutenant in the Royal Naval Air Service. With the war on and airships a higher priority, the War Office streamed Wallis back into dirigible designing. During downtime, he also taught and completed his engineering degree by correspondence at the University of London.

By the time he married Molly Bloxom in 1925, he'd become assistant chief designer at Vickers, where he helped design the framework for the R100 airship, but the crash of R101 that killed forty-eight crew in 1930 put an end to the company's airship program, and Wallis moved to Vickers's aviation design centre at Weybridge the same year. Life at the Wallis home raced ahead as rapidly as Barnes's career at Vickers through the 1930s and toward the outbreak of the Second World War in 1939. He and Molly had purchased White Hill House, a large Tudor home at Effingham, in Surrey. They eventually had four children of their own, but then adopted the two children of Molly's sister when she was killed in a wartime air raid. At his home, nestled on grounds adjacent to a golf course, Barnes helped raise the children; he was a strict but caring father who filled any spare time wood carving, playing golf, listening to music, and bell ringing at the local church.

Meanwhile, at work he assisted in the production design of the Vickers Wellesley light bomber, and in 1936 the company's long-range Wellington bomber. His unique geodesic "basket weave"[5] design fashioned lightweight alloy pieces into a latticework airframe capable of housing plenty of fuel and bomb payload while giving its aircrew the best chance of surviving flak and fighter attack and getting home safely. One of Wallis's co-workers considered him among the most respected aeronautical engineers of his time.

"He reckoned he could do anything he wanted to do if he gave enough thought to it, provided he did not upset any basic laws of physics," contemporary draftsman Norman Boorer commented. "He did not let problems stand in his way."[6]

The concept of destroying or disabling the reservoir dams along Nazi Germany's industrial Ruhr River Valley did not come from Barnes Wallis's drafting table. It was not his idea. It emerged from Britain's experience in the Great War. At the war's end in 1918, Major General Hugh Montague "Boom" Trenchard, the first chief of RAF Air Staff, concluded that the morale effect of aerial bombing an enemy outweighed the physical twenty to one and, should the need arise, the Royal Flying Corps (later the RAF) would have to develop "long-distance aerial operations against an enemy's main source of supply."[7] That's when the military bureaucracy, including a department called the Industrial Intelligence in Foreign Countries Committee, chaired by experienced bureaucrat Sir Maurice Hankey, joined the discussion.

As war loomed again in the mid-1930s, the committee began to gather data outside Britain; it considered potential warfare with certain countries, drafted strategic policies to wage it, and identified possible targets for Bomber Command to attack.[8] As early as 1937, Air Staff considered thirteen plans, known as the Western Air Plans; one of them called for attacking the oil supplies in the Ruhr River Valley. Bomber Command, the RAF group responsible for implementing the plan, chose nineteen power plants and twenty-six coking plants as potential targets. It predicted that 3,000 aircraft sorties over two weeks could bring the enemy's entire war production to a halt, at an estimated cost of 176 bombers.[9] At six crewmen per Wellington bomber, that would cost well over a thousand RAF lives.

Another advisory group, called the Air Targets Sub-Committee, proposed a more realistic plan that would ultimately become the core of Operation Chastise on May 16–17, 1943, striking just two targets—the Möhne and Sorpe Dams. From the sub-committee's research, Hankey surmised that such an attack would cause widespread and chaotic flooding, cease or severely interrupt electricity generation, and cut off the flow of water as a coolant to industrial facilities downriver. He then added the Eder Dam, as well as locks, aqueducts, and canals, to the list of potential enemy targets.

The Air Ministry, the government department established in 1918 to supervise civil and military aviation in Britain, contributed to the strategic discussion by analyzing the types of dams targeted, as well as the nature of the weapon required to breach them. In October 1937, its report concluded that a gravity-type dam, including those on the Ruhr, could not be successfully breached even if attacks created fissures in its wall. The following year, 1938, Air Vice-Marshal W. Sholto Douglas chaired a midsummer session of the committee, reinforcing the notion that certain reservoirs were the enemy's Achilles heel, perhaps a slight exaggeration of the facts.[10] However, the committee did address the damaging impact that breaching the large reservoir dams in the Ruhr River would have on railways, bridges, pumping stations, and industrial chemical plants below the dams.

Thus the Air Ministry began to weigh the relative importance and difficulties of successfully breaching gravity and earth dams (the Möhne and Sorpe, respectively). The gravity dam consisted of a masonry (stone and concrete) construction, roughly triangular in shape (broad at the base, narrow at the top), that was held in position by its own weight,[11] therefore protecting itself against the horizontal force of the water; sluices about halfway up the face of the dam allowed quick drainage of water in an emergency. Meanwhile, the earth dam relied on a vertical concrete or clay wall stabilized by banks of earth that tapered away on both sides.[12] Flooding over the top of the dam was prevented by allowing water through a sluice; at the same time, excess water could trickle through minor cracks in the wall, but with loam mixed into the earth on the reservoir side, the dam was self-sealing. As far as Bomber Command was concerned on the eve of the Second World War, neither the Möhne nor the Sorpe appeared to be an easy target, even though the German authority responsible for them—Ruhrtalsperrenverein—warned as late as August 29, 1939, that "several bombs dropped twenty to thirty metres [24 to 33 yards] away from [a gravity] dam which explode below the water-line . . . might cause the wall to collapse."[13] However, five days later, September 3, when Britain declared war on Germany, neither the protection nor the destruction of the Ruhr River dams seemed a high priority among war strategists on either side.

As the Second World War began, British politicians and military leaders had far more pressing issues to address than the feasibility of destroying gravity and earth dams in the middle of Germany. Nevertheless, the Air Ministry Bombing Committee hadn't lost sight of the Möhne, Eder, and Sorpe Dams as priority military targets. Indeed, in July 1940, Air Vice-Marshal Norman Bottomley, Assistant Chief of the Air Staff (ACAS), and Air Chief Marshal Sir Charles Portal, Chief of Air Staff (CAS), echoed the conclusions of the July 1938 Bombing Committee in both consideration of the Möhne Dam as a primary target for destruction and the belief that success was "by no means impossible provided the correct weapons are available."[14] Both men made the case for overall approval of the operation, encouraged the development of aircraft and bombing technology to make it work, and called for the creation of a special unit within Bomber Command to accomplish the task.

MEANWHILE, IN THE FIRST MONTHS OF THE WAR, Vickers and its staff of production crews and designers, including Barnes Wallis, had their hands full. Rex Pierson, the company's chief designer and the brains behind Britain's Vimy heavy bomber in 1917,* had the majority of draftsmen and engineers at the firm answering the Air Ministry's urgent call for a new heavy bomber (to replace the Wellington), which would be named the "Windsor." It would employ Wallis's patented geodesic interior design, with a pressurized crew cabin. Its four Rolls-Royce Merlin engines would allow the aircraft to fly at more than three hundred miles per hour and up to altitudes of 40,000 feet, and to carry an 8,000-pound bomb load.

Because he was assistant chief designer, Barnes Wallis had some latitude to think about the slightly more long-range and larger picture. The space he needed to explore such things came both with his "assistant" job title and with circumstances. When Luftwaffe bombs began falling on and around London, Vickers moved its design offices from Weybridge to the Burhill Golf Club. There, on the first floor of the clubhouse, in the relative peace of the country and away from the day-to-day bustle of the main Vickers production office (not to mention the Air Ministry), Wallis began to think beyond aircraft design and function. He recognized that modern warfare depended on industrial production—largely the manufacture of steel—which in turn depended on sources of power. He considered that the optimum attack against the enemy would disrupt its war effort or, if possible, destroy at source its ability to fight. He deduced that coal mines, oil fields, and reservoir dams were therefore high-priority targets, and

---

* The Vickers Vimy aircraft achieved additional notoriety in June 1919 when John Alcock and Arthur Brown, former Royal Flying Corps pilots of the Great War, flew their modified bomber from St. John's, Newfoundland, to County Galway, Ireland—the first transatlantic airplane flight in less than seventy-two consecutive hours.

that his job was to design potentially war-ending weapons to destroy them.[15]

"The first thing an engineer would think of as an effective way of stopping a war, would be to stop the supply of steel," Wallis said. "And the estimate is that roughly a hundred tons of water is necessary to produce one ton of steel."[16]

And so Barnes Wallis went back to school—all by himself—to study bombs, their behaviour, their chemistry, and their physics. He also researched data on the construction of German gravity, multiple-arch, and earth dams; in particular, he tracked down reports on file at the Institution of Civil Engineers and the Ministry of Aircraft Production (MAP) about the civil engineering of the power facility some thirty miles east of the main centres of Ruhr River industry, namely the Möhne Dam. As buried in the minutiae of bomb research that Wallis became, he also recognized the need to develop contacts—allies in government and the military who would transform his theories into action. Through a mutual friend, for example, Wallis met G/C Fred Winterbotham. An aviator himself, Winterbotham had served in the Royal Flying Corps in the Great War and then, at the behest of the RAF, moved about Europe, among other things, meeting and spying on senior Luftwaffe commanders just prior to the Second World War. Then in his forties, Winterbotham moved to MI6 as head of air intelligence and consequently into the trusted inner circles of power in Britain—at the Air Ministry and even the Prime Minister's Office. Winterbotham and Wallis met numerous times both professionally and at Wallis's home, Winterbotham sharing what German intelligence he could and Wallis offering his research and projections. Winterbotham sensed he needed to introduce some of Wallis's well-organized hypotheses to people in high places, including Winston Churchill's scientific advisor Lord Cherwell (Professor Frederick A. Lindemann).

With the Battle of Britain raging over southern England in mid-1940, Wallis tested scale models of his design in the wind tunnel of the National Physical Laboratory at Teddington. Then he made a new contact in A.R. Collins, a scientist in the Concrete Section at the Road Research Laboratory in Harmondsworth, west of London. With Collins, Wallis broached the subject of bombing attacks against three targets—the Tirso Dam, in Italy, and the Eder and Möhne Dams on the Ruhr River—suggesting that if a squadron of aircraft dropped ten-ton bombs in the reservoir upstream from the dams, there was "a reasonable chance" at least one bomb might land within 150 feet of it.[17] For testing purposes, the laboratory decided it would build a 1:50 scale model of a masonry gravity dam, using the Möhne as an example—including its main wall, sluices, and towers; then, to accommodate the scale, the test would employ a two-ounce charge. After their first planning discussions, to make his objective crystal clear, Wallis left behind a German publication for Collins's lab team about gravity dam construction, *Gewichtsstaumauern und Massive Wehr*, which specifically contained the dimensions of the Möhne.

A month later, Collins reported back to MAP that the two-ounce charge had delivered promising results; the test indicated "severe damage" would be done to the dam.[18] The clutter mounted on Barnes Wallis's desk. He had gathered policy and strategic papers from intelligence committees, target committees, aeronautic research committees, and bombing committees as well as offshore source material in books and periodicals. He had reviewed the contingencies of the Western Air Plans and the assessments of ordnance authorities, and had listened to the cause-and-effect analysis of both veterans and junior officers serving in the RAF. He had gathered and evaluated the experiments of independent research laboratories across the country on reservoir dams, explosive devices, and aviation technology. And he had poked and prodded countless layers of government and military bureaucracy, trying to find support for his own theories and projected outcomes. Wallis knew how devastating the elimination of the Ruhr reservoir dams could be to German war industries, and how valuable to British morale. But after many months of digging and quietly campaigning, he'd still not found answers to questions he'd been asking since the mid-1930s. Where was the Möhne Dam most vulnerable? How much explosive would accomplish a breach? What kind of aircraft could deliver the blow?

Suddenly, some clarity came to Wallis at the very heart of his dilemma. In each scenario to take down the Möhne, destruction had depended upon either the amount of explosive or the proximity of the blast to the dam. Up to that point in his investigation, he had sensed that to undermine the dam would require a direct penetrating hit or such powerful shock waves nearby that the resulting vibration of the structure itself would bring it tumbling down; in the latter case, the destructive vibration would have to come by way of concussion through the air.

That's when Wallis recalled an incident involving London's Waterloo Bridge, where the concrete piles driven into the bed of the Thames River kept shattering repeatedly. An engineering journal, published in 1935, had investigated and determined that the massive drop-hammers pounding the bridge piles into the bottom of the river had caused the tops of the piles to explode upward. The physics of the mysterious pile disintegration illustrated that each blow to the top of a concrete pile sent a shock wave down the pile; when the wave hit the blunt resistance of the clay river bottom, it reverberated back up the pile at 15,000 feet per second, and with the drop-hammer momentarily off the top of the pile, there was nothing for the vibration to rebound from again, so it dissipated into the air. In other words, the shock wave had first created compression in the pile, followed by tension in the pile. The civil engineering journal concluded that the concrete resisted the crush of compression reasonably well but withstood the stretch of tension poorly. Wallis calculated that he needed to create tension in the masonry of the gravity dam. If he succeeded, the impact on the dam would be seismic, much like an earthquake. He needed to create an earthquake bomb![19]

So Wallis began to consider the design of a bomb that was as heavy as possible, as aerodynamic as possible, and dropped from as great an altitude as possible. His calculations and drawings delivered a hypothetical bomb. It weighed ten tons (containing seven tons of explosive). Its steel casing was as aerodynamic as the R100 airship exterior he'd designed in 1930. Dropped from 40,000 feet, it would accelerate to a speed of 1,440 feet per second (982 miles per hour) and penetrate to an average soil depth of 135 feet. The resulting explosion underground, if close to or touching the concrete of the dam, would cause the tension his theory called for, a seismic reaction, and cause substantial damage—in this case, an earthquake beneath the dam. Wallis surmised further that even a near miss at the dam site so deep in the ground would cause such a subterranean blast that the dam would either be shaken to pieces or fall into the cavern created by the blast. And because Wallis had also weighed the effectiveness of anti-submarine depth charges, he wondered whether shock waves triggered by a bomb underwater might have similar effects.

The problem that Wallis and RAF Bomber Command continued to face, however, was that the aircraft available at the time—such as the Wellington, the Manchester, even the four-engine Stirling or the Halifax—could not carry the ten-ton explosive required. And so the scientist who commanded some sense of the future while maintaining a firm grasp of the present set about the task of designing the ideal bomber for the RAF, in a document entitled *Bomber Aircraft: Determination of the Most Economical Size*. In short, he made the case that larger machines could be constructed more cheaply and deliver more punch than the equivalent in smaller aircraft. Wallis's paper arrived on the desks of some higher-ups, including Sir Henry Tizard, chief scientific advisor to the Ministry of Air Production; Norbert Rowe, director of technical development at MAP; and G/C Ralph Cochrane, who would eventually call on Guy Gibson to train and lead Bomber Command's attack on the dams. Bureaucracy took over again. Some higher-level Air Ministry and Air Force officials called for even larger bomber designs than Wallis had in mind—six-engine bombers, not four—while skeptics said Wallis's ideas were flawed by putting too many eggs in one basket. It looked as if Wallis was back to square one.

* * *

IN THAT AUTUMN OF 1940, EVERYTHING CHANGED. The Scandinavian countries had fallen to German invaders. So too had Belgium and France. Britain had fought back sufficiently to withdraw much of the British Expeditionary Force from Dunkirk in May 1940 and had temporarily fended off the Luftwaffe in the Battle of Britain that summer. Then, within days of Hitler's mid-July directive to launch the all-out invasion of Britain, Barnes Wallis's efforts to draw attention to his long-range ideas of putting Germany out of the war found an unexpected ally in an unlikely place. On July 19, 1940, he was called to an interview with the UK Minister of Aircraft Production, Lord Beaverbrook. Wallis didn't know it, but his friend Fred Winterbotham had campaigned to get him the interview. Wallis expected to be questioned about ways of preventing enemy aircraft from landing in open spaces around Britain, in the event of an invasion attempt. He was wrong.

"Will you go to America for me?" Beaverbrook asked at the outset of the meeting.[20]

"I'd rather stay here for you, sir," Wallis answered, somewhat puzzled.

"What would you do for me here?"

"Build you a ten-ton bomb and a Victory bomber to carry it, sir," Wallis said, digging in.

"What would that do?"

"End the war," Wallis offered, and then he pointed to the papers under his arm. "An earthquake bomb. I've got it set out here."

Beaverbrook seemed to ignore Wallis's pitch and handed him material from the United States to study regarding pressurized cabins for high-altitude flight; then he told the engineer to come back with answers the following day.

Lord Beaverbrook, a Canadian-born businessman named William Maxwell Aitken, grew up in Ontario and New Brunswick, ever focused on enterprise. With business interests as wide-ranging as insurance, debt collection, newspapers, hydroelectricity generation, cement and steel manufacturing, and securities, Aitken was a millionaire by age thirty, in 1908. Then, looking for new challenges, he moved to Britain, where he entered politics, winning in the general election of 1910. Aitken continued his successful run in business, investing in such firms as Rolls-Royce, the aero-engine builder, and buying such newspapers as the *Daily Express* and the *Globe*. During the Great War, the Canadian government placed him in charge of the War Records Office in London, recording in art, photography, and film the experiences of Canadian soldiers on the Western Front. During the war, Aitken resigned his seat so another Member of Parliament could seek election and accepted a peerage—as first Baron Beaverbrook—while focusing on his newspaper empire. In spite of the fact that Beaverbrook wielded the full power of his newspapers to support Prime Minister Neville Chamberlain's appeasement policies, in May 1940, when Winston Churchill came to power, Beaverbrook was appointed Minister of Aircraft Production, just two months before his meeting with Barnes Wallis.

On July 20, 1940, when Wallis reappeared at Beaverbrook's office with answers to his priority questions from the previous day about high-altitude flight, Wallis explained to the minister that he had already equipped a Wellington with pressurized compartments. Then Beaverbrook curiously returned to

Wallis's construction proposal from the day before. "What about a ten-ton bomb?"

Wallis was succinct in telling Beaverbrook that his idea would smash war production of the Third Reich, but that it would also require men and aircraft to accomplish.

"A ten-ton bomb and a bomber twice the size of anything else sounds like something in the distant future," Beaverbrook said.

"I've got drawings for two-ton and six-ton bombs on the same principle," Wallis offered. "My Wellingtons can carry the two-tonner all right. The new four-engined ones can carry the six-tonner. They'll be operating in a year."

"Well, I'll see my experts about it," Beaverbrook said finally, "[but] I don't like your chances."

Before departing from that second interview with Beaverbrook, Wallis left behind his written proposal, entitled *High Altitude Stratosphere Bomber*. It provided an overview of what Vickers Aviation called its "Victory" bomber. Wallis's specs showed, as yet only on paper, that the bomber would fly at 40,000 feet, reaching maximum speeds of 330 miles per hour at 35,000 feet, with a range of 4,000 miles and would deliver a 20,000-pound bomb load. Even though Wallis's documents were purely hypothetical at this stage, Beaverbrook did instruct Air Vice-Marshal Arthur W. Tedder, who was responsible for research and development, to co-operate with Wallis. That instruction gave Wallis just enough of a foot in the door for his theories to begin to attract attention inside the corridors of power.

But the entire scheme teetered that autumn. Barnes Wallis learned that his best-placed ally, AVM Tedder, was about to be posted to the Middle East. Meanwhile, with Vickers' chairman Sir Charles Craven on the inside at MAP, Wallis learned that while one air marshal expressed support for his monster bomb idea, another was equally skeptical, since no bomber existed capable of carrying the device. But by January 1941, Beaverbrook had re-entered the picture; he'd recalled that Wallis had worked on a pressurized Wellington bomber for high-altitude flight and so directed Vickers to continue research "on your fifty-ton bomber."[21] The timing proved perfect for Wallis, who was writing a comprehensive summary of his research and development from the previous year.

In *A Note on a Method of Attacking the Axis Powers*, completed in March 1941, Wallis laid out his full thesis. The introduction offered diagrams of what he'd learned about strategic bombing, showing the enemy's natural sources of power—oil wells, gasworks, hydroelectric facilities—and therefore its ability to wage war. He compared the difficulty of attacking war factories scattered across the countryside versus those clustered near the fuel that powered them. Where war production was concentrated, he wrote, it was more vulnerable. These industries could be attacked with very large bombs, delivered by larger aircraft designed and built in the United Kingdom. Then followed eight chapters, including thirty-two pages of diagrams, five appendices, and eight tables of data—117 pages overall—in which Wallis made the case for attacking the Ruhr River dams with his shock-wave or earthquake bomb. Ultimately he spelled out how "concrete structures which are quite unharmed by a charge bursting in air, are destroyed by an equal charge at the same distance, when the explosion occurs in deep water or in earth."[22] If the destruction of such hydroelectric catchment areas could be accomplished, Wallis wrote, it would mean "RENDERING THE ENEMY UTTERLY INCAPABLE OF CONTINUING TO PROSECUTE THE WAR."[23]

Wallis's report, once circulated, sparked reaction throughout officialdom. Indeed, because he'd passed it among as many as seventy scientists, politicians, and military figures, Wallis received a visit from a secret service agent and was told to cease and desist from such activity. As spring arrived and Wallis's *Note* began to move through the layers of Air Ministry bureaucracy, research began moving on another front. Yet another committee, this one at the Ministry of Aircraft Production, was organized by the director of scientific research, Dr. David R. Pye, who had convened four civilian scientists at the Road Research Laboratory in Harmondsworth, a network of offices and experimentation sites, including water tanks, wind tunnels, and other outdoor labs, by this time working exclusively for MAP. This new group, the Aerial Attack on Dams Advisory (AADA) Committee, began to review, among other things, the 1:50 model experiments that scientist A.R. Collins had conducted during the summer of 1940 at Harmondsworth.

Since those early model trials, in which Collins had concluded that a comparable charge would inflict "severe damage" on such full-scale facilities as the Möhne and Eder gravity dams, plans had remained on the backburner to purchase the unused Nant-y-Gro Dam in the Elan Valley of Wales for larger-scale, more realistic experiments. That same spring of 1941, however, as Tizard campaigned for the Ministry of Home Security to agree to hand the over Nant-y-Gro Dam to MAP for the bigger tests, Air Staff announced its final decision on both Wallis's deep-penetration bomb and the Victory bomber. There was no interest in a specialized big bomber designed solely to carry one big bomb. Four months later Vickers abandoned the Victory bomber entirely. The end of the monster bomb and Victory aircraft project was unquestionably deflating, but coincidentally, Wallis received good news on another front. And this proved critical. The Road Research Lab released a second evaluation of the tests that Collins had conducted on the 1:50 scale-model gravity dam—the one built to mimic the Möhne Dam—the previous February. When Collins and his team examined the model, they discovered that the explosion had damaged it more extensively than they first realized; further, if they placed a charge closer to the underwater base of the dam, destroying it seemed more likely.

It was beginning to dawn on Wallis that getting a bomb with sufficient explosive capacity as near as possible to the dam was both the problem and possibly the solution. Whether dropped from 20,000 feet and penetrating 130 feet underground or launched like a missile across the water, the bomb's proximity to its target remained the key. Thus far, no bomber existed that was capable of dropping the earthquake bomb and having it penetrate the earth deeply enough to do the trick. And any theoretical attack at water level, using a missile or skimming torpedo, would likely be foiled by the maze of torpedo nets the Germans had long since laid across the reservoir upstream from the dam.

In the middle of 1941, the Aerial Attack on Dams Advisory Committee convened to discuss, among other things, A.R. Collins's model gravity dam experiment and the potential experiments on the Nant-y-Gro Dam. It became clear in Collins's damage assessments that he had focused largely on the least and most effective explosives used—gelignite and plastic, respectively. In a report submitted in the fall of 1941, Collins indicated that a 15,000-pound charge detonated a hundred feet from the water-side face of the dam would cause damage, but that the static forces of the water, caused by gravity, might prove just as effective. Collins seemed to hold out some hope that plastic high explosive might compensate for the distance from the target and still deliver a breached dam.

And so, in December 1941, as the AADA Committee considered whether or not to go ahead with a blast test on an existing gravity dam, the entire initiative seemed to hang in the balance. All of Barnes Wallis's research, experiments, paper writing, and contact building had come to a crossroads. He had to come up with something, some way of solving that fundamental bomb-delivery problem, and he needed a big idea fast.

THE INSPIRATION FOR THE BOUNCING BOMB, WHICH some say is more legend than truth, came on the backyard patio at the Wallises' Effingham home in the spring of 1942. Easter vacation brought the entire Wallis family together—Barnes and Molly and their own four children, as well as their two adopted nephews. The gathering sparked backyard games, among them daughter Elizabeth's pastime of flicking glass marbles across the surface of a water tub. Perhaps taking note of the physics, not just the play, Wallis considered the action of the marble: if thrown at a low angle, the marble would skim across the water in the tub and come to rest against the side of the tub;

if thrown with high velocity, the marble might skip over the tub wall to the patio surface beyond. For scientist Wallis, the marble bouncing on the water became less a game and more a potential solution to a problem.

"I had the idea of a missile, which if dropped on the water at a considerable distance upstream of the dam," he wrote, "would reach the dam in a series of ricochets."[24]

In reaching this conclusion, Wallis might have considered the work of noted nineteenth-century gunnery expert General Sir Howard Douglas. Writing in *A Treatise on Naval Gunnery* in 1855, Douglas analyzed the ricocheting action of a cannonball on water, provided the surface was smooth and the trajectory below three or four degrees.[25] Thus, on the backyard patio Wallis enlarged the children's game by devising a catapult, firing the marbles at a low angle off the surface of the tub and watching them repeatedly bounce across the water and over a piece of string strung above the water. The game and the science came together to give Wallis a means of designing a bomb that bounced over the surface of the water—and, most importantly, over the anti-torpedo nets—to reach a target.

Wallis described his discovery to his friend G/C Winterbotham, who was intrigued but cautioned Wallis to take more time working on the idea before revealing it. Wallis did share the anecdotal trials with George Edwards, a colleague at Vickers. Edwards was an experimental manager by profession and a talented cricketer in his spare time; he shared with Wallis his spin-bowling techniques, illustrating that the more backspin he applied when throwing a cricket ball, the higher it bounced when it hit the ground. Not entirely sold on the technique, Wallis took his catapult and sample spheres to nearby Silvermere Lake. He discovered that a ball that was unspun when it hit the surface of the lake might skip a handful of times, but one shot while spinning skipped thrice as many times. In May, Wallis returned to his writing table to design and describe a spherical bomb with a double skin—the inner skin containing the explosive, the outer providing a layer of air around the charge.

"I discovered that you can make a sphere run along the surface of water in a series of bounces, if you impart to it before it is released a very high degree of . . . backspin," he explained later. "Curiously enough . . . with backspin or undercut on it, a sphere hitting the ground will bounce backwards, but if dropped on the water, it will run forwards."[26]

One piece of the puzzle was still missing, the question Wallis had posed since the beginning: how much charge and at what distance from the dam would generate the equivalent of an earthquake sufficient to weaken and breach the dam? The answer emerged thanks to A.R. Collins's group and its scale-model testing at the Road Research Laboratory and, ultimately, at the Nant-y-Gro Dam in Wales. In April, using the dam model in the laboratory, the team detonated a device eighteen inches below the surface and nine inches from the dam wall; it caused damage, but no breach. Collins concluded again that a single charge of less than 30,000 pounds—exploded a distance from a gravity dam measuring 150 to 200 feet high—would not destroy the dam. The "distance from" specifically tugged at Collins's mind. Tasked with the job of taking apart the remains of the laboratory model, Collins decided to see what a contact explosion, a charge exploded while submerged and touching the dam wall, might do. The resulting explosion sent masonry debris thirty feet in the air and immediately punched a hole in the model dam through which water gushed as the model came apart. Next, the team travelled to Wales to try a similar test at Nant-y-Gro—a gravity dam thirty feet high and 180 feet long—understanding that to generate just a crack or a crater in the dam would not be enough.

"We had, in effect, to use a battering ram rather than a hammer or pick-axe," Collins explained.[27]

And so, on July 24, 1942, the team of army engineers suspended a five-hundred-pound anti-submarine mine on a scaffold almost eight feet below the surface of the Nant-y-Gro reservoir. With high-speed film running and scientists, including Barnes Wallis, gathered to view the results, the engineers detonated the mine. With the explosion, the surface of the water suddenly whitened as the impact of the blast pushed water skyward into a spout. The size of the spout caught Collins off guard, and his finger momentarily slipped off the movie camera button. Moments later, a hole appeared in the dam on the air side of the wall and water gushed through with tremendous force. Collins could now apply his results to a gravity dam of any size and height—in other words, he now knew that a 7,500-pound contact charge detonated thirty feet below the reservoir surface could blow a hole through about forty-four feet of dam wall. This was comparable to the Möhne and Eder Dams, and it wouldn't require a monster bomber for delivery.

The ripple effect, both literally and figuratively, gave Barnes Wallis's theories the credence they had not enjoyed since he had first shared the idea of breaching the Ruhr River dams with Collins, Winterbotham, and others back in 1940. The Nant-y-Gro experiments confirmed that a bomb, acting like a depth charge but weighing much less than Wallis's original ten-ton earthquake bomb, and therefore well within the carrying capacity of the four-engine Lancaster bombers rolling off the assembly line that very autumn, would deliver the devastating blow to Nazi Germany's industrial heart that the British Air Ministry and all its various departments had been debating for nearly a decade.

"The whole success of the operation," Wallis explained later, "depended on inventing a weapon which would go hopping along the surface of the water until it struck the freeboard of the dam, the part projecting above the surface, and sank and gradually paddled itself . . . up against the dam face."[28]

Remarkably, while A.V. Roe was indeed rolling Lancasters off its production line at Woodford, Barnes Wallis's bomb prototype remained little more than Elizabeth's ricocheting marbles in the family's backyard at Effingham. By October 1942, however, Wallis had gone to an engineering company to help him construct spheres—the casings for the bouncing bomb—that were four foot six inches in diameter. He'd also had a Wellington bomber modified with an underside hydraulic device that rotated the sphere just before it was released to ensure that it would bounce when it hit the water. As smoothly as the planning was going, there remained political and administrative turbulence all around him. Wallis had learned that Lord Cherwell continued to downplay the value of a raid on the Ruhr dams to Prime Minister Churchill. And there appeared to be a tug-of-war going on between the Royal Navy and the Air Force for ownership of the weapon; eventually, two versions of Wallis's bomb were up for consideration—a lighter bomb to be delivered by Mosquitos, code-named "Highball," and a larger, heavier weapon to be dropped by the Lancasters, code-named "Upkeep."

The powers that be—MAP, the Air Ministry, the (Royal Navy) Admiralty, and Vickers—agreed to let Wallis conduct trial drops of the prototype spheres on the Fleet, behind Chesil Beach. Throughout December 1942 and January 1943, Wallis conducted the trial flights with Mutt Summers in the pilot seat and Wallis as bomb aimer, while a camera filmed every low-level drop. With each trial, he tested a different version of the bomb—smooth and dimpled steel casings; the same, only with additional ribs for strength; and wooden spheres that contained equipment to record the impact on the water.[29] With every drop, Summers and Wallis altered the sphere type, the air speed, and the revolutions per minute (rpm) of backspin on the bomb. Water in the Fleet was shallow enough that Wallis could retrieve each sphere after every trial for post-mortem analysis. By January he was showing the motion-picture film of the trials to Vickers, the Air Ministry, the Ministry of Aircraft Production, and RAF and Admiralty personnel; meanwhile, he had written another paper, *Air Attack on Dams*, in which he reiterated the revelations of the tests on the dam in Wales, the impact the attack would have on Ruhr Valley industry, and the need to give equal attention to development of the smaller Highball and the larger Upkeep, with necessary modifications to the Lancaster bombers to achieve the objective. In one disheartened moment of doubt, sensing that the whole project was about to die, Barnes Wallis wrote to his friend and confidant G/C Fred Winterbotham at Air Intelligence on February 12.

"We have just worked out some of our results from the last experiment at Chesil Beach," Wallis wrote in desperation.

"Sufficient bombs for the Lancaster experiment (if, say, thirty machines were to be used) . . . can be completed within two or three weeks." He signed off with an additional handwritten plea: "Help, oh help."[30]

February proved pivotal to the entire dams raid scenario, not so much on the technical front as on the political one. When it became clear that development of Upkeep would require not only design modifications to Bomber Command's Lancasters but also the assignment of a full squadron of them to the operation for a number of weeks, Air Chief Marshal Harris reacted. He called the idea "tripe of the wildest description."[31] On February 15, Harris faced Wallis and Summers, roaring at what he called "you damned inventors" and warning them, "My boys lives are too precious to be thrown away by you."[32] Harris then entreated those at the Air Ministry and MAP to block any plan to reduce Bomber Command's capability by assigning bombers to Upkeep. Further, on February 18, Harris wrote to Air Chief Marshal of Air Staff Sir Charles Portal complaining about "panacea mongers" careering around the Ministry of Air Production recommending the sidelining of Harris's precious Lancasters. He ripped apart every aspect of the Upkeep proposal—the claims of its easy integration with Lancaster technology, the promise of its ballistics, and the timeline for delivery—and he concluded that "I'm prepared to bet my shirt . . . that it could never work."[33]

Meanwhile, at the corporate offices of Vickers on February 23, Wallis's ego and project took more criticism from his boss, Sir Charles Craven. The CEO berated Wallis for, in Air Vice-Marshal Francis Linnell's words, making a nuisance of himself at the Air Ministry, offending Air Staff, and damaging the Vickers corporate interests. After his dressing down, Wallis offered to resign.

"Mutiny!" Craven shouted at him, punctuating his accusation by pounding his fist on the desk.

Wallis left the room to compose himself, sensing that the chain of command, from Vickers's Craven to the Air Ministry's Linnell and Portal, had turned thumbs down on the entire dams raid concept.

In fact, however, Portal had received credible endorsement of Upkeep prior to Harris's "bet my shirt" memo, by way of the Air Vice-Marshal of Intelligence at the Air Ministry, Frank Inglis. Through an equally respected intelligence channel, Air Intelligence, Inglis had obtained strong support for Wallis's *Air Attack on Dams* document and trials film. The author reminded Inglis of earlier correspondence about "an invention" that could strike "any target where there was from a quarter to one mile of approach water surface."[34] He added that Prime Minister Churchill had been involved (an aside that was completely untrue), and he wondered whether the Air Ministry and the Chief of Air Staff (Portal) knew just how far the development of the invention had progressed. He added that there was great danger the Royal Navy might use this extraordinary weapon against enemy shipping prematurely instead of within a coordinated RAF plan, in effect implying that it was Inglis's duty to get *Air Attack on Dams* to Portal pronto. The letter had come from none other than G/C Winterbotham, from one intelligence officer to another. And it worked.

On February 19, the day after Harris's "bet my shirt" memo, CAS Portal wrote back to the head of Bomber Command, offering his respect for the Air Marshal's opinions of technical and operational matters and admitting that Highball and Upkeep might come to nothing. Nonetheless, he added, he didn't feel as if he should refuse Air Staff interest in the weapons. That day Portal also saw Wallis's trial film and assured Harris he would assign only three Lancasters to the project, but he also told Harris, "If you want to win the war, bust the dams!"[35]

On February 25, Barnes Wallis, just days earlier fearing that all hope was lost for Upkeep, learned that the bouncing bomb was suddenly back in the picture. Mysteriously, within a week, what had been three Lancaster bombers assigned to Upkeep became thirty. On February 26, Wallis was in the office of Air Vice-Marshal Francis Linnell at MAP in London. He had claimed the bouncing bomb could be ready in two months.

"Could this be done?" Linnell asked Wallis.

"Yes," Wallis said, "it could."

THAT EXPERIMENTAL SPHERICAL DEVICE, FALLING from the belly of a Wellington bomber and hopping over the surface of the Fleet off Chesil Beach—Upkeep—was the very thing that W/C Guy Gibson watched on film on March 24, 1943, at Barnes Wallis's lab inside the Burhill clubhouse. In the presence of his Mutt and Jeff acquaintances that day, in those few seconds of viewing those top-secret motion pictures, Gibson witnessed the culmination of years of research, campaigning, politicking, and trial and error, accomplished mostly by a patriotic scientist intent on driving Germany out of the war the best way he knew how. However, for both Gibson and Wallis there remained huge obstacles to accomplishing the military objective that would become known as Operation

Chastise. For the scientist, much refinement of the device lay ahead; for the wing commander, there was the task of finding the skilled airmen to deliver the blow. They each had just over seven weeks in the spring of 1943 to pull it off.

CHAPTER THREE

THE PLAN

Momentous. Dream-like. Majestic. A grey ghost. The arrival of the dirigible R100 in Canada in 1930 inspired reporters who saw it to wax eloquent, with one Toronto *Globe* journalist describing it as "a delicate silver fish against the deep rich blue of the sky, with coloured port and starboard lights like rubies and emeralds."[1] Another publication likened it to "a galleon of the air, some fairy boat of the Arabian nights."[2] The Vancouver *Sun* described its flight as "stranger than the fantasy of the floating island in Gulliver's Travels."[3] And perhaps most enthusiastic of all, the *Canadian Forum* said, "The machine age, which has filled our lives with noise and stinks and soul-cramping ugliness, can also give us things as poetically romantic as the R-100."[4] On August 1, 1930, the airship, making its maiden transatlantic flight, came into view over the St. Lawrence River on its way to Montreal. At nearby St. Hubert, Quebec, hundreds of spectators, many having slept in their cars overnight, honked horns and shouted out their excitement at the early-morning sight.[5] The goodwill flight of Britain's R100—including thirteen days flying through the skies of southern Ontario to Niagara Falls and back—seemed to herald a new era in aviation and even empire-building.

He may not have intended it, but Barnes Wallis, the designer of the bouncing bomb that would soon alter the tempo and focus of the Second World War, in his unique contribution to the creation of the R100 had also manufactured a tie to Canada and the Commonwealth that would ensure the delivery of his radically new weapon to its target in 1943. Born a novelty of lighter-than-air flight in France in 1783, then a symbol of human ingenuity in industrialized nineteenth-century Europe, the hot-air balloon, or dirigible, in the early twentieth century had emerged to represent power and nationhood. Indeed, during the Great War, Zeppelins bombing Allied troops and British cities had become a statement of German air supremacy. By the time Wallis joined Vickers in the mid-1920s, the competing dirigible manufacturers of the day on both sides of the English Channel had already built as many as 154 airships.[6] German and British firms raced to design and launch newer, sleeker, faster airships and just as quickly showcased them during highly publicized flights over Europe and across the Atlantic to North America. The Americans would also get involved in the 1930s, when the US Navy built the rigid airships *Akron* and *Macon*. Airship rollout suddenly represented a nation's technological advancement, its mastery of the air, and a significant deterrent to potential enemies.

Barnes Wallis found himself in the middle of an airship-building frenzy. During the interwar period, just as the

British Air Ministry considered potential bombing targets in the event of another war with nations on the Continent, so did that same government department also assume control of airship construction and service. Work on two British airships—the R100 and the R101—commenced in 1926, the former using Wallis's internal alloy design. The framework of the R100 consisted of sixteen longitudinal girders made of Duralumin connecting fifteen polygonal transverse frames held in place by wire bracing. Then, hydrogen captured inside a network of gasbags made of cattle intestines and covered in a cotton outer skin (all together ten acres in size) provided the airship's lift. The belly of the ship housed a lavish passenger cabin, and with Wallis's aerodynamic exterior and its three petrol-powered engines, the R100 emerged from its assembly plant in Yorkshire, England, in 1929 as the fastest and most modern way to travel on the planet.

In anticipation of the R100's maiden transatlantic flight, Mackenzie King, the Canadian prime minister, promised an appropriate welcome, including a new mooring mast at St. Hubert (near Montreal) worth $143,000. He also offered an invitation to delegates of an imperial air conference, as well as facilities to handle the hundreds of thousands of spectators expected to turn up when the airship toured Canada. Even though he had recently been defeated in a July federal election, King's expectations were realized. As many as 30,000 people had travelled to St. Hubert to witness the R100 link with Mackenzie King's prized mooring mast. And the excitement didn't end there. Throughout the dirigible's public-relations tour in the skies over southern Quebec and Ontario, up to 1.5 million Canadians were treated to the spectacle of a 720-foot-long airship gliding overhead. Commentators and politicians capitalized on the R100's visit to proclaim the supremacy of its British design, its safe and speedy transatlantic crossing, and its potential to unify the Commonwealth.

"[It's] the consummation of the combined efforts of the British and Canadian governments to provide, by air navigation, yet another avenue of trade and commerce between this country and the old land," Mackenzie King told reporters.[7]

The former prime minister already had an abiding respect for Britain as the leader of the Commonwealth; this was solidified at the Imperial Conference in 1926, when Canada gained Dominion status. But the arrival of Barnes Wallis's R100 in the skies over Quebec and Ontario in 1930 reinforced King's sense of Canada's military connection to Britain—particularly training pilots in the event of war. King acknowledged that from as early as 1917, Canadian flying schools had trained pilots for the Royal Flying Corps. And with hostilities looming again as he was returned to office in 1935, the prime minister considered proposals to expand aircrew training in Canada. Based on a memorandum from a Canadian veteran of the RFC,[*] King spelled out the strategic advantages of transforming the country into a hub of military aircrew training.

Canada was geographically close enough to the United Kingdom, and even closer to the industrial resources of the United States, but far enough from the war in Europe to carry out flight instruction in skies free of combat and in condu-

---

* G/C Robert Leckie was one of eight hundred Canadians who joined the Royal Naval Air Service during the Great War and was one its most distinguished flying-boat pilots. Then, as a representative of the RAF back in Canada, he researched and helped to organize Canadian military aviation in the interwar period.

cive climatic conditions. Canada already had a government-subsidized network of twenty-two flying clubs from coast to coast where elementary flying instruction was well established. And a training scheme based in Canada would attract more Canadian applicants to the RAF.[8] While King preferred, and campaigned for, greater Canadian control of the training plan to ultimately bolster a fledgling RCAF, he anticipated Britain's desperate need for qualified airmen, a fact made abundantly clear in 1939 when the United Kingdom declared war on Germany. Three months later, with representatives from Britain, Australia, and New Zealand visiting Ottawa, the prime minister co-signed into existence the British Commonwealth Air Training Plan. It would make Canada, according to King, "one of the greatest air training centres of the world."[9]

The BCATP at the outset would standardize the training of Commonwealth aircrew for military service in the Second World War. In its five-and-a-half-year lifespan—from December 1939 to March 1945—the BCATP would expend about $2 billion in the training of aircrew from nearly every nation of the free world.[10] The Plan would build, expand, occupy or rent as many as 230 different training locations from Atlantic to Pacific and in every province of the Dominion. The product of its training—nearly a quarter of a million air and ground crew—would spearhead the major Commonwealth land and sea operations to take back North Africa, Europe, and areas of the Pacific Rim. It would supply Bomber Command with the trained airmen for a third of a million sorties,[11] and for Fighter Command up to ten times that many. It would help to supply Ferry Command with trained pilots and navigators flying military aircraft built in North America to operational bases in Britain. Because the Plan also attracted American aviators before the US entered the war in 1941, it trained nearly 2,000 aircrew who, after Pearl Harbor, would return to the US and form the nucleus of the US Army Air Force. And by March 1943, when W/C Guy Gibson began assembling his top-secret squadron, it would supply fifty-six airmen, nearly half of the 133 flyers, that the wing commander needed to carry out the dams raid.* The BCATP would, in Winston Churchill's words, be "one of the major factors, and possibly the decisive factor of the war."[12]

On Sunday evening, December 17, 1939, not coincidentally the prime minister's birthday, Mackenzie King addressed the Canadian people in a national broadcast, stressing the important role the BCATP would play in the war.

"Let there be no mistake about the significance of the present war," he announced on the Canadian Broadcasting Corporation (CBC) radio network. "It is a desperate struggle for existence itself. On its outcome will depend the fate not of Canada alone, nor even the British Empire, but of humanity itself."[13] He continued: "The aim in short is to achieve, by co-operative effort, air forces whose coordinated strength will be overwhelming."[14]

In all likelihood, neither Barnes Wallis nor Guy Gibson heard Prime Minister King's patriotic speech on the CBC that December night. Nor might they likely have ever considered the impact of its promise. But King's parliament, his Commonwealth colleagues, and ultimately the British

---

* Of the aircrew Guy Gibson chose to fly the dams raid, eleven pilots, two flight engineers, twelve navigators, seven wireless radio operators, ten bomb aimers, and fourteen gunners had been trained in Canada.

Air Ministry all recognized the priceless value of the British Commonwealth Air Training Plan. They understood the value of an unrelenting flow of qualified aircrew to front-line combat stations in Britain, and, in time, that those pilots, navigators, and gunners would ensure that experienced Lancaster crews could be assembled for operations such as Barnes Wallis's bouncing-bomb attack against the Möhne, Eder, and Sorpe Dams on May 17, 1943.

THE TORONTO THAT WITNESSED THE ARRIVAL OF THE dirigible R100 on that August morning in 1930, like the rest of the country, welcomed the relief that such a spectacle provided. Floating overhead the Royal York Hotel and the Canadian Bank of Commerce tower, two of the tallest buildings in the British Empire, the cigar-shaped airship stopped most downtown residents in their tracks. Some ran outside in their pyjamas to watch the majestic dirigible pass. Others listened to the voice of Foster Hewitt—a hockey broadcaster normally heard on air shouting, "He shoots! He scores!"— give colour commentary of the event on the Toronto *Daily Star*'s national broadcast network.[15] Taking some of the agony out of the Depression, the R100 was a glorious distraction from deflating currency, food scarcity, crowding in the city, and the general unemployment that was already plaguing North America.[16]

For working-class families in the city, this first summer of the Great Depression was a real trial. And the MacLean household on Wallace Avenue in Toronto's Junction area was typical. The breadwinner in the family, James MacLean, fortunately had a job. He worked as a steamfitter at the nearby Goodyear Tire and Rubber plant, while his wife, Edith, and their children were at home. Their elder son, Don, had been born in April 1916. As a teenager in the 1930s, he grew to be tall, athletic, and, among other things, his mother's able assistant in managing the household budget.

"He was a detail guy," Don MacLean's son Bill pointed out. "Absolutely meticulous."[17]

"Granddad [James] would come in the door," added Don MacLean's other son, Jim. "He'd hand over his pay envelope to my grandmother. She would give him a small allowance. And that was it."[18]

Then mother Edith, daughter Isabel, and son Don would head off to a local store to buy household groceries. The three proved to be so precise in their purchasing estimates that whenever they arrived at the store checkout to pay their bill, the cashier would say, "So, how much do you owe us for groceries today, Mrs. MacLean?"

The MacLean home often housed more than just the immediate family under its roof. On occasion in those difficult times, James would bring home a friend in need to sit down to a welcome home-cooked meal. His wife didn't mind if their modest home seemed more like a boarding house than a single-family dwelling. "Just tell me the numbers," Edith would tell her husband, "and I'll throw more potatoes in."[19]

Wherever their son Don's organizational and financing skills came from, his ability to plan ahead served the family well beyond household budgeting. As a teenager going through Bloor Collegiate Institute in the 1930s, he worked part-time at a butcher store and did other odds-and-ends jobs to help put his older sister Isabel through secretarial school and eventually his younger brother Herb into the engineering program at the University of Toronto. Meanwhile, Don took advantage of one additional talent to help him secure work. Nearly six feet tall and weighing 185 pounds, he played hockey at an elite Junior A level, so when he received his teaching certificate at Toronto's Normal School, he relied on athletic skill to stickhandle his way into some of his teaching jobs. Often when Don applied for a school position, the interview question wasn't "How well do you teach?" but "Do you play hockey?" Just before the war, he got work teaching in two Ontario communities—Powassan and Coboconk—mostly because each town's hockey team needed him on the ice as much as it did in the classroom.

The MacLean family had no patriotic attachment to Britain or the Empire; indeed, their Scottish ancestors had been among the victims of the Highland clearances in the eighteenth century, when British rulers evicted Scottish tenants from their Highland crofts. And while there was certainly propaganda and peer pressure for young unemployed or unattached men in Toronto to sign up, Don Maclean admitted that some youth—in both English- and French-speaking Canada—felt a genuine neutrality at the start of the war.

"We had a lot of pacifist feeling in the '30s," he said. "But I think we were convinced when we entered the war that we were fighting for survival."[20]

Don enlisted in the RCAF in 1941. It didn't take long for Aircraftman Second Class (AC2) MacLean's sense of purpose—or his meticulous nature—to find a home. After a stint at Manning Depot, where he and thousands of other recruits were barracked in the livestock barns at the Canadian National Exhibition, he learned how to march, to salute, and to bring his eyeballs around with a click.[21] Then he was posted to Initial Training School (ITS). As a sprog (novice) air observer, MacLean dealt with compasses, sextants, and drift recorders that tested his skill at calculating air and ground speed and tracking a course on a map, but all from a classroom. For the former teacher, keeping track of things came relatively easily. But by November, now Leading Aircraftman (LAC) MacLean had been shipped to No. 9 Air Observer School (AOS) at St.-Jean-sur-Richelieu, Quebec, and he was soon airborne in twin-engine Avro Anson training aircraft. With his pilot instructor, whom MacLean referred to in his logbook as "Mr. Leach," the young trainee faced what the syllabus considered the most exacting task in a bomber.

"Mentally [the observer] must always be on the alert. He must estimate and plot the course, be able to take snap readings, [and] judge weather conditions," the syllabus explained. "Above all he must never make mistakes."[22]

It's no surprise that former schoolteacher MacLean felt at home working out such aeronautical problems as the effect of crosswinds and varying altitudes on the Anson as he and his taxi pilot practised a series of manoeuvres and exercises while airborne. On January 7, 1942, MacLean and his pilot even joined a search for a missing aircraft in eastern Ontario. MacLean adapted quickly to the primitive navigation computers, position graphs, tables and charts, and maps. He soon realized, however, as did every observer trainee, that direction-finding radios and astro-observations were valuable aids, but not fallbacks.

"A navigator could not assume that the stars would always be visible, or that electronic devices would be free from enemy interference," syllabus documents pointed out. "Dead reckoning remains the basis of the navigator's training and his work."[23]

Like all his course mates, MacLean had to face an additional reality of airborne training. Computing and plotting in the comfort of a classroom was one thing, but could a novice navigator deliver both speed and efficiency without sacrificing too much of either while airborne? Could he remain focused and deliver the precision an aircrew needed, given the cramped and often uncomfortable quarters of a military aircraft? Could he ignore the negative effects of cold temperatures or nausea inside the plane and the distraction of engine noise and still make his calculations quickly and accurately? Often it would be up to men such as Mr. Leach, the pilot flying the trainee on his practice circuits, to report on the work and attitude of a student observer in flight.

"To qualify for their job, [observers] had to have a sound knowledge of navigation, or else a strong homing instinct and more than an ordinary amount of patience," the syllabus required,[24] and often it would be up to the experienced Anson pilot to offer a final on-the-job assessment of a trainee's performance.

By early February 1942, after about twelve weeks at No. 9 AOS, LAC MacLean had clocked just shy of the prescribed sixty hours and received a "certified" rating in his logbook from his chief instructor.[25] Then it was on to Jarvis, Ontario, home of No. 1 Bombing and Gunnery School. Flying in Fairey Battle trainers, he completed air-to-air gunnery exercises, passing with an above-average grade of 75 percent. Along the way,

LAC MacLean had also studied and passed tests on meteorology, aircraft recognition, current affairs, physical education, and sending and receiving Morse code at a speed of at least eight words per minute. By April, MacLean had completed the course and earned his observer's brevet—a badge showing a single wing attached to an O. That month, MacLean and his class were sent to No. 2 Air Navigation School at Pennfield Ridge, New Brunswick, specializing in astro-navigation, or observing via the stars.

His meticulous nature must have paid off there too. While most aircrew upon graduation were sent overseas en masse by troopship, the RCAF posted Sgt. Don MacLean to a Ventura medium bomber for delivery to Britain. So, on May 22, 1942, MacLean and his pilot, Flying Officer (F/O) Vaclav Korda, took off from Dorval, Quebec, and over eight days flew to Gander, Newfoundland, to Reykjavík, Iceland, and on to the United Kingdom, MacLean navigating all the way. The posting illustrated not only that BCATP instructors had confidence in their top observer graduates, but also that the Air Force could trust MacLean in the right-hand navigator's seat enough to ferry Crown property to a war zone.

Just past his twenty-sixth birthday, when his Ventura landed at the RAF station in Prestwick, Scotland, Don MacLean had become one of the first seven hundred observers the BCATP had trained and delivered overseas during its first eighteen months of operation. In the ten months that followed, F/Sgt. Maclean would navigate bombers—Manchesters and Lancasters—through day and night training flights, dropping mines in enemy shipping lanes, and on high-altitude nighttime bombing runs to German targets—

eighteen combat operations in total—before being assigned, on March 31, 1943, to a crew for the dams raid. And yet, throughout those ten months, no matter how confident he felt about his skills or his experience as a combat navigator or how trusting he was of the crewmen around him, on every training flight, every bombing operation, he carried with him a foreboding premonition.

"I'm not going to live 'til the end of the day," MacLean always said to himself.[26]

IF DON MACLEAN GRAPPLED WITH A FEAR OF FLYING throughout much of his BCATP and combat careers, the man who piloted most of the bombing operations that MacLean navigated appeared to be fearless. Joseph Charles McCarthy was born in August 1919 in the hamlet of St. James on Long Island, New York. As a teenager, he sprouted to an athletic height of six foot three and a weight of 225 pounds. When his mother died in 1930, Joe and his brother, Frank, were raised by their grandmother, staying in the Bronx most of the year and on Long Island in the summer. Naturally Joe took to the water and used his strong build as a swimmer to pick up spending money by serving as a lifeguard at the beach on Coney Island and swimming competitively.

During the Depression, Joe and friend Don Curtin found themselves drawn to the hubbub and odd-job potential of Roosevelt Field airport on Long Island. With its history of training pilots for the US Army in the Great War, as well as being the starting point of Charles Lindbergh's solo trans-atlantic flight in 1927, the airfield attracted the two Long

Island youngsters repeatedly. Joe and Don talked themselves into enough pickup work around the field that they were able to buy flying lessons. In 1939, when the war in Europe broke out, McCarthy presented his basic flying credentials to officials of the US Army Air Corps. Three times he applied for combat training and three times he was refused. The two young American novice pilots watched in frustration as the Axis powers marched across Europe while the United States stood by. And there, stranded at Roosevelt Field on Long Island, they might have remained were it not for the Allies' nascent air training plan in Canada, its insatiable appetite for capable aircrew trainees, and the memory of a dashing American fighter pilot in the First World War.

Among the war stories that would-be pilots McCarthy and Curtin no doubt heard during hangar flying—when inclement weather or aircraft repairs kept planes on the ground at Roosevelt Field—was that of Clayton Knight. A New Yorker like Joe and Don, Knight was enjoying a flourishing art career in 1917.[27] But like McCarthy did in 1940, Knight in 1917 felt conflicted by the horrific stories of wartime conditions in Europe and his country's insistence on staying neutral. So, at age twenty-seven, when he learned that his college education allowed him entry into the US Army's Signal Corps Aviation Section, near Roosevelt Field, Knight became one of 150 American pilots sent to England for service in the Royal Flying Corps. His wartime sorties as pilot of an Airco DH9 biplane took him over enemy lines on bombing, reconnaissance, and photography missions, until he was shot down over German territory in October 1918. He survived the crash and imprisonment, convalescing at the end of the war in Britain. In addition to Knight's exploits, what likely attracted McCarthy and Curtin to his story was the veteran's efforts to secure the next generation of Americans the same avenue to wartime service that he had found.

On the very night that Britain declared war on Germany in 1939, the US president reassured isolationist camps in America that his country would remain neutral. However, during his regular fireside chat on national radio, Franklin Roosevelt added a caveat: "Even a neutral cannot be asked to close his mind or conscience."[28] Consequently, a week after Canada officially joined Britain in the Second World War, American volunteers began arriving at US–Canada border crossings ready to enlist in the RCAF, which caught the attention of Clayton Knight's RFC squadron mate W.A. "Billy" Bishop. The former fighter ace had recently received figurehead status as Air Marshal in the RCAF, in charge of recruitment. But with the BCATP suddenly drawing heavily on Canada's limited reservoir of experienced pilots, and with American manpower potentially available to bolster the ranks of the RCAF and RAF, Bishop realized the opportunity. He dialled up his former comrade-in-arms Clayton Knight, who was in Cleveland attending air races. Knight happened to be dining with Thomas J. Herbert, the attorney general of Ohio.

"That was Billy Bishop," Knight explained to Herbert after the call. "He wants me to help him . . . smuggle pilots up to Canada."

"As attorney general," Herbert sputtered, "I should be the last to know about this. . . . America is neutral!"[29]

Nevertheless, in the interim, Ian MacKenzie, the Canadian defence minister in Mackenzie King's cabinet, bestowed RCAF wing commander status on another Canadian veteran of the

Royal Naval Air Service from the Great War, Homer Smith. And with Smith supplying funds, Bishop the authority as head of recruitment, and Knight the American portal, at an office in the Waldorf Astoria in New York City, the search for American prospective pilots began—although, in cloak-and-dagger style, correspondence among the parties referred to the Air Marshal as "Mrs. Bishop" and the RCAF staff officer processing American recruits as "Mr. P. Jones."[30] Secrecy was imperative to disguise any Canadian government involvement in the smuggling so as not to embarrass President Roosevelt.

Then, in May 1940, the landscape shifted. As the German blitzkrieg pushed RAF resources to the limit and BCATP officials recognized that their courses had plenty of AC2s but not nearly enough instructors, the Air Council in Canada called an emergency meeting. Attending were RCAF, BCATP, and Canadian airline representatives, as well as Clayton Knight and Homer Smith. The latter two listened as the others lamented that they might be able to scrounge two dozen pilots from Canadian sources. When it was his turn to speak, Knight disclosed that his office had already compiled a list of three hundred experienced American pilots ready to move quietly across the border. The Clayton Knight Committee was born.[31]

With headquarters at the Waldorf Astoria, other committee offices opened in Atlanta, Cleveland, Dallas, Kansas City, Los Angeles, Memphis, San Antonio, San Francisco, and Spokane. None of the offices could advertise, but their presence stimulated word-of-mouth attention and their brochures sent to aviation schools and airports across the United States prompted applicants to seek pilot positions in both British and Canadian aviation. The committee staff could arrange for medicals, flying tests, and documents to get to Canada. On the surface, the call went out for American civilians who could serve as flying instructors and taxi pilots in the elementary flying schools and air observer schools of the BCATP. The committee realized, however, that many recruits wanted a direct line to the RCAF at the service flying schools and bombing and gunnery schools, and ultimately to combat in the skies over Europe. By the end of 1940, 321 Americans had crossed the border, while 105 applicants had been rejected. In New York City the following spring, Joe McCarthy and his friend Don Curtin were both out of work and considering their options; they decided to try their luck with the RCAF.

"Don and I boarded a bus and headed for Ottawa," McCarthy said.[32]

They crossed the St. Lawrence by ferry, received help from customs officials for connections to Ottawa, spent their first night in a YMCA, and arrived at the RCAF recruiting office on May 5, 1941. They were welcomed but told to return in six weeks for processing.

"Don and I responded that we didn't have the money to return again, so if the air force wanted us, they had better decide today," McCarthy said.[33]

The warrant officer must have recognized McCarthy's determination; by the end of the day he'd processed the two Americans and a dozen others and sent them immediately to Manning Depot in Toronto. Among myriad details, McCarthy and Curtin were vaccinated, had their hair cut, and received their AC2 uniforms. As initial indoctrination, the recruits learned to clean latrines, march on the parade grounds, and complete guard duty. Though the threat was negligible, McCarthy was

shipped to Sydney, Nova Scotia, to keep a watchful eye—
four hours on and four hours off—over the facility's hangars,
runways, and aircraft lined up on the tarmac. At ITS back in
Toronto, McCarthy and Curtin found that their pilot training
at Roosevelt Field came in handy, and by August 1941 they'd
received their LAC rating and had arrived at No. 12 Elementary
Flying Training School (EFTS) at Goderich, Ontario.

At No. 12 EFTS, McCarthy and Curtin joined as many
as ninety fellow trainees in a program that required them
to master the syllabus in seven weeks, about 180 hours of
ground instruction and fifty hours in the air (half with an
instructor in the second cockpit, half solo).[34] While half the
LACs logged their first hours in a two-seat, single-engine Fleet
Finch with their instructor, the other half worked on ground-
school subjects—engines, airframes, theory of flight, airmanship, navigation, signals, and armament. In order to hasten
their understanding of the basics of needle, ball, and air-speed
instrument flying, EFTS students clocked many ground hours
aboard Link Trainer simulators. The system expected a pupil
to fly solo shortly after eight hours of dual instruction. LAC
McCarthy soloed on day eight of the seven-week course. On
September 26, 1941, he and Curtin moved on to No. 5 Service
Flying Training School (SFTS) at Brantford, Ontario.

All aspects of instruction accelerated at the service level.
On the ground, the original curriculum of basic airmanship
had meteorology, photography, and reconnaissance added to it
and lots of additional hours in the Link Trainer. In the air, flying time grew to one hundred hours, half dual and half solo.[35]
And as McCarthy and Curtin moved to twin-engine Anson
aircraft, air speeds increased from the Finch's eighty-five miles
per hour to nearly two hundred miles per hour. Meanwhile,

McCarthy also became aware that demands for qualified bomber and fighter pilots overseas, and for teaching pilots within the BCATP in Canada, had put a severe strain on the supply of qualified instructors. To compensate, administrators of the Plan began plowing top graduating students back into the program to instruct, in order to keep pace with the growing number of schools, courses, and cadets. Joe McCarthy had no interest in becoming an instructor.

"He sort of faked it," his son Joe Jr. said years later. "[Joe] made sure that he wasn't the best guy around, so that he wouldn't get nailed for instructor duty."[36]

To complicate things, just before McCarthy and Curtin were to receive their graduation wings at the end of their course, Japanese warplanes attacked the US naval base at Pearl Harbor on December 7, 1941, and overnight the United States came into the war. Original arrangements between the Clayton Knight Committee and the RCAF had assured American volunteers that they did not have to renounce their US citizenship, and that they could freely transfer to American armed forces if or when the United States became a belligerent. At the time of the Japanese attack, 6,127 Americans were serving in the RCAF.[37] Sometime later, a train left Washington on a cross-Canada trip to collect Americans who wished to return home. Joe McCarthy and Don Curtin were not among them. By the time the train re-entered the United States a few months later with 1,759 Americans bound for service in the US Army Air Force,[38] the two eager New Yorkers had been commissioned in the RCAF; they had crossed the Atlantic aboard troopships to begin advanced and operational training unit (OTU) flying for combat duty in RAF Bomber Command.

They had barely begun their OTU training, on Handley Page Hampdens, when there was a sea change of administration and strategy above them. A string of largely ineffective bombing operations in previous months, combined with heavy losses over German targets, had sparked much debate among high-level RAF, War Cabinet, and Air Ministry officials. The validity of maintaining a large bomber force faced critical review. Defenders of RAF Bomber Command insisted that "it is in bombing, on a scale undreamt of in the last war, that we find the new weapon on which we must principally depend for the destruction of German economic life and morale."[39] New aircraft, better performance, greater bombing capacity, and new navigational aids were nearly in the RAF's hands, proponents said, and Bomber Command seemed the only arm of Britain's war effort able to strike Germany from the west to give the Russians some relief to the east.

While nobody said it aloud, the initiative to bomb individual factories or military targets would have to be abandoned and the general destruction of German cities would have to become Bomber Command's new objective. Churchill did not agree to redirect resources to build Bomber Command's proposed force of 4,000 bombers, but he did support its continued strategic role.[40] Thus, in February 1942, bomber aircrews got a new "area bombing" directive and a new director, as Sir Arthur Harris became Air Chief Marshal of Bomber Command. By spring and summer, Harris had approached Churchill and Chief of the Air Staff Sir Charles Portal with a bold new idea of amassing a force of 1,000 bombers to attack a German city.

The plan would affect all bomber crews, veteran and novice alike. Pilot Officers McCarthy and Curtin had not yet completed their OTU training when each received word he would fly in a large formation bombing run at night from their RAF Cottesmore station against the city of Düsseldorf. McCarthy's sortie proved uneventful. Curtin's was just the opposite. Both on his way to and from the target, Curtin's Hampden took fire from enemy fighters, but he pressed on. The attack wounded both his rear gunner and his wireless radio operator, and the cordite from a bursting shell temporarily blinded Curtin himself. Anti-aircraft fire again struck his Hampden over Holland, wounding his navigator; still, the skipper safely landed his beaten-up aircraft back in England.

"In this, his first operational flight," his DFC citation later read, "Pilot Officer Curtin displayed great courage, determination and devotion to duty."[41]

From their days as boys on Long Island to their decision to accept help from the Clayton Knight Committee and enlist as Americans in the RCAF, through their BCATP training, graduation, and commissioning, and on to their posting to Britain, Curtin and McCarthy's lives as bomber pilots had progressed virtually in tandem. They had even logged time together in Airspeed Oxford trainers in March 1942. But on ops in the fall of 1942, the two pilot officers were posted to different squadrons—Curtin to 106 Squadron at Coningsby, and McCarthy to RAF No. 97 Squadron at Woodhall Spa. Each got his fair share of hair-raising combat time over occupied Europe—laying mines ("gardening") in enemy shipping lanes, corkscrewing away from night fighters and anti-aircraft fire over fortified German cities, and diving away from defensive searchlights. Sometimes, however, the worst enemy on ops was a natural one. On their first op, on October 5–6, 1942, a raid to Aachen, McCarthy and his crew took off in thunderstorms over Lincolnshire. Six other Lancasters crashed before the bomber stream was even formed over the North Sea.

In a later letter home, McCarthy's flight engineer, Bill Radcliffe, from New Westminster, British Columbia, reported St. Elmo's fire around the aircraft. "When we got up to 10,000 feet, we ran into an electrical storm," he wrote. "It sure was pretty at first, seeing sparks and flashes all over the windscreen and flashes all over the wings and fuselage. And the tips of the props were glowing."[42]

But high altitude and humidity also brought icing. No matter how much McCarthy attempted to climb above the storm—to 15,000 or 16,000 feet—the weather worsened. And with every surge in the electricity in the atmosphere, the Lancaster lit up with sheet lightning. In such abysmal flying conditions, the German counterattack was negligible. But because the bomber's radio and flight instruments were failing in the weather, McCarthy found a hole in the clouds and used an estimated time of arrival to drop the bomb load. The trip home proved even more difficult. More ice formed on the aircraft and it lost 14,000 feet of altitude in no time. When McCarthy managed to regain control of the bomber, the rapid temperature change cracked the Perspex windows and blew holes two feet across in both sides of the fuselage.

"I was scared," Radcliffe continued. "I thought for sure we had been hit. My navigator's log, pencil, and instruments just vanished outside. . . . I looked out and saw we were skimming the treetops of France."[43]

Over the channel, McCarthy nursed the Lancaster up to a more comfortable altitude, but with their radio not working, they couldn't communicate their situation to anybody on the ground. McCarthy finally managed to find Woodhall Spa and circled the Lancaster over the airfield for thirty minutes before bringing down the bomber safely via signals. When Radcliffe inspected the damage, he discovered that the icing had broken their radio aerial and punched it through one of the Lancaster's Perspex blisters. He wrote home that he felt relieved to find that other crews had experienced much the same sort of perilous trip.

"Mac is a wizard at handling the machine," he wrote to his family. "If it hadn't been for him . . . I think if I had to go through those storms on every trip, I'd be grey before I'm twenty-four."[44]

That trust worked both ways, however. As *Q-Queenie*'s flight engineer, Sgt. Radcliffe had earned his share of respect from his aircrew comrades. With his ancestry in England, Bill had left British Columbia in 1939 and travelled overseas to enlist in the RAF. Initially a ground-crew mechanic, in July 1942 he jumped at the chance to train in Wales to become a flight engineer, joining McCarthy that September. But in addition to his patriotism and skill, Radcliffe brought one more asset to each op. His father back in New Westminster had sent Bill a five-inch-tall stuffed panda bear; on each of his bombing trips, Radcliffe tucked the toy into the top of his flying boot. Chuck-Chuck became the crew's lucky mascot.

More pragmatic but equally valued on McCarthy's crew, rear gunner Dave Rodger had his own lucky charm. But the candy-cane striped Algoma Steel hockey jersey he wore on every op, not coincidentally, also provided the peacetime steel-worker some much needed warmth in the unheated rear gun turret. Rodger had come to the war from a polar-opposite working environment—the open hearth at the Algoma Steel mill in Sault Ste. Marie, Ontario. In the fall of 1942, with so many of his friends joining up, Dave did too. His scores at the RCAF bombing and gunnery school at Jarvis, Ontario, put him in the top 10 percent of his course, and he was quickly shipped to Britain for further training. Just before he left, however, he sent Nell Barbet, his fiancée, a cedar chest with a note that said, "You've got to marry me."[45]

Nell interpreted Dave's gift for her trousseau as a serious "Wait for me," so she wrote to him nearly every day he was overseas. She added, "I sent him parcels, chocolates, and one time some dice."

"I lost all my money," he told her later, but F/O Rodger enjoyed a run of good luck where he needed it, on bombing runs over enemy territory in the rear turret of McCarthy's Lancaster.

Luck ran out for McCarthy's best pal, Don Curtin, on February 21–22, 1943, when they both flew in the combined 97 and 106 Squadron attack against Nuremburg; Curtin's Lancaster was one of nine bombers that did not come home. For some time, McCarthy's comrades at the squadron managed to keep Curtin's death a secret. Perhaps it was no surprise they were successful; Joe McCarthy seemed so deeply preoccupied with the job at hand. Over the next month, he and his crew completed operation numbers twenty-five through thirty-three, most in Bomber Command's new offensive against coke plants, steelworks, and synthetic oil plants in Germany's Ruhr River Valley. McCarthy would earn a promotion to flight lieutenant and receive a DFC. But what came next for the man they described as "the big blonde American" would test all his skills, fortitude, and good luck.[46]

* * *

THE FACT THAT ARTHUR HARRIS WAS NOW BOMBER Command's commanding officer on the front lines in the United Kingdom meant more than just a shift in strategy from pinpoint to area bombing. The new chief's thousand-bomber ops suddenly put more pilots, more navigators, and every available aircraft in harm's way more often. Every operation meant all hands on deck, from the cockpit to the ground crew on the flight line. From February 1942 on, the operational system was stretched thin, and the ripple effect of his decision carried across the Atlantic to Canada's air training scheme too. Not only did the BCATP have to ratchet up production of qualified aircrew, it also had to alter the skills of many graduates. The officials who assessed both the needs of Bomber Command at the front line and the efficiency of the BCATP behind it decided that most of the growing heavy bomber squadrons needed a new crewman; henceforth a Lancaster crew would consist of pilot, navigator, wireless radio operator, one or two gunners, and a new technician who would pay full attention to the bombs hitting the target.[47]

"The navigator had more than enough to do," Air Marshal Harris explained, "to get the aircraft within a few miles of the target, especially when making the run-up [and] the work left him no time to get his eyes conditioned to the darkness . . . before trying to spot the aiming point."[48]

The man with his eyes peeled in the darkness, focused on the target, would from then on be known as the air bomber (or bomb aimer). Among the first Canadian recruits to move into that new category was a young British Columbian. Born in Nanaimo in 1922, John Fraser got his high-school matriculation and then, just before the war, went to work in the BC lumber industry as a stenciller with Alberni-Pacific Lumber. He enlisted in the RCAF in May 1941, and like many other Western Canadian volunteers, he experienced the cow barns at Brandon and guard duty at Saskatoon before the BCATP streamed him into bomb-aimer training. After ITS, Fraser joined an expanded course at No. 4 Air Observer School in Edmonton, then an elongated stint at No. 8 Bombing and Gunnery School in Lethbridge. Between mid-September and the end of December 1941, he'd completed practice flights during which he read maps, worked beside navigators, directed cross-country flight paths, and then directed bombing runs at the end of each flight. By early 1942, Fraser had completed his training with an advanced course at No. 1 Air Navigation School at Rivers, Manitoba.[49] In many respects the bomb aimer had to become the bomber crew's jack of all trades, a reality F/Sgt. Fraser would soon discover.

On April 15, 1942, amid a flood of BCATP graduates, bomb aimer Fraser arrived at the RAF's personnel receiving centre in Bournemouth, on the south coast of England, ready for his posting and operational training. It was just weeks ahead of Bomber Harris's first "Thousand Bomber Raid" on Cologne, in May 1942, and then against Essen and Bremen in June, and other German cities well into August. Posted to RAF No. 50 Squadron in November 1942, Fraser flew his first combat operations as bomb aimer with Lancaster pilot F/L Norman Schofield against enemy targets in Italy, France, and Germany. They were not cakewalks—in particular, the January 1943 raid to Berlin.

"The kite was a mess of holes," he wrote to his mother, Ethel May, later.[50] Their Lancaster fuselage had sustained numerous hits from anti-aircraft and night-fighter shells—some, Fraser said, "you could put your head and shoulders through."[51] During the attack, the crew's rear gunner took cannon shells through his arm and ankle, and was attended to by the wireless radio operator with coffee and oxygen. But the crew's safe return to England was more seriously threatened by the shrapnel that had severed rods running the length of the fuselage that controlled the bomber's elevators and rudder. And solving that problem required the crew to jury-rig bits and pieces of equipment to keep the aircraft flying.

"Pop [Schofield] and I held the nose of the plane down with a haywire scheme, with the trailing aerial wire," Fraser said, "while the flight engineer joined the wires to the [elevator] controls in the back."[52] For six hundred miles en route home, Schofield and Fraser grappled with the flight controls. Then, making the final run toward an emergency landing in the United Kingdom, they realized the exploding shells had punctured the compressed air tanks that lowered the landing gear. Schofield managed to jar one wheel down and, with no brakes, bounced the battered bomber into a mudhole that finally brought it to a stop. All survived.

"That trip looks better in my log book than it did then," Fraser said.[53]

Schofield and Fraser flew a full tour together—thirty ops—with 50 Squadron. Coincidentally, one of the other bomber crews on the Berlin raids included Guy Gibson. Fraser's service as a bomb aimer above and beyond the call no doubt factored in the wing commander's invitation to Fraser, and fellow Canadian navigator F/O Ken Earnshaw, in April 1943 to fly that one last operation that AVM Ralph Cochrane of 5 Group

Bomber Command had described as "perhaps one of the most devastating of all time."[54] Indeed, it would have deadly consequences for both Canadians.

The introduction of the bomb aimer to aircrew trades wasn't the only modification to the British Commonwealth Air Training Plan in 1942. The evolution of the bombers these aircrew would fly over enemy territory shook up BCATP planning and syllabuses too. Indeed, just as British aviation designer Roy Chadwick realized that the demands of war required he modify and enlarge his twin-engine Manchester bomber into the four-engine Lancaster, so too did they necessitate another change in the bomber's crew requirements. No longer would there be two pilots in the cockpit, but rather a pilot and a flight engineer. That final Lancaster crewman would, under ideal conditions, have skill as an aero-engine mechanic and become the pilot's assistant, monitoring fuel consumption, attending to airborne engine problems, and, if necessary, fly the aircraft.[55] The flight engineer had to master a variety of jobs and respond proficiently and calmly to any number of emergencies in the air.

Few men recruited into the Air Force met these requirements as well as Charles Brennan. Around the turn of the nineteenth century, his parents eloped from England to Western Canada, where Charlie was born in 1916. From their Calgary home, his father ran a saddlery business until 1928, when the family narrowly escaped a fire that destroyed all they owned. With few alternatives, the family returned to England, living with an aunt in Leeds. When the war came, Charles quickly enlisted to train as ground crew. He married his long-time girlfriend, Freda Pemberton, and in 1942, when the RAF needed aero-mechanics to train as flight engineers, he was accepted.

No sooner had he graduated from his course than he was posted to 106 Squadron and crewed up with British pilot John Hopgood, on August 14, 1942.

They were both finishing training stints—Brennan as a flight engineer trainee at RAF St. Athan and Hopgood as an instructor assisting pilots making the transition to heavier bombers. The Lancaster was the common denominator. And they both arrived at 106 Squadron to begin operations with Lancs that summer. Brennan's baptism of fire came the next night, when he and Hopgood flew a sortie over Düsseldorf on August 15; visibility was poor, the bombing scattered, and two Lancasters were lost, but Hopgood's plane and crew got home safely. By October 1942, when Hopgood had completed thirty-two operations and Brennan sixteen, the RAF posted them both to instructing duties on Lancasters. They were soon noticed by the powers that be. Hopgood's quiet authority and good nature and Brennan's efficiency under fire impressed W/C Guy Gibson. The three would soon be reunited in a combat operation that would secure the wartime legacy of the Lancaster and its bomber crews.

A COMMON THREAD THROUGH THE LIVES OF SO MANY of the airmen who wound up together on the dams raid in 1943 was growing up in the Depression. Though most were born as the Great War ended, or in the early 1920s, it was the Dirty Thirties that had shaped these young men's attitudes, their prospects, their experiences, and their fortunes. If they had education, the Thirties had often forced them from school to help feed their families even before they left home. If they had work, economic conditions meant it was short-term or temporary; up to 30 percent of the North American adult population was unemployed through the decade. If they had hopes and dreams, most had to wait for better times. But just like Joe McCarthy and Don Curtin who as boys ferreted out nickels and dimes with gofer work at Roosevelt Field, Fred Sutherland got piecemeal work by hanging around the riverside in Peace River, Alberta, where northern bush flyers regularly landed their float planes. But unlike Joe and Don—who'd only heard about the likes of aviation legends Charles Lindbergh, Amelia Earhart, and Wiley Post passing through Roosevelt Field—Fred actually got the chance to rub shoulders with a legend from the world of frontier flying. "I had my first ride in an airplane with Punch Dickins," Sutherland said.[56]

A town of roughly nine hundred souls during the Depression, Peace River survived on commerce associated with the riverside, whether the steamboats that brought people and supplies or the float planes that landed, loaded, unloaded, fuelled up, and took off to the next port of call in the North. In those years, when government airmail, mining company prospectors, hunting parties, and even medical supply contracts became the bread and butter for frontier flying companies, bush pilots proved only as successful as their flying skills in the air and their resourcefulness on the ground. The day that bush pilot Clennell Haggerston "Punch" Dickins[*] faced three star-struck kids at the riverside—Fred and a couple of his childhood pals—chomping at the bit to get in his Bellanca float plane, he realized an opportunity. He

---

[*] Clennel Haggerston Dickins, OC OBE DFC, had plenty of nicknames: North American Indigenous people called him "Snow Eagle"; northern Europeans knew him as "White Eagle"; newspaper reporters dubbed him the "Flying Knight of the Northland." But most just called him "Punch."

offered to take the boys up for a few minutes over the town if they could scrape up the airfare.

"I went to my dad's [doctor's] office and asked him for the three dollars," Sutherland said, remembering the experience from his thirteenth year. "Another of the kids, Jim Hannah, went to his dad at the drugstore; he gave him three bucks too . . . And Punch took three of us up at the same time. I think he went over the town two or three times. And that was it. I figured I'd be a bush pilot."[57]

But these were the Thirties, and even though his father, Fred Sr., was the town doctor, attending to the medical needs of a place as busy as Peace River, funds for things beyond the basics didn't exist. Fred Jr. remembered his father often being called away in the middle of the night, travelling for miles out of town through the snow in an open horse-drawn cutter to deliver a baby, set a broken bone, or deal with myriad emergencies. His wife, Clara, a Woodland Cree, feared the cutter would skid off the road and her husband disappear on his way home. Many were the days when Doc Sutherland might attend to thirty people and only have a dollar in pay to show for it. Nevertheless, the couple provided for their two daughters and a son, and Fred Jr. grew up getting by at school but emerging more comfortably as a tough defenceman for the Peace River Stampeders hockey team. When the Second World War came, Fred had just turned sixteen.

"I was worried that the war would be over before I got a chance to get into it,"[58] he said. His mother didn't like the idea of his joining, but his father, a former medic in the Great War, seemed to feel that if a young man didn't join the army when a war was on, then he wasn't good for much. Fred's passion for planes pushed him to the Air Force, so he left for Edmonton in 1941; at the train station somebody nicknamed him "Doc" Sutherland after his dad, and it stuck.

Once he was processed, AC2 Sutherland headed for the Manning Depot at Brandon, Manitoba, where he was housed with 5,000 other eager sprog airmen. They got their uniforms all right, but then the recruits spent hours memorizing the King's Rules and Regulations, marching, conducting rifle drills, and parading, often through the streets of the city. Like so many BCATP centres, those on the Prairies were just getting under way, and by the winter of 1942 the system was clogged with enlistees with nowhere to go. Doc knew he didn't have sufficient education to become a pilot; he'd have to sit tight and wait his turn. Then somebody came looking for volunteers.

"Anybody want to go straight to air gunner?" he said. "Don't have to know Morse code. Let us know if you want to go."

Fifteen of the AC2s volunteered right away, including Doc Sutherland, and they were immediately shipped to No. 2 Bombing and Gunnery School at Mossbank, Saskatchewan, for the six-week course. Brandon's depot might have been struggling to keep up with the flow of recruits, but the facility at Mossbank faced even greater challenges. One headache planners had not anticipated, particularly on the Canadian prairies, was the lack of an adequate water supply (45,000 gallons required per day at each bombing and gunnery school) and a system to deliver it. By the time Sutherland and his course arrived at Mossbank, the closest drinkable water came from a well seven miles away. Trucks regularly hauled water for drinking, cooking, and firefighting; since metal piping was not available, a makeshift underground line of wooden staves bound together with hoops delivered the water, although not always with sustained pressure. In 1942 the federal government found a partial solution, installing an indoor pool whose water could be used for either swimming or fire protection.[59] Need, apparently, proved to be the mother of BCATP invention.

Meanwhile, AC2 Sutherland also learned to improvise. From January 19 to February 16, 1942, he was airborne twenty-one times getting his air-to-air gunnery training. Some of his earliest flights aboard Fairey Battles required Sutherland to fire at a cotton drogue target (a kind of windsock) on the end of a cable towed by another Fairey Battle. The weapon was a gas-powered Vickers machine gun; the gunner fired a hundred rounds at the drogue passing alongside from the rear-facing gun position, which was open to the air of a Saskatchewan winter's day. But the cold wasn't the worst problem.

"The bullets had paint on them, so if you had red-painted shells, they knew who'd made the holes in the drogue. And they counted how many hits you had," Sutherland said. "But the guns were mostly worn out, so there wasn't much accuracy."[60]

After his nearly twelve hours of freezing aboard open Fairey Battles, when the instructors reviewed Sutherland's scores from the drogue hits and movie film shot of his sequence of firing—air-to-ground and air-to-air—he had scored better than average. Those scores alone would have given him the grades to advance, but instructors had other evidence of Sutherland's marksmanship. During ground training inside a hangar set up like a skeet-shooting range, and using a .22 rifle about fifty feet away, gunnery students learned how to shoot at a moving target. Sutherland had plenty of experience from hunting geese and deer in the backcountry of Peace River with his father.

"I'd hit twenty-five out of twenty-five," he said. "Some of the guys going through were missing quite a few of the clay pigeons. . . . To show the others, the instructor got me to shoot at the ones they didn't break. The idea was to learn to put a lead on the target, shoot ahead of it."[61]

Before Doc Sutherland had his graduating gunner's brevet stitched to his RCAF tunic and sailed from Halifax to Glasgow, he'd managed to honour one other personal commitment: he'd purchased a ring and given it to his girlfriend, Margaret Baker, the daughter of a local bank manager in Peace River. They'd shared a quiet engagement when he was back home on leave during training, and despite the uncertainty of the times, they promised to write each other as often as they could throughout Sutherland's service overseas.

During the spring and summer of 1942, F/Sgt. Sutherland completed operational training on Whitley, Hampden, and Manchester bombers, moving to four-engine Lancasters at 1654 Heavy Conversion Unit in Wigsley during August. As well as finding his way around a new heavy bomber, the young gunner had to find his way into a larger Lancaster crew. Sometimes squadron commanders simply let unassigned aircrew loose in a briefing room or hangar to figure out on their own who would "crew up" with whom. It was a little like couples sizing each other up at a dance.

The first unattached crewman Sutherland met was Henry "Harry" O'Brien, a gunner from Regina, Saskatchewan. They'd actually gone through some of their BCATP training together on the Prairies and knew that Lancs required a pair of gunners. O'Brien broke the ice by saying, "Where do you want to go?"[62]

"I'd like to go into the top turret," Sutherland said.

"Good. I'd like the rear turret," O'Brien said.

That was simple enough. Next the gunners approached an older airman who they learned had been raised in Lincoln, not far from their Wigsley heavy conversion station. He'd lost his father in the Great War and worked in a number of businesses before joining the RAF in 1940. At thirty years of age, Edward Cuthbert Johnson already had a commission and a number of ops as a navigator under his belt.

"I don't like being called Cuthbert," Johnson told them. "Call me 'Johnny.'"

O'Brien and Sutherland agreed. Then the threesome approached another navigator, whom Johnny Johnson knew, a former Lloyd's insurance salesman named Sidney Hobday. Johnson and Hobday had wanted to crew together, but both couldn't be navigators, so Johnny offered to serve as bomb aimer on the new crew. Hobday agreed to be navigator. Next they overheard a reference to a quiet, rather standoffish Australian pilot. "This guy's looking for a crew," somebody said. It turned out that Les Knight already had a fellow Australian, Bob Kellow, as his wireless radio operator. So, within an hour, the six individual airmen had effectively assembled all members of a Lancaster crew, except for a flight engineer.

"We had trouble with the engineers," Sutherland said. "Awful troubles."[63] On a training flight aboard a Manchester soon after, an interim flight engineer absent-mindedly turned off the flow of fuel to the aircraft's two engines as the bomber passed a church steeple in the final approach to a landing. The bomber came down like a stone, barely missing the church. All survived, but the plane was a write-off. They tried a second engineer, and he didn't work out either. Finally they found Raymond Grayston, a motorcycle enthusiast who'd trained in England to be a flight engineer; he rounded out the seven-man complement needed to operate the new Lancasters, just as the crew was posted to 50 Squadron at Swinderby in September of '42.

Sutherland's crew commenced almost nightly flights, for familiarization at first, but then operations that autumn to bomb targets at Turin and Genoa in Italy; St. Nazaire and Lorient in France; and Bremen, Wismar, Kiel, Essen, Düsseldorf, Hamburg, Cologne, and Berlin in Germany. Through the clear plastic bubble over his 360-degree rotating mid-upper turret, Doc Sutherland could see every moment of every raid. He said he rarely had to fire his .303 Browning machine guns, but when he did, the bullets were daylight tracers that flamed out at a thousand yards; every time he pulled the trigger, tracers— at twenty bullets a second—blazed out in front of him like flames shooting into the night. "The point was they were a scare tactic," Sutherland said, "but the only person who was scared was me."

Sutherland admitted that most of his crewmates learned as they went, recognizing landmarks at night, spotting fighters, judging distances, enduring anti-aircraft flak, and hiding their fears. On some nights, fighting back the panic was tough, but one who seemed impervious to all the strain was Doc's pilot, Les Knight. On one trip, another Lancaster in their formation was coned; an enemy master searchlight from the ground locked onto the aircraft and every other light and gun homed in on the doomed plane. From his perch atop the Lanc, Sutherland watched as the other bomber exploded and crashed. Then, the same night, Sutherland's bomber was coned. Just as suddenly as the lights fixed on them, Sergeant Pilot Knight put their Lancaster into a steep dive, nearly straight down. Hobday claimed later that the air-speed indicator at his navigator's desk indicated 450 miles per hour. But having escaped the coning, it was up to Knight to bring the 40,000-pound bomber out of its rapid descent. Sutherland recalled the exchange between pilot and flight engineer on the intercom as the two men struggled at the Lanc's controls.

"Pull it out," Knight implored his engineer. "Trim it out . . ."

In his panic the flight engineer trimmed the tabs the wrong way.

"No, no," Knight corrected. "The other way . . ."

Finally Sutherland felt the bomber respond and eventually level off, just as features on the ground became distinguishable in the dark. "Scared the hell out of me . . . but it was an unbelievable piece of flying."[64]

On March 23, 1943, Fred Sutherland and his aircrew comrades returned from a bombing operation against the German dry docks and U-boat pens at St. Nazaire, France. They had officially completed twenty-four ops (Knight had done one before crewing up on the Lancaster) over enemy territory, six ops short of a full tour of duty. The commanding officer of 50 Squadron, Squadron Leader (S/L) Peter Birch, had written an assessment in Sutherland's flight logbook: "Has shown efficiency as a gunner." Then the CO presented Les Knight's crew with an offer.

"There's an RAF officer forming a new squadron," Birch

said, "and he wants an experienced aircrew."

The seven men were attentive but wondered what Birch was up to.

"If you decide to transfer over and start a new tour," he said, "we'll finish your current tour at twenty-five trips. You can start a second tour, and in twenty trips you'll be finished all your ops."[65]

It didn't take Doc Sutherland and his comrades long to consider the offer. They would be credited with one full tour of thirty trips after flying only twenty-four. They clearly got along and worked well together. They didn't want to be separated or to have to join a different, maybe inexperienced crew. And the prospect of a shortened second tour appealed to all of them. When they gave S/L Birch their affirmative answer, they asked about the new squadron. It didn't have a number yet, Birch told them, but its commander was Guy Gibson. Four days later, they arrived at Scampton air station with twenty other Lancaster crews. Nobody knew the nature of the next op. Nobody knew its ultimate objective at that point, not even Gibson. But their new CO was about to push them and their capabilities in a way no other had. Along with navigator MacLean, pilot McCarthy, bomb aimer Fraser, and flight engineer Radcliffe, gunner Sutherland would rely heavily on his BCATP training and the life lessons of the nighttime ops he'd experienced thus far to help him survive this next, mysterious op. History would judge their performance.

CHAPTER FOUR

"A TREE IN THE MIDDLE OF ENGLAND"

A BOMBING OPERATION TO BERLIN WOULD BE stressful enough for any Bomber Command airman, but on March 27, 1943, just moments before the op briefing for pilots and navigators about specific targets, numbers of aircraft on the op, weather conditions en route, and likely enemy response over the German capital, the commanding officer of RAF No. 44 Squadron pulled pilot Ken Brown aside.

"Report to my office immediately after the briefing," John Nettleton VC told Brown.[1] And when the sergeant pilot from Moose Jaw, Saskatchewan, arrived at his CO's office, the exchange that followed gave the young Canadian pause, probably when he least needed it. "You are to be transferred to a new squadron," Nettleton announced to Brown. Whether the directive was designed to intrigue or inspire Brown is hard to say, but it did spark the pilot's natural sense of loyalty.

"Sir, I'd rather stay here and finish my tour for Forty-Four," he responded.

"That's impossible," Nettleton said. "It's a name transfer and I can't do anything about it."

Brown had no alternative but to obey his CO's orders. After that night's trip to Berlin, twenty-two-year-old Brown and a crew he'd only recently assembled, and with whom he'd flown only four previous sorties, would be sent to another squadron. End of conversation. The combat op to "the Big City"[2] that night involved 396 bombers, including Brown's Lancaster, but it had not gone well. The Pathfinders—the aircraft and crews flying in advance of the bomber stream to pre-mark the targets with coloured flares—had missed the objectives by a large margin, and the only real damage inflicted on the ground was the accidental bombing of a Luftwaffe supply depot southwest of the city. Bomber Command lost nine aircraft and crews, while the rest of the bomber stream, including Ken Brown's Lancaster, returned safely from the misdirected bombing run. Three days later, he and his crew packed up their gear and received one final comment from CO Nettleton: "You're going to be the backbone of this new squadron." It did seem odd. Brown admitted that he had much less experience than other combat pilots on the squadron. Nevertheless, as ordered, he led his crew off to join a new, as yet unnamed squadron in an operation they would never forget.

KEN BROWN WAS A CRACK SHOT. UNLIKE SOME YOUNG-sters at that time, he could handle a shotgun and knew how to drive a car. He was also a quick study. And as a consequence, he figured his qualifications would almost certainly mean, when the time came, that the Air Force would train him as a fighter pilot. As it turned out, his entry into the war tested his patience as much as his skill. In 1941, Brown left home in Moose Jaw, Saskatchewan, intent on serving his country in the cockpit of a Spitfire. But at that time, the air war over Nazi-occupied Europe needed bomber pilots more desperately than it needed fighter pilots. So, after Brown's initial training in Canada, the RCAF sent him to RAF No. 19 Operational Training Unit at Kinloss, on the north coast of Scotland, and from there to flying Whitley bombers out of the St. Eval aerodrome in southwest England as part of Coastal Command.

While at St. Eval, Brown crewed up with navigator Dudley Heal, wireless radio operator Herbert Hewstone, bomb aimer Stefan Oancia, and gunner Grant McDonald, the last two being fellow Canadians. Bomber Command eventually came knocking and shipped Brown, still a flight sergeant, to 1654 HCU for Lancaster training. During his upgrade to Lancs, Brown's crew expanded to include flight engineer Harry Feneron and gunner Don Buntaine. Early on at HCU, Brown took instruction from Harold "Mick" Martin, an Australian pilot famed for his skill in flying at low altitude and for eluding night fighters. In fact, during an aircraft affiliation exercise, Martin showed Brown some of his evasion techniques and then turned to his heavy-conversion student.

"OK, young fellow," Martin said, "let's see what you can do."[3]

Without skipping a beat while in mid-air, the two men exchanged seats, and Martin heard Brown mutter under his breath, "Anything you can do, Buster, I can do too."[4] Which he did. Brown always seemed competitive, always eager to test himself, and never afraid to take on a challenge to his ability or will, even in the face of authority.

On February 5, 1943, Brown's crew was posted to 44 Squadron to begin combat operations. Brown flew his inaugural sortie as "second dickey" (standing behind the pilot observing the way he performed) on a raid to Wilhelmshaven, but then had to wait a month before rejoining his own crew for its first op together, a bombing run to Munich on March 9; that night, some of Brown's evasion practice paid off when his bomber was coned over the city and he managed to dive away from the searchlights. Four more bombing ops followed. Then came the off-course op to Berlin on March 27 and the immediate reposting to Scampton and the mystery unit—identified only as Squadron X—assembling there.

The aerodrome that had overnight become home to Squadron X had a history as long as wartime aviation in Britain. Spread across nearly 360 acres of Lincolnshire countryside near the east coast of England, the airfield had opened in 1916 as a defensive station to meet the threat of German Zeppelins bombing British targets. Late in the Great War, Scampton had served as a training depot but in 1919 was returned to farm production. By 1936 an RAF expansion program saw new construction on the original site—four hangars and an array of brick buildings that housed station offices, the officers' mess, the sergeants' mess, and general airmen's quarters. On September 3, 1939, just six hours after war was declared, RAF No. 49 Squadron and 83 Squadron at Scampton had delivered the first RAF offensive of the campaign—nine Hampden bombers off to do a sweep over Wilhelmshaven—led by rising-star pilot Guy Gibson. But not long into the war, "Sunny Scampton"—

the facetious nickname acknowledging that aircrew stationed there hardly ever saw clear sky overhead—seemed to fall under an operational cloud too. Bomber Command had moved all squadrons—except RAF No. 57 Squadron—elsewhere, so that when the newly assigned crews of Squadron X began arriving, late in March 1943, the place seemed empty.

The buzz of twenty-one Lancaster bomber crews—147 men initially—landing at Scampton brought the place to life again. On March 21, now Wing Commander Gibson—DFC and bar and DSO—took charge of Squadron X. Three days later seven of his chosen crews arrived, the next day seven more, and by March 31 the final seven, including Ken Brown's crew, had landed. Among the pilots Brown met were men from 106 Squadron, including F/L Dave Shannon, the son of an Australian Member of Parliament, wearing Royal Australian Air Force (RAAF) insignia; F/L John "Hoppy" Hopgood, a talented musician from Surrey, England; and F/Sgt. Lewis Burpee, a fellow Canadian. All three former 106 men sported service decorations—DFC, DFC, and DFM, respectively.

Two other Canadian sergeant pilots arrived: Vernon Byers from RAF No. 467 Squadron and George Lanchester from 57 Squadron. From the same squadron came P/O Geoff Rice and F/Sgt. Ray Lovell, with relatively few ops under their belts, but also Britons F/L Bill Astell DFC and S/L Melvin Young, affectionately known as "Dinghy"; the former Oxford rowing blue had twice ditched a bomber into the sea, but he had two tours and two DFCs to his credit. From 44 Squadron came F/L Harold Wilson with relatively little combat experience. Acquisitions from 50 Squadron included a few more Australians: P/O Les Knight, with a full tour now to his credit, and F/L Mick Martin DFC, the low-flying expert. Also from 50 Squadron came S/L Henry Maudslay DFC, an Etonian with more than forty ops behind him. Meanwhile, RAF No. 61 Squadron had supplied Australian F/L Norman Barlow DFC; 49 Squadron had contributed sergeant pilots Cyril Anderson and Bill Townsend, while P/O Warner "Bill" Ottley DFC came from RAF No. 207 Squadron. From 97 Squadron had come the only Royal New Zealand Air Force (RNZAF) pilot, F/L Les Munro DFC, plus F/L David Maltby DFC, and US-born RCAF F/L Joe McCarthy DFC.

McCarthy's rear gunner, Dave Rodger, figured he got the nod to join the new squadron because his records showed he had better-then-average night vision. Rodger summed up his first impression of Scampton when he said the gathering reminded him of "an All-Star [National Hockey League] team—lots of medals, tons of operational experience and ability, but no real squadron spirit."[5]

Herbert Hewstone, known as "Hewie" to everybody aboard Ken Brown's Lanc, was a Londoner. One of a household of seven children and the son of a general store owner in the British capital, Hewstone didn't mince words. And when Brown's crew entered the hangar for one of W/C Gibson's first briefings, wireless operator Hewstone recalled his former CO Nettleton's remark about Brown's crew being "the backbone" of this new squadron. "Skip," he said to Brown, "if we're the backbone of this squadron, we must be damn close to the arse end."[6]

Brown didn't have to be bludgeoned with that fact. There in the briefing, within the wingspan of a Lancaster, mingled airmen wearing enough military decorations to make his head spin—eleven Distinguished Flying Crosses and four Distinguished Flying Medals, as well as W/C Gibson's Distinguished Service Order. In addition to the array of awards and service ribbons, Brown was introduced to what seemed a virtual League of Nations of pilots, including twelve RAF, five RCAF, three RAAF, and one RNZAF skipper. Along with the prestige of his new assignment, Brown quickly discovered, came responsibility and a new level of discipline. A demonstration of the latter resulted from his very first encounter with his new CO. When Brown and his crew arrived at Scampton, they followed the lead of others awaiting their first instructions and sprawled on the grass in front of the building housing the crew room. Eventually word circulated to assemble for the briefing in No. 2 Hangar, so Brown and his crew made their way in. The young Canadian was not the last into the briefing, but he did close the door behind him.

"Brown," Ken heard W/C Gibson call out from the front of the hangar, "report to my office after the briefing."[7]

Then, as he had several times during those first days with pilots, navigators, bomb aimers, wireless radio operators, flight engineers, and gunners taking up residence at Scampton, Gibson gazed out at his Squadron X aircrews. He noted that they looked young, carefree, and eager to hear why they had been gathered together. It was a short inaugural speech.

"You're here to do a special job," he began. "You're here as a crack squadron. You're here to carry out a raid on Germany which, I am told, will have startling results. Some say it may even cut short the duration of the war . . ."[8]

Fred Sutherland, the front gunner from Les Knight's Lancaster crew, remembered that first assembly of Squadron

X and all the decorations on the other airmen's chests too. He sensed he was in for something very exciting and dangerous. "You don't ever think about getting killed, but on this operation the chances seemed pretty good you would."[9] Doc Sutherland sensed too that in every aspect of this new posting, Gibson meant business. He was the boss.

Gibson went on to explain that he couldn't reveal the target or the location, or any other operational details. About the first days of their work at Scampton, he only told them that every crew would have to practise low flying all day and all night, until they could do it blindfolded.

"If I tell you to fly to a tree in the middle of England," he emphasized, "then I will want you to bomb that tree. If I tell you to fly through a hangar, then you will have to go through that hangar, even though your wingtips might hit either side. Discipline is absolutely essential."[10]

George "Johnny" Johnson, Joe McCarthy's bomb aimer, said Gibson's reputation had preceded him. Nobody could argue with his service record, and Johnson had heard that the wing commander didn't even bother to record absolutely every sortie he'd flown.[11] Johnson said Gibson was bombastic and arrogant, but with that kind of record, he had every right to be.

Gibson finished his inaugural pep talk by demanding that everything they did at Scampton had to remain a secret. Nobody could say anything away from the station. Not even in pubs at night was the subject of squadron activity to be mentioned. And if asked, even by other airmen, they were to keep their mouths shut about the nature of their work. Secrecy was the first and last order. Above all, it appeared,

Gibson expected the ultimate in obedience and loyalty in the air and on the ground. F/Sgt. Ken Brown became Gibson's first scapegoat for the level of discipline expected of everyone on the base. When the Canadian pilot arrived at the wing commander's office, as ordered before the briefing, the adjutant marched Brown in. Gibson told him he was on charge for being late for a briefing. Brown thought for a second that Gibson was kidding, but when the Wingco read out the charge, he realized otherwise.

"Do you prefer a court martial or my punishment?" Gibson asked.

"I'll take your punishment, sir," Brown said.

"Fine. You'll wash all the windows on the outside of the briefing room and the inside of the briefing room. All after duty hours."[12]

Some aircrew said that Gibson had it in for "colonials." But Brown wasn't the only one in Gibson's sights when it came to order and discipline. From the moment he arrived at Scampton, the wing commander chafed at the neglect and shortcomings of the place. There were no parachutes, no Mae Wests, and he found the offices cold and devoid of necessary furniture. When he learned that the adjutant Bomber Command had assigned to Scampton wanted to live away from the station barracks, Gibson dismissed him as "a last war man." Further, the new CO decided to take his high standards of discipline into the married men's quarters; he therefore cancelled all leave. When Joe McCarthy and his crew arrived from 106 Squadron at Woodhall Spa on March 25, his British bomb aimer, George "Johnny" Johnson, suddenly realized he had a problem; he'd made a commitment to marry his fiancée, Gwyn Morgan, in Torquay on April 3. His promise contravened Gibson's no-leave orders.

"We are joining this new squadron, but it's only for one trip," Johnson wrote his fiancée. "Don't worry. I'll be there on the third."[13]

"If you're not there on the third," she wrote back, "don't bother to contact me again."

Despite serving as a member of the Women's Auxiliary Air Force (WAAF) and understanding regulations fully, Gwyn seemed to have drawn a line in the sand for the twenty-one-year-old RAF airman from Lincolnshire. Johnson's hands were tied. Cancelled leave was cancelled leave. McCarthy responded the only way he knew how. He gathered his six crewmates, marched up to Gibson's office, and demanded to be seen. With an entire crew on his doorstep, Gibson must have sensed it was serious.

"The thing is, sir," McCarthy explained, "we've all just finished our tour and we are all entitled to a week's leave."[14]

Gibson listened while McCarthy's crew, mostly NCOs, probably wished they were anywhere else but in the CO's office.

"My bomb aimer is due to be married on the third of April." He paused. "And let me tell you, he *is* going to get married on the third of April!"

A few uncomfortable moments passed in silence. Then Gibson looked up. "Very well. You can have four days. Dismissed."

Despite the predictable number of last-minute stumbles that a wartime wedding inevitably faced, Johnson arrived on time. Gwyn and Johnny enjoyed a one-day honeymoon. And by Monday morning, McCarthy's entire crew, including

Johnson, was back on base and in the thick of training for a second tour of duty.

Some of Gibson's call-ups to join Squadron X had far less experience than decorated pilots such as Hopgood, Martin, Maudslay, McCarthy, and Young, but the wing commander considered their respect for discipline and their desire to fly with a crack squadron as key criteria for joining. Vernon William Byers fell into that category. Byers was born in 1919 in Star City, Saskatchewan, and as a young man worked as a farm labourer, construction worker, and miner. Wanting to join the Air Force but unable to qualify when the war began, Byers signed up with the army in 1941, but eventually he earned a transfer to the RCAF, graduating with his BCATP wings the following year. During his training at 1654 Heavy Conversion Unit in Wigsley, he was crewed up with some of the men who would serve with him later on the dams raid, including flight engineer Alastair Taylor, navigator Jim Warner, wireless operator John Wilkinson, and gunner Jimmy McDowell, a fellow Canadian from Port Arthur, Ontario.

Sgt. Byers began operational duties in February 1943, flying second dickey on a couple of ops over France and Germany that winter. On just its first bombing op to Stuttgart, Byers's aircraft lost power to the rear turret; that meant McDowell had to swivel the turret by hand. Nevertheless, Byers's crew pressed on and successfully dropped its bombs. In March, when Gibson invited an experienced 467 Squadron crew to join his special operation, part of the crew, including the pilot, turned him down; that's when Gibson took note of Byers and his crew and their record of determination and awarded them a spot with the new squadron.

"A good type of NCO who is fully capable," wrote Gibson in his recommendation for Byers's commission in April 1943. "He keeps his crew in order, is punctual, and understands discipline."[15]

With a record of just three combat operations, Vernon Byers, the twenty-four-year-old bomber pilot from Saskatchewan, and his green crew had earned a blessing from the CO and joined the elite combat team for the mission ahead.

PART OF W/C GIBSON'S SENSE OF SELF-ASSUREDNESS no doubt came from the choices he'd made for his own crew on Squadron X. His wireless operator, F/L Robert Hutchison, from Liverpool, had served sixteen ops with his skipper at 106 Squadron, so "Hutch" was an obvious call-up. P/O Fred Spafford, from Adelaide, Australia, had served half a year with 50 Squadron as a bomb aimer and had received a DFM and a commission, so "Spam" had credentials strong enough for Gibson's liking. As far as gunners were concerned, Gibson couldn't ask for much better than F/L Richard Trevor-Roper, from the Isle of Wight; he had more than fifty ops under his belt and a DFM, so he became Gibson's gunnery leader. One of two Canadians aboard Gibson's Lancaster was front gunner George Deering. Born in Scotland but raised in Toronto, in his first year with RAF No. 103 Squadron, Deering completed a tour and was commissioned just before Gibson claimed him for his crew. Meanwhile, Sgt. John Pulford was the man at Gibson's right hand. The flight engineer from the district of Hull had served in the RAF literally from the ground up. He started as a motor mechanic with ground crew and then, in 1942, he re-mustered and had accumulated thirteen ops in the new position of flight engineer by the time he reached Scampton and was posted to Gibson's Lancaster. The final link, Gibson's navigator, Torger "Harlo" Taerum from Canada, was a story unto himself.

The eldest of three sons and a daughter, Harlo was born on the family farm near Milo, in southern Alberta, in 1920. But before he was a teenager, his role as an older brother took on even greater significance; in 1931 his father, Guttorm, drowned in a swimming accident on nearby Lake McGregor.* Suddenly Harlo faced the challenge of simultaneously helping his mother raise his siblings, carrying out most of the farm chores, and maintaining his grades at the Lake McGregor elementary school.

Nevertheless, young Harlo excelled at just about everything he tried, obtaining "the highest number of passes during a single term since the school's inception."[16] He kept up his academic standing at Milo High School, completing three subjects in grade eleven and eight in grade twelve during the same school year, while also excelling in sport as "a track, baseball, and rugby football star."[17] After Harlo graduated in 1938, the family moved to Calgary, where he accepted work as a labourer while taking radio correspondence courses; he had hopes of joining the Air Force the following year. Harlo had never been to Norway, the birthplace of his parents, but Hilda Taerum watched her eldest son grow increasingly anxious about the state of things in the old country.

---

* On June 4, 1931, the *Vulcan Advocate* reported that on the previous Sunday winds had suddenly increased on the lake, which served irrigation canals in the district. The rough waters capsized a raft where two fishermen had cast their lines; they were immediately in distress. Guttorm Taerum and two others, fishing at the water's edge, swam out to the raft, but in the panic both Taerum and the man he was attempting to rescue, Henry Olson, sank and drowned in sixteen feet of water.

"When Norway was invaded by the Germans [in 1940] and reports began to filter through of the manner in which his father's people were being treated," she said, "Harlo enlisted in the RCAF."[18]

His BCATP service records show that he began training as an AC2 on July 22, 1940, five weeks after the evacuation of Allied forces and the royal family from Norway. Within a month Harlo was a Leading Aircraftman (LAC), by November he'd risen to a technical sergeant, and by February 1941 he'd been posted to No. 1 Air Observer School at Toronto's Malton Airport. There he routinely flew as a cadet observer aboard twin-engine Ansons, learning map reading, night flying, cross-country navigation, search and interception techniques, and reconnaissance photography. By the middle of the year, he'd also completed training at No. 1 Bombing and Gunnery School near Jarvis, Ontario, and the Advanced Air Navigation course at Rivers, Manitoba, with across-the-board high percentage grades. Then, on June 7, 1941, during a ceremony in Toronto, he received his RCAF navigator's brevet, pinned to his tunic by none other than Air Marshal Billy Bishop VC.

While most BCATP aircrew graduates would next have received embarkation leave for a brief visit home, followed by train tickets to Halifax for the transatlantic crossing aboard a troopship, Harlo Taerum got different orders. In late July, his mother opened a postal telegraph from him that read simply: "LEAVING MONDAY NO ADDRESS NOT PHONING LETTER FOLLOWING LOVE HARLO."[19] Hilda later learned that the RCAF authorities had sent her son to the military airfield at Gander, in the Dominion of Newfoundland, where he crewed up with Captain H.C. Moody to fly a coastal reconnaissance bomber, the Lockheed Hudson, from North America to Britain. On August 9, when the pair landed in Prestwick, Scotland, they learned they'd completed the trip in a record-breaking time of ten hours and forty-four minutes. Such were the signs that the RCAF had welcomed into its combat arsenal an above-average serviceman—indeed, a navigator on a mission.

His final training phase brought F/Sgt. Taerum to the operational training unit at Upper Heyford through the summer and fall. On January 2, 1942—with about 130 hours' experience in daylight flying and half that many flying at night—Taerum commenced combat operations with RAF 50 Squadron, based at Swinderby, England. He'd been paired with a Rhodesian skipper, F/O Norman Goldsmith, aboard Hampden bombers. Night after night throughout the month, the duo joined high-altitude bombing operations against Cologne, Brest, and Wilhemshaven, as well as low-level "gardening" flights over enemy shipping lanes of occupied Europe.

Along with the standard date, hour, aircraft numbers, and duty references, Taerum's flight log entries regularly included references such as "attacked and hit by night-fighter," "caught in searchlights," and plenty of "hit by flak."[20] But his logbook also recorded additional exercises, such as low-level blind approaches and lots of night-flying training. One time, his exercise even attracted an extra passenger. Sydney King, a ground crewman with "B" Flight at 50 Squadron, got permission to join Goldsmith and Taerum on one of their flight tests. King sat strapped in as the Hampden crew practised cross-country low-level flying at altitudes less than two hundred feet—at night! "This rare opportunity to go hedge-hopping was too good to miss," King wrote years later.[21]

The young Canadian navigator's acumen at day and night flying also caught the eye of his commanding officers. In July 1942, Taerum and Goldsmith (by now a flight commander) joined a conversion flight at 50 Squadron, advancing from twin-engine Hampden bombers to four-engine Lancasters. Within weeks F/Sgt. Taerum was not only learning to navigate these larger, more sophisticated bombers to targets at Düsseldorf and Bremen, but he was also instructing other navigators on the new equipment. Taerum had now accumulated more than 175 hours of daylight flying time and nearly 225 hours in the air at night. In January 1943, he navigated two bombing ops over Berlin with one of the most experienced pilots on the squadron, F/L Mick Martin.

The twenty-five-year-old RAAF pilot had completed a total of thirty-six combat operations—thirteen with RAF No. 455 Squadron and twenty-three with 50 Squadron—and the previous fall had been awarded the DFC. Martin had limited respect for authority but total respect for his wartime profession as bomber pilot. Flying was a skill never mastered but always tested. And in turn, he insisted on rigorous flying standards among the Bomber Command crews with whom he served.[22] If he'd learned one thing trying to bomb targets, it was that flying effectively at a low level increased his odds of surviving anti-aircraft or enemy fighter fire. His crews had to get used to the close proximity of treetops outside their gunnery or bomb-aiming bubbles; indeed, on one operation, Martin's Hampden bomber came home with a local power line cable wrapped around a wing.[23] On Martin's recommendation, just a couple of weeks after Martin and Taerum had worked together on the Berlin ops, Guy Gibson filled the final vacancy aboard his Lancaster.

"Terry was one of a number of [RAF] 50 Squadron aircrew hand-picked to join 617 Squadron under Guy Gibson . . . selected to be navigator in the CO's aircraft," wrote Sydney King, Taerum's ground-crew mate. "[It was] surely recognition of the fact that [he was] the best among the best."[24]

FOR A WARTIME BOMBER COMMAND STATION, AS W/C Gibson had already discovered, Scampton was woefully under-equipped that winter of 1942–1943. Even though the hangars, administrative buildings, and aircrew quarters were only ten years old, many were rehabilitated First World War huts and barracks with many shortcomings, including no furnishings and little hot water. The base already housed 57 Squadron, there since the previous September, and with a full new squadron moving in, there would hardly be enough liveable space unless Gibson made changes. Such logistical chaos landed in the lap of F/Sgt. George Powell, whom Gibson had recruited from 57 Squadron to become chief administrator and disciplinarian for Squadron X. To "Chiefy" Powell fell the responsibility of acquiring both the support staff and the facilities Scampton would need in the coming weeks; he was soft-spoken but, according to Gibson, "was something of a psychoanalyst [who] interviewed his men kindly, getting the best out of them."[25] From the moment he arrived, all day, every day, Chiefy interviewed the seven hundred men who would serve the new squadron as riggers, fitters, signallers, armoury crews, radar specialists, and other ground-crew roles.

Among those he interviewed and acquired was Canadian Sergeant Hugh Munro, a radar specialist from the RCAF.

Munro, it turned out, was more than a technician. When he arrived at the aircrew quarters, he realized he would have to use some amateur psychology to meld this mishmash of Scots, Rhodesians, Canadians, Welshmen, and Englishmen into a cohesive unit. Each night before the nearly exhausted Scampton ground crews retired, he put them through a calisthenics routine. To one newcomer, the odd sight of ground crew leaping and flailing their arms left the impression he'd stumbled into a local mental institution, but Munro convinced him and he "soon joined our lunatic actions."[26]

Meanwhile, any resistance that Chiefy Powell faced in the acquisition of squadron paraphernalia evaporated in a single stroke. Air Ministry officials finally began to accept the existence of a new squadron, outlined its orders, and addressed its critical needs. At an ad hoc meeting on March 25, the Air Ministry had designated Squadron X top priority for any and all requirements. It had reported that Vickers and A.V. Roe promised to have all the Type 464 Lancasters—twenty of them—modified to carry the bouncing bomb, and to have them delivered to Scampton by mid-April and early May. It had also given the dams raid an official code name—Operation Chastise—and the squadron of Lancasters and their crews an official numeral. Since all squadron numbers up to 299 were taken, the 300s designated for overseas squadrons, the 400s assigned to Canadian and Australian squadrons, the 500s to RAF training squadrons, and 600 to 616 given to pre-war auxiliary squadrons, that left 617 free. In addition, the code letters "AJ" were allocated and would be painted with the RAF roundel on the fuselage of each Lancaster, followed by each plane's letter code.

After Gibson's series of short talks with members of his aircrew, he gathered the ground crews in the hangar. This time, to be seen and heard, he jumped onto the hood of his Humber and repeated his cryptic predictions about shortening the duration of the war and the need for discipline on the station.[27] Then he handed over the floor to G/C Charles Whitworth, who was given the job of galvanizing the non-flying airmen for the challenge ahead. Some recalled that Whitworth's talk inspired more squadron spirit than anything Gibson had said. Whitworth asked the men to consider a scene from Noël Coward's 1942 feature film *In Which We Serve*. He asked them to recall an exchange between Coward, as commander of a Royal Navy destroyer, and one of his onboard crew.

"What is the secret of an efficient ship?" the commander asks.

"A happy ship, sir," the seaman answers.[28]

Whitworth repeated that he hoped for the same kind of atmosphere on the new squadron. He suggested that to ensure things ran smoothly, all levels on the station had to "bind" together—and that it was a two-way bargain. "I can promise you," he said finally, "that if you don't bind me, I won't bind you."

Even as Gibson and Whitworth laid the foundation for a healthy squadron spirit, the Air Ministry and RAF decision-makers were determining the next steps in the process. They announced that Gibson was to be awarded a bar to his DSO, and then, two days later—March 27, 1943—passed him his written "most secret" orders for Operation Chastise.

"No. 617 Squadron will be required to attack a number of lightly defended special targets," the orders stipulated. "These attacks will necessitate low-level navigation over enemy territory in moonlight with a final approach to the target at 100 feet at a precise speed, which will be about 240 miles per hour."[29]

The orders went on to direct crews to prepare for delivery of the bouncing bomb not more than a mile from the target and within forty yards of the prescribed release point. It indicated that Lancasters would take off from the Scampton aerodrome at intervals of about ten minutes and attack the target inside enemy territory. What wasn't immediately obvious was that the secret operation called for delicate high-speed, low-level flying throughout the mission—perhaps six or seven hours continuously—crossing the North Sea, racing over enemy territory, descending even lower when attacking the target, and then back to base. Flying just off the deck all the way, the operation planners surmised, would help the bombers escape radar detection, dodge anti-aircraft or night-fighter fire, and increase the element of surprise. The Air Ministry recommended that training commence immediately over water on nine suitable lakes and reservoirs located in Wales and the North Midlands. Indeed, the very afternoon that Gibson had welcomed his aircrews, he dispatched one of them into the skies above the lakes to photograph their surrounding topography as a reference for the rest of the squadron. Finding and flying to Gibson's "tree in the middle of England" was to begin in earnest right away.

In a way, Barnes Wallis had already found his training tree. Earlier that month, the Ministry of Aircraft Production had chosen the location to conduct trial drops of Upkeep prototypes: Reculver Bay, a quiet stretch of coastline in Kent. Wallis, assisted by one of his design team, Herbert Jeffree, had successfully run Upkeep on a spinning device on the ground—five hundred revolutions per minute. But now, over Reculver, crews would test the spinning apparatus built into the bomb bay of the new Type 464 Lancasters and conduct actual drop tests of the trial bombs, called "stores," on the waters of Reculver Bay. By mid-April the Type 464 Lancs had undergone customized changes themselves. A.V. Roe and Vickers crews had removed the Lancaster's mid-upper turret and faired over the opening. Then, instead of attaching bomb-bay doors in its belly, they installed a set of caliper arms in the sides of the fuselage; V-shaped and positioned toward the front of the bomb bay, the apparatus was connected to a drive belt and hydraulic motor (normally used to open and close the bomb-bay doors) that would rotate Upkeep to the prescribed five hundred revolutions per minute. It would be the wireless radio operator's job to operate the motor, which had borrowed the rev counter from a motorcycle to show Upkeep's rpms. The first modified Lancasters arrived at Scampton on April 8, and the twentieth (and last) one on May 13, three days before Operation Chastise.[30]

TWO MEMBERS OF THE NEWLY CHRISTENED RAF NO. 617 Squadron needed little encouragement or inspiration to achieve G/C Whitworth's prescribed esprit de corps. Life before the Air Force had already done that. And it made them nearly inseparable aircrew comrades. Abram "Albert" Garshowitz was born in Hamilton, Ontario, in 1920; he was the ninth of twelve children born to immigrants from Russia. Frank Garbas was born in 1922, one of nine children in a Polish family that also lived in Hamilton. Both boys grew up in the north end of the city and on weekends and after school found their way to the community focal point, Eastwood Park. A piece of reclaimed land on the city's harbourfront, the park became the home to some of Hamilton's most competitive hockey, baseball, football, and rugby teams. Albert and Frank were friendly rivals in the Hamilton Junior Rugby League. After graduation, Albert worked in his grandfather's furniture store and Frank worked for the Otis elevator company.

When Canada declared war on Germany, both Garshowitz and Garbas enlisted as soon as they were eligible, and both were streamed as wireless operator/gunners in the RCAF. Garshowitz felt so strongly about the need "to fight for the country" that when he completed his BCATP courses in Canada, his family travelled to his graduation at Trenton, Ontario, even though the wings ceremony was the same day as his brother David's bar mitzvah. Overseas in 1942, both Al and Frank trained at different OTUs until Garshowitz convinced his pilot, F/Sgt. Max Stephenson, to have his old friend join their training crew.

"The [new] gunner is from our fair City of Hamilton," Garshowitz wrote home that October. "I used to play football with him for Eastwood Park. . . . He's a swell fellow. His name is Frank Garbas."[31]

The Lancaster crew Frank Garbas joined included bomb aimer Don Hopkinson, a former cricketer from Royton, Lancashire; Richard "Dick" Bolitho, from Northern Ireland; and Floyd Wile, a navigator from Canada. Wile had grown up on a farm near Scotch Village, Nova Scotia, working in his father's lumber mill, which specialized in the manufacture of berry boxes for fruit produce in the Annapolis Valley. He originally enlisted in the Canadian Army, like his older brother Raymond (with the Princess Louise Fusiliers), but re-mustered in the RCAF in 1941. His instructors described LAC Wile as "quiet and plodding,"[32] but he placed near the top of his observers' class in February 1942 and later that year got his posting overseas. At 19 OTU in Kinloss, Scotland, as navigator, he also joined F/Sgt. Max Stephenson's aircrew. All that fall, the Stephenson crew gelled in the air—piling up daily and nightly hours training on Whitley bombers—and on the ground too. They were young, working hard and playing hard.

"Here [at Kinloss] we raise Hell and murder," Garshowitz wrote his siblings back home in Hamilton. "The first three days here, we were put on charge three times. [But] since we are sergeants they can't CB [confined to barracks] us. They can't take our stripes from us, because we need them to fly."[33]

In December 1942, the Stephenson crewmen left Kinloss station and its Whitley bombers behind and moved to heavy-conversion training on Lancasters. They acquired a seventh crewman, flight engineer John Kinnear, and within a month had accumulated sufficient hours on the four-engine heavies to go on operations. Suddenly the relatively safe circuits over England, air firing at mock targets, bombing practice runs, and night-flight tests of operational training ended. The Stephenson crew was posted to RAF No. 9 Squadron, at Skellingthorpe, for combat sorties. The war came into sharp focus immediately. During that winter, Al Garshowitz lost two friends on bombing ops over Europe. He attended the funeral of longtime family friend F/Sgt. Ralph Frank, as well as that of a friend from his own squadron and barracks.

"When I heard that Jimmy got it, I felt sick to my stomach,"

Albert wrote his sisters. "That very morning he'd come in to borrow my Canadian comics. Who will be next? Who knows?"

It wasn't long before he found out. At Skellingthorpe, Max Stephenson's crew had to wait for its skipper to complete one final test of leadership and endurance—an actual bombing sortie as second dickey, on this occasion serving as flight engineer with a more seasoned crew. But that Lancaster didn't make it back—shot down that night over Duisberg and the entire crew killed. The operations of one night suddenly left six men in search of a new pilot leader. But as quickly as it had lost Max Stephenson, his crew was transferred to 57 Squadron at Scampton, where its members were reassigned to pilot Bill Astell.

Born on April 1, 1920, Astell had an advantaged childhood as the son of a textile manufacturer in Manchester. Studies at various schools culminated in 1933 at Bradfield College, where he acquired wanderlust, finally arriving back home in May 1939. That summer he joined the Royal Navy but by fall had transferred to the RAF; they streamed him for pilot training and shipped him to Rhodesia, and he quickly advanced from elementary to service flying training on Airspeed Oxfords. "I am pretty certain to be put onto bombers," he wrote, "which is what I always wanted."[34]

Astell was independent and tightly focused on his military aviation career. Upon graduation, when he learned he'd been given a commission but no new uniform with which to display his promotion, he adroitly sewed epaulettes on his sergeant's tunic. He couldn't quite improvise his way back to Britain, so he had to contend with an operational training posting to the Mediterranean. They first sent him to RAF

No. 148 Squadron on the island of Malta in January 1941, then to Kabrit, Egypt, supporting the British 8th Army. Over the desert he concluded his conversion to Wellington bombers, conducting air-sea rescue searches, night flying and landings, and eventually "the Mail Run" flights from Kabrit over enemy ports in search of targets and back. At the end of May 1942, he and his crew were sent to attack an enemy airfield at Derna, Libya. During the sortie, a night fighter returned fire three times, forcing Astell to crash-land in the desert near Martuba. Estimating that he was 120 miles behind enemy lines, he set off with his navigator—hiding in caves, stealing rations, impersonating German signallers, and crossing minefields—before arriving back at Kabrit airfield, five days overdue. The RAF awarded him a highly appropriate DFC, but the unofficial "Order of the Winged Flying Boot" also honoured him with membership in the "Late Arrivals Club."

"On 1st June 1942, when obliged to abandon his Aircraft, on the Ground or in the Air, as a result of unfriendly action by the enemy," the citation read, "[Astell] succeeded in returning to his Squadron, on foot or by other means, long after his Estimated Time of Arrival. IT IS NEVER TOO LATE TO COME BACK."[35]

Back in England by October 1942, F/O Bill Astell saw his first Lancasters up close and described them as "simply enormous machines." Following some instruction on four-engine aircraft and air gunnery and a refresher on beam-approach flying, he got acquainted with the Lancaster that was assigned to him. He also had to familiarize himself again with maritime conditions, not desert ones—although he had done some superb low-level flying below sea level over the desert. On

January 25, 1943, he reported to 57 Squadron at Scampton, where he was assigned a "headless" crew—flight engineer Kinnear, navigator Wile, bomb aimer Hopkinson, wireless operator Garshowitz, and gunners Bolitho and Garbas—who had just lost their pilot, Max Stephenson. And so Bill Astell began his second tour with a brand-new crew. According to Garshowitz's flight log, the blended crew seemed to move smoothly into operations, flying a series of local test flights, night flights, and cross-country exercises in early February 1943. Their first combat op took them to the German navy dry docks and U-boat pens at Lorient, France. And while RAF protocol generally frowned upon personal comments in a flight log, Garshowitz, now a warrant officer, couldn't resist. "Easy target," he noted in his log.[36]

Seven sorties followed through February and March, including one to Milan, which Garshowitz called a "Good target," and another to Hamburg, where they lost use of a starboard engine. On March 5, they joined Bomber Command's first night operation in the Battle of the Ruhr Valley with an attack on Essen, and Garshowitz penned into his log, "Hottest yet." The crew chemistry must have become apparent. Their skipper had been promoted to flight lieutenant and they had accumulated fifty-one operational hours in just their first month together. That's when they got the call from Guy Gibson to join 617 Squadron. Garshowitz wrote to his family: "I'm in a new squadron now, a newly formed squadron, that is highly secret. When the time comes for me to spill the beans, you'll all know. But for the present, let's keep it that way. . . . We're doing a lot of flying, but only exercises."[37] Indeed, when the wing commander wrapped up his comments that first day in Scampton's No. 2 Hangar, he called on F/L Astell, as Deputy Flight Commander, to take the lead in the new training regimen.

"Bill, I want you to take your crew and to fly over every lake you can see in England, Scotland and Wales and take photographs of them," Gibson had said. "Let me have the photographs in thirty-six hours."[38]

Garshowitz logged an hour and forty minutes with F/L Astell as pilot on March 29, and another hour with F/L Shannon as pilot on March 31. He also packed a camera of his own aboard the Lancaster as he and his fellow crewmen conducted their low-level, nighttime, and practice bombing exercises over the British countryside. Such activity, no doubt, would have riled their CO as a potential breach of security, but the daylight images taken inside Astell's and Shannon's Lancasters captured the workmanlike attitude of the 617 Squadron crews as well as their apparent demeanour of youthful assurance.

REVIEWING THE PHOTO RECONNAISSANCE RETRIEVED by Astell's crew that last week of March, W/C Gibson chose to personally overfly some of the proposed water reservoirs that he and the rest of the squadron would use for trial runs simulating low-level attacks over water. On March 28, he took his two best pilot friends, Melvin Young and John Hopgood, aboard his own Lancaster to the Derwent Reservoir, a lake in the Pennine Hills of north-central England. The high ground that surrounded the reservoir immediately demonstrated the kind of delicate flying that would be required to descend quickly and fly low over the reservoir. When Gibson's aircraft got there, some industrial haze from the steel mills of nearby Sheffield hung in the air, but Gibson eased his Lanc down to about 150 feet above the lake at 240 miles per hour. So far, so good. But when Gibson repeated the run a few hours later, at dusk, the evening fog and the absence of light had changed everything. For example, Gibson noted later, the water, which had been blue in the daylight, turned black at dusk, so water and sky seemed as one. Even more alarming, the Lanc's altimeter couldn't register accurately the few feet between aircraft belly and water surface. *G-George* nearly hit the water during the dusk descent.

"Christ! This is bloody dangerous," bomb aimer Spam Spafford blurted over the intercom.[39]

Quickly regaining some altitude, Gibson commented to Young that unless the squadron's Lancasters had a way of reading their altitude above the water more accurately, the operation would be impossible.

"Why must we fly at this dead height?" Hopgood asked.

"The scientist I met told me that in order to make his weapon work, we would have to fly within a few miles an hour, at the right air speed, and within a very few feet of the right height," Gibson said. "That's our problem."

The problem gained magnitude the following day, March 29, when Gibson was called away from Scampton for another meeting with AVM Ralph Cochrane, the CO of 5 Group headquarters at Grantham. Cochrane had received delivery of three large packing cases, all labelled "very fragile." Cochrane and Gibson took screwdrivers to the case lids; when they lifted the tops away, inside each case sat a model of a dam in perfect detail. At that point Gibson's only reaction was relief. "It's not the *Tirpitz*," he thought. After some examination of the models, Cochrane sent Gibson on his way in a communications airplane, back to Barnes Wallis's office at Burhill for clarification.

Unlike their first meeting five days earlier, when Wallis seemed perturbed that Gibson had been blindsided by the whole enterprise, this time the scientist was glad to see the wing commander and immediately asked how the Lancaster trials were going. Gibson explained that flying as low as 150 feet above water at night felt nearly impossible. The altitude of bomb delivery would come later, however. Wallis first reminded Gibson of the models he'd just seen and explained how his bouncing bomb might knock down the massive dams of the Ruhr Valley. He gave Gibson a précis of the research, writing, and rationale he'd developed over the previous six years to attack and destroy the Möhne, the Sorpe, and the Eder Dams. He reiterated the importance of the structures—industrially, militarily, and emotionally—to the German war effort, and therefore their priceless value as targets to the Allies. Then the scientist drew Gibson's attention to photographs he'd compiled in a book; they included some of the images of the breaching experiments conducted in 1942 at the Road Research Lab and the Nant-y-Gro Dam in Wales.

Finally he updated Gibson on the evolution of Upkeep itself. By this time Wallis's primitive weapon sketches had evolved into the building of prototypes. Back in February, the original design Wallis had in mind was a nearly spherical steel weapon measuring seven feet six inches in diameter. But when Ministry of Supply experts told him the dies for such a steel casing would require two years to produce, Wallis turned to a smaller, cylindrical design instead. The bouncing mine would have a

ATTACKING THE GRAVITY DAM

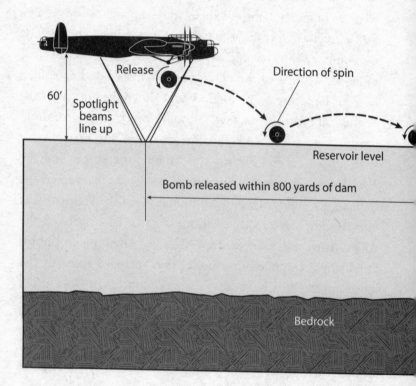

Release

Direction of spin

60'

Spotlight beams line up

Reservoir level

Bomb released within 800 yards of dam

Bedrock

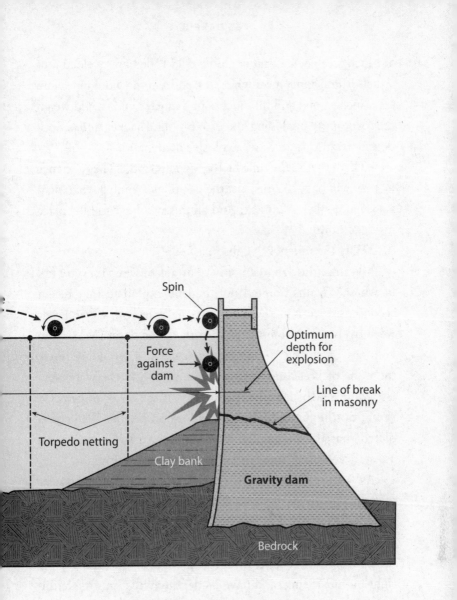

Spin

Optimum
depth for
explosion

Force
against
dam

Line of break
in masonry

Torpedo netting

Clay bank

Gravity dam

Bedrock

3/8-inch steel jacket that could be cold-rolled and welded into a fuel-drum shape; meanwhile, the entire mine would measure sixty inches long and fifty inches in diameter and would weigh 9,250 pounds (including the 2,650-pound jacket and 6,600-pound Torpex underwater explosive contents).[40]

"Then, there's the time factor," Wallis said. "The ordnance factory will have to construct the weapons. You'll have to plan a special method of attack. And all this will have to take place inside a month."[41]

"Why the urgency?" Gibson asked.

"Because the dams can only be attacked when they are full of water," Wallis pointed out, and he explained that recent reconnaissance had revealed that the reservoir water levels were twelve feet from the tops of the three dams. Maximum volumes of spring runoff in the reservoirs would improve the odds of breaching the dams, he said, and the water levels would reach their maximums about the week of May 13 to 19, during an advantageous full-moon period. Wallis predicted that the moonlight would give aircrews some visual assistance getting to the target and bombing it at night.

As for the logistics of the bomb drop, and with the near miss the previous night over the Derwent Reservoir on his mind, Gibson raised the issues of proper altitude, appropriate air speed, and dropping the weapon the right distance from the dam so that Upkeep would stop bouncing at precisely the right moment, sink, and have its depth-charge sensors detonate the explosive to breach the dams. Wallis warned that if the mine was dropped too early—more than about eight hundred yards from the target—then it wouldn't bounce close enough to the dam wall to do the job. And if the weapon came down too late, the mine might hit the top of the dam and explode under the Lancaster's tail.

If all went according to plan, Gibson wondered, how far behind the speeding Lancaster would Upkeep explode? Wallis calculated about one hundred yards and added that the underwater explosion of the mine, at that distance, meant the concussion wouldn't affect the bombers and that the parapet of the dam wall would offer the aircraft further protection. With a first viewing of the dam models and all these logistics in his head, Gibson quietly left Burhill with his black Labrador retriever in tow and flew back to Scampton, writing later about the state of the operation and his resolve: "The limitations seemed almost impossible. But all we could do was to try."[42]

As the bar to his Distinguished Service Order indicated, W/C Gibson had accumulated an extraordinary 174 operational sorties by early 1943. His experience in the cockpits of every British bomber in the RAF arsenal seemed second to none. But the day before examining the models of the Ruhr River dams and listening to Barnes Wallis's rationale for breaching them, Gibson had nearly plunged his Lancaster into the Derwent Reservoir, because flying so close to the surface at dusk made it nearly impossible to discern where the water ended and the sky began. In other words, even the man leading Operation Chastise seemed unsettled by the challenge of ensuring that all twenty-one of his crack aircrews could safely fly nearly thirty tons of attack bomber at nearly maximum speed, at nearly minimum altitude, in nearly complete darkness to a target in the middle of Germany and back. But with all the cards now on the table, Gibson sensed he could sharpen the aircrews' focus, narrow the margin of error, and give each member of the raid team a fighting chance to reach the objective, deliver the blow, and survive.

From that moment on, since he knew where and what the targets were—but still couldn't share that top-secret information with anybody—Gibson would direct his crews to fly mostly over British lakes. He used the excuse that the lakes and surrounding hillsides provided the crews with valuable landmarks that navigators and bomb aimers could use to cross-refer with their map plotting or instrument readings. So, as April arrived and marginally better weather, the 617 aircrews filled their days with more low-levels and cross-countries and mock bombing runs two and three and four times per day.

Since many of the aircrews were from towns and counties within flying distance of Scampton, it was not unusual for the practising bomber crews to show off their skills in front of the relatives when an opportunity presented itself. When he knew their flight path would take the crew of Vernon Byers near his hometown of Morayshire, flight engineer Alastair Taylor convinced his skipper to fly their Lancaster particularly low, or "beat up," his home out in the country. Based on Taylor's next letter to his mother, they'd done a pretty impressive job.

"I hope we didn't scare you too much last Monday," Taylor wrote. "I saw you and Aunt Julia just in front of the house, but I could not pick Dad out anywhere, so [I] thought he would probably be at a pig sale."[43]

These proved particularly tough days for the wing commander, who worked by day in his office chasing the paper associated with the squadron and then took his own crew out in the evening to train for their role in the coming operation. They flew up the west coast of England over the Western Isles of Scotland, well into the night. It didn't seem to bother his crew, who recognized the seriousness of the work, one commenting, "It's a good thing flying with the Wingco—it keeps us off the booze."[44]

Meanwhile, the Air Ministry and the RAF brain trust were hard at work addressing some of the problems that Gibson and Wallis had identified during their most recent meeting at Burhill. To help simulate, in daytime, the nighttime flying that the crews were told Operation Chastise would require, the 617 airmen borrowed several accessories from the US Army Air Force, including amber-tinted goggles and blue celluloid that could be fitted to the windscreen and side windows of the Lancasters; this "synthetic night flying equipment"[45] helped them rehearse reading maps at night.[*]

Then, on a day in April when Gibson was flying his desk in his office at Scampton, not his Lancaster, he received a guest— W/C Charles Dann from the Ministry of Aircraft Production. With few pleasantries, Dann began talking about the sighting difficulties that 617 aircrews faced on the Eder and Möhne Dams raid. He added that one bombsight being considered, the latest anti-submarine device, would not work. The context suddenly dawned on Gibson.

---

* One of the so-called RAF backroom boys was Charles Harold Wood, a civilian photographer in Bradford, England. For personal use, Wood had designed glasses tinted to register only sodium light. For RAF flight training during the war, crews applied a blue filter coating to the inside of the aircraft windscreen; the pilot in turn wore amber-coloured goggles—combined, these measures turned day into simulated night. Wood was later awarded the Most Excellent Order of the British Empire for his work.

"How the hell do you know all this?" Gibson asked in a bit of a panic.[46]

Dann tried to calm Gibson. As the supervisor of aeronautics at the Aircraft and Armament Experimental Establishment in Boscombe Down, and as a bomb-sighting expert, he had been cleared to know the secret. "No one else knows," Dann said.

The two wing commanders then settled down to discuss the problem of knowing when and at what distance from the dam to release Upkeep from the Lancasters. Based on reconnaissance photography, they knew that the two Möhne sluice towers sat roughly seven hundred feet apart, so Dann began to sketch a makeshift rangefinder. He concocted a triangular wooden sight (shaped almost like a slingshot) with a viewing peephole at the end of the single prong and a nail protruding from each end of the double prongs. He postulated, with appropriate mathematical scales worked out, that the bomb aimer viewing through the peephole on the single-prong end of the device would see the upright nails on the two prongs line up with the sluice towers of the Möhne; at that moment, he calculated, the bomber would have reached the spot on the bombing run to release Upkeep and have it bounce to a near stop at the dam wall. Gibson handed Dann's drawings to a corporal and had the instrument section build a bombsight prototype within half an hour.[47]

At least one other navigational problem remained, the one that, according to Wallis, had given Gibson pause on his last visit to Burhill—dropping Upkeep from the proper altitude. Somebody had suggested dragging a trailing wire with a heavy weight that would guide the pilot and navigator to the correct height over the water, but that idea was tossed out. Melvin

Young had wondered about electric altimeters, but Gibson worried that the high ground surrounding the targets might interfere with their accuracy. As with Dann's wooden bombsight, however, a relatively simple solution would present itself. Benjamin Lockspeiser, who directed Scientific Research at MAP, hatched the idea of placing two angled spotlights—one fore and one aft—beneath the Lancaster such that when they converged on the water they created a figure-eight pattern on the surface, showing that the aircraft had reached the desired altitude.

The optical altimeter, as it was known, had been tried with flying boats when chasing U-boats, but open water proved too choppy for the spotlights to register clearly enough on the surface. Lockspeiser suggested that the calmer waters of the reservoir might reflect the spots more clearly and prevent the bomber crews from colliding with the water. The Royal Aircraft Establishment (RAE) at Farnborough in Surrey began testing right away. Designers ultimately chose Aldis lamps to be mounted on the underside of the bomber. On April 4, S/L Henry Maudslay and his navigator, F/O Robert Urquhart, flew Lancaster *Z-Zebra* to Farnborough to test the new spotlight system. They had both come through the upgraded British Commonwealth Air Training Plan in Canada that had raised the standard of each of their aircrew positions; Maudslay, from the United Kingdom, had experienced more instrument flying than previous pilots, for example, and Urquhart, from Saskatchewan, had completed observer, bombing and gunnery, and additional navigation training before receiving his observer's brevet. By the time they arrived at 617 Squadron, Maudslay and Urquhart both

DAMS RAID
LANCASTER

had a tour to their credit. Both had also been cited for a DFC, but only Maudslay had received one.

At Farnborough, *Z-Zebra* had the Aldis spotlights installed. They placed one under the port side of the Lanc's nose, facing down and aft, while they positioned the second centrally in the rear of the bomb bay, facing down but aimed forward. This way, navigator Urquhart, positioned at the cockpit's starboard plastic blister, could see the convergence of the two spots on the water below and report the aircraft's exact altitude so Maudslay, in the pilot's seat a few feet from him, could make adjustments. Eventually the two spotlights were adjusted so that the front Aldis was set at a 30-degree angle and the rear Aldis at a 40-degree angle. Maudslay and his *Z-Zebra* crew tested the system over the Channel south to Farnborough for about forty-five minutes. With the lamps set to converge when the Lancaster was at an altitude of 150 feet, Maudslay and Urquhart returned to demonstrate in front of the CO.

"It was dusk when he came whistling across the aerodrome with his two thin beams of light shining down," Gibson described later. "He looked so low . . . if he turned onto his side one wing would rip along the ground."[48]

Maudslay and Urquhart explained to Gibson that the Aldis lamps gave instant readings for the navigator to call out to the pilot, allowing him to concentrate on his instrument flying. A few days later all the aircraft were fitted with optical altimeters and, using the convergence system, all the crews were accurately roaring low over water and land to within two feet of the 150-foot ideal altitude. What haunted Gibson, however, was the realization that at night, lights shining beneath a bomber made it an obvious target for German gunners on the ground.

Experience became the core principle at Scampton. Occasionally during the run-up through April, Gibson had to let go some of the crews he'd recruited, specifically Ray Lovell's (replaced by Bill Divall's crew) and George Lanchester's—in the latter case because Gibson wanted to replace the navigator but the crew refused to be broken up. Meanwhile, other airmen with plenty of depth in their logbooks arrived to fill any gaps among the remaining Lancaster aircrews. Among them was navigator Ken Earnshaw, who came to 617 Squadron on April 29, 1943. Another product of the British Commonwealth Air Training Plan, Earnshaw was a born learner and, as it turned out, a teacher. As a boy growing up in Ohaton, Alberta, Ken rode on horseback five miles to school. Later, when he earned his teaching certificate, he cross-country skied to the Whitebush School near Bashaw, where he taught for a year.[49] Earnshaw was nothing if not thorough.

In June 1941, when he enlisted at the RCAF recruiting centre in Edmonton, he wrote in his attestation papers that he was "single" and "played softball moderately."[50] In answer to the question "Are you in debt?" he first wrote "No," then crossed it out and admitted, "Yes. Owe $20 on radio to [department store] Robert Simpson Company." He scored high in bombing and gunnery, air observer school, and navigational training, and graduated high enough to earn a commission as well. While still training at No. 3 Air Observer School in Regina, he got permission to go home so he and his girlfriend, Mary Heather, could marry. They corresponded nearly daily, including when the new F/O Earnshaw arrived overseas in May 1942 and realized why he needed to serve.

"The government has taken over most of the hotels and is

using them to billet the Canadian airmen," he wrote from No. 3 Personnel Reception Centre in Bournemouth, England. "We saw some of the bombed places. They were really smashed up. . . . When we saw all of the damage that Jerry had done,* it made us all glad to be over here and perhaps get a chance to get even . . ."[51]

During the autumn of 1942, Earnshaw completed operational training and heavy-conversion training and began service as navigator with 50 Squadron, flying operations aboard Manchester bombers from Swinderby to targets in Europe. His pilot was Norman Schofield and his bomb aimer was fellow Canadian John Fraser; they would eventually serve together in the dams raid. In less than six months as a crew they had flown nearly a full tour—twenty-four operations—and had survived their share of tangles in enemy airspace. He shared as much as the censors would allow in his correspondence home to his parents and Mary.

"Before we went on leave we had two very exciting trips to Germany," he wrote in February 1943. "On the first, our bomber was hit by heavy flak. We got several holes in it, but no one was hurt. A few days later, we went out and got a dose of it. First flak got us, and then a fighter . . . Our mid-upper gunner was hit and our plane was riddled with bullet holes. . . . I guess as long as one is around to tell of these things, they really aren't that bad, are they? Ha! Ha!"[52]

---

* Following the Battle of Britain, the Luftwaffe shifted its tactics from carpet bombing British cities to individual *Jagdbomber* (fighter-bomber) sorties, called "tip and run" attacks, on British targets, including military installations, railways, gas holders, and locations such as Bournemouth, where large concentrations of aircrew were billeted.

In April, just before he and Fraser left the squadron for a well-deserved inter-tour leave, Earnshaw wrote home that he'd flown bombing operations over Berlin three times and to Essen four times. For his service he finally got his flying officer's stripe, which, he satirized, "means another 75 cents a day, so it's OK, I guess." And when Air Force mail delivered a colour photo of his wife, Mary, he confessed to his parents in a letter written over several days that "I'm half afraid I'll be afraid to speak to her when I do get back. Good bye. Love from Ken."[53]

Nearly a month into the low-level training with 617 Squadron, pilot John Hopgood suddenly needed an experienced navigator and a bomb aimer to fill vacancies in his crew. Here was demonstrated the true value of the BCATP; though they had not once flown with the decorated British skipper, Earnshaw and Fraser's training and experience spoke volumes about their adaptability to the job at hand. In reviewing 50 Squadron's service records, Gibson and Hopgood took note of Fraser's thirty trips and Earnshaw's twenty-four, so on April 29, just over two weeks before Operation Chastise was expected to launch, the two Canadians were invited and assigned to Hopgood's Lancaster, *M-Mother*.

By the end of April it seemed that British skies had never been busier, with low-flying Lancasters diving, climbing, and criss-crossing the countryside. As an indication of the experience piling up, in less than a month most of the 617 crews had accumulated between twenty-five and forty hours of training flights; as a squadron that amounted to nearly 1,000 training hours in total, *and nearly all below 1,000 feet*. American Joe McCarthy had completed 36.45 day hours and 12.3 nighttime.

New Zealander Les Munro was right behind, with 35.3 hours daytime and 15.35 at night. Then followed Australian pilot Norman Barlow, with 27.35 by day and 15.35 by night. Canadian pilot Vernon Byers topped them all, with over 50 hours in daylight and about 15 night-flying hours. Gibson and his crew, not surprisingly, had flown fewer than 20 hours in daylight and 4.5 at night.[54] Just how valuable such intense and repetitive low-level training was proving to be is illustrated in a series of exchanges between W/C Gibson and the Canadian who seemed to be his nemesis, Ken Brown.

The flight sergeant and his all-non-commissioned crew had done their fair share of hedgehopping while stationed at Scampton. On sixteen of the thirty days in April, Brown had piloted his Lancaster and crew through 39.15 hours of cross-country, bombing, and spotlight-testing runs—plus eleven hours at night—all at altitudes no higher than five hundred feet.[55] And when he wasn't airborne in a Lancaster for four days in mid-April, Brown added another twelve practice runs at Fulbeck station, an RAF base that specialized in blind-approach training. As Brown remembered it, Gibson told his Lancaster pilots to conduct their low-level training over England by flying cross-country patterns at about two hundred feet above the ground. The pilots also knew that Gibson had assigned members of the Royal Observer Corps to record and report all their flying altitudes. About three days later, Brown noted, the low-level ceiling was reduced to 150 feet, which brought his Lancaster, *F-Freddie*, low enough to be skimming treetops and roofs. In fact, on one training trip, Brown was flying so low that his bomber was heading straight for an RAF aerodrome hangar under construction, so he pulled up the aircraft to about two hundred feet and watched as the building crews scattered out of the way. Brown found himself in front of Gibson yet again.

"What were you doing going over the hangar?" Gibson asked.[56]

"I thought it was a good idea." Brown shrugged.

"Two hundred feet? Hardly! You'll do that one again."

The next day, Brown's cross-country route took him over the same aerodrome hangar. This time he and his crew could see roofers at work on top of the building. Not particularly fazed, Brown gently nosed the Lancaster down to nearly grass level and came up over the top of the hangar the way a fighter aircraft might. Brown's Lancaster crew watched with some amusement as the roofers came tumbling off the building and scattered in all directions yet again. That prompted another session with his wing commander.

"Brown, I said low, but not that low!" Gibson admonished.

But that slap on the wrist to Brown may have just been for show—to prove to the public that Gibson was keeping his crews in check. Scampton went so far as to task one of its intelligence personnel, WAAF Section Officer Fay Gillon, to notify military and civilian populations where and when Lancasters from 617 Squadron might be roaring at low levels through their part of the country. What's more, the day-in, day-out low-level flying was apparently taking its toll. As the weeks of repetitive night and day training went on, Scampton's medical officer (M/O), Malcolm Arthurton, received a steady stream of aircrew complaining of airsickness. Not willing to jump to any conclusions, Dr. Arthurton got permission to tag along on one of S/L Henry Maudslay's cross-country exercises.* Maudslay flew his Lancaster, *Z-Zebra*, through some gusty winds that buffeted the bomber severely.

"Low flying experience. Weather bumpy," Arthurton recorded in his log on April 25, 1943. "Airsick after half hour."[57] From then on the squadron doctor seemed more sympathetic when 617 crewmen arrived at his sickbay door.

Meanwhile, the trials with the Lancasters dropping Upkeep prototypes had begun on April 13 on Reculver Bay. Each test experimented with the Lancaster flying at a different airspeed or a different altitude, or with Upkeep revolving at different rpm. On April 24, the entire dams raid initiative faced yet another make-or-break moment, when Barnes Wallis and W/C Gibson met to view the trial results motion-pictures and analyze the designer's latest evaluation. Wallis showed Gibson the results of dropping Upkeep at 150 feet at a certain speed that might prevent Upkeep from disintegrating; likewise, he showed what happened at forty feet at a certain speed. All of Wallis's trials came down to one formula that he estimated would deliver Upkeep to the target.

"The best height to suit your aircraft is here at the 60-feet level at 232 miles per hour," Wallis said. He asked, "Can you fly at 60 feet above the water? If you can't, the whole thing will have to be called off."

---

* Military training and low-flying antics went hand in glove at Scampton. No. 617 Squadron brass received a continuous flow of complaints from civilians blown off their bicycles or having to retrieve stampeding livestock after Lancasters roared overhead at treetop height. Once Henry Maudslay came back to base with foliage adorning his bomb-bay doors, while Joe McCarthy's bomb aimer, Johnny Johnson, admitted that his skipper flattened tulip fields near Spalding with "the slipstream and prop wash" of their low pass, and he flew under the electrical power lines at the town of Sutton Bridge, then pulled up "to clear the bridge."

Gibson said that he considered 150 feet low, but 60 feet very low. A slight hiccup and a bomber and crew would crash into the water. "We will have a crack tonight."

Back at Scampton, Gibson alerted the crews to adjust the Aldis spotlights beneath the Lancasters to criss-cross at sixty feet. He sent David Maltby up for a trial over one of their practice zones—Eyebrook Reservoir (a.k.a. Uppingham Lake). Then Gibson took his crew over the same waters while Uppingham was still calm. He worked with his navigator, Harlo Taerum, who directed him to say "Go down" calmly but to yell "Go up" if he dropped below the desired altitude. That night the spotlights worked perfectly. The desired speeds and altitudes were achieved. In the last days of April, all the crews tried and accomplished it.

"We can do it," Gibson told Wallis. It was May 1, 1943, fifteen days before the dams raid.

CHAPTER FIVE

"RACEHORSES STANDING IN THE PADDOCK"

WHEN HE RECEIVED THOSE VERY RARE FORTY-eight-hour leaves from Scampton, Robert Kellow, the wireless radio operator serving on Les Knight's Lancaster crew at 617 Squadron, looked forward to his visits with family relations in London. Born in New South Wales, F/Sgt. Kellow had been trained in Canada by the British Commonwealth Air Training Plan, like nearly 10,000 other Royal Australian Air Force volunteers. In January 1942 he'd finally arrived in the United Kingdom and had crewed up with fellow Royal Australian P/O Knight and then been posted to 50 Squadron. It was there, having completed twenty-five ops late in March, that Knight's crew received the offer of a shortened tour if they agreed to do a special trip with 617 Squadron. Naturally, members of Kellow's extended family, especially his aunt in London, became curious about his wartime exploits.

"Where have you been?" his aunt asked during one of his visits.[1]

"We've been to Berlin . . . " Kellow offered.

"No, where have you been this last month?"

"Just flying around England," Kellow explained honestly. "Just training for something."

"Well, what're you doing?" she asked, getting a little frustrated with his evasiveness. "Us taxpayers are paying for all this petrol you're using. What are you training for?"

"I don't know," Kellow said, ending the discussion.

In fairness, even as late as the first week of May 1943, Kellow didn't know much more than he'd admitted to his aunt. As it was for the other members of the squadron's flight crews, information was emerging on a need-to-know basis only. And there was precious little, it seemed, that Kellow needed to know. He and the rest of 617 aircrew understood it would be a low-level operation, over water, and likely at night. And it would be happening soon. In addition to the rest of the operational details, Kellow also didn't know that he'd already been recommended for a Distinguished Flying Medal for his skill as a wireless operator under fire, and perhaps indirectly for helping to keep the lid on as much of the 617 secret activities as he knew.

At her home in Calgary, Alberta, Hilda Taerum had dutifully inserted all correspondence from her son, P/O Harlo Taerum, into a treasured scrapbook. There were postcards from the BCATP stations in Ontario and Manitoba where her son had trained. Included was a photo of Air Marshal Billy Bishop pinning a navigator's brevet onto her son's tunic at his graduation in 1941, as well as telegrams from his operational station with 50 Squadron and from when he received his commission. Out of habit, Harlo Taerum, who was now training as W/C Gibson's navigator, rarely offered tangible information about his service. The coming operation was no exception.

"Best wishes from your loving son. Everything fine," was all he wrote in a telegram to his mother on May 9, one week before the raid.[2]

As Guy Gibson had stressed from the very beginning, nothing could be leaked outside the Scampton station. It could jeopardize everything. So, on May 5, when the wing commander joined a top-secret meeting at the Air Ministry on King Charles Street, Whitehall, in London, to discuss the status of Upkeep and Operation Chastise, the first order of business was an actual breach of security. Gibson had learned that one of 617 Squadron's armament officers, sent to RAF Manston near Reculver Bay, had accidentally witnessed some of the development work on Upkeep; he'd seen sectional drawings, maps of the Ruhr River Valley, and a number of other details associated with the planned sortie. That meant that the armament officer knew more about the operation than most of the senior pilots of the 617 Squadron aircrews. Gibson complained that such a breach had let down the team, but he was reassured that the documents involved would be confiscated and the leak sealed.

Also on the agenda at that Whitehall meeting were the latest Upkeep trials and the status of water levels behind the Ruhr dams. The latest reconnaissance images—photos shot on April 4–5, 1943—showed that water levels at the Möhne were two feet below the lip of the dam. Barnes Wallis, who also attended the meeting that day, pointed out that as the spring wore on, water would be drawn from the reservoirs, causing the levels to drop ten feet per month. That, he stressed, would diminish Upkeep's effectiveness. Wallis asked for more up-to-date reconnaissance but also informed those present about the latest on Upkeep's rollout and testing; they were grappling with the problem of balancing a spinning Upkeep in the calipers under the Lancasters, but he predicted all would be ready by May 14 or 15. AVM Ralph Cochrane, of 5 Group, told the meeting that the 617 crews were trained and ready to go. It was then decided that the operation—bombing the Möhne (code-named Target X), the Eder (Target Y), and the Sorpe (Target Z)—should go ahead on or about May 14 or 15.

Gibson emerged from the meeting recognizing that it was time to move the training of the remaining nineteen Lancaster crews up a notch, to tactical training as a squadron. In other words, with Operation Chastise just ten days away, it was time to conduct dress rehearsals, simulations with everybody involved. Aircrews would still not be told what the targets were. Pilots and navigators would still not know where in enemy territory they were headed. Crews would still have to operate in a virtual vacuum regarding what Upkeep was designed to do. Their job was to pilot, navigate, communicate, and defend aboard their aircraft under a security blackout that kept them as much in the dark as anybody else.

A letter home from Canadian bomb aimer Vincent MacCausland to his family illustrated the effect of the blackout, and also the intensity of each crewman's view of the operation. "You are perhaps wondering what I am doing here," MacCausland wrote his mother in Tyne Valley, Prince Edward Island, in mid-April. "There is really no need to feel over anxious to know that I am back again for my second tour . . ."[3]

A graduate of the BCATP's air observer school at Malton, of bombing and gunnery training at Jarvis, complete with bomb-aimer training with the RCAF in 1940, MacCausland had served in the United Kingdom for a year. By 1941 he'd become a flying officer and had done a full tour on bombers with 57 Squadron at Scampton. In mid-April 1943, with S/L Melvin Young seeking an experienced bomb aimer to fill a vacancy, MacCausland was drafted into the decorated pilot's crew. Like all the others, MacCausland knew little or nothing about the actual operation, but he was still clearly motivated to meet its challenge.

"I [have] had the privilege of joining a well-experienced crew and on aircraft that one dreams about," his letter continued, "and we are on revision and conversion for the next month before going over with a few bundles for the square-heads. I know that you will be feeling most anxious . . . but the time will soon pass and I know that God will be especially with us, as we were blessed in that first tour."

Expressing his apparently abiding faith that all things would come to pass as they should, using the code common among most airmen overseas to minimize any danger he might face, bomb aimer MacCausland wrote in a style he hoped would prevent his loved ones from worrying. Sugar-coated or not, however, the nature of 617 Squadron's work could not be minimized. It had a more visible impact on gunner Harvey Glinz. Born in 1922, the son of a letter carrier in Winnipeg, Manitoba, Harvey Sterling Glinz matriculated and went to work as a clerk in a Hudson's Bay Company department store. After his nineteenth birthday in 1941, he enlisted in the RCAF and apparently won favour with his recruiters as "a neat, clean, athletic man, sincere and a worthwhile addition to aircrew."[4] Appropriately, Glinz's BCATP assessors streamed him into training as a wireless radio operator and gunner. He graduated at the head of his air gunnery class and was immediately posted overseas for operational training. He landed at 61 Squadron in October 1942. First as a fill-in, then assigned to an American RCAF pilot, Glinz accumulated ops quickly, but it took a while for a youth raised in arid prairie air to adjust to the maritime weather in Britain; he suffered from catarrh and ear infections, excess mucus buildup in the ear, nose, and throat.

Tougher to cope with were the aircraft mishaps he survived—crashes on his second and fourth ops. Not surprisingly, these incidents triggered some anxiety for the young airman, and he sought medical assistance. After some rest and reassessment from an RAF medical board, Glinz was cleared for a return to active duty—a decision he'd wanted—just as W/C Gibson began to organize his secret squadron at the end of March 1943.

"He has an opportunity of being crewed up with an experienced pilot in whom he has every confidence," the medical assessor wrote of Glinz's chance to fly with Gibson's hand-picked aircrews. "This crew is being posted to another unit to form a new squadron."[5]

F/O Glinz rejoined some of his former 61 Squadron aircrew on their way to Scampton; they were crewed up with F/L Norman Barlow DFC in 617 Squadron. And there were no further reports of anxiety in Glinz's file. In fact, his bombing and gunnery expertise was welcomed in the new squadron. He became the "A" Flight gunnery leader at 617, chosen for the position from among gunners who had already completed their full tours. Glinz managed to cope with the pace and tension of the seven-week training stint ahead of the raid, although Barlow and his Lancaster crew once again experienced some challenging flights. On April 9, during an extremely low-level cross-country outing, Barlow's Lancaster ran into a flock of birds, brushed treetops, and smashed the front blisters in which bomb aimer Alan Gillespie and front gunner Glinz were positioned. Despite yet another near miss, front gunner Glinz, like everyone at 617 Squadron, was learning to cope. "He appreciates that his symptoms are nervous in origin, but thinks that he can make the grade and complete his tour," concluded his medical officer.[6]

Glinz's skipper, F/L Norman Barlow, carried with him a unique story, as both a civilian and an airman. Born in 1911 in a suburb of Melbourne, Australia, Barlow grew up in a storied family that owned and operated a popular motor-car business. In 1926, when Norman's older brother Alec teamed up with adventurer Francis Birtles for Australia's Darwin-to-Melbourne motor-car race, the family business sponsored the pair; in their British Bean roadster, *Sundowner*, they completed a record-breaking dash across 3,379 miles of the continent in eight days and thirteen hours. Then, following accusations of fraudulent dealings during the 1930s, Barlow's father took his own life. Norman took over the car dealership.

When he enlisted in the Royal Australian Air Force in 1941, Barlow already had his private pilot's licence, so he was transferred to Canada, along with 4,000 other Australians over the duration of the BCATP, for military pilot training. He received his graduation wings and a commission in January 1942 and by the fall of that year had embarked for the United Kingdom and been posted on Lancasters to 61 Squadron. He crewed up aboard Lancasters with a diverse group at Syerston station.

Navigator Philip Burgess, flight engineer Leslie Whillis, and rear gunner Jack Liddell were all officers from the United Kingdom. Bomb aimer Alan Gillespie, also a British officer, had previously received the DFM. Wireless operator and fellow Australian Charles Williams had, like Barlow, received a DFC. Front gunner Harvey Glinz, also an officer, was the sole Canadian aboard. Several of Barlow's crew had accompanied him during their first full tour of bombing operations, during which Barlow was commended in his DFC citation for setting "a magnificent example of courage and determination."[7] Barlow's crew would soon be the occupants of modified Lancaster *E-Easy*, preparing for the launch of Operation Chastise.

DURING THE FIRST WEEK OF MAY, THOSE MODIFIED Type 464 Lancasters began arriving at Scampton, delivered by special pilots.[8] The moment they pulled into the flight line, they became the centre of attention. F/L C.C. "Capable" Capel and the engineering crew took close looks at the absence of a mid-upper turret. And for ground crew, who had checked the ailerons, rudders, elevators, undercarriage, and instruments of their beloved Lancasters for many months, these Type 464s looked oddly misshapen. The new-look bombers stopped Harold Roddis, a twenty-year-old RAF ground crewman, in his tracks. "The neat lines of the Lancaster [were] completely destroyed," he said.

Some members of the ground crew went even further and suggested that the Lanc, having lost a great chunk of its underside, looked as if it had had an abortion. "Thereafter, they became known to us as 'Abortions.'"[9]

Not long after Roddis and his fellow ground-crew mates had digested that odd sight, onto the airfield came long eight-wheeled trucks, their cargo hidden under tarpaulins.[10] When the armourers pulled the covers away, ground crew were introduced to the component that would fit into the cut-out undersides of the Lancs where the now aborted bomb-bay doors had once hung. Most were painted red at that point. These were the shiny, just-off-the-line Upkeep mines. "Even then," Roddis said, "I could not believe . . . this 'dustbin-shaped' object . . . was a bomb."[11]

The final phase of training, Gibson decided, should involve simulations of the actual operation. Up to ten aircraft at a time would join exercises over Uppingham Lake (Eyebrook Reservoir) and Colchester Lake (Abberton Reservoir). To help focus the crews, on May 5 targets were erected on the dam wall at Uppingham. The crews would practise their techniques of travelling cross-country at a low level, arriving over the target with precision, and being called in to launch individual bombing runs over the lakes, although no bombs would actually be dropped. The Lancasters would then fly a route back to base over Wainfleet in order to drop practice bombs; then, on their return to Scampton, they would conduct a final low-level run across the airfield to check the calibration of the Aldis spotlights and then land. Gibson calculated that Uppingham Lake had much the same shape (although it was a good deal smaller) as Möhne Lake, while Colchester offered the calm waters they might expect in front of the Eder Dam. The wing commander had stretched the point slightly. Uppingham did look like a smaller version of the southern part of Möhne Lake, but the flat surroundings at Colchester did not replicate at all the narrow confines of the Eder reservoir, and the eighty-four miles between the two make-believe British objectives did not match the shorter distance between the two actual German targets.

Synchronizing all elements of the simulated attacks posed a new challenge, but by early May most of the aeronautics were in place. Crews had worked with the amber-tinted goggles and blue windscreens that approximated moonlit night conditions. They had experience with the optical altimeter, using the Aldis lamps aimed at the reservoir surface to guide them to the exact altitude over water. Most of the bomb aimers had adapted to the Dann rangefinder, but several had refined the sighting gear they would use during their simulated attacks.

Canadian navigator Revie Walker and British bomb aimer Len Sumpter had improvised aboard F/L Dave Shannon's *L-Leather* Lancaster. They recognized the difficulty that a bomb aimer faced when attempting to steady the wooden device with one hand to view through the peephole while keeping the other hand free for the bomb-release mechanism. In addition, if winds were buffeting the Lancaster around the sky or the pilot had to make evasive manoeuvres en route to the target, holding a viewing device steady hardly seemed practical.

Daniel Revie Walker was no stranger to improvising. Born in the Rocky Mountain town of Blairmore, where collieries and lumber mills were prevalent, young Revie got work in the Alberta forestry service. An early riser, a go-getter, and a child raised during the Depression, Walker had a waste-not, want-not attitude about life and living. At home and on any job, Walker followed a cardinal rule. "There was just one way to do things," Revie's son John noted about his father's approach to work. "It wasn't worth doing anything the sloppy way, the shortcut way. He just did things the right way."[12]

No doubt his instructors at Air Observer School, Bombing and Gunnery School, and Advanced Navigation School appreciated his dedicated approach. He raced through training and graduation in 1940–41, and while he was at No. 22 Operational Training Unit, his temperament and abilities were so highly valued that the RAF trainers seconded him to instruction. He arrived back on ops just when Dave Shannon needed a reliable navigator to join Gibson's 617 Squadron. F/O Walker fitted right in.

When faced with the dilemma of trying to free the bomb aimer's hands on his way to the target, Walker and Sumpter concocted a sighting device of their own. They drew two blue Chinagraph marks on the clear panel in front of the bomb aimer's position. With a string attached to each side of the panel and drawn tight against the bridge of his nose, lying flat and stable on the floor of his position in the Lancaster, the bomb aimer could support himself with his forearms, line up the towers using the marks and the taut string, and then release the mine at the right moment. This steadier, equally reliable ranging device was adopted by several other crews for the operation. As Walker's first DFC citation acknowledged, "First on Hampden aircraft, then Manchesters, and Lancasters, he has navigated his aircraft to targets [including] Brest, Mannheim, Düsseldorf, Bremen, Wismar, Stuttgart . . . and secured photographs of the aiming point, displaying great navigation ability and with his pilot F/O Shannon has achieved considerable success."[13]

Meanwhile, the 617 Squadron navigators had come up with what they thought was a more economical method for map-plotting the Lancasters' progress from takeoff to target and back. Since most or all of the flying would be low-level, some of the navigators suggested that they trim the maps they carried on the op to cover just the width of the flight plan; they then put their narrower maps on a pair of rollers that could scroll the less cumbersome map across the navigation table. Don MacLean, whose job it was to get Joe McCarthy and his *Q-Queenie** crew to target and back, worried about the narrower map. "This was a dangerous business," MacLean decided. "If you go too far off track then the roller maps would become useless."[14]

It's quite possible that F/Sgt. MacLean's healthy skepticism about the rollers came partly as a result of the non-operational side of his life at Scampton. While training at 617 Squadron, he'd become acquainted with Josephine Tear, a WAAF at the station. Perhaps he viewed a more cautious approach to the operation as an insurance policy for a safe return to base and to Corporal Tear.

"I decided to stick with straight scale maps of 1:500,000, which is the half-inch map," MacLean said.[15] It turned out to be a choice that would mean the difference between life and death on the operation to come.

MacLean's crew mate, rear gunner Dave Rodger, had made a custom change of his own in the rear gun turret of their

---

* When aircrews were assigned to aircraft, they immediately transposed the registration letters on the aircraft fuselage into an identifier for their bomber. Since Joe McCarthy's Lancaster's registration letters ended in Q, his crew created the alliteration *Q for Queenie*, or *Q-Queenie*, as its identifier.

Lancaster, removing a portion of the Perspex panelling in front of the gunsight to give him unrestricted vision. He recognized the problems that low flying posed for all the Lancaster crews. "You didn't know what was coming . . . until it went by."[16]

Along with improvisation at Scampton came interruption. On May 6, the day after his meeting at the Air Ministry, Gibson had to play host to Air Force dignitaries. That day, Hugh Montague "Boom" Trenchard, Marshal of the Royal Air Force and founder of the RAF in 1918, toured the station; the significance of the visit escaped no one. Soon after, Arthur Harris, CO of Bomber Command, also dropped in. The visits did much to inflate the squadron's sense of self-importance, but nothing to sustain the momentum of training. The short interruption made Gibson's conference with senior staff that same day all the more relevant. Present were his most trusted pilots, station engineering officer F/L C.C. Capel, armament officer F/L Henry "Doc" Watson, and, as always, the station mascot, Gibson's black Lab.

Issues discussed ran the gamut. The structural changes in the Type 464 Lancasters, for example, eliminated the mid-upper turret and moved the gunner to the nose gun position, just above where the bomb aimer lay prone. Since he would be there for the duration of Operation Chastise, S/L Melvin Young, piloting *A-Apple*, suggested the squadron engineers manufacture a support for the gunner's legs, so that he'd be more comfortable and the bomb aimer "wouldn't have to put up with the smell of his feet."[17] F/L Dave Shannon, skipper of *L-Leather*, wondered about radio telephony (RT)—how the crews would communicate with each other during the operation. Gibson suggested that crews use existing TR1196 radio

During the Allied bombing of German war-production plants in the spring of 1943 (BACKGROUND), Lancaster pilot Lewis Burpee (TOP, third from right) flew nearly a full tour—twenty-five sorties—with the same aircrew, (ABOVE, LEFT TO RIGHT) Gordon Brady, Ginger Long, Guy Pegler, Ed Leavesley, and George Goodings. Bomb aimer Jimmy Arthur (INSET) joined Burpee's crew in time for the secret attack against the Ruhr River dams on May 16–17. Guy Gibson (RIGHT) volunteered to lead the specially trained bomber squadron; in turn, he chose 132 other airmen for what most considered a suicide bombing run—the Dam Buster raid.

Designer Barnes Wallis (RIGHT) made his earliest mark in aviation by creating the polygonal framework of the British dirigible R100—seen here on its maiden transatlantic flight over Toronto's Royal York Hotel on August 1, 1930.

To topple the Möhne and Eder hydroelectric dams in Nazi Germany, Wallis tested his bouncing-bomb prototype, dropping it from a Wellington bomber over Chesil Beach off the south coast of England. He also experimented with explosives at the Nant-y-Gro Dam in Wales in 1941. But his plan would never have reached the prime minister without the assistance of Canadian Lord Beaverbrook (ABOVE LEFT) or intelligence ally Fred Winterbotham (BOTTOM LEFT).

Many Air Force volunteers who served on the dams raid in 1943 learned the basics of air warfare at schools of the British Commonwealth Air Training Plan in Canada. John Fraser (LEFT) came from BC's lumber industry to become a bomb aimer. (TOP, LEFT TO RIGHT): Dave Rodger left work at Algoma Steel to serve as a gunner; Ontario senior hockey player Don MacLean became a navigator; former Coney Island lifeguard Joe McCarthy came from the United States to become a pilot; and Bill Radcliffe, from British Columbia, served as a flight engineer. Fred Sutherland (BOTTOM RIGHT) was a crack shot as a hunter in Peace River, Alberta, and so was streamed into air gunnery aboard Fairy Battle training aircraft (BOTTOM LEFT). All were trained in Canada. All became Dam Busters.

Initially, Air Marshal Arthur Harris (FAR LEFT) viewed the bouncing-bomb concept as "tripe of the wildest description." Once Harris had been convinced, it was Air Vice-Marshal Ralph Cochrane (LEFT) who oversaw training and testing of Wallis's bomb.

Each Type 464 Lancaster had its mid-upper turret and bomb-bay doors removed to make way for a cradling mechanism for the Upkeep mine (LEFT). Dropping the 500 rpm reverse-spinning bomb, while flying at 235 mph, sixty feet off the water, presented additional dangers: the resulting water plume could destroy the bomber's tail section. The sequence above shows a practice bombing run at Reculver Bay, with the bouncing bomb coming ashore on target (NEXT PAGE, MIDDLE LEFT) in April 1943.

Canada was well represented on the dams raid. Rugby rivals in Hamilton (TOP LEFT, LEFT TO RIGHT), Frank Garbas and Al Garshowitz came through training in Canada to serve on the same Dam Busters bomber, May 16–17, 1943. Meanwhile, from Saskatchewan, both Ken Earnshaw (TOP RIGHT), who married his sweetheart before going overseas, and Robert Urquhart (BOTTOM RIGHT) served as navigators on the dams raid. Vincent MacCausland (ABOVE RIGHT), from Prince Edward Island, wrote home before the raid that "we're going over with a few bundles," while Canadian Harlo Taerum (BOTTOM LEFT, FAR RIGHT), from rural Alberta, navigated the lead bomber piloted by Guy Gibson (top of ladder).

On the same day that the sixteen surviving Canadian (and one American) Dam Busters returned, they were photographed on the airfield: (ABOVE, BACK ROW, LEFT TO RIGHT) Stefan Oancia, Fred Sutherland, Harry O'Brien, Ken Brown, Harvey Weeks, John Thrasher, George Deering, Bill Radcliffe, Don MacLean, Joe McCarthy (American), and Grant McDonald; (FRONT ROW, LEFT TO RIGHT) Percy Pigeon, Harlo Taerum, Revie Walker, Chester Gowrie, and Dave Rodger.

On their return, the dams raid crews were debriefed (ABOVE LEFT); navigator Harlo Taerum sits second from the right, while Air Marshal Arthur Harris (standing left) listens. As well, after the raid, on May 27, 1943, at the 617 Squadron air base in Scampton, King George VI (ABOVE RIGHT) greeted Australian pilot Les Knight.

Queen Elizabeth (BOTTOM LEFT) congratulated American-born RCAF pilot Joe McCarthy. Among those lost in the eight Lancasters that crashed on the operation (RIGHT), navigator Floyd Wile (INSET) was killed in action with fellow Canadians Garbas and Garshowitz when their aircraft struck a hydro pylon in Germany.

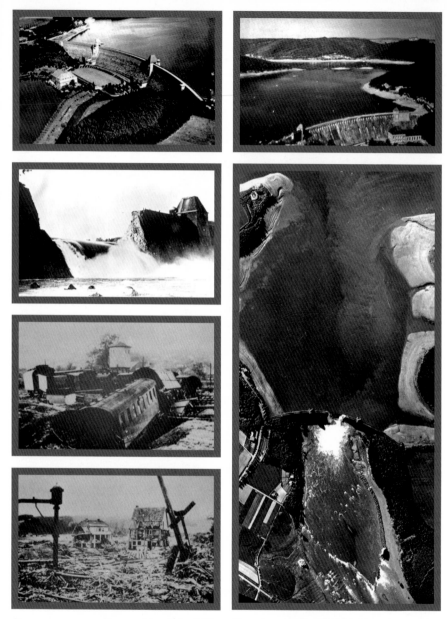

German war strategists considered the Möhne Dam (TOP LEFT) and Eder Dam (TOP RIGHT) untouchable and left them weakly defended. Allied Lancasters breached the Möhne (MIDDLE LEFT AND RIGHT AERIAL) at 12:52 a.m., May 17, 1943, and the Eder at 1:53 a.m. Later that day, reconnaissance photos taken at 30,000 feet showed "a torrent with the sun shining on it." In the Ruhr River Valley, below the Möhne, the rush of water reached a height of thirty-three feet and extended nearly a hundred miles. Below the Eder, more than five billion cubic feet of water gushed down the valley for two full days. The deluge killed 1,400 people and wiped out factories, town buildings, bridges, railway lines, farms, and livestock. An eyewitness said it was "as if Niagara Falls had been unleashed."

sets, but on the first rehearsal that night, the sets failed to deliver clear signals air-to-air. An urgent call went to the Royal Aircraft Establishment at Farnborough, and the next day twenty VHF sets arrived and were installed in the Lancasters within three days, a feat Cochrane said was an indication of "the drive and enthusiasm" of Capel's engineers.[18]

Gibson's dress rehearsals yielded mixed results. The first, because of the RT communication problem, ended in disarray. The next, with the VHF communications in place, went more smoothly for the formations. While the hangars buzzed with riggers, fitters, and instrument technicians, Gibson received valuable intelligence. Meteorology officers had reported that recce aircraft flown well beyond Norway had spotted little to indicate any major fronts entering the weather picture for days. And images from reconnaissance over the Ruhr River showed water levels about five feet from the tops of the dams, just about optimum conditions for the bouncing mine. Of perhaps greater concern, the Ruhr recce photos also showed that German troops had been at work around the Möhne Dam. They had removed the roofs of the two sluice towers and installed a platform and an anti-aircraft gun on the northern tower, three anti-aircraft guns near the compensating basin, and what looked like a search-light position as well. They still had no direct contact with such intelligence, but the aircrews of 617 Squadron all sensed that the operation was close at hand. It might be hours or just a few days away.

Not knowing and not telling took their own toll. From the beginning of its weeks of training, 617 Squadron had shared the Scampton station with 57 Squadron, which was also flying operational bombers. Naturally there was talk and occasionally strained encounters between the two squadrons. John Fraser, John Hopgood's bomb aimer, noted that 57 Squadron "used to think we were a bunch of idle sons-of-guns, sitting around doing nothing, not part of the real war effort."[19] But on occasion when the neighbouring aircrew officers got together in a station watering hole, the idle chatter boiled over. A couple of nights before the operation F/L Joe McCarthy recalled a drinking session among the officers of the two squadrons. The issue of 617's apparent non-combatant role in the war became a bone of contention and a pushing match resulted. "[We] ended up taking the pants off the boys in the other squadron," McCarthy said, "and throwing them out the window, [so] they were running around in their shorts."[20]

W/C Gibson arrived and broke up the disturbance, telling his officers to get to bed. "It was just a pre-warning," McCarthy said. "He wanted to make sure we'd be in good shape."[21]

Among the pilots Gibson watched as a kind of barometer of the state of his squadron was a fellow pilot from his 106 Squadron days. Lewis Burpee—like Gibson's closer friends Hopgood, Martin, and Maudslay—was well-educated. Burpee had completed a degree at Queen's University back in Canada, had earned his pilot's wings via the British Commonwealth Air Training Plan, and, in Gibson's command at 106 Squadron, had finished a tour and earned a Distinguished Flying Medal for his "coolness and courage."[22] Consequently, when Gibson was recruiting crews from 106, he'd invited Dave Shannon, John Hopgood, and Lewis Burpee to his new Squadron X.

Gibson appeared to show interest in more than just his pilots' performance as Lancaster skippers; he considered himself best qualified to know when his aircrew deserved awards and promotions too.

"This Canadian is an excellent type of NCO," Gibson noted when Burpee's name came up for a commission that spring of 1943. "But [he] should be given more experience of service life before being given a commission."[23]

It appeared the powers that be felt differently, and shortly after the Canadian pilot joined 617 Squadron, with 650 hours of wartime flying,[24] a full tour in his pilot's log, and a DFM, Burpee became a pilot officer. Nevertheless, Gibson wasn't sure that the scholarly Burpee was coping very well with the daily routine and pressures at Scampton, especially when it came to balancing his married life with his service life. "He [has] just married a young English girl," Gibson wrote, "and was busy trying to find her a house not too far away. He [finds] it a very difficult job."

It was likely quite the opposite. Lillian Burpee's correspondence with her husband's parents in Ottawa suggested that she had settled quite comfortably into their lodgings in Newark, Nottinghamshire, not far from the 617 air station. While her husband trained at Scampton, Lillian maintained their household—shopping, corresponding, and cleaning their clothes—quite smoothly, so much so that she bragged to her in-laws that "We've set the fashion at the camp—they're ALL trying to get rooms for their wives up here."[25] What posed perhaps the greatest difficulty might have been her husband's commute, the twelve and a half miles from Scampton to Newark by bicycle. However, one more pressing development was preoccupying the young Canadian pilot about this time: Lillian was pregnant with their first child.

At any rate, by the first week of May 1943, Gibson's hard-working squadron was approaching 2,000 hours of flight training. The wear and tear, the strain, and the repetitiveness of the regimen were starting to show. "All the boys [are] rather like a team of racehorses standing in the paddock," Gibson noted, "waiting for the big event."[26]

No doubt with Burpee's distraction and the general welfare of his squadron in mind, the wing commander called a short pause in the grinding routine that his crews had maintained since the last days of March. Gibson himself was showing the strain too; he admitted to being irritable and visited the medical officer for advice on treating a boil on his face; M/O Malcolm Arthurton had recommended a couple of weeks off. Gibson just laughed in his face, but he allowed his squadron aircrews three days' rest to attend to personal lives, blow off a little steam, and bond with each other a bit more.[27] The coming days would test them, Gibson knew, but he emphasized again the necessity of abiding by his strict secrecy rules during the short break. In that atmosphere of resting and bonding, P/O Vernon Byers and a couple of his crew decided to spend their short leave together.

Pilot Byers and rear gunner Jimmy McDowell were compatriots. They had both worked in the Canadian North—Byers as a miner in northern Manitoba and McDowell as a miner in northern Ontario. Byers had trained in the BCATP as a pilot, McDowell as an air gunner. They had also survived some tough raids together, including the one to Stuttgart during which McDowell's rear turret hydraulics failed and he'd been forced to rotate the turret manually. Byers's crew had experienced an odd turn prior to coming to Scampton; two members, Neville Whitaker and Charles Jarvie, had agreed to swap places, leaving a bomber piloted by Sgt. Herbert Vine, which was subsequently shot down over Wilhelmshaven. With its short but often unnerving ops history, Byers's crew took heed of Gibson's offer of a three-day-leave.

Since all but two of Byers's crew were British, most of the men scattered to family homes across England and Scotland. Not wishing to leave his comrades stranded, wireless operator John Wilkinson invited Byers and McDowell to come home with him to Antrobus, in Cheshire, several hours west of Scampton. There, on the Wilkinson family farm, the two Canadians enjoyed restful sleep away from the barracks, home-cooked meals, conversation about anything but air training, and a birthday party—on May 2, 1943, John Wilkinson turned twenty-one. Three days later, they were back in the air with their newly reconfigured Lancaster, *K-King*.

MEANWHILE AT RECULVER, UNDER BARNES WALLIS'S supervision, the trials continued with the "dustbin-shaped" bombs. Beginning on May 11, some of the senior pilots from 617 Squadron flew the first test drops with inert Upkeep mines (filled with concrete, not explosive). F/L Martin, F/L Hopgood, and W/C Gibson took off from Scampton that afternoon, landing at RAF Manston station, where inert Upkeeps were loaded into the bellies of their Lancasters. Flying in formation up the Kent coastline, they simulated their bombing runs just after six o'clock. Gibson dropped his Upkeep from sixty feet, perpendicular to the shoreline; it bounced across the water for six hundred yards and then between the two screens that approximated the Möhne towers. Wallis, viewing from church ruins on top of a nearby hill, assessed Upkeep's performance as "one hundred per cent successful."[28]

The next day, F/L Dave Shannon flew his crew and *L-Leather* Lancaster through the same simulation. Shannon reported that "nine thousand pounds of bomb spinning at 500 rpm meant there was a juddering effect" on the Lancaster;[29] it felt like driving down a cobblestone road, but it was nothing they couldn't handle. However, they had conducted the trial by flying straight and level, not taking into account manoeuvring the Lancaster quickly over hillsides, quickly descending to the required sixty feet, and steadying the aircraft to drop Upkeep at precisely the right spot. Meanwhile, bomb aimer Sumpter and navigator Walker tried out their modified range-finding device but unfortunately dropped the mine too soon; it didn't reach the shore. To further complicate things, during their test runs, F/L Les Munro and S/L Henry Maudslay both released their inert Upkeeps too low, and the resulting splash plume damaged their tailplane sections. Maudslay had the medical officer back with him on one of those last simulations. This time, knowing how airsick he'd become during his first low-level trip, M/O Malcolm Arthurton carried anti-airsickness pills. The dams raid was just two days away, but he, like the rest of the squadron, still had no idea what the target was.

"We took off at 2150 hours and flew for four hours," Arthurton wrote. "I have not the foggiest notion where we were nor exactly what we were doing. . . . People said very little [but] I realized there was something in the wind."[30]

As the final tests involving the inert Upkeeps wound down at Reculver Bay, on May 13, Gibson left Scampton for a flight offshore. This time he wasn't in charge of piloting the Lancaster to deliver the bomb but flew alongside in a second Lancaster, watching the first descend to the allotted height and release a live Upkeep mine in a mock attack. The spinning mine slipped perfectly onto the ocean surface, skipped for about eight hundred yards, and then disappeared beneath the surface. Seconds later, the spot where Upkeep was last seen churned as if struck by an earthquake, followed by a column of white water that plumed up a thousand feet. The hydrostatic trigger had detonated this active Upkeep and demonstrated the weapon's explosive power.

Adamant that he had to have as many of his squadron crews as possible in the air for a full dress rehearsal, Gibson called for a tactical raid exercise on May 14. Circumstances meant several aircrews could not participate; Maltby's Lancaster *J-Johnny* was away from the station that day, and several other crews had not yet been given Type 464 Lancasters, so they flew their older Lancs. Nevertheless, the last full simulation went ahead on Uppingham and Colchester Lakes. Gibson assessed them as fully successful. The next day, May 15, the air officer commanding No. 5 Group of Bomber Command, AVM Ralph Cochrane, arrived at Scampton and personally informed W/C Gibson the squadron was to launch the operation the next night. Not long after Cochrane's personally delivered go signal, an all-white Red Cross Wellington landed at the station and Mutt Summers and Barnes Wallis stepped out. All the threads were coming together.

Now the pressure was on Gibson to compose the operation order—the final plan for the way the dams raid would unfold. But just as he did, he received bad news from both the repair depot and sick bay. Maudslay's damaged Lancaster would not be ready for the operation, and it appeared that illness had felled both F/L Wilson's and P/O Divall's crews; coincidentally, that left an equal number of Lancs and crews—nineteen. Gibson assembled his senior pilots—Maudslay, Hopgood, and Martin—and the squadron's bomb leader, F/L Bob Hay, who would also serve as bomb aimer on Martin's crew, to review the plan. With less than twenty-four hours before the start of the operation, Gibson revealed the identity of the targets to his senior pilots. They then considered 617 Squadron's ultimate strategy, timing, and routes to target. For the pilots present, including F/L Joe McCarthy, this was the first word they'd received of the actual targets they would strike since arriving at Scampton seven weeks earlier.

"I didn't know about [my] target until [that] afternoon of [May] 15," McCarthy said. "They revealed that the targets were the dams and there were models of the dams. . . . We reviewed the routes to see if we could find any flak spots or any danger areas."[31]

The force, consisting of nineteen Lancasters, would depart Scampton in three waves. Because it would follow a longer, more northerly route, the second wave would leave first, beginning about 9:30 p.m. About ten minutes later, at 9:40, flying more directly to the enemy coast, the first wave would take off in sections of three aircraft, so that both waves (fourteen

Lancasters) would be airborne by ten o'clock. The third wave of five bombers would leave an hour later (about midnight) at one-minute intervals. All the Lancasters would cross the North Sea at an altitude of sixty feet. They would continue to fly at low altitude over the Continent, although the flight leaders could climb to five hundred feet to get a visual bearing, if needed.

The first wave would consist of pilots Gibson, Hopgood, Martin, Young, Astell, Maltby, Maudslay, Knight, and Shannon, sent to attack the Möhne Dam. Once that first target was breached, the first wave would carry on to the second target, the Eder Dam, and then, if available, on to the third target, the Sorpe. The second wave would consist of pilots McCarthy, Byers, Barlow, Rice, and Munro. Its job was to act as a diversion and to attack the third target, the Sorpe Dam. Gibson hoped the second-wave diversion would split any enemy night-fighter force; in addition, when it arrived at the Sorpe, it would fire off Very lights and create a further disturbance, drawing enemy response away from the attack of the first wave. The second-wave attack on the Sorpe would also require dropping—without spinning—Upkeep mines parallel to the earthen dam, not at right angles to it. The third, reserve wave, consisting of pilots Townsend, Anderson, Brown, Burpee, and Ottley, would fill in any gaps left in the first two waves.

For F/L Joe McCarthy the parallel bombing of his target, the Sorpe Dam, was a revelation. "I could see that I was going to have a little problem with [the Sorpe], but I didn't really figure that it was going to give me as much problem as it eventually did."[32]

It was in a moment of relative complacency that some-body noticed a dropped thread. The first and third waves were

ATTACKING THE EARTH DAM

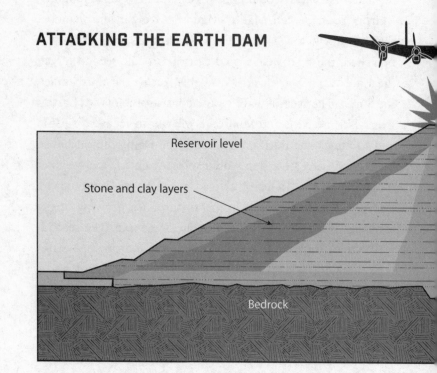

Reservoir level

Stone and clay layers

Bedrock

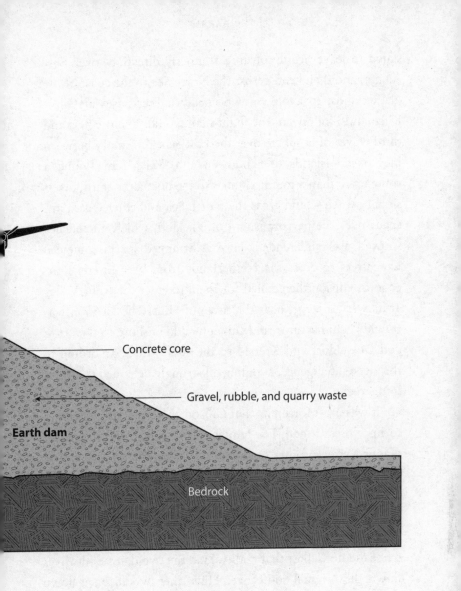

Concrete core

Gravel, rubble, and quarry waste

Earth dam

Bedrock

slated to leave Scampton in a southerly direction, over East Anglia, and then head across the North Sea to the coast of the Netherlands; to avoid known enemy fighter bases at Gilze-Rijen and Eindhoven, the flight plan would take the first and third waves of bombers over the East Scheldt estuary between the coastal islands of Schouwen and Walcheren. Taking a route more than a hundred miles to the north, the third, diversionary wave would cross the North Sea and enter Dutch airspace over the narrow island of Vlieland, which intelligence showed was undefended. Having arranged for his nineteen Lancasters to cross the Netherlands from two different directions, Gibson then called for them to enter the Ruhr Valley at its western edge, near the town of Hüls. The location was roughly equidistant from Mülheim and Duisburg to the north and Düsseldorf and Krefeld to the south, thus, according to the latest intelligence, avoiding all strongly defended positions in the region.

It was most fortunate that Gibson chose this time to reveal to his closest friend, F/L Hopgood, both the targets and the planned attack routes contained in the operation order. The flight lieutenant's own experience revealed a vital piece of anecdotal intelligence that no officials had caught. Hopgood knew that the Germans had taken special measures to protect a rubber factory on the outskirts of Hüls, and the latest flak maps did not reflect that reality. Had the two dams raid waves flown the original route over Hüls, they would have flown right into a dangerous anti-aircraft position, despite all efforts to avoid one. Gibson immediately changed the intended flight route, moving both waves north to avoid that part of the industrial Ruhr River completely.

It was after midnight when the operation orders meeting broke up. As it did, G/C Charles Whitworth came up to Gibson. "Look here, Guy," he said, "I'm awfully sorry . . ."

He told Gibson that his dog, the squadron's mascot, had been run over by a car earlier that night. The black Lab had died on the spot. The CO was surely shaken by the personal blow—the dog had been Gibson's constant companion from the time it was a puppy at 106 Squadron—but with the impending Operation Chastise weighing heavily on his mind, there seemed very little room for grieving the loss of his canine sidekick. That night, sensing that some might want the assurance of a full night's sleep, the station doctor handed out sleeping pills to those who wanted them. For a while, Gibson lay awake in his room, considering whether his dog's death was a bad omen; he spent his last waking moments that night "looking at the scratch-marks on the door . . . and feeling depressed."[33]

BOMB AIMER JOHN FRASER HAD ONLY JUST JOINED 617 Squadron, with fellow Canadian Ken Earnshaw, when the Type 464 Lancasters began arriving that first week of May. So changes seemed to be coming at him all at once—the extremely low flying, the abnormal secrecy, and even the Dann rangefinder, although he seemed to adapt quickly to that. But Fraser, who'd done thirty trips with pilot Norman Schofield at 50 Squadron, also had to get used to a brand-new aircrew at Scampton. Perhaps the upheaval and serious nature of the impending operation nudged him to make a change in his personal life as well. He and Doris Wilkinson, a British secretary he'd met at Finningley, had fallen in love. The couple had received special permission for a day off to get married on April 29, just eighteen days ahead of Operation Chastise. At one point in their courtship, John wrote to Doris about his Bomber Command family.

"There is one Australian P/O DFM in the crew called Tony [Burcher], one Scot P/O DFM called George [Gregory], a sergeant wireless op called Minchie [J.W. Minchin], a navigator called Ossie [whom Earnshaw soon replaced], engineer sergeant called Charlie [Brennan], a Canadian who came over here seven years ago and settled in Leeds [in] an attempt to colonize this country, the pilot called 'Hoppy' F/L [John Hopgood] DFC and bar, and me."[34]

This was the typical makeup of so many of the aircrews in Bomber Command—an Australian, a Canadian, a Scot, several Brits, all fitted together like components of a machine—but each was an airman trained mentally and physically to contribute to the machine's optimum performance. Here were seven men from different walks of life, varied social standing, and disparate cultural backgrounds brought together by circumstance in a Lancaster bomber. But several years of preparation—initial training in far-flung regions of the globe, crewing up in the United Kingdom to build the chemistry of a combat team, and rehearsing to carry out a critical sortie—had given 617 Squadron combat-ready airmen. It was up to each of those crews to then fulfill one of the toughest assignments of the war, an operation some later called suicidal. And the irony of it all was that none of the crews was to know, until just hours before they climbed aboard their modified Lancasters, what and where their target was . . . or how deadly the risk.

As Dave Rodger, rear gunner aboard Joe McCarthy's bomber, had so aptly put it, "We were seven men against the Reich."[35]

CHAPTER SIX

"BIG DO ON"

IF ANYONE COULD BE HAPPY THAT SUNDAY, MAY 16, had finally arrived, it was the Scampton meteorological staff. As the weather recce flights had been predicting, a high-pressure weather system had remained lodged over northwestern Europe and the British Isles for most of May, which meant the Met Office could reliably say that skies would stay clear over the next twenty-four hours. A hot, sunny day would be followed by a clear night lit by a full moon—exactly the conditions the dams raid aircrews would need. However, with the exception of Gibson and his senior pilots—the flight leaders—most of those taking their breakfast in the Scampton mess that morning—porridge, sausage, toast and jam—still didn't know yet that the dress rehearsals were done. The op would be today. W/C Guy Gibson had risen early and gone right to his office to wade through the paper chase of war. Breaking with the routine established over the previous seven weeks, Gibson told his adjutant, Harry Humphries, to draw up battle orders, but to issue them as a night-flying program. Not training, but flying.

"Is it for training?" Humphries asked.

"No," said Gibson, and he looked into his adjutant's bewildered face. "We are going to war, but I don't want the world to know about it."[1]

Humphries, detail man that he was, had begun processing what Gibson's last statement meant to him and to the squadron.

"Just make out a night-flying program," Gibson said, and added, "All who should know will receive their orders verbally."[2] The wing commander then left his office to await the official typewritten operation order from 5 Group headquarters. When it arrived at 11 a.m., Scampton, while still not officially on battle alert, was alive with preparations. It was pretty hard not to notice in No. 2 Hangar and around the Lancasters on the perimeter of the airfield, that crews had jumped into high gear. Bowsers pulled up alongside the Lancs to pump fuel into their wing tanks. Armourers loaded full belts of tracer bullets, so that when they were fired in the night the bursts would look as if the gunfire were heavier. And the modified trolleys bombed up the Lancasters with Upkeeps, as well as illuminating flares in case crews needed to light up their targets. At the same time, the compasses aboard the Lancasters needed attention. Instrument technicians had to swing the compasses—that is, register each aircraft compass's true north reading both without the mine in place and (since the mine had plenty of metal in it) when it was installed in its carrying calipers.

* * *

CANADIAN GROUND CREW SERGEANT HUGH MUNRO, who had helped organize lodgings when the men and equipment arrived back in March, noted that the activity in the hangars, the offices, and all along the flight line was no ordinary simulation.

"Your sixth sense told you that this was *it*, by the way the crews acted," Munro wrote.[3] The RCAF radar specialist recorded, as if for posterity, that if it were just another exercise the air and ground crews tended to be relaxed and talkative, but "if it's the real thing, there is tension in the air, as well as a general quietness in communication." Munro sensed it was the latter.

The wing commander had also received the latest reconnaissance photography from the Ruhr; F/L Frank "Jerry" Fray, the recce pilot from RAF No. 542 Squadron, had flown his high-altitude Spitfire IX over the region and returned with photos that showed the defensive positions on the dams had not changed and, perhaps more important, that the water levels remained high behind the dams, exactly where Barnes Wallis had hoped they would be. Wallis himself had arrived in time for the late-night briefings with the senior pilots the day before but had slept in until 10 a.m. on May 16; he would be called upon shortly to reveal all to the awaiting aircrews. With two crews out with sickness and one Lancaster irreparable, the operation would have exactly nineteen modified Lancasters for nineteen available aircrews; but it also meant there were no backup aircraft, should there be an emergency as aircraft and aircrews made last-minute preparations. One Type 464 was available at Boscombe Down, so it was immediately flown to Scampton as the reserve Lancaster.

By noon, for at least the 133 aircrew involved, all the wraps began coming off the secrecy of the targets, the routes across enemy territory, and the timing of the entire operation. The countdown to the evening takeoff had begun. Just nine and a half hours until the squadron's intense training regimen was to be put to the test. Gibson now briefed his pilots and navigators in front of tables displaying the models of the Möhne and Sorpe Dams, while alluding to the walls now covered in maps and reconnaissance photographs; the model of the Eder had been ordered but didn't arrive at Scampton until September 18.[4] All of this was still a surprise to many who'd trained and wondered since the end of March what the operation was all about.

In a separate briefing, the 5 Group chief signals officer, W/C Wally Dunn, met with the wireless radio operators to go over their operational details. Through the afternoon, bomb aimers and gunners joined pilots and navigators to study the dam models, maps, and photos together. F/Sgt. Robert Kellow, the Canadian wireless operator aboard P/O Les Knight's Lancaster *N-Nuts,* expressed the feelings most aircrew had. Once he knew their low-level operation would take them right down the Ruhr River Valley, where Bomber Command crews had been sustaining heavy casualties since early March, he was curious about the kind of reception the Germans might give them.

"We had been given to understand that probably there was not too much danger," Kellow said. "We were going to fly low. We were going to be down below radar pickup. The only thing we would have to do was watch for power lines." Squadron commanders explained that the Möhne Dam would be defended, but because the approach to the Eder was a difficult dogleg turn over the water, RAF intelligence suggested the Eder might not be so strongly defended. Kellow said his superiors added that "the Germans apparently must have felt [enemy aircraft] would have been crazy to try to get to the dams."[5]

Among those studying the models and photographs on display in front of the crews for the first time, Neville Whitaker, the bomb aimer with Vernon Byers's *K-King* crew, took his time. The thirty-three-year-old from Lancashire was among the eldest of the aircrew with 617 Squadron. He'd already become a chartered accountant and had worked for a musical instrument dealership prior to the war. He'd enlisted with the local Blackpool Regiment and then, in 1941, transferred to the RAF. As a graduate of observer school, he had been posted to 467 Squadron and assigned to pilot Herbert Vine. Following a crew swap, Whitaker joined Byers; Vine's crew was lost over the North Sea soon after. As a bomb aimer he was meticulous, and during the afternoon briefing he pulled out an envelope from a letter he'd just received and began jotting down locations—waypoints in Holland and Germany for which he and his navigator would need specific coordinates.

"Stavoren . . . Harderwijk . . . Doesberg"—locations in the Netherlands on his flight path—he noted in pencil, and at the bottom of the envelope he wrote the coordinates for the German objectives: "Rees . . . Ahlen . . . Target X . . . Target Z."[6]

Loading the 9,250-pound Upkeep mines into their carriages on the underside of the Lancasters was not the sort of operation many of the regular staff at Scampton had ever witnessed before. So, as some of the Type 464 Lancs underwent the bomb-loading process, station personnel gathered round to watch. Bomb aimer John Fraser recalled that one of the Scampton station intelligence officers, a WAAF, was at some point invited into the cockpit of *P-Popsie*, F/L Mick Martin's Lancaster.*

"The bombing force had used a glider release inside the aircraft, as an emergency release for the bomb," Fraser said. "Wondering what it was, she pulled the glider release and this 14,000-pound [*sic*] bomb fell from its calipers."[7]

The bomb hit the ground with a thud. Fraser said he'd never seen an aircrew evacuate an aircraft or a ground crew disperse quite as quickly as in that panic-filled moment. F/L Martin was next seen on a dead run to get an armament officer. Doc Watson arrived a few minutes later and announced to all within earshot, "Flap's over. It's not fused," meaning that Upkeep's detonation fuse wasn't activated.[8] Once the armourers had reinstalled Martin's Upkeep, they painted the secret weapon black.

The ripple effect of Air Force bureaucracy and procedure began to move outward from Scampton. Just after 1 p.m., Bomber Command headquarters requested Fighter Command to launch intruder operations over the Continent in order to draw German night fighters away from 617's attack routes through Holland to the Ruhr. Also overnight, Wellington, Stirling, and Lancaster bombers would conduct "gardening" operations off the Frisian Islands and in front of the ports of Brest, Lorient, and St. Nazaire. By 2 p.m., May 16, signals had

---

* References suggest that Section Officer Fay Gillon was the WAAF involved. Her experience and stature as an officer in Intelligence Operations gave her access to much of 617 Squadron's secret activity. Indeed, she was aboard F/L Mick Martin's final dress-rehearsal flight on May 14, 1943. She was also present when Martin's *P-Popsie* received its Upkeep, and in the cockpit may have inadvertently pressed the glider release.

been sent to USAAF, Fighter Command, Coastal Command, and other bomber stations across the British Isles, warning of special ops that night.

Then, at 3:15 p.m., 5 Group headquarters contacted the CO at Scampton with the final op orders: "Code name for 5 Group Operation Order B.976, is Chastise," the telex message read.[9] For the first time, Bomber Command had issued both the code number (the only title the op had until then) and the code name. A cypher despatch—"Executive Operation Chastise 16/5/43"—arrived next, meaning that 617 Squadron Lancasters were now under direct orders to take off that evening to complete the manoeuvres they had practised for seven weeks, this time as an attack on the major reservoir dams of the Ruhr River Valley. With that, the senior officers at Scampton could assemble all aircrew for a final general briefing. The call was issued over the public-address system at 6 p.m.

Minutes later, as the last of 133 airmen clambered their way into the room, a door closed behind them, with Service Police preventing any further entry. Opposite the doorway, the wing commander sat with other senior officers and Barnes Wallis, whom Gibson introduced. For some of the station's aircrew, it was the first time they'd heard their CO utter the words "the operation to attack the great dams of Germany." He added that all the secrecy meant this raid against the dams could only be done once; a second attempt would have the enemy fully armed and ready. When it was his turn to address the aircrews, Wallis emphasized—as he had so many times before—the economic impact that taking out the Ruhr dams would have on the German war effort. He reviewed the prerequisites for effective delivery of Upkeep—spinning at 500 rpm, dropped from 60 feet, at 230 miles per hour. He went through it all again, perhaps with some relief that the day of the actual operation had finally come. Finally, Wallis summed up 617's role in Chastise.

"You gentlemen are really carrying out the third of three experiments," Wallis told the airmen. "We have tried it out on model dams, also one dam one-fifth the size of the Möhne dam. I cannot guarantee it will come off, but I hope it will."[10] With those final words of background and encouragement Wallis sat down to gaze across the sea of young faces in front of him. Up to that moment, most of the squadron's bomber crews had never known the word *Upkeep*, nor the notion of perhaps taking Germany out of the war. And they certainly hadn't known Barnes Wallis—the gentle, white-haired scientist who had designed this entire scheme and presented it to them that evening. It was just the latest of many revelations that would preoccupy them for at least the next twenty-four hours of their lives.

"It was like when you'd go in to write a school exam. Everybody's tense," said Fred Sutherland, from P/O Les Knight's *N-Nuts* crew. For the front gunner, who had just turned twenty, every piece of information at this briefing—just hours before they launched the op—was entirely new. "Everybody was pretty apprehensive about going over at low level and dropping this spinning bomb."[11]

As Joe McCarthy recalled, Wallis appeared to be a "very mild and meek gentleman."[12] One of the officers present overheard Wallis comment softly in front of the assembled airmen, "They must have thought it was Father Christmas speaking to them."[13]

The CO of 5 Group, AVM Ralph Cochrane, next addressed the briefing with a review of the three designated waves and their intended targets—first wave: nine armed bombers destined for the Möhne, Eder, and Sorpe Dams; second wave: five Lancasters heading for the Sorpe only; and third wave: the last five aircraft in reserve. He completed his remarks with a confident exclamation point: "this attack will succeed!"[14] Then Gibson stood up and for nearly an hour went back over the running order again. He emphasized the need for radio silence. He reviewed the known enemy defences and night-fighter locations, no doubt reminding many of the bomber crews present of the Ruhr's "Happy Valley" moniker. On a more optimistic note, the weather remained ideal—skies would be clear, moon full, and winds negligible. Gibson finished by stating that no Upkeep mine was to be brought back to England. At about 7:30 p.m., some ninety minutes after it began, the squadron-wide briefing came to an end and the crews dispersed from the room and fanned out across the flight line into the early evening sunlight. It was two hours to takeoff.

In the mess, aircrews sat down to their evening meal. The mess staff recognized the significance of the fare they were asked to prepare—bacon and eggs, a luxury in Britain and an indication that a serious op was about to happen—but made no comments. Chiefy Powell had the mess staff also ensure that coffee, sandwiches, and fruit would be available for aircrews during the flight. Then, most of 617 operational crew retired to their quarters, taking the time that remained before takeoff for themselves.

For all the married men at 617 Squadron—including Canadians Lewis Burpee, John Fraser, Charles Brennan, and

Ken Earnshaw—there would be no time, or permission, for last words with wives. Any last correspondence, including wills and letters home, could be written but not posted or transmitted on this day. Doc Sutherland thought about writing to his fiancée back home in Peace River, Alberta, but realized there was too much on his mind about the raid, and that he couldn't distract himself with a letter to Marg Baker. All outside calls were now prohibited, to family or anyone else. Station security even had Scampton WAAF Ruth Ive tapping all telephone calls that night, listening for indiscretions and disconnecting any such calls.[15] The station was physically and electronically locked down. Gwyn Johnson, Johnny's wife of just over a month, noted that a friend at nearby RAF Hemswell, a bomber training station, had come off duty early. When Gwyn, a WAAF at Hemswell, asked why, her friend said, "We've all been stood down. Nobody's flying tonight from anywhere except Scampton. . . . They must have a big do on."[16]

Sometime after supper, F/L Bill Astell's crew enjoyed a few minutes of thoughts not associated with Operation Chastise. On their last leave before the op, Scottish flight engineer Richard Kinnear, as well as Canadians Floyd Wile and Albert Garshowitz, had travelled to nearby Kimberley, home of a thriving brewing industry. They were a crew who enjoyed spending leisure time together and mixed in some good-natured fun when they could. They kidded the youngest member of their crew, twenty-year-old gunner Frank Garbas, because he'd recently "tore the whole side of his face" during his first ever shave.[17] In these final minutes before takeoff, as they gathered beside their Lancaster *B-Baker*, W/O Albert Garshowitz took a piece of chalk, walked up to the crew entry in the fuselage, and, at the expense of his non-officer rugby pal from Hamilton, Sgt. Garbas, wrote over the doorway, "Officer entrance only." Then, on the Upkeep in the belly of their Lanc, Garshowitz further inscribed a Churchillian epithet that likely reflected his crew's youthful confidence and anxiety about the night to come: "Never has so much been expected of so few."[18]

BY EIGHT O'CLOCK No. 2 HANGAR BEGAN TO BUZZ again. Crews arrived, some on foot, others on bikes, to collect supplies and gear. In the crew room they gathered the usual equipment—jackets, boots, gloves, helmets, goggles, and parachutes. Somebody pointed out that the squadron would be flying so low that even if a bomber survived a collision or crippling anti-aircraft fire, nobody would have sufficient time to clip on a parachute pack, scramble to a hatch, exit, survive the two-hundred-miles-per-hour slipstream, *and then* pop a chute. But training superseded all, this night; they gathered their parachutes anyway. Around the crew room and out on the grass, the Chastise flyers put on the faces they sensed would get them through the waiting. When he finished crossing off all the necessary items on his checklist, Adjutant Harry Humphries captured the demeanour of the aircrews in his squadron diary. "Most of them wore expressions varying from 'don't care a damn' to the grim and determined," he wrote. "On the whole, I think it appeared rather reminiscent of a crusade."[19]

Just before 8:30 p.m., W/C Gibson pulled up in front of No. 2 Hangar in his car. He climbed out, followed by his entire crew. Humphries, in addition to noting the faces of the squadron aircrews, recorded that the squadron CO stood among his men looking "fit and well and quite unperturbed." As the crews milled next to the flight trucks, long-time comrades F/L John Hopgood and W/C Guy Gibson shared a last few minutes in the crew area. Gibson asked Humphries to ensure that there'd be plenty of beer for a party when they all got back. "Hoppy," Gibson called to his friend, "tonight's the night. Tomorrow we will get drunk."[20]

Not wanting to reveal anything but confidence, Gibson soon announced that it was time to go. He joined others heading to the trucks that would taxi the aircrews in the first and second waves along the perimeter track around Scampton airfield to their respective Lancasters. Among other things, Gibson thought about family; his Lancaster's registration letters, AJ-G, matched his father's initials, and May 16 was his father's birthday. He thought about his canine pal, killed by accident the night before; Gibson had asked that the dog's body be buried on the grounds in front of his office at midnight, about the time the first wave would reach its target. And he wondered about his own fortunes; on this trip, as he always did, Gibson wore a Boy Scout badge on his right wrist as a lucky charm. Accompanying Gibson, AVM Cochrane and a photographer watched the aircrew prepare to board *G-George* and ensured that the CO was captured on film atop the entry ladder.

Along the perimeter, other crews and their gear were disgorged by the flight trucks to await the signal to board, start their Lancaster engines, and prepare for takeoff. Outside F/L John Hopgood's *M-Mother*, bomb aimer John Fraser and navigator Ken Earnshaw shared their feelings about the op. The two Canadians had served together in 50 Squadron, and both had come over to 617 Squadron partway through the training period to join Hopgood. With them, the two airmen brought substantial hours of experience—Fraser and Earnshaw had flown thirty operations together. Still, as close as they were, Earnshaw occasionally caught Fraser off guard with his predilection for predicting the outcomes of combat operations. It happened again this night as the two men stood waiting for the signal to get underway.

"Ken, what do you think of tonight?" Fraser asked his buddy.[21]

"Well, I think perhaps we might lose eight tonight . . ." Earnshaw said, and before Fraser could react to the high casualty prediction, Earnshaw went further. "And, you know, I think we might go ourselves." That was the last spoken aloud about his premonition, least of all in front of their pilot, Hopgood.

At ten minutes past nine o'clock, W/C Gibson's wireless operator and the squadron's signals leader, F/L Robert Hutchison, fired a red flare into the evening sky. The Lancasters, until now idle and waiting, began to stir. Earlier, F/L Munro had been sitting on a deck chair at the hangar casually reading a magazine, but in the cockpit of *W-Willie,* preparing to take off in the second wave, he was all business. He had a wartime record equal to any in experience and experiences. He had enlisted in the Royal New Zealand Air Force, been trained in Canada, and survived nineteen ops, the mechanical-failure crash of a Wellington, and a near miss low-flying over a Royal Navy convoy during 617 training. And as recently as May 12, during a practice drop of an inert Upkeep on Reculver Bay, the resulting splash plume had damaged the tailplane of Munro's Lanc, but he'd landed the bomber safely.

Operation Chastise seemed risky, but no more so than any other wartime op. Munro's wireless operator/air gunner, Sgt. Percy Pigeon, from Williams Lake, British Columbia, had flown with the same skipper since the summer of 1942, completing twenty-three bombing ops with him. With nearly two hundred hours of daytime flying and 213 hours at night recorded in his log before Chastise, Pigeon too was an experienced airman. In the cockpit, Munro was running up the Lancaster's engines while flight engineer Frank Appleby began his pre-flight checklist. The remainder of the crew—navigator Grant "Jock" Rumbles, bomb aimer James Clay, and gunners Bill Howarth and Harvey Weeks—donned helmets, plugged in, and checked in on the intercom. As usual, his fellow crew members had shoehorned F/Sgt. Weeks, all six feet of him, into the Lancaster's rear turret.

Next to them on the flight line, F/L Joe McCarthy and his flight engineer, Bill Radcliffe, had begun a similar pre-flight ritual in *Q-Queenie*. Even though they were in the second wave, their northern route would take them over a greater distance than the first wave, so they were scheduled to take off first. Like Munro, McCarthy had a tour to his credit, as well as a DFC. He'd just learned this day that his target would not be the Möhne or Eder Dam, but the Sorpe, and that he'd have to improvise on some of his recent low-level training to attack not perpendicular to the dam but in line with it; and instead of spinning backwards, his Upkeep would have to remain motionless during the drop to ensure that it sank on impact.

No doubt McCarthy reflected on his lifelong friend Don Curtin, killed during 106 Squadron's operation against Nuremberg in February, and how they'd hoped to complete their RCAF service together before heading home to the United States. But that was history. With recently married bomb aimer Johnny Johnson, meticulous navigator Don MacLean, and wireless operator Len Eaton, who was thirty-seven and the oldest airman on the raid, as well as reliable gunners Ron Batson and Dave Rodger, McCarthy had come out of the briefing concerned but confident. Plus, he knew *Q-Queenie* also had Bill Radcliffe's lucky "Chuck-Chuck" panda mascot tucked into the flight engineer's flying boot.

But suddenly things started to unravel. Radcliffe and McCarthy spotted a coolant leak on *Queenie's* outer starboard engine. The skipper realized that would scupper their participation in the op. "For Christ's sake!" McCarthy called to his crew. "Everybody out! And let's get over to the reserve [Lancaster] before some other bugger does and we don't get to go!"[22]

It took only a few seconds to register on the members of McCarthy's crew that the one reserve Type 464 Lancaster, flown in from Boscombe Down that morning, was their only hope of going on the raid. So everybody began grabbing gear and making for *Queenie's* exit. In the confusion of seven aircrew dashing around, tossing all their equipment out doors and windows, flight engineer Radcliffe caught his parachute on a window hook; even in the slight breeze the chute billowed and enveloped McCarthy as he dashed toward the flight offices in search of Chiefy Powell.

"What's the matter?" Powell called out.

"My bloody aircraft is U/S [unserviceable]. I've got to take the spare."

Adjutant Humphries joined the exchange, noting that McCarthy was out of breath, his shirt soaking wet from his exertion, and his large hands clenching and unclenching spas-modically.

"Where are those . . . compass adjusters?" McCarthy added in total exasperation. Before the Lancaster could take off, the pilot and navigator would need an instrument tech-nician (compass adjuster) to give them correction cards that informed the crew about the way their new aircraft's normal magnetism would deviate compass readings.

"Calm down, old boy," Humphries told McCarthy. "You'll make it."

Powell responded and returned with the compass cards. "Here you are, sir."

Meanwhile, the crew without a home had made its way to the reserve Lancaster, *T-Tommy*, and hurriedly loaded their gear aboard. As pilot McCarthy and navigator MacLean arrived to work out the details on the compass cards, rear gunner Dave Rodger realized he had his own problems. In *Queenie*, their now unserviceable Lanc, he had altered his rear gun turret by removing a panel of clear Perspex in front of the gunsight to give him an unrestricted view around his end of the Lancaster. He wanted to replicate that arrangement in the new aircraft; so, during the general delay, Rodger found some volunteer ground crew to help him rip out the panel in *Tommy* so that the new turret felt like the old.

As all of this went on, around 9:30 p.m., the first four Lancasters assembled at the downwind edge of the station and prepared to take off from the grass airfield—first Barlow's *E-Easy*, next Munro's *W-Willie*, then Byers's *K-King*, and finally Rice's *H-Harry*—one by one. Ten minutes later Gibson in *G-George*, Martin in *P-Popsie*, and Hopgood in *M-Mother* took off together in a Vic (V) formation of three. Ten minutes after that, Young in *A-Apple*, Maltby in *J-Johnny*, and Shannon in *L-Leather* did the same. The final three bombers in the first wave taxied to the same spot on the airfield just before ten o'clock, and then Maudslay in *Z-Zebra*, Astell in *B-Baker*, and Knight in *N-Nuts* also formed up and took off together.

"I had never seen Lancasters take off in formation," said rear gunner Grant McDonald, watching from the flight line next to his Lanc, *F-Freddie*.[23]

Two minutes later, just after 10 p.m., McCarthy's Lancaster powered up and lumbered to the edge of the Scampton airfield. *T-Tommy* was fully fuelled, bombed up, and thirty-four minutes behind schedule, and its crewmen were eager to catch the second wave they were supposed to be leading. Now McCarthy and Radcliffe faced what all of the pilots and flight engineers had during the past half-hour—taxiing to the down-wind edge of the field, throttling up, and taking advantage of what little breeze there was to get off the ground before running out of airfield. Like the other cockpit crews this night, McCarthy looked apprehensively through the windscreen to the hedgerow at the end of the field. "It looked a thousand feet tall!"[24] Nevertheless, a few seconds later, *T-Tommy* was airborne.

Operation Chastise was underway.

WITH TWO WAVES OF OPERATION CHASTISE BOMBERS thundering barely a hundred feet above the North Sea toward the enemy coastline, those most responsible for the attack—Arthur Harris, Ralph Cochrane, and Barnes Wallis—convened thirty miles away at St. Vincents, in Grantham. There, at the headquarters for 5 Group of Bomber Command, they would receive Morse code messages from the 617 Squadron crews about their progress in the raid. All three men—the two senior RAF officers responsible for the aircrews, and the scientist who'd designed their weapon—plus the regular officials who occupied HQ during a combat sortie, made their way to the underground operations room connected by a passageway to the main headquarters of the building. In the ops room, one wall was adorned with a large map of Europe as well as a list of the bombers involved and their status. As Harris, Cochrane, and Wallis waited for news, WAAFs and other HQ staff worked on headsets, while on a dais off to the side, W/C Wally Dunn, the chief signals officer, sat next to a telephone. The moment each Morse message from the squadron radio operators was decoded and verified, it would be delivered to Dunn by phone and passed verbally to those gathered in the underground HQ. All communications in this room on this night had tension and concern written between every line.

If Barnes Wallis's "Help, oh help" plea, scrawled in a memo to his friend and ally Fred Winterbotham, had ever needed to be heeded, it was now.

CHAPTER SEVEN

THE GAUNTLET

N O ROUTE INTO EUROPE IN MAY 1943 OFFERED an intruding air force a free pass to the target. No matter how stealthy the preparations, no matter how low-level the flight path, no matter how great the speed or complete the radio silence, no matter how favourable the weather conditions, danger awaited any intruder. On most nights when RAF Bomber Command operated in the skies over occupied Europe, German anti-aircraft guns—some 10,000 of them across northwestern Europe[1]—posed a significant threat to bombers flying at altitudes of 20,000 to 24,000 feet. But against aircraft entering their airspace at treetop level, and at nearly 250 miles per hour, German high-altitude weapons were at a disadvantage; they found it difficult to track or catch up to intruders. On the other hand, light anti-aircraft batteries—German Flak 30 or Flak 38 batteries, the latter firing twenty-millimetre shells at 480 rounds per minute[2]—could challenge an aircraft travelling closer to the ground. Such were the batteries entrenched on land and aboard gunboats along the Dutch coast, and many of the Flak batteries were guided by airborne radar, ground control, and powerful searchlights. The same German-occupied territory over which intruders might fly also bristled with bases of Luftwaffe night-fighter aircraft—Messerschmitt Bf 110s and Junkers Ju 88s—that were regularly dispatched when German radar, Freya, detected an attack. There was good reason for Allied strategists to call Hitler's fortifications along the coasts of France, Belgium, and the Netherlands "Fortress Europe."

The trick for the Lancaster aircrews in all three waves of Operation Chastise was to bring their seven weeks of low-level practice to bear while running the gauntlet to the dams. By keeping their Lancasters below the effective range of German radar—well under 1,000 feet—and eluding enemy airborne radar trackers who might be scanning higher altitudes and miss the exhaust trails from lower-level aircraft, the dams raiders had a chance of flying past the outer rim of German defences undetected. The downside of hugging the surface of the North Sea was that the curvature of the earth put the bombers out of touch with GEE; this radio guiding system allowed an RAF navigator to pinpoint his own bomber's location by reading radar pulses sent out from three ground stations in the United Kingdom. Without GEE, a navigator had to rely on map reading (impossible over open water) or more likely DR, dead reckoning. And if a navigator managed to remain relatively accurate via traditional methods, crosswinds could cause drift by pushing even a heavy bomber sideways and off course. To compensate, 617 Squadron navigators tossed flame floats from the aircraft so that the rear gunners could determine how much the bomber was drifting.

On the first leg of the outbound sortie, the one natural factor that W/C Gibson and his senior pilots expected would give some advantage turned against them. Clear skies and the rising moon would give all airborne crews the best view ahead. But the twilight on the western horizon and the growing brightness of unexpected aurora borealis had a deadly side effect: the northern lights tended to silhouette the vanguard of each Lancaster wave, despite it being just a few feet off the North Sea.

"The sun had set when we reached the enemy coast," said James Clay, the bomb aimer aboard *W-Willie*. "There was a little gloomy moonlight."[3] Prone in the nose of the Lancaster and with likely the best vantage point—looking ahead through the clear Perspex blister—Sgt. Clay likely spotted the Dutch coast before anyone in his Lanc. Since the second-wave bombers had all departed Scampton separately, they approached the Frisian Islands on the northernmost coastline of Holland in staggered fashion. But the winds over the North Sea had pushed at least one of the second-wave bombers over Texel Island, south of Vlieland Island. Texel proved more heavily defended. At about eleven o'clock, as they made landfall over the islands, aircrews of the second wave began taking flak from German light anti-aircraft guns located on the island. Clay concluded that the twilight or the intensifying northern lights must have silhouetted their aircraft against the western sky. Then Clay reported seeing "someone to starboard skim the water and send up a plume of spray."[4]

To the right of *W-Willie*, P/O Vernon Byers in *K-King* must have realized that he was not crossing Vlieland and felt the need to get a more accurate bearing to continue to the target. So, clearing the island and, he assumed, out of range of the Texel batteries, he climbed over the Waddenzee for a better look. At about 450 feet above the water, Byers's Lancaster became a more visible target to the flak guns on Texel. Edmund Mantell, one of the German gunners stationed on Texel, had his eyes trained on the horizon, spotted the Lancaster, and, with his 10.5-centimetre flak gun at a nearly flat trajectory, opened fire.[5] A burst from his gun hit the aircraft. It exploded and its pieces sent up that plume of water on the surface of the polder that bomb aimer Clay had seen. The crew that had accumulated the least number of previous combat operations on the squadron but the most low-flying training hours from Scampton, the one that had just celebrated the twenty-first birthday of its youngest member, John Wilkinson, was gone in a moment. At 10:57 p.m., Byers and the crew of *K-King* disappeared into the Waddenzee,* eighteen miles west of Harlingen, Holland. They were the first 617 Squadron fatalities in the dams raid.

At nearly the same moment that Clay spotted *K-King* splash into the sea, his aircraft, *W-Willie*, passed low over the centre of Vlieland, where the German flak battery spotted the Lancaster and opened fire. The skipper, Les Munro, saw tracers headed toward his bomber, and then his headset went dead— no intercom and no VHF. Staying low over the Waddenzee beyond, Munro circled to assess the damage, but without intercom the crew was forced to shout over the noise of the Merlin engines. At the top of his voice, Munro instructed flight engineer Frank Appleby to get their wireless radio operator,

---

* When the pieces of *K-King* descended into Waddenzee, among them the unexploded Upkeep, it took four weeks for the mine cylinder to sink to a depth sufficient to trigger its explosive.

Percy Pigeon, to ensure that rear gunner Harvey Weeks was uninjured, and then to check if intercom and VHF could be restored. Presently Pigeon came forward to say the flak had punched a hole in W-Willie's fuselage and destroyed its distant-reading compass just forward of the crew door, leaving the communication lines a mass of severed wires. The skipper scribbled a note and handed it to Appleby to take to Clay in the nose of the bomber. If they continued, all the communications among the crew to get to the target and to assist Clay in dropping Upkeep with precision would have to be done without intercom. "Intercom U/S [unserviceable]. Should we go on?" Munro had written.[6]

As a fighting unit, the crew of W-Willie had nearly twenty operations under its belt. Based on their bombing experience, Munro's aircrew members sensed that if it were a high-altitude job, they could probably improvise communications to complete the bombing run. But flying at sixty feet and at over two hundred miles per hour, in an operation that demanded pinpoint accuracy and split-second communications, without at least intercom, they were hamstrung. "We'll be a menace to the rest," Clay wrote back to Munro.[7]

Moments later, still circling low over the Waddenzee, Munro made the decision. With their chances of completing the operation nullified, he turned his Lancaster for home, his Upkeep mine undelivered.

Crossing into enemy territory over the outer islands of the Waddenzee proved no easier for the crew in H-Harry. Like the other members of the second wave crossing the North Sea just above its whitecaps, navigator Richard Macfarlane had to rely on dead reckoning to get there. Then, just a couple of minutes short of Vlieland, *H-Harry*'s aircrew also reported sighting Byers's bomber explode and crash. Following much the same path as the others across Vlieland, pilot Geoff Rice managed to elude the island flak batteries with low-flying manoeuvres, but he was so low that on one occasion he had to pull up to dodge protruding dunes on the island. Once across Vlieland, Rice turned southeast over the Waddenzee, much the same as the others had. He was flying toward the Afsluitdijk dike, straight into the rising moon.[8] As a consequence, accurate visual reference on the surface of the Waddenzee proved difficult. Again GEE was not available, so Macfarlane and rear gunner Stephen Burns collaborated on a flame float to check the aircraft's drift.

Flight engineer Edward Smith was about to call to Rice that his altimeter was registering zero feet when the crew felt a violent jolt, and then another as Rice attempted to regain control of *H-Harry* over the water. The first collision with the surface of the water had ripped the Upkeep mine from its calipers and sprayed water up into the bomb bay. The second impact—caused by the mine exiting and pushing the tailwheel up through the fuselage, which demolished the lavatory—sprayed sea water and disinfectant from the Elsan toilet up to the roof of the cabin, cascading back into the rear turret.

"You've lost the mine," reported one voice on the intercom.

"Christ!" added Stephen Burns from the rear turret. "It's wet back here!"[9] He was now up to his waist in water and debris, but his head remained above water.

The crew of *H-Harry*, like the men aboard *W-Willie*, considered what further contribution they might be able to make to the operation to destroy the Sorpe, and reached the same conclusion. They would be no help, and possibly a hindrance. Rice turned *H-Harry* northwest to retrace his path for home, this time flying low between the islands of Texel and Vlieland and escaping detection by any of the islands' flak batteries. With one crew lost and two on their way home, only McCarthy's replacement bomber *T-Tommy*, still half an hour behind what was left of the second wave, and Norman Barlow's *E-Easy* remained to attack the Sorpe Dam. Fortunes for the second wave would now go from bad to worse. Miraculously, *E-Easy* had cleared Vlieland, the Waddenzee, and the Zuiderzee without a scratch. Once over enemy territory, the crew had armed the Upkeep mine by triggering its fuse but maintained radio silence as the bomber approached airspace just across the Dutch border, near Rees, Germany, east of the Rhine.

At ten minutes before midnight, two and a half hours into their outbound flight toward a rendezvous with the Sorpe on the Ruhr River, and maintaining their prescribed speed and altitude, Barlow's Lancaster crossed a German railway line and was suddenly confronted with a span of hydroelectricity lines strung between massive pylons. Either Barlow didn't have sufficient time to react at the flight controls, or nobody aboard *E-Easy* spotted the low-level obstruction in the moonlight in time, but the Lancaster plowed into the lines. At her farm home near Haldern-Herken, young Johanna Effing heard the plane crash and dashed up from the cellar to see an inferno in the field in front of her house.

"An aircraft flying from the west . . . hit the top of a 100,000-volt electricity pylon and crashed into the field," she reported. "[We] saw the field in front of us blazing fiercely."

The explosion and crash had killed all aboard, but remarkably, Effing continued, "a huge bomb had rolled out fifty metres [164 feet] from where the plane crashed."[10] *E-Easy*'s Upkeep came to a stop, unexploded.

Only one Lancaster from the entire second wave remained in action. It appeared that any success this night against the Sorpe Dam now depended entirely upon Joe McCarthy's crew, and *T-Tommy* was still a quarter of an hour behind everybody, flying over the Zuiderzee and oblivious to the setbacks the second wave had sustained.

THE SAME WINDS THAT HAD PUSHED THE FIRST FOUR second-wave aircraft off course for their approaches over the Frisian islands of Vlieland and Texel affected the first of the first-wave Lancasters too. Guy Gibson's *G-George*, John Hopgood's *M-Mother*, and Mick Martin's *P-Popsie* bombers arrived off the Dutch coast at about eleven o'clock, but 120 miles south of the Frisians. They had hoped to emerge from their crossing of the North Sea to enter enemy airspace between Walcheren and Schouwen Island in southwest Holland. Instead they flew directly across Walcheren and South Beveland province and consequently straight onto Freya radar screens and into the gunnery sights of a heavily defended stretch of occupied Holland. Leading the formation of three, Gibson alerted his RCAF front gunner, George Deering, a man with thirty-five operations to his credit. But he didn't have to fire a shot. In minutes they had passed over Walcheren—because of its seaside dikes perhaps the only place in Europe where, flying so low, *G-George* was actually flying below sea level. Over the East Scheldt estuary, Gibson took the aircraft up to three hundred feet so navigator Harlo Taerum could get his bearings.

"There's the windmill and those wireless masts," Taerum said. "We must have drifted starboard." He gave his skipper a new heading.[11]

Finding these landmarks also allowed bomb aimer Spam Spafford to bring his navigational invention into play. Since the majority of the dams raid operation was low-level, he'd trimmed their maps to get rid of the excess paper outside their planned flight path; then he'd loaded the narrower map like a scroll stretched across a flat surface, allowing the navigator to see only the important features—railway lines, canals, and high-tension wires along their route—as they approached them. He guided Gibson, and the two other Lancasters still flying in perfect formation with them, to Roosendaal, where three railway lines intersected, then eastward, using a canal as a roadmap to take them to the Rhine River. Again the three Lancasters flew so low and so quickly that there was no enemy response from the ground for much of the way. But Gibson's skill at keeping *G-George* just off the deck more than once prompted his bomb aimer in the nose of the Lancaster to shout at him. "Power lines. Pull up!" Spam would call out.[12]

From Roosendaal, Gibson's trio of Lancasters followed the planned route. They sighted and followed the Wilhelmina Canal running eastward, strategically taking the bomber formation between two night-fighter airfields at Gilze-Rijen and Eindhoven. At a T junction in the canal system, the bombers picked up the Rhine River in the moonlight to a point where the river turned at Rees, the very spot where a few minutes later

Barlow's *E-Easy* would crash into the hydro pylon. Gibson continued to lead his trio on its low-level pass through that part of the German frontier, which "seemed dead"—without movement, without flak. Inevitably, from time to time, the group drifted off its intended flight path, and this caused problems. Between Bocholt and Borken they ran into light flak and plenty of searchlights scanning the sky. Then, near the Dülmen Lakes, Hopgood ran into trouble. *M-Mother* received a burst of anti-aircraft fire that penetrated the Lancaster from the nose, across its portside wing and into the cockpit. Front gunner George Gregory died in that burst of shells.

"Look at the blood," Charlie Brennan called out to his pilot, who'd been hit too. The Canadian flight engineer pulled out a handkerchief to attend to Hopgood's head wounds. He was no medic, but Brennan's training had taught him to respond to every emergency in the cockpit. Besides, he and Hopgood had served nearly a year together in Bomber Command; they were good friends as well as comrades-in-arms.

"I'm okay," Hopgood told Brennan.

Tony Burcher, the rear gunner, listened on the intercom as an exchange between Hopgood and Brennan ensued about their options.

"Should we go on?" Hopgood asked, but he didn't waste any time answering his own question. "I intend to go on because . . . we've come this far."[13]

Somehow Hopgood continued to fly the bomber as Brennan applied pressure with his handkerchief to stem the bleeding. At one point Burcher felt the bomber dip suddenly—even from its extremely low elevation—to fly under a set of high-tension wires.

"There's no good taking this [Upkeep] back with us," Hopgood continued. "The aircraft is completely manageable. I can handle it okay."

Navigator Ken Earnshaw made note of an additional problem, however. Since they'd left England, crossed the North Sea, skirted the Scheldt estuary, and penetrated the German frontier, the GEE radio pulses had intermittently assisted Earnshaw in his direction finding. Now enemy jammers seemed to be scrambling the GEE signal; keeping all three aircraft together would now become more difficult.[14] Nevertheless, Gibson, Hopgood, and Martin continued eastward in loose formation past Hamm, avoiding its well-defended marshalling yards, and away from the equally well-protected Hüls factories that Hopgood had warned them about. At Ahlen they turned south on the last leg of the outbound trip, past Werl and Soest into the Ruhr River Valley. The first three Lancasters of Operation Chastise were just minutes from the Möhne reservoir and dam.

IT WAS 11:12 P.M., ABOUT TEN MINUTES AFTER THE first three Lancasters of the first wave had penetrated the Dutch interior, when Dinghy Young's *A-Apple*, David Maltby's *J-Johnny*, and Dave Shannon's *L-Leather* bombers slipped into enemy airspace over the East Scheldt, roughly following Gibson's flight path. The east-west Scheldt estuary guided them over Tholen Island and inland toward Roosendaal, the same railway junction the earlier group had used as a landmark. Gibson's lead Lancasters had whizzed past without disturbing a single ground flak gunner, but the arrival of the second Vic formation drew a response.

Maltby's navigator, Vivian Nicholson, on his very first combat operation, kept meticulous, if brief, notes of the trip. "Evasive action,"[15] he wrote as his skipper dodged the flak coming their way. A while later, when he tried to make a GEE reading and it failed, he wrote, "Jammed. Something chronic."[16]

In formation off Young's other wing, pilot Dave Shannon pointed out later that the Air Force intelligence identifying concentrations of flak had not included Roosendaal as a hot spot. Searchlights managed to catch the Lancasters momentarily and Shannon saw tracers streaking up toward them. But thanks to their air speed and extreme low altitude, Young, Maltby, and Shannon just as quickly flew past the shafts of light and flak bursts and followed virtually the same track as Gibson, Hopgood, and Martin en route to the target area.

Before the attack could get underway, however, the tail-end group of three Lancasters needed to catch up with the first six aircraft in the first wave. At about 11: 21 p.m.—with Henry Maudslay piloting *Z-Zebra* in the lead, Bill Astell in *B-Baker* to his right, and Les Knight manoeuvring *N-Nuts* to his left—the final trio crossed into enemy territory, fused their Upkeep mines, and began picking their way eastward past the Scheldt estuary, across the occupied Netherlands, and over the German frontier. Fred Sutherland, the front gunner who'd fallen in love with bush flying as a kid, had no experience to compare with the likes of this trip aboard *N-Nuts*.

"We went low level—sixty feet above water or ground— all the way," he said. "Les [Knight] always had the aircraft trimmed nose light, so if there was an inattention, the plane would always climb instead of going in. It was really scary."

With the flip-down seat and special set of stirrups concocted to keep the front gunner suspended above the bomb aimer in the nose blister of his Lancaster, Sutherland and his bomb aimer comrade, Edward "Johnny" Johnson, never took their eyes off the view ahead. "Everybody—me, the pilot, the engineer, the bomb aimer—is looking out for high-tension wires. It was all industrial area, so everywhere there were high-tension wires. We were on constant lookout."[17]

Robert Kellow, *N-Nuts*'s wireless radio operator, couldn't assist Sutherland and Johnson as a lookout as their Lancaster hurtled low across the German countryside, so, watching through the aircraft's astrodome, he would warn his skipper if the Lanc were facing any attack from night fighters. To that point he hadn't seen any, but what Kellow did witness as the three Lancasters passed the town of Marbeck, east of the Rhine, was *B-Baker* to his left, struggling to catch up to the other two Lancs in the formation. On the ground in the rural country-side, the drone of passing aircraft caught the attention of the Thesing family and a nun working for the family as a maid.

Sister Roswitha Reiming happened to be outside at that moment. She saw the first two bombers pass low overhead, but the third appeared to collide with a hydroelectric pylon several hundred feet from the farmhouse. "Suddenly the air-craft was engulfed in flames," she said. "It rose a little, flew over our house and crashed in a field 200 metres [656 feet] away [and then] exploded and left a crater you could have put a house into."[18]

In nearby Marbeck the explosion set off air-raid sirens, brought searchlights to life, and set flak batteries firing into the sky. But the damage was already done. All Sister Roswitha recalled was an intense fire that seemed to light up the sky as bright as daylight. When Bill Astell's *B-Baker* hit the ground, all of its volatile contents—belts of machine-gun tracer bullets, flares, aircraft fuel, and eventually the 6,600 pounds of Torpex explosive inside the Upkeep mine—exploded, killing all aboard the aircraft. The concussion from the blast broke windows within a radius of 1.8 miles. The *B-Baker* crewmen, who had only recently lost their original skipper, Max Stephenson, were now all gone. As Albert Garshowitz had aptly scrawled on the Upkeep, so much had been expected of so few. It was just past midnight.

BACK AT SCAMPTON, FOLLOWING THEIR WINGCO'S orders, Chiefy Powell and Corporal John Bryden carried a bundle from the guardroom at the station.[19] It was the body of Guy Gibson's dog, which the wing commander had told Powell to bury about the time the first dams raid bombers were expected to reach their targets on the Ruhr River. In the moonlight, Powell and Bryden moved to the front of No. 2 Hangar. There, with Gibson's office window blacked out just above them, they sculpted a hole, buried the dog's body, and tapped a wooden cross, crafted by one of the station's air riggers, into the ground.

The burial went virtually unnoticed. It had been nearly two hours since the chaotic departure of Joe McCarthy's replacement Lancaster, *T-Tommy*, in mad pursuit of the first wave it was supposed to lead. But since it was midnight, activity at the station began picking up yet again. It was time for the third wave of Operation Chastise—the five remaining aircrews of the raid—to take off and provide backup wherever it might be needed. F/Sgt. Ken Brown's crew from *F-Freddie*, as well as F/Sgt. Cyril Anderson's *Y-York* crew, P/O Bill Townsend's *O-Orange* crew, P/O Bill Ottley's *C-Charlie* crew, and P/O Lewis Burpee's *S-Sugar* crew, gathered near No. 2 Hangar waiting for the flight trucks to carry them to their aircraft around Scampton's perimeter track. Just like Dave Rodger with his Algoma Steel jersey and Bill Radcliffe with his panda mascot, pilot Ken Brown took along a good-luck charm: a red, white, and green school scarf was wrapped around his neck as he boarded a flight truck en route to the waiting bombers. As Brown climbed aboard the crew truck, his glance caught that of fellow Canadian pilot Lewis Burpee.

"Goodbye, Ken," Burpee said to Brown.[20]

"Goodbye," Brown said, meaning "Until next time," but he immediately deduced from the tone of Burpee's voice that he really meant it as a last goodbye.

There were three crews loaded onto the truck that carried the twenty-one airmen to their waiting Lancasters. Brown's crew was the last to be dropped off, and when the transport let them off and pulled away, Brown noticed that his rear gunner, Grant McDonald, was just standing there quietly.

"C'mon, Mac," Brown called. "Let's go."

"Skip, you know those guys aren't coming back, don't you," McDonald said.

"Yeah, I know."

"Well, damn it," McDonald said angrily. He didn't have the completed tours of duty or decorations of so many others on the dams raid, but F/Sgt. McDonald understood the stakes. Statistics spoke for themselves. Fewer than half of the Bomber

Command aircrews flying nightly sorties over Europe survived their first thirty-op tours; only one in five got through a second tour of twenty combat operations. McDonald had said more than once that anybody who worried about ops probably had no business being on them.[21] And now, several hours into Operation Chastise, the aircrews of the reserve third wave were about to shoulder their share of the load.

For at least the first portion of the outbound journey, orders put the third wave under direct command of 5 Group headquarters; these directives were communicated by way of a special wireless transmission channel. In effect, this meant that the five aircrews—thirty-five men—whose battle briefing had prepared them to attack either the Möhne or Eder Dam, could at any moment be redirected to a target and enemy environment none of them anticipated. The one advantage they had, however, was intelligence transmitted from Gibson himself; just as the third-wave aircraft rumbled across the grass at Scampton, their CO had broken radio silence over Germany and told 5 Group headquarters of the danger posed by enemy gun emplacements and searchlights in the Bocholt-Borken area.[22]

By fifteen minutes after midnight, all five third-wave bombers had taken off and were headed southeast. First things first, Ken Brown decided: as soon as *F-Freddie* cleared the Lincolnshire coast, he brought the bomber down below a hundred feet and to cruising speed across the North Sea. As it had for the first-wave bombers, the trip over the water gave Brown and his crew about ninety minutes of prep time before they spotted the Scheldt estuaries of the Netherlands. In the front and rear turrets, Daniel Allatson and Grant McDonald tested their mechanics and machine guns. Flight engineer Harry Feneron and bomb aimer Stefan Oancia checked to see that the Aldis lights were focused at the prescribed sixty-foot level. And wireless radio operator Hewie Hewstone tested the motor that rotated Upkeep, which Brown said made the aircraft feel "like driving a truck over the rails of a railway, unbalanced as it was."[23]

More pressing, however, was the fact that when the third-wave pilots manoeuvred along the same corridor across Holland that Gibson, Hopgood, and Martin had found relatively free of anti-aircraft fire, they discovered that things had changed. By this time F/Sgt. Brown and P/O Burpee were flying together, and the Luftwaffe aerodromes at Gilze-Rijen and Eindhoven were on alert. Out of the darkness just beyond his rear turret in *F-Freddie*, Grant McDonald saw tracer bullets arcing up at him; enemy flak gunners had spotted them. Then searchlights began homing in. McDonald began firing back, hoping to destroy the light. Meanwhile, *S-Sugar*, off to McDonald's left, had strayed too close to Gilze-Rijen. With the German flak batteries and searchlights scanning the sky now at treetop level, they suddenly caught up to Burpee's Lancaster.

Herbert Scholl, a Luftwaffe wireless operator at Gilze-Rijen, reported hearing a bomber approaching from the west. The noise sent the searchlight crews into action. "I saw a searchlight beam suddenly come on and catch a four-engined plane, which couldn't have been more than twenty metres [66 feet] up," Scholl said. "The beam lit up like daylight . . . and caught the bomber more or less horizontally as it was coming in."[24]

Burpee reacted, trying to evade the bright lights that had caught his aircraft over the trees by bringing *S-Sugar* slightly lower, away from the searchlight. But the Lancaster clipped the tops of the trees between the airfield hangars and the searchlight tower; in seconds, the plane was descending deeper into the forest, tearing a huge swath through the trees. Ultimately the bomber crashed into a motor transport shed and came to a stop about 330 feet from the searchlight tower that had caught it in its beam moments before.

"There was this deafening explosion," Scholl continued. "The blast was so strong, that I and the other aircrews standing about 700 to 800 metres [2,296 to 2,624 feet] away . . . were almost knocked over."[25]

The gloomy goodbye that Lewis Burpee had given Ken Brown back at Scampton had been warranted. All aboard *S-Sugar* died in the ball of fire at Gilze-Rijen: navigator Tom Jaye, whom Burpee had relied on heavily throughout the Battle of the Ruhr; gunners Ginger Long and Gordie Brady, who'd flown with their skipper on all twenty-five ops he'd piloted; Sam Weller and Guy Pegler, Burpee's chosen wireless op and flight engineer; bomb aimer Jimmy Arthur, on just his second bombing sortie ever; and Lewis Burpee, just commissioned and with his wife, Lillian, expecting their first child later in the year. All gone in a flash.

But there was nothing for Brown's crew or the other three reserve crews to do but press on deeper into enemy territory. The Germany that Gibson had noted seemed "sleepy" as he passed over it earlier that night was now awake and restless. As Brown and P/O Bill Ottley in *C-Charlie* approached the final waypoint at Hamm, where the previous waves had turned south toward the Ruhr, they encountered another volley of light anti-aircraft flak and tracers.

"They were really waiting for us," Brown said. At the time, *F-Freddie* and *C-Charlie* were actually flying below the flak gunners. "They poured the flak down at us. They were on a bit of a lip as we went through the valley."[26]

As the gunners returned fire from the front and rear turrets of their Lancasters and the pilots attempted to outrun the ground fire, suddenly the flak caught Ottley's aircraft; first the plane's wing fuel tanks exploded, and then the Upkeep bomb. The valley just outside Hamm lit up in a blinding explosion as *C-Charlie* went down in a ball of orange flame, killing all aboard but the rear gunner, Fred Tees. Skipper P/O Bill Ottley died not knowing that the Air Ministry had recommended him for a DFC. Miraculously, as the pieces of *C-Charlie* tumbled to earth, Fred Tees was thrown clear and survived. Just before his bomber caught fire and crashed, Tees recalled hearing a muffled voice refer to the Möhne Dam on the intercom. But *F-Freddie* raced on. Brown and his crew had the Sorpe Dam as their objective, and they were still forty minutes away.

GERMAN SEARCHLIGHT CREWS AND FLAK GUNNERS ON the ground near Gilze-Rijen, in occupied Holland, had responded to the third-wave Lancasters with deadly force, but that was expected. Those batteries of the German XII Air Corps were defending a Luftwaffe aerodrome loaded with night-fighter aircraft. The call to battle stations there was a nightly occurrence. More than 124 miles to the east, however, atop the great dams of the Ruhr River, the atmosphere shared little or none of that intensity. Indeed, during March and April 1943, when RAF Bomber Command had launched its concentrated attacks on the major cities of the Ruhr, German military defence strategists had reassigned most of the barrage balloons and heavy flak guns away from the Ruhr water reservoirs and hydroelectric dams to protect those cities miles away. That decision had left Jörg Widmann, flak battery commander at the Möhne Dam, with only light anti-aircraft batteries—single-barrelled 20-millimetre anti-aircraft guns—in each of the dam's two towers, and several more guns below the dam.

"Flak Sanatorium," the Luftwaffe gun crews called their posting on the Möhne, meaning "no threat, no action" in such an out-of-the-way location. Nevertheless, Leutnant Widmann kept his limited armament and crews ready, just in case.

About a quarter past midnight, W/C Gibson's *G-George* crested the last ridge and entered the Ruhr River Valley. Aside from the maps, photos, and models he'd studied, it was the first time he'd laid his eyes on the Möhne reservoir and the dam, certainly from that altitude. He thought it appeared grey and unconquerable.[27] Mick Martin and his crew aboard *P-Popsie* had arrived moments before. When John Hopgood's *M-Mother* also entered the airspace above the reservoir, the three pilots flew a circuit around to gauge distances and defences. Their air intelligence information was dead accurate. There were no balloons to block their bombing runs. They could see no searchlight positions. And while photo reconnaissance had indicated the presence of light anti-aircraft gun emplacements on the sluice towers at either end of the dam, the bombers' arrival hadn't yet drawn any response.

Eleven minutes after Gibson, Hopgood, and Martin arrived over the reservoir, so too did Dinghy Young, David Maltby, and Dave Shannon. Gibson didn't have the latest on who'd survived the outbound journey and who hadn't, but his squadron strength was significantly diminished. There was one bomber and crew gone from the first wave (Astell's *B-Baker*). Two crews had been lost from the second wave (Byers's *K-King* and Barlow's *E-Easy*), as well as the two from that wave (Munro's *W-Willie* and Rice's *H-Harry*) that had been forced to return to base. Thus, before its first attack on the dams, Operation Chastise was down to fourteen aircraft and ninety-eight men. Gibson next made a dummy run over the dam without indicating his intended attack direction, speed, or altitude. The feint flypast did attract some return fire from the guns positioned in the Möhne sluice towers. Aboard *L-Leather*, Dave Shannon's navigator Revie Walker made note of it. "Light flak is a very distracting thing to aircrew at night," he said. "If it wasn't so lethal, it would be a beautiful sight to see, the flak bursting in all its various colours."[28]

"God, this light flak gives me the creeps," Gibson said on his intercom.[29]

"Me too," another crewman echoed.

In short order, Gibson had figured out his strategy. Each Lancaster would attack on its own, beginning its run with a flight path over the reservoir; then, flying from the south toward the Heversberg promontory, a tree-covered point that nearly divided the reservoir in half, the pilot would use the bush on the promontory to shield his approach and throttle to the right air speed; and finally, with the dam just under a mile away, the Lancaster would hop over the promontory, line up the dam with correct speed and altitude, and drop the Upkeep, leaving enough distance for the mine to bounce to the wall.

"I suppose we had better start the ball rolling," Gibson said, and then he spoke on the radio transmitter to Hopgood. "Hello *M-Mother*. Stand by to take over if anything happens."[30]

"Okay, Leader," Hopgood called back. "Good luck."

Gibson began another approach—not a dummy run but the real thing. He guided *G-George* along the sleeve of the reservoir and over the promontory until the last stretch of water toward the dam opened up in front of him. By this time, navigator Harlo Taerum had turned on the Aldis lights to talk Gibson down to the prescribed altitude above the reservoir surface. Gibson told John Pulford, his flight engineer, sitting to his right, to clock his speed. He was sixty feet above the reservoir and flying at 230 miles per hour.

The sight of a low-flying aircraft in the moonlight homing in on his position caught German gunner Karl Schütte off guard. Then the beams of the Lancaster's Aldis lamps appeared in the darkness over the reservoir. "The monster . . . raced at zero feet across the lake towards the centre of the dam," Schütte noted, and his battery opened fire.[31]

As enemy flak raced up toward *G-George* from the sluice towers, gunner George Deering returned fire with his tracer bullets. Then, with Upkeep spinning at the proper reverse revolutions per minute, Gibson called on bomb aimer Spam Spafford to eyeball the distance through the Perspex and, with his own custom-made range finder, drop the bomb. For Gibson, the bombing run was a storm of impressions: Pulford beside him calling numbers, the smell of burned cordite, the dam wall racing toward him, the chatter of his gunners answering the anti-aircraft fire coming from the dam towers, and finally his bomb aimer's call.

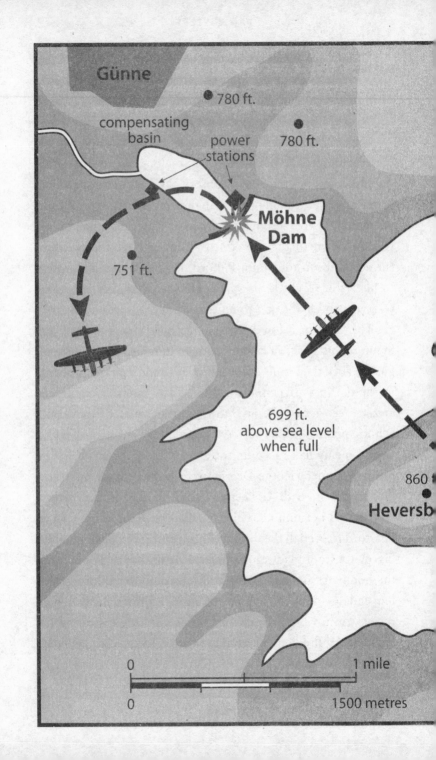

Günne

780 ft.

compensating
basin

power
stations

780 ft.

Möhne
Dam

751 ft.

699 ft.
above sea level
when full

860

Heversb

0   1 mile

0   1500 metres

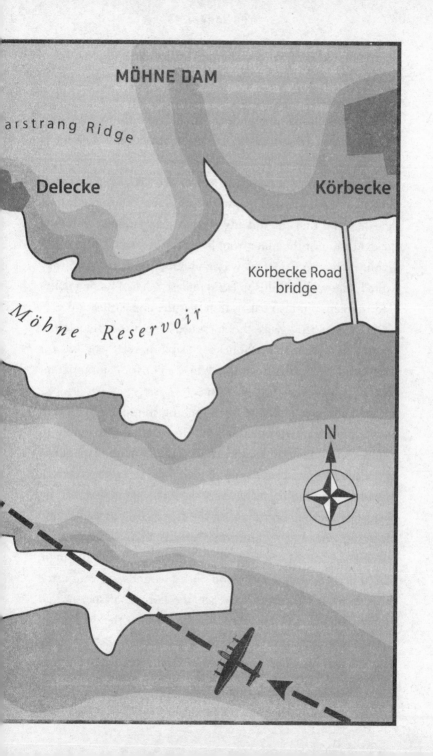

"Mine gone!" Spafford shouted on the intercom.[32]

As *G-George* passed over the top of the dam with just a few feet to spare and Gibson rapidly manoeuvred the bomber to clear the hilltops surrounding Möhne Lake, Gibson remembered Richard Trevor-Roper still firing at the sluice towers as the bomber climbed. The rear gunner reported that the mine had bounced three times and sunk. Wireless operator Bob Hutchison fired a red flare into the air, signalling to the rest of the squadron that the mine was gone. Then they all watched the explosion of the mine from beneath the surface of the reservoir, a thousand feet of water pluming upward. And they waited, and waited. Gibson felt immense relief at having delivered Upkeep, but also frustration that the dam still stood.

"Goner 68A," was the message Hutchison reluctantly sent on his VHF system. Goner for "Upkeep released," six for "exploded five yards from the dam," eight for "no apparent breach," and A for "target Möhne."

Four minutes after the first bombing run, just after 12:30 in the morning, Gibson called on Hopgood and his crew to follow through with a second attack. The remaining members of the squadron circled the outer rim of the reservoir to watch *M-Mother*'s bomb run. They saw the Aldis lights switched on by navigator Ken Earnshaw as the Lancaster descended and picked up speed at its attacking velocity and altitude. In the cockpit ahead of Earnshaw, flight engineer Charlie Brennan, who'd been attending Hopgood's head wounds, now adjusted the Lancaster's throttles to reach the correct airspeed. And Hopgood lined up *M-Mother* for a final run at the dam.

At the tower battery, NCO Schütte tried to direct fire at the next bomber now lining up the dam. The defenders were now familiar with the attack strategy, so the flak gunner ignored the beams of light streaming down from the Aldis lamps and concentrated his fire on the aircraft itself. He was firing at the bomber on virtually a flat trajectory. "I saw our tracers striking home," Schütte said. "The flames flickered and got bigger."[33]

And since *M-Mother*'s front gunner Gregory was dead, a victim of the earlier engagement near the Dülmen Lakes, *M-Mother* had no answer for the incoming enemy flak. The only man left in the forward blister was bomb aimer John Fraser, lining up the towers for the right distance to drop the mine. "I had just reached the point where I felt we should go around [for another attempt] and we were hit by the flak," Fraser said.[34]

The bomb was released, but with the aircraft in peril, the precision of the drop was lost and the mine came down late, bouncing over the top of the dam and falling toward the power station beyond. By this time, one of *M-Mother*'s port-side engines was dead, the other ablaze, and fire was spreading rapidly. Ordering his crew to abandon the aircraft, Hopgood tried desperately to gain altitude to give his crew a chance of bailing out. That proved extremely complicated for rear gunner Tony Burcher; with the inner port engine out of commission, thus cutting off the hydraulics to his turret, Burcher cranked the turret around by hand, crawled to his parachute, and, once it was in place, made his way to the crew door on the starboard side. There he found wireless operator John Minchin trying to get out. While Hopgood continued to nurse the crippled bomber higher, Burcher pushed Minchin out the door and in the same thrust pulled the ripcord on Minchin's chute.[35]

John Fraser, farther forward in his bomb aimer's blister, was oblivious to the struggles at the crew door as he made preparations to escape through the hatch beneath him. He reached for his breast parachute and quickly strapped it on. Then he pulled the escape-hatch door loose and peered into the darkness beyond.

"I knelt, facing forward over the escape hatch, looked down, and I saw that the trees looked awful damn close," Fraser said. "I figured I couldn't jump out and pull my chute. So, I thought the only thing to do was to pull the ripcord and let the pilot chute go out first, and let it pull the chute out and me after it. That's what I did and rolled out. The tail wheel whizzed by my ear. I swung to the vertical and within two or three seconds I touched the ground."[36]

At the starboard crew door, the only man left outside the cockpit was Burcher. He too looked down and judged that the ground was too close for him to survive a jump. So he pulled his own ripcord and crouched in the doorway holding the blossoming chute; suddenly, the explosion of the rest of the aircraft at his back blasted him out into the open air, several hundred feet above the ground. "While I was in the air, before I touched the ground," Fraser concluded, "the aircraft crashed about 1,500 or 2,000 feet away from me."[37]

As a final statement from *M-Mother*, its Upkeep came spinning over the top of the dam wall and down toward the power station next to Möhne's compensation basin; its self-destruct fuse was triggered the moment the mine left its calipers, and when it exploded it caused a massive fire amid the transformer oil in the power station. It had blown, just not in the right place. The message sent to Grantham was "Goner 58A"—

Upkeep exploded fifty yards from the dam, with no apparent breach. The radio transmissions among the first-wave aircrew went silent. On top of absorbing the sight of *M-Mother*'s demise, the next attacker had to wait, as Hopgood had, until the smoke cleared and the turbulence on the surface of the reservoir settled.

The destruction of the power station had helped, indirectly. Loss of power cut the communications between the German gun positions, and the explosion sent debris crashing down on the south battery, putting it out of commission. However, during the lag in the action, the remaining gunners in the north tower had ample time to reload and refocus on the next solo bomber. Gibson realized that attacking the dam alone was too risky. On the next run in, he would fly in tandem with the Lancaster carrying the Upkeep to draw the tower gunners' fire. It was nearly 12:40 a.m. when Mick Martin and *P-Popsie*, with *G-George* ahead and slightly to the right, began the third bombing run against the Möhne. The approach drew plenty of fire, but none that inflicted the serious damage sustained by Hopgood's aircraft. With his Lancaster racing to the dam at 217 mph and his Upkeep spinning at 480 rpm, squadron bombing leader Bob Hay released the mine. But it veered off to the left of the trajectory slightly, bounced to within twenty yards of the dam wall, sank, and exploded moments later. A third signal, "Goner 58A," repeated the "no breach" result.

A fourth run sent Dinghy Young and the *A-Apple* crew hurtling toward the dam. This time Gibson circled to the north of the reservoir as Taerum flicked the Aldis lights on and off to draw ground fire, while Martin flew to Young's starboard side. As he had promised in his letter home to family in Prince Edward Island, bomb aimer Vincent MacCausland had indeed delivered "a few bundles" to the enemy. The Upkeep bounced three times, went straight into the centre of the dam, sank, and exploded. The crew of *A-Apple* could not have delivered Upkeep with more precision. Again a plume of reservoir water shot a thousand feet up into the moonlit sky above the dam. Everybody watched closely as Young manipulated *A-Apple* away.

"I think I've done it!" Young called out as he pulled *A-Apple* across the brow of the dam and then up over the adjacent hills.[38] But the result appeared the same, and so the message sent back to 5 Group headquarters was the same too: "Goner 78A." No apparent breach. Then Gibson called on his fifth flight mate, David Maltby, and his *J-Johnny* crew to make their run . . .

In the underground operations room at 5 Group headquarters in Grantham, some 375 miles away, Barnes Wallis had started to pace. In half an hour of attacks, it appeared that the first wave had only managed to violently churn the waters of the Möhne reservoir near the dam, nothing more. The response to the uncomfortable question he'd asked himself for months—would this experiment work?—kept coming up negative. Only now, since the scientist had grown to know and respect the young men risking their lives over the Möhne that night, his doubts had become a more personal fear: had he sent them all to die in vain? The ops room communications had now decoded four "no breach" signals from the skies over the Ruhr. Wallis was imagining the worst.

For much of the night, Grantham's attention seemed focused mostly on Targets X and Y—the Möhne and the Eder.

But about the same time that Gibson, Hopgood, and Martin entered the valley around the Möhnesee, Joe McCarthy and his *T-Tommy* crew had arrived over the Ruhr River Valley and above Target Z, the Sorpe Dam. They'd pulled off a miraculous catch-up job. When McCarthy and his crew had crossed the Dutch coastline, they were a mere seventeen minutes behind the rest of the second wave, having left Scampton more than half an hour behind the previous four Lancasters. Squeezing as much speed as he could out of the Merlin engines, flight engineer Bill Radcliffe had managed to shave sixteen minutes off the North Sea crossing. Meanwhile, right at McCarthy's back, Don MacLean had worked feverishly at his nav table, plotting his pinpoints, fixes, position lines, and any drift to get *T-Tommy* to the Frisians exactly according to the briefing.

Then McCarthy called on his own experience as a low-level flyer and a few natural elements to get to the target as quickly as he could. "There were two large sand dunes right on the coast which I snuck between, and got to the Zuiderzee without any damage," McCarthy said. "We flew so low, we actually used trees and hills to escape from searchlights and the ack-ack firing at us."[39]

McCarthy proved so deft at the art of zigzagging his way over the Dutch and German countryside at treetop level that his gunners—Ronald Batson in the front turret and Dave Rodger in the rear—spotted German night-fighter aircraft cruising a thousand feet above them, oblivious to the Lancaster's passage beneath. At 12:30 a.m., when *T-Tommy* finally crested the hill-tops surrounding the town of Langscheid and the Sorpe reservoir beyond, McCarthy was surprised to find none of the rest of the second wave in the area; he had no idea that Munro and

Rice had been forced to return to Scampton, nor that Barlow's crew had crashed and Byers's crew had been shot down on their way to the target. To add to the discomfort of finding none of his comrades either attacking or circling the area, the hour had brought on a heavy mist over the valley, including a shroud of fog over the dam itself. As Barnes Wallis had described at the briefing all those hours ago, *T-Tommy* didn't have to spin Upkeep for the greatest effect on this earthen dam, nor did the crew have to attack the dam at right angles, but rather parallel to the wall of the dam itself.

"Jeez," McCarthy said on his first pass. "How do we get down there?"[40] The Sorpe wall was about 2,000 feet long, the longest of the dam targets in the May 16–17 raid, but hills around the reservoir rose up steeply, hundreds of feet, right from the water's edge. Completing a parallel run and dropping Upkeep about halfway along the dam would require a surgical descent, rapid levelling off to deliver the mine parallel to the dam wall, and then an equally quick ascent to exit the valley and clear the hills. The dam hardly needed armament to defend it; the landcape seemed to protect it naturally.

"I had to come over a hill in the town (Langscheid), which was on the edge of the dam . . . get my aircraft down to the level that I required in the distance that was available. I had about a quarter of a mile to get down from 250 feet, level out, and drop my weapon," McCarthy recalled.[41]

The town itself was nestled around a sizable church with a prominent steeple; McCarthy realized he could use the church spire to line up his run over the town and down to the dam. The same spire could assist his bomb aimer, Johnny Johnson, as well; all he needed was the proper altitude and speed and a perfectly parallel run along the wall of the dam. But as helpful as the steeple might be to mark his entry to the dam site, it was definitely in the way; there was some discussion about setting it ablaze to knock it down, but that idea was abandoned.[42]

McCarthy had the relative luxury of facing no flak, no searchlights, and, so far, no night-fighter aircraft over the Sorpe. Having come this far, he wanted to make sure the Upkeep was delivered where it would do the most damage, just to the reservoir side of the dam at about the centre. He made several circuits, attempting to descend quickly enough and low enough to release the bomb and still leave enough time to pull up and out of the valley. Each time, he and Johnson, who would release the mine, needed to know that conditions were perfect. Otherwise, one or the other called off the pass as a dummy run. "Nine times I called dummy run," Johnson said. "It didn't do the morale of the crew much good, but I knew that if we had to do it, we had to do it properly."[43]

Each pass, Johnson got McCarthy to line up the port engines with the dam wall so that when Upkeep was released, it would come down on the water side; this would allow the mine to sink to the prescribed depth before it exploded and allow *T-Tommy* to get out of the way, even though both mine and aircraft would continue travelling in the same direction. On the tenth time, it worked.

"Bomb gone," Johnson shouted.[44]

"Thank Christ for that," came Dave Rodger's voice from the rear turret. He felt the jar of Upkeep's release and from his vantage point watched the bomb bounce and then sink. And as McCarthy accelerated and climbed to avoid hitting the valley hillside, Rodger watched the results.

925 ft.

Melschede

N

Langsch

1115

SORPE DAM

Sorpe Reservoi

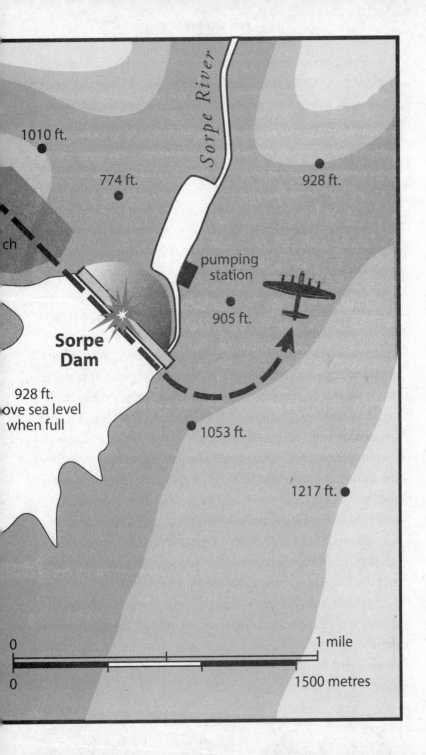

1010 ft.

774 ft.

928 ft.

Sorpe River

ch

pumping
station

905 ft.

**Sorpe
Dam**

928 ft.
ove sea level
when full

1053 ft.

1217 ft.

0

0

1 mile

1500 metres

"The explosion was right against the face of the dam," Rodger said. "It went up and up and up and I'll bet the spout was about 700 feet in the air. . . . When [we] swung back over it, the water was coming down and we were running through rain. . . . The whole side where the bomb was dropped . . . the bricks, the mortar, big concrete blocks, it just turned them upside down."[45]

T-Tommy completed its attack just before one o'clock in the morning. That left two third-wave bombers to try to finish the job at the Sorpe. But the fog that had presented McCarthy with visibility problems intensified with each passing minute. Just after 2:30 in the morning, Cyril Anderson piloted his *Y-York* Lancaster over the Ruhr Valley, trying to find his target. In addition to the thickening fog over the target and surrounding area, he encountered navigational problems and couldn't pinpoint the dam. To add to *Y-York*'s problems, its rear turret was also out of commission. Rather than risk disaster in the fog, he turned for home with a live Upkeep still tucked in the Lancaster's belly. A short time later, Ken Brown and the crew of *F-Freddie* managed to find the Sorpe and began to reconnoiter the same fog-filled valley for their attack. On his first dummy run, just as McCarthy had, Brown tried to position himself to enter the valley by using the spire of the Langscheid church as a guidepost. He found himself at ground level behind the dam, having to climb almost a thousand feet and then having to turn and descend abruptly to make the bombing run.

"It didn't do my nerves any good," he said. "Because I was on top of the trees, I had to do a flat turn. I couldn't move the wing down to [bank]. I had to stand on the rudder to get around and then we were down in the valley again."[46]

In a series of additional dummy runs, Brown called on his wireless operator, Hewie Hewstone, to drop flares at intervals along the dam to help guide them during their actual bombing run. Eventually, on his sixth pass, Brown managed to descend through the mist to the prescribed sixty-foot altitude and a speed of about 180 miles per hour; bomb aimer Stefan Oancia dropped the mine. Again the explosion shot water skyward a thousand feet and inflicted more damage to the crown of the dam, but Oancia had to radio back "Goner 78C"—that the mine had exploded in contact with the wall but it had not breached the dam.

As F/L David Maltby brought *J-Johnny* into position over the reservoir for the fifth run against the Möhne Dam, he worried that the full moon behind him was silhouetting his aircraft perfectly for the German gunners in the remaining north tower anti-aircraft battery. To allay Maltby's fears slightly, Gibson called on Mick Martin's *P-Popsie* to flank Maltby's approach on the port side while he positioned *G-George* on his starboard side. All three flew at the dam together. There was still flak fire coming from the north tower; as well, members of German gunner Karl Schütte's battery crew—whose south tower anti-aircraft gun was disabled—began firing at the inbound bomber with their carbines from atop the parapet of the dam itself.[47] It was ten minutes before 1 a.m. when Maltby jockeyed *J-Johnny* to 223 miles per hour and into position at the prescribed sixty feet above the reservoir surface on his final race to the reservoir wall. Suddenly, everybody's attention was drawn to the centre of the dam.

"The crown of the wall was already crumbling," Maltby realized. "[There was] a tremendous amount of debris on the top . . . and a breach in the centre of the dam."[48]

Maltby was already committed to releasing the mine, but he was able to shift the direction of his run slightly left of the apparent breach to augment the impact of his Upkeep on the target.[49] The bomb bounced four times, hit a part of the dam that hadn't fallen away in the breach, sank, and exploded seconds later, adding to the turbulence at the centre of the dam. Gunner Schütte saw the breach developing and shouted to his battery crew, "The wall's had it."[50] He didn't want to be there if the bombers launched yet another attack and run the risk of getting sucked into the water rushing through the hole in the dam.

While it seemed initially that Dinghy Young's claim that he'd "done it" was premature, when Gibson looked at the fifth rising spout of water behind the dam and the reservoir water gushing through the growing breach, he saw a gap one hundred yards across and growing. The three previous Upkeeps that had exploded just underwater next to the reservoir wall had done their work. Barnes Wallis's design and prediction had been vindicated; the collective quake beneath the water and against the Möhne's submerged wall had delivered sufficient tension to the masonry and weakened the dam enough to let the force of the water do the rest. The Möhne was crumbling. Gibson watched in awe; he later said the water and the moonlight reminded him of "stirred porridge" cascading through the air to the valley below. This night, he and his squadron had unleashed a surge of destructive power that was now crashing toward key war-production plants of Germany's Third Reich.

Gibson suddenly realized that Dave Shannon had already moved to the far end of the Möhne reservoir to deliver a sixth Upkeep; he abruptly called him off. Silence on the aircraft radios was suddenly broken; there was hooting and hollering. The rest of the flight—*A-Apple*, *N-Nuts*, and *L-Leather*—came down from the adjacent hills and joined *G-George*, *P-Popsie*, and *J-Johnny* circling over the scene. At four minutes to one o'clock, Bob Hutchison, Gibson's wireless radio operator, fired off the coded signal that the Möhne Dam had been breached. At Grantham, Chief Signals Officer Wally Dunn called for a verification. Moments later, when Hutchison repeated the signal, Dunn announced the news to a breathless operations room. The confirmation of the breach sent Barnes Wallis, hands in the air, dancing around the room.

"It worked! It worked!" Wallis kept shouting.[51]

There were congratulations all around. Even Arthur Harris, who had once described Wallis's plan as "tripe of the wildest description," shook the scientist's hand and said, "Now you could sell me a pink elephant."[52]

Amid the euphoria above the Möhne and back at Grantham, the leader of the dams raid took stock. As he watched the valley beneath him swallowed by the gushing reservoir water, in the moonlight Gibson saw debris in the growing flood—bridges, railways, viaducts, buildings—all tumbling like toys in a wall of water. Through the growing fog and rising water, he could see automobile headlights racing away from the surge of water, then overtaken, then submerged and gone. Three miles beyond the valley, he could see the crumpled wreckage of John Hopgood's Lancaster, its fuel and ammunition still burning in a red glow on the ground. While his good friend had not survived, Gibson would learn later that two aircrew—John Fraser and Tony Burcher—had parachuted outside the river valley and would become prisoners of war. Allowing all this to sink in, Gibson rallied his flight. The raid was still not complete. He told Mick Martin and David Maltby to head for home and instructed Dinghy Young (whose mine had been expended against the Möhne) to help him lead the remaining aircrews still carrying their Upkeeps—Henry Maudslay's *Z-Zebra*, David Shannon's *L-Leather*, and Les Knight's *N-Nuts*—to attack Target Y. The Eder Dam was fourteen minutes away.

Actually locating the Eder proved difficult. The night had brought a new foe into the picture. McCarthy had fought his way through ten passes over the Sorpe to penetrate it. But it was now about 1:30 in the morning, and mist was collecting in pockets over the Eder reservoir, hiding some of the most challenging terrain that low-flying bombers would have to thread to get to the dam. Approaching from the northeast, the 617 pilots had to descend over a castle atop a ridge down to the reservoir surface, make a nearly ninety-degree dogleg turn to port over the Hammerberg spit, and, in about half a mile, level off to the prescribed altitude and speed to deliver the mine. Finally, seconds after the release, skirting the top of the dam, the pilots had to make a rapid, steep climb to clear the hilltops beyond the dam. The Eder Dam had no apparent gun emplacements to defend it; the natural topography was perhaps enough.

"I'll fire a red Very light right over the dam," Gibson told his crews, hoping that would guide them to the target. Then he called on Shannon's *L-Leather* crew to attack.

Shannon decided to make a dummy run to get a better sense of the time and space he'd need to complete all the manoeuvres, deliver the mine, and emerge safely from the valley. After his quick descent over Waldeck Castle, Shannon used the spit as a marker to make his hairpin turn to the left but levelled off above the sixty-foot mark, tried to correct his altitude, and realized he'd run out of yardage to the dam. Gibson watched Shannon hit full throttle; the Merlins were under such terrific strain to pull the 40,000-pound aircraft and its 9,250-pound Upkeep out of the valley that they emitted sparks. Shannon apologized for the awkward run and made four more attempts, trying to "get used to this place."[53] But he couldn't, not yet, anyway.

"I'd made five runs and was getting somewhat frustrated, as no doubt the rest of my crew, because we had been unsuccessful either from height or speed," Shannon said. "Gibson, who was getting a little perturbed about the time that dawn would come up, called in Henry Maudslay."[54]

Maudslay took Z-Zebra along exactly the same path that Shannon had blazed five times. As experienced as he was, however, Maudslay didn't fare any better making the sharp turn to the left over the spit and, in the space remaining, bringing the Lancaster down to the desired altitude in time to deliver the mine to bounce to the dam. He tried again but pulled away a second time without dropping the mine. Gibson gave the lead back to Shannon, and this time the descent, the turn to port, and the levelling out resulted in an approach to the dam at 240 miles per hour at sixty feet.

"Height spot on," called navigator Revie Walker.

"Everything's fine here," called out bomb aimer Len Sumpter, and he released the Upkeep. It bounced twice, hit the

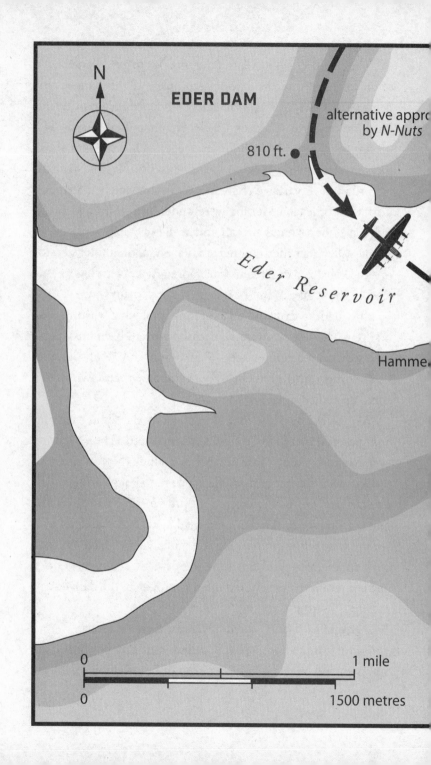

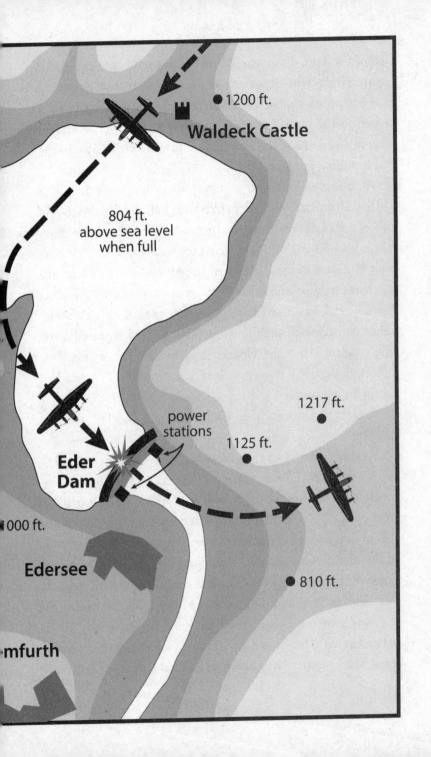

wall of the dam, disappeared into the reservoir, and exploded, creating the plume of water the aircrews were now expecting as a matter of course. Shannon felt certain they'd caused a breach in the dam. But with no physical evidence, they had to send a code back to Grantham indicating no breach on the first bombing attempt.

At fifteen minutes to 2 a.m., Maudslay conferred with Robert Urquhart, his navigator, and John Fuller, his bomb aimer, and began his third attempt at the dam. The other crews that could do so, through their Perspex, watched Maudslay pilot *Z-Zebra* to the dam. It appeared to Robert Kellow, the wireless operator aboard *N-Nuts*, that they'd made a perfect drop. There was a red flare indicating that *Z-Zebra*'s bomb aimer had released the mine, but then Kellow reported a terrific orange flash. The Upkeep had hit the top of the dam and exploded. What wasn't clear was whether *Z-Zebra* had escaped the inferno.

"Henry!" Gibson called on his radio. "*Z-Zebra*, are you o.k.?"[55]

At first there was no answer, then a faint "I think so . . . Stand by," from Maudslay. An awkward and uncomfortable silence followed. Nobody saw wreckage or heard distress calls. *Z-Zebra* had disappeared without a trace. When the smoke cleared, Hutchison sent the all too familiar code of the night, "Goner 28B," signalling that the mine had been released, that it had overshot, and that there was no breach. For Gibson, two daunting factors loomed. To the north, the sky was growing lighter; their cover of darkness was giving way to dawn. They'd run out of time. Just as pressing, Gibson knew the squadron was down to its final Upkeep; Les Knight and the crew of *N-Nuts* represented the last chance to breach the Eder.

Given all they'd witnessed this night over the Ruhr—Bill Astell's crew crashing into high-tension wires at Marbeck, Hopgood's going down over the Möhne, and now Maudslay's disappearance beyond the Eder—confidence among members of Knight's crew was at low ebb. Knight's front gunner, Fred Sutherland, admitted he was worried. Though he'd had his Browning machine-gun handles in a death-grip most of the night, Sutherland hadn't fired a single shot. And even as Knight lined up a dummy run over the reservoir, Doc scanned the dam for anti-aircraft guns. "I didn't see anybody firing or even running," Sutherland said. He was just listening intently on his headset. "All I remember then was the intercom talk, that was all."[56]

The chatter on the radio receiving transmissions from the other crews had everybody advising pilot Les Knight about his attack strategy; it must have been one distraction too many. Knight called to wireless operator Robert Kellow: "Switch [the radio] off." Knight had now been at the controls of *N-Nuts* for more than three hours, hedgehopping, circling, and constantly preparing for his commander's call to attack. Thus far, he'd remained in reserve. But experience had also taught Knight to adapt. He'd watched Dave Shannon and Henry Maudslay crest the valley over the castle, attempt to descend quickly, then bank severely to the left while decelerating and finish the run to the dam at the requisite speed, altitude, and attitude. Shannon had done five dummy runs, Maudslay two. In those precious minutes of observing and listening to the others, Knight had found perhaps a better way to get the job done.

"We didn't use the route over the castle," Fred Sutherland recalled. "Les went to the north and came down a small ravine instead."[57] Knight had found a small indentation in the shoreline of the reservoir, not quite wide enough to bring *N-Nuts* right down to water level, but enough of a depression in the hillside to permit a less radical descent, without having to execute a perilous low-level turn, and on a line that gave the pilot and bomb aimer a continuous, straight-on view of the dam, with a short hedgehop over the spit and then a smooth and direct run at the wall. "Les did one dummy run," Sutherland said. "And I remember bomb aimer [Johnny Johnson] and [Les] saying on the run, 'We can do it from here.'"[58]

It was eight minutes to 2 a.m. when P/O Knight brought *N-Nuts* down over the ravine on the north side of the reservoir. Using the cut in the hillside to descend more evenly to the required altitude, Knight now listened to his crew on the intercom to help jockey *N-Nuts* into position for the final leg of the run. Flight engineer Ray Grayston called out the bomber's airspeed so that Knight could keep the aircraft close to the prescribed 230 mph. Wireless operator Robert Kellow confirmed that Upkeep was spinning at the required 500 rpm in its calipers. Once the bomber had made the last quick hop over the Hammerberg spit, navigator Sid Hobday guided Knight to the altitude where the Aldis spotlights converged exactly sixty feet below the Lancaster. Bomb aimer Johnson used his Dann rangefinder to line up the Eder's towers to drop the Upkeep at the correct distance from the dam.

"Let's ride," Johnson said, and the mine was gone. The squadron's final Upkeep aimed at the Eder Dam made three textbook bounces, coming to a halt against the wall slightly to right of centre, where it sank. "When [Johnson] called, 'Bomb gone,' we went into a steep climb with the throttles pushed through the gate," Sutherland said. "Everything worked perfectly."

The last crewman over the dam was rear gunner Harry O'Brien, looking directly at the face of the dam. He had a bird's-eye view of the results. "The column of water that came up [was] as high as the hill, around a thousand feet," he said. "I had no idea that all this water could come up towards me in the tail end of the Lancaster."[59]

Meanwhile, Kellow was standing with his head in the blister of the astrodome, looking back and down at the dam as Knight nearly put the bomber on its tail with acceleration to climb out of the valley and over the hills. "[The dam] was still intact for a short while," Kellow said. "Then, as if some huge fist had been jabbed at the wall, a large almost round black hole appeared and the water gushed as from a large hose."[60]

"It's gone!" shouted Jack Buckley aboard Shannon's *L-Leather*. And once Knight had cleared the hilltop beyond the now disintegrating dam, on came the radio aboard *N-Nuts*, where shouts were erupting from every man on the aircraft and from every crew across the flight. Bob Hutchison sent the code word "Dinghy" to 5 Group back at Grantham, meaning Eder breached. Grantham called for confirmation and Robert Kellow transmitted "Goner 710B," confirming mine dropped, exploded on contact, with large breach. So captivated was Les Knight by the surging water that he flew low-level, following the flood and debris down the valley, until his wing commander came on the R/T.

"Good show, boys," Gibson said.

Like pilot Knight, gunner O'Brien seemed mesmerized by the apparent tempest they'd unleashed on the Ruhr Valley. Gibson's congratulations on the radio snapped him back to attention. And as O'Brien settled his 210-pound body back into his uncomfortable and vulnerable gun position in the rear turret of *N-Nuts*, he realized that the surviving aircrews of Operation Chastise faced one last hurdle this night.

"We'd been flying for [four] hours," O'Brien said. "We still had a long way to go [to get home.] We were all hoping that our luck was going to hold out."[61]

CHAPTER EIGHT

"APRÈS MOI LE DÉLUGE"

I F THE TRIP OUTBOUND FROM SCAMPTON WAS HAZ-ardous for the dams raiders—dodging German gun emplacements, evading night fighters, and flying lower than Freya, the German radar, and sometimes even lower than treetops and hilltops—the homeward-bound trip proved equally so. Springtime brought shorter nights over the Continent, so by the time the 617 aircrews had completed their bombing runs in the early hours of May 17, the eastern horizon had brightened enough to silhouette the Lancasters heading for home, the way the aurora borealis had on their way to the targets. And any element of surprise, if it existed at all, had diminished substantially. If nothing else, word of the attack on the dams would soon spread and trigger alerts across occupied Europe between the Ruhr and home.

When Lancaster *T-Tommy* finished its work at the Sorpe Dam, just after 12:45 a.m., navigator Don MacLean noted in his navigator's log the time, the bomber's air speed of 180 mph, and the altitude from which they'd dropped the Upkeep. Then finally he wrote, "Bomb's gone."[1]

A few minutes later, when pilot Joe McCarthy called for a course back to the Möhne on their way home, MacLean gave him a heading of twenty-eight degrees north-northeast so that they could see for themselves what the breach of Target X looked like. McCarthy figured they might be one of the last crews from 617 Squadron across the now draining reservoir and could therefore make mental notes of its impact for a debriefing to Air Force intelligence later. Then McCarthy called on MacLean again, for a course that retraced the route that Gibson and the first wave had used coming into the Ruhr. That course, much shorter than the more northerly second-wave route, had delivered the first wave relatively unscathed; it made sense to try to retrace that route home. As they flew northward toward Ahlen, *T-Tommy*'s front gunner, Ron Batson, spotted what looked like an enemy troop train chugging along in the open. They would soon overtake it.

"Hey Skip, can we shoot it up?"[2]

"Well, OK," said McCarthy, knowing that *T-Tommy*'s guns had been pretty much silent all night long. "Go ahead."

In the bomb aimer's blister in the nose section of the Lancaster, Johnny Johnson had a pretty clear view of what followed. As Batson began firing from the front gun position and Dave Rodger from the rear turret, they suddenly realized that what looked rather like a troop train was in fact an armoured one. "The train's response to our .303 [bullets] was a little heavier," Johnson said.[3]

"I started pumping away at [this gunner on the train] and he was pumping at me," Rodger said, adding that his aircraft was bouncing around so much at low level that neither side appeared to do the other any damage. "And we pumped at each other for about two miles. As soon as I stopped, he stopped. I wish I'd stopped a heck of a lot sooner."[4]

Return fire from the German train gunners turned out to be the least of *T-Tommy*'s concerns. Pilot McCarthy had no sooner outrun the harassing fire from the armoured train when he looked ahead of him through the windscreen. According to MacLean's calculations, they were still flying the reciprocal course, the exact reverse of the one that Gibson had used to sneak into the Ruhr virtually undetected earlier in the raid. But what should have been a corridor of uninhabited darkness on the ground and sky suddenly loomed brighter and brighter. They weren't heading east of the city of Hamm, as MacLean had plotted, but straight over it and into the gunsights of a phalanx of anti-aircraft batteries. It was almost exactly the same location where Bill Ottley and the crew of *C-Charlie* had been shot down earlier that night when the third wave was en route to the dams.

"The sky opened up in front of us with searchlights and guns firing at us," McCarthy said. "We were off course."[5]

In an instant, McCarthy pulled the Lancaster into a 180-degree turn and began to circle, maintaining his one-hundred-foot altitude as he and MacLean tried to figure out where they were. Quickly the navigator calculated that they were eighteen degrees off course. And McCarthy realized why.

"When we got this new aircraft the night of the raid," McCarthy said, "they had swung the compasses of the aircraft to make sure they were accurate," compensating for the impact that Upkeep's steel casing would have on their compass's reading of true north. "So naturally, when the bomb [was dropped], the magnetic differences had swung the compass . . ."[6]

Even though MacLean thought he had set his course for home, he had forgotten that Upkeep's magnetic force on the aircraft's compasses was now absent, putting *T-Tommy* eighteen degrees west of its intended heading and flying right into the teeth of Hamm's defensive anti-aircraft guns. As McCarthy completed his third circle a hundred feet off the deck, waiting for MacLean to set the corrected course, he felt a sudden jerk on the controls and heard a thud behind him. On the intercom he checked to see if anyone had been hit. All seemed okay. It was during this navigational crisis that Don MacLean's forethought *not* to use the narrower scrolling maps across the navigation table emerged as his wisest decision of the night.

McCarthy let MacLean know he now considered *T-Tommy*'s compass readings suspect. Instead of using its readings to backtrack along the route that the first wave had used to enter enemy territory earlier that night, McCarthy suggested to MacLean that he map-read the way out by backtracking along their original second-wave route in. Fortunately MacLean had been using the maps with the wider perspective, and he plotted a new course back the way they'd come—across the Zuiderzee, if possible around its coastal defences, and finally taking the northernmost route over the North Sea for home.

Just as he had on the eastbound route to the target, *T-Tommy*'s flight engineer Bill Radcliffe coaxed the Lancaster's four Merlin engines to deliver every ounce of speed possible on the westbound route home. They were now trying to outrun the dawn creeping across the eastern horizon behind them. So often had McCarthy and Radcliffe flown together that the pilot fully expected his engineer to err on the side of saving fuel. But out over the open Zuiderzee, the crew heard an unexpected dialogue between pilot and flight engineer on the intercom.

"Hadn't you better cut [the engines] back a little?" McCarthy warned.

"Don't you go worrying about those Merlins," Radcliffe came back. "They're doing real fine. Just you get us the hell out of here before sunup."[7]

They weren't out of the woods yet. As they were crossing the Dutch coast, a German gunner spotted their low-level path over the treetops and opened fire. Rodger found himself saying, "It's going to be the next one, the next one," but soon the Lanc was out of range and on its final leg over the North Sea, making a beeline for home.[8] Because they had chosen a different exit route from the one in the original flight plan, they suddenly found themselves at an extremely low level thundering over a convoy that included warships; McCarthy worried aloud about "trigger-happy" naval gunners, but *T-Tommy* raced through faster than any gunner's reaction time could catch them. Still, the final test of man and machine confronted McCarthy on his approach to Scampton aerodrome. When he lowered the Lanc's landing gear, the right strut was minus a tire. The thud he'd heard when they were circling near Hamm was a piece of shrapnel that had come through his forward right landing gear, pierced the top of the wing (narrowly missing the fuel tanks), smashed into the astronavigation equipment over Don MacLean's head, and landed on his desk. After the panic of changing airplanes at the last minute, followed by five and a half hours of stressful flying to the target and back, McCarthy now had to land his Lancaster without a tire on his right-hand landing gear.

"Joe managed to hold the [starboard] wheel up by applying aileron until we were just about stopped," Dave Rodger said. "We just spun around once," and came to a stop.[9]

Meanwhile, Don MacLean never said a thing about the close encounter with the shrapnel that had come to a stop on his navigation table a couple of hours earlier. When *T-Tommy* spun to a halt at 3:23 in the morning on the airfield at Scampton, he just scooped up the sheets of his navigational plotting paper—his record of the raid for his flight log and the debriefing to come—and then joined the crew of *T-Tommy* making a quick exit through the crew hatch, just in case their Lancaster was in danger of catching fire from that final ground spin. Not long afterward, MacLean took out his pencil and signed the final sheet of his navigation notes into history. "17:5:43," he wrote in large numbers, indicating the date—May 17, 1943—followed by, "F/Sgt. D.A. MacLean."[10] But neither entry looked particularly historic. Both the date and his signature were shaky and uneven, as if scrawled by a man who'd repeated to himself before every sortie, "I'm not going to live 'til the end of the day."[11]

As MacLean completed the op entries in his flight log, Bill Townsend and the crew of *O-Orange* had just delivered the final Upkeep to their target in the Ruhr; at about 2:20 a.m. they had received a signal to set a course for an alternative target, the Ennepe Dam. Also facing the problem of dense fog over the Ruhr River, Townsend mistook the earthen Bever Dam for the Ennepe; it would have required a line of attack much like the two drops against the Sorpe, so *O-Orange*'s bombing run resulted in little or no damage. His work done, however, Townsend turned and raced for home.

About forty-five minutes behind *T-Tommy*, the surviving Lancasters of the first wave moved across the Zuiderzee as well. Guy Gibson's flight engineer, just like Bill Radcliffe, had turned a blind eye to any kind of fuel conservation. Meanwhile, *G-George*'s navigator, Harlo Taerum, had plotted the shortest route home too, including passage across the Dutch coast at Egmond aan Zee, where Gibson's past experience told him there was a gap in enemy defences. Still, Taerum advised his wing commander to keep his altitude down. At about 3 a.m., he reported, "Fifteen minutes to go" to the coast of Holland.

By this stage of the operation, Lancaster crews were choosing courses and flying tactics that suited the conditions and that might expedite their passage home. The first wave, which had already lost *B-Baker* on its way to the dams and *M-Mother* during the attack on the Möhne itself, would sustain two more losses as the surviving Lancaster crews raced westbound. Over the Eder Dam, *Z-Zebra* had seemed to disappear as its Upkeep hit the top of the dam and exploded. But Henry Maudslay's faint apparent "Stand by" radio transmission suggested the pilot was attempting to thread his crippled ship through searchlights, night fighters, and flak en route home; just after 2:30 a.m., however, the aircraft was hit by anti-aircraft fire and crashed near Emmerich, Germany. Meanwhile, *A-Apple*, following its role in the attacks at both the Möhne and Eder

Dams, made its way to an exit course over the Zuiderzee; like Gibson, Dinghy Young was experienced at searching out the gaps in coastal defences, but when Gibson tried raising his comrade on the radio, as they were heading out of enemy territory, there was no answer. Just before 3 a.m., flak batteries on the coast of the Netherlands, near Castricum aan Zee, had brought down *A-Apple*; all members of Young's aircrew, including his Canadian bomb aimer, Vincent MacCausland, were lost.

The homeward-bound flight for Ken Brown and the crew of *F-Freddie* proved no cakewalk either. They too had chosen the Zuiderzee route, hoping to dodge the night fighters, but by the time they reached it, about 4 a.m., enough light from the dawn made the mud of the Zee indistinguishable from the sky. It was all Brown could do to keep his Lancaster below the sightlines of German gunners around the inland sea, no higher than he'd been flying on the final runs at the Sorpe to stay off enemy radar. But despite maintaining his altitude and keeping his cockpit top below fifty feet above the Zee, about fifteen minutes into the crossing, searchlights found them and *F-Freddie* began taking cannon shells through its canopy and along the length of its fuselage. Brown had only one choice.

"I'd been told by a famous wing commander in the RAF, 'If you're low, never pull up. If you're low, never pull up.' So, I put her down ten feet. When we came across, their gun positions were on the sea wall, so they were firing slightly down at us. . . . They couldn't believe we were lower than they could fire."[12]

Brown's gunners—Daniel Allatson in the front turret and Grant McDonald in the rear—couldn't believe they were firing up at the German guns either. As Brown pulled up only slightly to crest the last battery of guns on the coast, he watched the defenders either falling because they'd been hit by his Lancaster gunners or jumping to save themselves. Then, just as suddenly as it had come into view and taken fire, *F-Freddie* had hopped over the coastline and left the enemy batteries behind. Like McCarthy, Brown opened his throttles wide and raced out over the North Sea for home. Meanwhile, he went on his intercom to check for any wounded crew and damage. Eventually Brown came to Hewie Hewstone, the wireless operator who'd once wisecracked that if they were considered the backbone of this secret squadron, it was likely the part of the backbone closest "to the arse end." When Brown asked for damage status, Hewstone quipped, "Well, Skip, come on back and crawl in and out of the holes!"[13]

Finally, over the British coast, *F-Freddie* navigator Dudley Heal gave Brown his final course heading for an approach to Scampton. Instinctively the pilot opened his radio and identified himself. "This is *F for Freddie*," Brown reported.

A momentary pause. Then the voice of a WAAF from Scampton control tower came on the air, "Hello, *F for Fox*."

It was May 17 and all call signs had changed overnight. But that was just the protocol. Scampton had been receiving Operation Chastise Lancasters sporadically all night long, but not without a few frightening moments. Just after midnight, Les Munro managed to get *W-Willie* on a final approach to Scampton. The Lancaster still carried an Upkeep in its calipers hanging from the bomb bay, but its radio equipment had been blown to bits by enemy flak on the outbound journey over Holland, so radio operator Percy Pigeon had no wireless means of communication with wireless operators on the ground. Munro headed straight for the airstrip. He had no way of knowing that on the same approach, and just above him, Geoff Rice had been given clearance to land *H-Harry*. But Rice's bomber had mechanical problems too, given that it had accidentally bounced off the water in the Waddenzee, lost its Upkeep, and nearly drowned its rear gunner. Damaged hydraulics aboard *H-Harry* meant Rice had to use an emergency compressed-air bottle to lower his undercarriage and that he had limited manoeuvrability with his flap controls; he also had no tailwheel, since it had been ripped off in the low-level collision with the water. Fortunately, pilots Munro and Rice saw each other and both landed their damaged Lancs safely.

Ken Brown landed *F-Freddie* at 5:33 in the morning. Within seconds, flight engineer Harry Feneron was out the crew door and, upholding one of his post-op rituals, kissing the ground in gratitude. At about 6:15, when *O-Orange* touched down safely with Bill Townsend at the controls, something slowly dawned on F/Sgt. Brown: of the nineteen aircraft in the raid, he and his crew had been the third last to leave, and yet here they were back at Scampton. Around him sat only ten other Lancasters. On the ground were Gibson's *G-George*, Maltby's *J-Johnny*, Shannon's *L-Leather*, Knight's *N-Nuts*, and Martin's *P-Popsie*—that is, five of the original nine in the first wave—as well as McCarthy's *T-Tommy* and the heavily damaged *W-Willie* and *H-Harry*. That meant only three of the five from the second wave had arrived home safely; from his own third wave, Brown counted his Lancaster as well as Cyril Anderson's *Y-York* and Townsend's *O-Orange*, three of the original five.

"Wonder where the other fellows landed?" Brown thought. Unless they had landed elsewhere, and under the circumstances that was quite possible, it appeared that eight aircraft were missing, along with their fifty-six aircrew! Out of his cockpit, back on terra firma, and at first commiserating with his six *F-Freddie* comrades, Brown's eyes eventually settled on the 617 Squadron riggers, fitters, bomb loaders, bowser workers, and WAAFs standing on the sidelines.

"The ground crews of all the aircraft were . . . long-faced, tears running down their cheeks," Brown said. "We couldn't quite believe there were so many missing."[14]

As base personnel began to gather around the surviving Lancasters, it began to dawn on Herbert Jeffree, one of Upkeep's design specialists working with Barnes Wallis, that the station had an unacknowledged problem. Out on the perimeter there sat two parked Lancasters, *W-Willie* and *Y-York*, with two live mines hanging from calipers in their bomb bays. Their combined explosive power, if let loose, posed a legitimate threat. When he dashed to the scene, Jeffree had no way of knowing whether the fuse mechanisms in either of the two Upkeeps were damaged, or whether he needed to sound alarms to evacuate while the mines were carefully defused. When he spotted armourers working on one of the mines, he realized that they had the situation in hand.[15]

MEANWHILE, THOSE MOST RESPONSIBLE FOR OPERATION Chastise—Barnes Wallis, Air Marshal Arthur Harris, and AVM Ralph Cochrane—had travelled from Grantham to Scampton to watch the last of the third-wave Lancasters touch down. This part of post-op—noting the number of surviving aircrew versus those lost on the sortie—was routine for the two RAF commanders. But for Wallis, facing the human balance sheet for a combat operation was entirely new. As an engineer, he rejoiced in knowing that his theories, his designs, and his unique technology had proven themselves on the battlefield. For more than three years he had focused heart and mind on convincing government, military, and corporate decision-makers that he had a significant weapon against Germany's industrial might. But it was only in the final days before the 617 Squadron airmen took off for their targets on the Ruhr that Wallis realized the potential human cost attached to the dams raid. Just hours earlier, he had finally met Gibson's flight leaders—Dinghy Young, Henry Maudslay, John Hopgood, and others among the aircrews—and put faces to their names.

"Where are they?" Wallis kept asking. "Where are all the others?"

Mutt Summers, his long-time friend and test pilot at Vickers, tried to console him. "Oh, they'll be along. Give 'em time."[16]

Ultimately, recognizing that his creation had taken with it eight Lancasters and possibly the lives of their fifty-six men proved shattering to the sensitive scientist.[17] For him, the arithmetic was basic. More than 40 percent of the aircrew members who had volunteered or been assigned to Operation Chastise were gone. The numbers left Wallis distraught. Cochrane tried to reassure Wallis that the "percentage losses" were worthwhile.[18] Harris commented that "Bomber Command in particular and the United Nations as a whole owe everything to you . . . for the outstanding success achieved."[19]

Wallis kept a brave face, mingling with the surviving aircrew through a meal at Scampton. Later in the day, he went to the Vickers factory at Castle Bromwich, then to the Air Ministry offices in London, and finally retreated to his home at Effingham that evening. In the day and a half since he'd briefed the crews, followed their progress from the operations HQ, attended their return home, and done the rounds away from the base and returned home, Wallis had not slept. He was drained physically and emotionally. And he blamed himself for the aircrew casualties.

"For me the success [of the operation] was almost completely blotted out by the sense of loss of these wonderful young lives," Wallis later wrote to Cochrane. "I do hope that all those concerned will feel that the results achieved have not rendered their sacrifice in vain."[20]

Before the aircrews left the perimeter at Scampton airfield, RAF photographers arrived to assemble the men, virtually fresh from their combat operation, for group pictures. One image showed eight of the thirteen Australians who'd participated and survived the raid. In another group photo, fifteen of the twenty-nine Canadians in the operation, and American Joe McCarthy, posed for the camera. They were still in their battle dress, the NCOs with wedge caps and officers with officers' hats. In the shot, taken with a Lancaster's props behind them, prairie gunners Doc Sutherland and Harry O'Brien stood side by side. Bomb aimer Stefan Oancia, pilot Ken Brown, navigators Harlo Taerum and Revie Walker, and flight engineer Bill Radcliffe still had intercom lines strung around their necks, while rear gunners Harvey Weeks, George Deering, and Dave Rodger, navigator Don MacLean, wireless operator Percy Pigeon, and pilot Joe McCarthy still had their Mae Wests slung over their shoulders. A few of the men appeared to be smiling, although more likely it was the bright sunlight making them squint. Absent were their thirteen countrymen killed over occupied Europe just hours before the photo was taken. F/Sgt. Oancia's description of the moment offered an appropriate caption to the image. "I [had] a feeling of great relief," he said, "and tiredness because we'd been under terrific tension for more than twenty hours."[21]

Routine required aircrews to attend a debriefing session. Amid the din of the room, airmen gulped down mugs of coffee or tea. There was a tot of rum available. But the essence of this moment was for intelligence officers to interview crews about the targets, the flak, the mine drop, and any recollection of the downed bombers for the records. In one unfortunate exchange during the debrief, W/C Gibson queried the pilots who had brought home their Upkeep mines, including Les Munro, whose radio was destroyed by flak; Gibson commented critically, "Oh, you were too high," and turned away without giving Munro a chance to respond.[22] For some of the seventy-seven combat-weary airmen, a post-mortem attended by the highest-ranking RAF officers they'd ever seen seemed surreal. Cochrane and Harris even conversed with some of their Chastise bomber crews. Following the Q-and-A session, most aircrew moved off to their respective messes for a morning meal. The mess staff couldn't hold back the tears at the sight of so many empty chairs.

Fred Sutherland relished the chance to enjoy a breakfast of two UK delicacies—bacon and eggs. Then he retired to his NCO barracks to finally sleep. His *N-Nuts* gunnery partner, Harry O'Brien, wasn't ready to rest. "We were excited and wanted to talk about it," he said. "We were just sorry that all the crews hadn't been as lucky as we had been."[23] It was when Sutherland entered the crew barracks, which included a dormitory, that the cost of the raid hit him hard. "Some of us lost roommates and some lost their best friends that night."[24]

The officers on the station had a different mess, where membership was rigidly enforced; their decompression from the raid had a very different atmosphere about it. RCAF F/L Joe McCarthy could barely move through the room, there were so many cases of beer on the anteroom floor, and their numbers grew as the party ramped up. Somebody was dispatched to the WAAF officers' quarters to invite them, whether they cared to or not, to join the festivities.[25] Most did. Meanwhile, McCarthy's rear gunner, F/O Dave Rodger, had run into fellow Canadian officer Doug Warwick, who was with the squadron but not on the raid. Rodger knew Warwick could play the piano and demanded that he provide some music, as up-tempo as possible for as long as possible. "Every time he wanted to quit," Rodger said, "we'd make him play more boogie-woogie."[26]

P/O Harlo Taerum found a quiet moment amid the excitement. He hadn't written to his mother in a few days. His responsibilities for the operation and the demands of his navigational prep aboard Gibson's lead Lancaster had occupied most of his attention and time. Now he composed a page or two and posted them to Hilda Taerum back in Calgary. "It was by far the most thrilling trip I have ever been on, and I wouldn't have missed it for anything. We all got back in the mess about 5:30 in the morning and then we really did relax."[27]

By 8 a.m., the unexpected silence of that Monday morning out on the Scampton airfield struck Canadian sergeant Hugh Munro, one of the station's radar specialists. As they always did when bombers returned from overnight operations, he and other members of the maintenance crews had assembled in No. 2 Hangar, gathering their tools and preparing to head for the field perimeter to assess the state of their squadron's aircraft inventory. Sgt. Munro found it hard to fathom why there were so few Lancasters parked around the station that morning.

"It struck us how quiet it seemed to be at the dispersal points," Munro said. And when they reached the Lancasters parked willy-nilly on the perimeter, they couldn't believe their state, with "flak holes through the fuselage of such a size that you could put your fist through them."[28] Even though Operation Chastise was long over, and with the eleven surviving Lancasters scattered around the base perimeter, Munro still did not know that his aircrews had just returned from a secret overnight raid on the Ruhr River dams. "The vacuum in which we were operating," Munro continued, "soon was filled with the announcement that someone had heard on the radio about the raid."[29]

The world first learned about the dams raid during a public event at the Royal Albert Hall in London that same Monday, May 17. In an event previously arranged by the British government to honour wartime ally Norway on its annual Constitution Day, the secretary of state for air, Sir Archibald Sinclair, rose to address King Haakon VII of Norway and the Crown Prince (then in exile in London).

"I have got great news for you today," Sinclair announced to the dignitaries and hall audience. "Bomber Command, the javelin in our armoury, struck last night a heavy blow of a new kind at the sources of German war power. The two greatest dams in Germany . . . were breached by bombers despatched by Air Chief Marshal Harris. . . . It is a trenchant blow for the victory of the Allies."[30]

Following the secretary's enthusiastic announcement to the Norwegian delegation, the Air Ministry released an official communiqué broadcast by the BBC: "In the early hours of this morning, a force of Lancasters attacked with mines the dams of the Möhne and Sorpe reservoirs. These control two-thirds of the water storage capacity of the Ruhr basin. . . . The Eder dam was also attacked and reported breached."[31]

The press joined the chorus of superlatives the next day. In a lead printed in the *Daily Telegraph* in Manchester and London on May 18, 1943, the newspaper declared, "With one single blow the R.A.F. has precipitated what may prove to be the greatest industrial disaster yet inflicted on Germany in this war." Not to be outdone, the *Illustrated London News* ran a story with the title "A Titanic Blow at Germany; RAF Smash Europe's Mightiest Dams." *Punch* magazine contributed a cartoon with the headline "The Song of the Ruhr," showing three sirens atop rocks about to be submerged by rising floodwaters. The front page of the *Ottawa Evening Journal* employed two-inch-high bold type on its front page, declaring the "Great Ruhr Dams Smashed . . . Tons of Water Sweep Down Valleys." Right below the headline, the paper published a photograph of one of the raid's participants, hometown flyer P/O Lewis Burpee, and the caption "Son of Mr. and Mrs. Lewis A. Burpee has been awarded the D.F.M."[32] The *Journal*'s editors had not yet learned that their hero of the day had died in the operation.

Meanwhile, most newspaper accounts around the world published reconnaissance photographs retrieved by RAF Spitfire pilot F/L Jerry Fray; he'd taken off just after 7 a.m. on May 17 to shoot images of the aftermath of the raid.

FOR THE PEOPLE WHO READ THOSE NEWSPAPERS IN THE days following the raid, Fray's aerial photographs barely began to illustrate the magnitude of the Ruhr River flooding. Black-and-white and one-dimensional, the reconnaissance images depicted the "smashing" and "flooding" described in the news copy from a detached 30,000 feet above the valley. In Fray's words, the scene was "a torrent with the sun shining on it."[33] Closer to the ground, however, the experience proved more catastrophic. Operation Chastise had indeed delivered the devastation intended, in some cases beyond its designers' wildest expectations. Only once in the previous century, during a massive natural flood in 1890, had residents of the Ruhr experienced such high water levels, and not with nearly the force that Chastise had unleashed by breaching the dams.

Below the waterline of the Möhne Dam, the Upkeep mines had torn a hole 249 feet across and seventy-two feet deep. And over the next twelve hours, 4 billion cubic feet of the 4.6-billion-cubic-foot capacity of the reservoir flowed through the breach.[34] The water gush formed a tidal wave thirty-two feet high through the narrow Möhne Valley, and the violence of the torrent destroyed buildings on the floor of the valley for forty miles and bridges for up to thirty-one miles; the breach caused flooding all the way to the junction of the Ruhr and Rhine Rivers, nearly ninety-three miles from the dam.

The destructive power of the Möhne flooding affected water and electricity supplies immediately, effectively washing away the two generating stations at the dam and tossing one of its twenty-ton turbines downriver like a toy. At nearby Günne, two sawmills were washed away. At Neheim, some eight miles from the dam, where the river flowed at its narrowest, the Brokelmann aluminum factory was destroyed, and nearby, a dozen armament factories manufacturing artillery shells, parts for U-boats and aircraft, small arms ammunition, and bunker reinforcement parts were either destroyed or severely damaged.[35] About six miles below Neheim, at Wickede, the Ruhrwerk, Wickede Eisen, and Stahlwerk factories and the Rödinghausen iron foundry were lost and the Soest water-works destroyed. And between Dortmund and Hagen, flood waters caused two railway tunnels to cave in.[36] The dams raid had destroyed eleven factories, severely damaged forty-one others, and slightly damaged thirty-three more.[37]

In the valley immediately below the dam, the deluge caused the greatest number of human casualties; nearly nine hundred people, including French and Belgian POWs, Dutch forced labourers, and Ukrainian women labourers, died in the flooding and destruction of the factory shelters. One Dutch worker heard "a violent rushing sound" as he ran from a bridge over the river for higher ground and then witnessed the bridge, full of people, swept away.[38] A Ukrainian worker responded to the warning alarm and dashed outside, where a guard cut the barbed wire for workers to flee up the hill, but "the water swept people's legs from under them. . . . They were pulling bodies out of the water for a week."[39] Where once had stood the town of Günne, after the flood *Todestal*, or "Death Valley," remained. One witness described the impact on the village of Himmelpforten "as if Niagara Falls had been unleashed"; in the seven-hundred-year-old Porta Coeli chapel, the priest kept ringing the bell in the steeple until "it tipped over and went under with one last muffled clang of the bell."[40]

A similar scene followed the breaching of the Eder Dam, where the Upkeep mines ripped open a V-shaped breach 230 feet across by seventy-two feet deep. Again the resulting deluge was augmented by the presence of 7.1 billion cubic feet of water in the reservoir; the breach unleashed 5.4 billion cubic feet on the valley below, not just for twelve hours, as at the Möhne, but for two full days.[41] The Eder valley stretched wider than the Möhne, and that reduced the overall strength of the water surge, but the greater volume of water still generated a tidal wave that affected towns and industries 250 miles below the dam as well as all the rich farmland—7,413 acres[42]—along its path; the year's planting had either been submerged or washed away.

Right at the Eder itself the flooding immobilized four power stations. A woodyard at Paul disappeared, and at Henschel the floods affected railway works as well as factories manufacturing aeroplane engines and army vehicles. The military airfield at Fritzlar was submerged, and the railway trestle at Giflitz, carrying the main line to Frankfurt, was washed away. The flood halted river transport, since all navigable channels on the Eder became blocked with more than 100,000 cubic feet of silt and the debris from destroyed buildings.[43] Meanwhile, at the Sorpe, while Operation Chastise did not break the dam, enough structural damage occurred that the reservoir had to be drained for repairs. Across the region, transportation of every kind by car, truck, or rail stopped dead as most infrastructure became submerged or eroded. At Herdecke, floodwaters on the Ruhr toppled a complete column of the sixty-year-old railway viaduct, leaving its rails suspended in the air, just as a train approached. Only the quick thinking of passengers, who pulled an emergency brake, saved the train from tumbling into the river gorge.

On Saturday, May 22, a mass funeral procession filled the streets of Fröndenberg, about twelve miles west of the Möhne reservoir. German government officials seized the moment to transform the burial of the town's dead into propaganda supporting the Third Reich. Authorities arranged for gun carriages to transport the coffins—adorned not with crosses but with swastika ribbons—escorted by muffled drums and armed guards to the town cemetery. There, district officials read eulogies that helped to channel the mourners' grief by encouraging the citizens to remain steadfast in their hatred of the Allied bombers, "those great birds of destruction flying over the village."[44] The death toll from the dams breach reached 1,400 people, including German citizens, prisoners of war, and forced labourers. And while the wheels of propaganda turned, so the German Ministry of Armament and War Production began to respond too. Wakened to news of the attack, Reich armaments minister Albert Speer immediately took a reconnaissance flight over the valley to assess its impact.

"[RAF bombers] tried to strike at our whole armaments industry by destroying the hydroelectric plants of the Ruhr," Speer recorded in his report to Hitler. He appeared more impressed with the carcasses of animals strewn along the valley than he was with the human habitation that had disappeared in the deluge. He ordered the immediate installation of protective flak batteries at the remaining German dams. The next day, he met with officials responsible for the delivery of gas, water, and electricity, noting with greatest interest that "the grave consequence [was] that industry was brought to a standstill and the water supply of the population imperiled."[45]

Speer then sought Hitler's approval to dispatch 7,000 workers to the scene to commence the cleanup; more importantly, he requested an additional 20,000 labourers for the rebuilding of the Möhne and Eder infrastructures—roads, bridges, and the dams themselves. By the time the armament minister had returned to Berlin with a complete assessment of damage and a more formal response, he optimistically predicted that all of those armament industries damaged would resume 50 percent production within days and full production within weeks. But neither Speer nor Reich minister for propaganda Joseph Goebbels was prepared to admit how much the shifting of the German workforce required to achieve such a miraculous industrial recovery would affect other vital projects, such as Hitler's high-priority Atlantic Wall along the Dutch and French coastline. Speer noted, as well, that the mobilization of the nation's civil and military engineers—Organisation Todt (OT)—was the first ever call to action within Germany, as opposed to elsewhere in the occupied territories of the Reich. Thus Operation Chastise had levelled one of the first offensive stabs at the Reich's industrial jugular, or what Barnes Wallis had originally described in his *Note* document of 1941 as "rendering the enemy utterly incapable of continuing to prosecute the war."[46]

Further, for days afterward, the dams raid generated significant turmoil among members of the German High Command
of the Armed Forces. Some tried to minimize the attack by
suggesting that "weak British flying formations" had entered
the Ruhr and "dropped a few bombs" that had damaged a
couple of reservoirs. But there was also criticism from within
that the Allied bombers had flown into German territory "and
were not detected" by night fighters or radar, and that only
one of the dams attacked had any anti-aircraft protection.
Goebbels did not point a finger at the Luftwaffe, but instead
at "treachery at work in the Reich," claiming the idea for the
raid had been fed to the RAF by a German Jewish refugee,
although his thesis was generally rejected. Ultimately, perhaps
the greatest reverberation of the dams raid carried to the very
top of the Reich hierarchy, planting doubt and concern in the
mind of the Führer himself. While others downplayed the lack
of Luftwaffe response on May 16–17, Hitler was furious at his
air force for being out of the picture during the entire episode.
And for some time afterward, the Führer referred to the raid
on the dams as "this disaster in the West."[47]

German intelligence did not remain in the dark for very
long about the design, function, or objective of the Upkeep
mines. On the night of the attack, either anti-aircraft batteries or high-tension wire pylons had brought down Lancasters
A-Apple, *B-Baker*, *C-Charlie*, *E-Easy*, *K-King*, *M-Mother*,
S-Sugar, and *Z-Zebra*. While all eight of the lost bombers had
gone down with violent explosions or as flaming infernos,
taking most of their crews (and, in three cases, the Upkeep
mines) to a fiery end, the mine aboard Norman Barlow's
E-Easy had separated from the aircraft but had not exploded.

Consequently, despite every effort by Barnes Wallis, Guy Gibson, Bomber Command, and all the Air Ministry to keep Upkeep under wraps, the years of secrecy evaporated in that unexploded Upkeep 165 feet from the burning wreckage of *E-Easy*. In Britain, MI5 quoted descriptions intercepted from German communications immediately after the raid that spelled out the nature of the bombs; and by early July, German reports showed drawings of the Type 464 Lancaster and its Upkeep mine (or *Britishe Rotations-Wasserbomben*), how it worked, the nature of its explosive, and the means of delivery. Remarkably, the one physical characteristic the early German reports either missed or misunderstood was the purpose of Upkeep's backspin and capacity to bounce on the water.

Nevertheless, Albert Speer put a completely different political spin on the raid, diarizing about the RAF's missed opportunity. "A few bombs would have produced cave-ins at the exposed building sites," Speer hypothesized, "and a few fire bombs would have set the wooden scaffolding blazing."[48]

THE RAF FOUND OTHER WAYS TO CAPITALIZE ON Operation Chastise. During the raid, early on the morning of May 17, when he had confirmation that his aircrews had breached both the Möhne and Eder Dams, Air Marshal Arthur Harris seized the moment and called Washington. Though it was late at night there, Harris felt compelled to convey the news to his prime minister, who was visiting the White House. Eventually he reached chief of the air staff Sir Charles Portal, who was travelling with Winston Churchill, and passed along the news. How auspicious for the political head of the British

Empire, with but a few pyrrhic victories (the Battle of Britain, the Battle of the Atlantic) in three and a half years of war against the Axis powers, to be able to announce to President Franklin D. Roosevelt that the Allies had landed a lethal blow against Nazi Germany's industrial heart. Coupled with the news four days earlier that Tunis had been wrested from the German army and that the Allies "were masters of the North African shore," this allowed Churchill to stand before radio microphones in the US House of Representatives on May 19 and offer a confident declaration that the Allies were on the offensive.[49]

"You have just read of the destruction of the great dams which . . . provide power to the enemy's munition works," Churchill announced during his fifty-minute address. "That was a gallant operation, [making] it impossible for Germany to carry on any form of war industry on a large concentrated scale. . . . We cannot doubt that it is a major factor in the process of victory."[50]

By the time Churchill had addressed politicians in Washington, F/Sgt. Johnny Johnson, *T-Tommy*'s bomb aimer, was enjoying his first leave away from Scampton since the beginning of May. Married to WAAF Gwyn Morgan only a little more than five weeks, Johnson decided to take his wife to the movies in neighbouring Lincoln. On the bus, passengers were all burbling about the latest news from the war—in particular, reports that the RAF had attacked dams deep in Germany. It began to irritate Johnson. "God, I wish they would shut up about it," he said to Gwyn.

"Why?" she asked.

"Because that was us," Johnson said.

"That was you? On the raid?"[51]

Johnson just nodded. It had been his first opportunity to tell her what he'd been up to the past seven weeks, and why he'd been so secretive. Johnson had the good fortune to return to his wife, and Gibson to his, to eventually share with them as much of the story as top-secret protocol allowed. But that wasn't the case for Charlie Brennan, Ken Earnshaw, or John Minchin, the aircrew lost aboard John Hopgood's *M-Mother*, or the skipper of *S-Sugar,* Lewis Burpee; their widows would learn of their husbands' roles in the dams raid for the first time and of their deaths all by way of Gibson's letters of sympathy. Lillian Burpee would give birth to their son on Christmas Eve 1943; she would name him Lewis Jr.

Even though 617 Squadron aircrew had received a week's leave, W/C Guy Gibson remained on the station (he hadn't taken a full leave since serving with 106 Squadron in March) to complete his correspondence to next of kin. While much of the content in the telegrams to loved ones followed a repetitive format, Gibson insisted on including personal observations about each aircrew man in each transmission. Among those telegrams was one he composed to Mary Earnshaw back in Calgary, about her husband, Ken, the navigator who had served with Gibson's close friend John Hopgood aboard *M-Mother*.

"F/O Earnshaw is reported missing as a result of May 16th operations against the big German dams," Gibson wrote. "It is possible that the crew were able to abandon the aircraft and land safely in enemy territory. . . . The captain of your husband's aircraft, F/L Hopgood, was an experienced and able pilot, and would, I'm sure, do everything possible to ensure the safety of his crew."[52]

W/C Gibson, assisted by Adjutant Harry Humphries, took several days to complete the telegrams sent to families of the men lost or missing—some fifty-six in all. In the course of those days when the surviving aircrews were on leave, Scampton station fell into an uncharacteristic wartime silence and stillness. But not for long. By May 20, three days after the raid, AVM Ralph Cochrane had contacted Gibson with the names of the 617 Squadron airmen to be recognized with Air Force citations. Thirty-four men would receive medals—Distinguished Service Orders for five of the pilots, ten Distinguished Flying Crosses, four bars to DFCs, eleven Distinguished Flying Medals, one bar to DFM, three Conspicuous Gallantry Medals, and a Victoria Cross for Gibson himself. But even before the official awards ceremony at Buckingham Palace later in the spring, Gibson learned that the royal couple would pay a visit to Scampton on May 27 to meet and mingle with the surviving aircrew.

Gibson's navigator, Harlo Taerum, captured the moment when he later corresponded with his mother in Calgary. "One morning, they woke me up and told me that I had been awarded the DFC," he wrote to Hilda Taerum. "We were ordered back to our station to meet the King and Queen. They had lunch with us in the officers' mess."[53]

Queen Elizabeth and King George VI arrived at the station about one o'clock and entered the officers' mess. Reverend Donald Hulbert, the padre at the station, presided, but his wife, Vi Hulbert, was asked to decorate the mess and provide the music. She found that mess staff had placed a silver model of a Lancaster in the centre of the main table. "I had several airmen fetch and carry vases and water for me," she said, "and I arranged a ring of displays in small deep red roses 'round the centre of this."[54] Then she assembled a choir of fifty people from the Suffolk parish, along with WAAFs and aircrew from the station, to provide accompaniment. After lunch, the King and Queen visited the ops room and examined F/L Fray's reconnaissance photos of the Ruhr before and after the raid. W/C Gibson showed the royals one of the briefing models he'd revealed to the aircrews the day of the raid. Gesticulating with his hands over the model, Gibson showed King George how each Lancaster had made its low-level attack on the dam.

Outside on the Scampton airfield, ground crew had painted straight white lines on the turf, like football field sidelines, to keep the inspection orderly. The dams raid crews organized themselves in lines behind their skippers; each of the pilots placed his toes on the white line and waited to be introduced to the royals as they passed. Official RAF cameras flashed and Pathé newsreel cameras rolled during the entire proceeding to capture the exchanges between aircrew and monarchs. When Gibson introduced the King to F/L Dave Shannon, he added that it was Shannon's twenty-first birthday. "You seem to be a very well preserved twenty-one," the King observed. "You must have a party tonight."[55]

The Queen followed along the white inspection line, oddly accompanied by an officer who did not know any of the airmen by name. When he came to P/O Les Knight and spotted his Australian shoulder flash, the escorting officer introduced him as a newcomer. "Settling down nicely?" the Queen asked politely.[56]

In front of F/L Les Munro, the officer again didn't know who he was. "Munro's my name," the New Zealander piped up.

The Queen also met the newly commissioned Harlo Taerum, Gibson's navigator, who was clearly overwhelmed by the experience, describing the Queen as "most charming and gracious." Writing his mother later he said, "It was really quite a day."[57]

During the visit, W/C Gibson showed King George two potential designs for a new squadron crest. One depicted a hammer severing chains that encumbered a figure representing Europe, and the motto "Alter the Map." The second showed three bolts of lightning breaking a dam and the words "*Après moi le déluge*," an apparent misquote from Madame de Pompadour's alleged declaration, "*Après nous le déluge*" (after us, the flood). King George appeared amused by the misquote but endorsed the second crest and motto as his preference anyway.

The festivities continued several weeks later, on June 21, when those designated to receive military decorations travelled by special train from Scampton for an overnight stay in London, and then to Buckingham Palace the next day for the investiture. Parties filled the night in London, but hangovers didn't appear to interfere with the palace ceremony the next day, when the Queen pinned the awards on 617 Squadron recipients, beginning with Guy Gibson's VC and the bar to his DSO; at that moment he became the most decorated airman in the Royal Air Force. Among the others recognized, seven RCAF airmen received honours: Distinguished Flying Crosses to front gunner F/Sgt. George Deering and navigator P/O Harlo Taerum; bar to the DFC to navigator F/O Revie Walker; Distinguished Service Order to pilot F/L Joe McCarthy; Conspicuous Gallantry Medal to pilot F/Sgt. Ken

Brown; and Distinguished Flying Medals to bomb aimer F/Sgt. Stefan Oancia and navigator F/Sgt. Don MacLean.

Red tape caused a hiccup in the process for MacLean. He learned that the Air Force had not processed his commission paperwork quickly enough; technically he had flown on the dams raid as a flying officer, though his rank had remained flight sergeant. Adjutant Harry Humphries offered to have MacLean's DFM changed to a DFC, consistent with his rank during Operation Chastise.

"Hell no!" MacLean said, and when photographers asked MacLean to pose for publicity shots, he insisted, along with his pilot, F/L McCarthy, and rear gunner, F/O Rodger, that his NCO crewmates Bill Radcliffe, Len Eaton, Johnny Johnson, and Ron Batson be included. And his skipper reciprocated. McCarthy refused to fly any aircraft without MacLean as its navigator; despite having Radcliffe's lucky panda mascot aboard their flights, the pilot considered MacLean his real lucky charm.

More celebrations followed the palace investiture when Lancaster manufacturer A.V. Roe staged a dinner and reception for the 617 Squadron award recipients. The thirty-four men were taken to the Hungaria Restaurant on Lower Regent Street for dinner and salutations; the menu headline read "The Damn Busters." Air Force brass Ralph Cochrane and Charles Whitworth attended, as did others involved in the bouncing-bomb design, including Mutt Summers, Roy Chadwick, and Barnes Wallis. Cigars and speeches followed dinner, when Gibson acknowledged all those from the squadron, and Wallis in particular for his work on Upkeep. Next to the dining tables, an easel displayed an aerial photograph of the breached Möhne

Dam and the empty Möhne reservoir that Wallis had been asked to bring to the dinner. Gibson autographed the image, as did other 617 Squadron aircrew. Wallis later wrote, "The shores of the empty reservoir are now adorned by signatures of the crews . . . a historical record of this outstanding accomplishment on the part of the R.A.F."[58]

NOT DEPICTED IN THE RECONNAISSANCE PHOTOGRAPH, but certainly on the minds of those celebrating that June night in London, was the crash site of Operation Chastise bomber *M-Mother*. Courageously piloted by John Hopgood until the blaze that was consuming the crippled aircraft finally tore it apart, the Lancaster's ascent away from the Möhne had allowed two of its aircrew—bomb aimer John Fraser and rear gunner Tony Burcher—to parachute to safety. F/Sgt. Fraser* managed to evade German ground forces and police for ten days, enabling him to travel some two hundred miles toward Holland. When he was captured near the Rhine River, the first stage of his interrogation took him to Dulag Luft, where he was held in solitary confinement for a week.

"Finally they found out where I'd come from," Fraser said. "And a German officer said this [dams] raid had accomplished as much damage as a hundred normal air raids. . . . I felt pretty darn good."[59]

---

* Most of John Fraser's records associated with the dams raid cite him as "flight sergeant" when in fact Air Force officials had awarded him a commission on April 12, 1943, a month before Operation Chastise. Consequently, German interrogators at Dulag Luft sent him to a prisoner-of-war camp for NCOs; in the spring of 1944, when his pilot officer rank caught up to him, the Luftwaffe transferred him to a POW camp for officers, Stalag Luft III, where the Great Escape had occurred on March 24.

News of the dams raid arrived at the home of rear gunner Jimmy McDowell in Port Arthur, Ontario, making an already tough day tougher. Jimmy's wife, Dorothea, and two young daughters had gathered for a wake following the death of Dorothea's sister Nora from cancer. As Dorothea served tea to the mourners, on May 18, 1943, a boy in a Canadian National uniform arrived by bicycle at their front door with a telegram. F/Sgt. McDowell was reported missing.

Word of her father's disappearance in an RAF bombing raid hit eight-year-old Marilyn especially hard. She recalled the night before her father left Port Arthur to rejoin his RCAF comrades for the transatlantic voyage to Britain in the summer of 1942; Marilyn couldn't resist.

"I curled up inside my father's sheepskin-lined flying suit on the floor and slept in it that last night," she said. The following day, as he was leaving for the train, Jimmy McDowell heard Vera Lynn on the radio singing "The White Cliffs of Dover." When Lynn sang, "And Jimmy will go to sleep in his own little room again," Marilyn remembered her father saying softly, "No, I won't."

McDowell's body was found floating in the Waddenzee near Harlingen, Holland, where his Lancaster *K-King* was shot down and sank on the outbound trip of Operation Chastise, on May 16, 1943. All seven crewmen on board had died. [60]

CHAPTER NINE

THE OP TOO FAR

I T WAS THE LAST PLACE HE WANTED TO BE. BUT ON this day, September 11, 1943, it was the first place he had to be. Standing tall, arms crossed in his Royal Air Force service dress uniform, his officer's hat pushed back slightly on his head and looking every inch the war hero he had become, W/C Guy Gibson leaned toward two microphones placed before him on the reviewing stand. One was connected to the public-address system at the military airfield; the other was about to broadcast his comments locally over radio station CFAC in Calgary, Alberta. Nearly encircling him on the podium sat military and civic dignitaries, including AVM G.R. Howsam and W/C C.F. Falkenberg, both of the Royal Canadian Air Force; Lieutenant G.R. McKay of HMCS *Tecumseh*, Royal Canadian Navy; and Andrew Davison, the mayor of Calgary.

Gibson would just as soon have been flying another op over Germany as be standing at microphones on a western Canadian airfield. Anywhere but here, he must have thought, was more appropriate for a leader of a combat squadron.

Calgary had buzzed all week in anticipation of his appearance. The *Calgary Herald* and the *Morning Albertan* had published the itinerary of his visit, the time of his address, and a list of those participating in the march past of Air Force personnel at Currie Airfield, home of RCAF No. 3 Service Flying Training School. All that Saturday, CFAC Radio had counted down the hours until the decorated wing commander arrived at this command headquarters of the British Commonwealth Air Training Plan. At 5 p.m., W.R. Irwin, CO of No. 3 SFTS, had ordered the security gates unlocked and opened to the public. Hundreds of civilians had strolled onto the tarmac and up to the flight line to get as close as possible to the yellow BCATP training aircraft—all neatly lined up for the special visit. Then, at six o'clock, an inbound military aircraft had touched down on the airfield runway, taxied to the flight line, and disgorged Guy Gibson—VC, DSO and bar, DFC and bar—there to represent 617 Squadron on a two-day ceremonial stopover in Calgary.

As excited as Air Force brass, city officials, and the media seemed about the visit, nobody felt the nervous excitement over Gibson's impending arrival more than the lone female member of the reception party waiting on the tarmac. Hilda Taerum had travelled from her home in the city out to Currie barracks that afternoon. Dressed in her light-coloured, trimly cut victory suit and lady's homburg, the bespectacled Mrs. Taerum smiled nervously amid the attention that suddenly came her way as the dignitaries arrived at the base and emerged from the Air Force transport. This was a moment Gibson had also anticipated from the beginning of his cross-Canada publicity trip.

"I'm awfully glad to meet you." Gibson smiled as he shook Hilda Taerum's hand there on the tarmac.[1] Newspaper reporters and Air Force photographers snapped pictures of Hilda Taerum responding in kind. She knew she was expected to speak, but not until called upon at the podium in the formal portion of the proceedings. "You are the living image of him, you know," Gibson continued, "or should I say he is the living image of you?"

Gibson was certainly in a position to know. He'd spent a significant portion of the spring—day and night—seated mere feet from Harlo Taerum, Hilda's son. For seven extraordinary weeks, from the end of March to mid-May, the two young aviators had shared the business end of a Lancaster bomber— Gibson as pilot, Taerum as navigator—preparing and carrying out the dams raid in the industrial heartland of Nazi Germany. Even four months after the fact, newspaper reporters and broadcasters were still eager to interview and feature members of the dam busters raid. Accordingly, Prime Minister Winston Churchill had dispatched W/C Gibson on a goodwill trip to North America, first to take a bow for his accomplishment, and then to state that Britain had turned the corner in this war. From then on, Churchill's unofficial envoy was encouraged to state unequivocally that the British Commonwealth and its allies were on the offensive.

Indeed, as he introduced Guy Gibson on the reviewing stand at the Calgary airfield that September evening, AVM Howsam wasted no time getting to the heart of his own pep talk. Howsam gestured to the BCATP aircraft, the personnel, and the barracks of the aircrew training facility around him and looked back to Gibson. "You have come here to tell our instructors and air crews things which they are very anxious to know," he said. "These are the things they are going to do in the future, like dam-busting, Cologne-busting, Hamburg-busting and finally busting Hitler's phony fortress of Europe," Howsam added.[2]

When it was his turn, Gibson spoke equally deliberately. Having been feted right across the country over the previous four weeks, the words rolled off his tongue perfectly. He kindly thanked Mayor Davison and the public for "coming out to look at me." Then, to curry favour from his Calgary audience, he added, "This is the first welcome of this type I have had since coming to Canada and I deeply appreciate it."[3]

Mindful of his audience beyond the microphones, W/C Gibson first offered greetings from the British prime minister and from all aircrew in Bomber Command, still fiercely focused on targets in enemy-occupied Europe. He noted that during a press conference held in Ottawa the previous month, Canadian prime minister Mackenzie King had referred to Gibson as the "dam buster." While it was not an original nickname, the wing commander was quick to transfer King's enthusiastic praise to all of his 617 comrades-in-arms. Repeatedly throughout the weeks-long tour he had handled questions from reporters about the death-defiance of the dams raid. He'd offered that every member of the Operation Chastise combat group had felt that "[dying] will not happen to me."

"But that raid on the dams was the one time . . . when you . . . when we knew that we were going to die, or not die, as the case may be," Gibson said. "You know, the hair which was hanging on our life was very thin. And then there's just a feeling of . . . a funny, empty feeling in the stomach, but not frightened."[4]

Such comments were perhaps the most candid the seemingly invincible RAF wing commander revealed during his whirlwind tour of North America. Since disembarking from the *Queen Mary* at Halifax, Nova Scotia, on August 4, the five-times-decorated wing commander had addressed banquets, fielded questions at Canadian government press conferences, and engaged in private conversations with Prime Ministers King and Churchill and President Franklin D. Roosevelt. He'd dashed to New York for a broadcast on WJZ Radio, visited recruiting centres, and survived motorcades and public appearances in Montreal and Toronto and at training stations all across western Canada. In Winnipeg, Gibson took time to visit the family of Harvey Glinz, the front gunner killed aboard Norman Barlow's *E-Easy* when it was lost on the dams raid. Still, the essence of his message to the audience of dignitaries and the public in Calgary was, as it had been at every stop, positive. Gibson assured Canadians that their families' commitment to the war effort had not gone unnoticed and that the dividend of their service and sacrifice would ultimately be realized.

"The creed of the bomber command is to hit Germany hard and thereby shorten the war," Gibson emphasized to his audience and the press. "There is no difference between a Canadian, an Englishman, a New Zealander or anyone else [in this war]. We are all . . . fighting under the same flag, against the same enemy and with the same planes. We're all damn good. That's why we're winning this war."[5]

At that point during his outdoor address, Gibson paused and turned to face Hilda Taerum, warmly indicating for any who didn't already know that the woman seated before them was the mother of the now famous Calgary Dam Buster Harlo

Taerum, whom Gibson and his squadron mates called "Terry" for short.

"Terry is a great boy," Gibson said across the microphones to Mrs. Taerum. "And a great navigator. He got the whole squadron to the dam."[6]

Hilda Taerum could not have beamed more proudly. She later told reporters that W/C Gibson's build, demeanour, and even his voice had reminded her of Harlo's mannerisms. It was the next best thing to having her son there, she said. And even if she recognized some exaggeration in Gibson's compliment—that the twenty-three-year-old navigator had personally directed all the Lancasters to their targets on May 16–17—Hilda Taerum could feel genuine pride in her son's skill and accomplishments. But now it was her turn to speak. All this time, she'd held the neatly folded eight-line speech she'd prepared for Gibson in her purse. Finally, invited to the PA and broadcast microphones, she unfolded her note and offered her tribute to the man, his mission, and his comrade-in-arms.

"I am really very thrilled," she said, looking straight back at Gibson. "I have been looking forward to meeting you. I feel as though I have known you for some time. Harlo has said so much about you in letters."[7]

Gibson responded with another warm nod. The thought likely crossed his mind that unless Allied censors had failed in their capacity to black out or cut out the names of officers, their locations, and their activities from servicemen's mail, an accurate description of the people at Scampton, the base of operations for 617 Squadron in Lincolnshire, England, and their wartime work would never have been allowed to get out, much less be shared with a navigator's mother in Canada.

"When you go back to England, Wing Commander Gibson, tell Harlo that we are all well at home," Hilda Taerum said finally. "This has been a real privilege, and one I will never forget."[8]

Tour organizers had scheduled a brief pause in the wing commander's hectic itinerary. Gibson spent part of the next day sightseeing around Banff in the Rocky Mountains. Later that Sunday, he met with Hilda Taerum again. At her home, away from the cameras and microphones, they had a more comfortable talk about events leading up to and including the dams raid. Gibson was able to share with her some of his impressions of the awards presentations that had followed in June at Buckingham Palace. Mrs. Taerum pulled out a prized album, full of wartime news stories, photographs, and letters from her son; she pointed out the one with an account of the aftermath of the raid. "We were just about mobbed for autographs afterward. The next thing was five days of leave in London . . . so we really had a time," Harlo Taerum had written his mother.[9]

Just before Gibson said his goodbyes, Hilda Taerum invited her son's CO to autograph the album full of clippings and correspondence. And since she'd also received several new photographs of the event at the Calgary training station the previous day, she asked Gibson to sign those as well; he obliged and then departed. That same day, Gibson took time to visit another Air Force family with a connection to the dams raid. LAC Robert Young was in the midst of his service training at No. 3 SFTS in Calgary. The recruit's older brother, S/L Melvin "Dinghy" Young, had piloted another 617 Squadron Lancaster that delivered its payload against the Ruhr Valley dams on May 16–17,

1943, but was subsequently shot down over the North Sea en route home. The sting of the dams raid losses, it seemed, was an ever-present part of Gibson's goodwill itinerary.

And the sting would return. Less than a week after W/C Gibson's visit to Calgary and his meeting with a most grateful Hilda Taerum, she received a telegraph hand-delivered from Canadian Pacific:

> REGRET TO ADVISE THAT YOUR SON FLYING OFFI-
> CER TORGER HARLO TAERUM DFC J ONE SIX SIX
> EIGHT EIGHT IS REPORTED MISSING AFTER AIR
> OPERATIONS SEPTEMBER FIFTEEN STOP LETTER
> FOLLOWS RCAF CASUALTIES OFFICER.[10]

So soon after the upbeat visit by W/C Gibson and all its positive coverage at the training base, on radio, and in the news-papers, Harlo Taerum was back in the headlines at home. "Calgary's Dam Buster Is Reported Missing," the local stories announced.[11] When Gibson learned that F/O Taerum was missing in action, he was in Montreal and immediately wired Mrs. Taerum at her home in Calgary*; he paid tribute to his navigator yet again, telling his mother, "He was a first-class man."[12]

THE BATTLE OF THE RUHR, WHICH HAD INCLUDED THE dams raid, continued into the middle of July 1943. The sta-

---

* For Hilda Taerum, the painful telegrams did not end with notification of her son Harlo's death. In February 1944, Hilda received word that her other son, Lorne, also an RCAF airman, had died on his first combat operation, when his Lancaster was shot down over Nijmegen, Holland.

tistics from the onslaught against the German industrial heart were staggering. Over 141 days and nights, Bomber Command had sent bomber operations to the Ruhr ninety-nine times at night and fifty-five times in daylight, for a total of 24,355 sorties, or bomber trips. The operations had dropped over 57,000 tons of bombs on the Ruhr centres and had sustained the loss of 1,038 aircraft, or 4.3 percent of its force.[13] By the end of the summer, Arthur Harris had called a pause in the Battle of the Ruhr, next focusing his attention on the larger German cities of Hamburg (in the late summer) and Berlin (in the fall).

But as W/C Gibson toured North America, the Dam Buster squadron, under new commander S/L George Holden, had not flown again until July 15–16, when it attacked electrical transformer stations in northern Italy; Arthur Harris had decided to keep 617 Squadron focused on what he called "independent precision raids."[14] And while that designation appeared to pay the veterans of the Dam Buster squadron all due respect, it also had a downside. Some Bomber Command squadrons, which continued to fly several operations a week, resented 617's favoured status. One 617 airman even composed a lament, including the lines: " . . . since [the dams] operation, 617's been a flop / And we've got the reputation of the squadron with one op."[15]

On August 30, 1943, the Dam Buster squadron had moved its Lancasters from the grass airfield at Scampton, a few miles away, to the long bitumen runways at Coningsby so that its bombers could take off with heavier bomb loads. A special new op was in the wind for 617. Amid a similar kind of secrecy that had preceded the dams raid, large trucks began arriving with tarpaulins draping their explosive contents. These were new, 12,000-pound, thin-cased, high-capacity "Blockbuster" bombs, the largest the RAF had ever carried, and they were designed to sever yet another industrial artery in Germany's industrial Ruhr Valley. By September 14, S/L Holden had drawn up plans for eight Lancaster crews to make a second low-level attack, this time on the critical Dortmund-Ems Canal, 150 miles of artificial waterway linking the Ruhr Valley to the sea, which that year carried thirty-three million tons of freight.

Near Ladbergen, the canal had an elevated section of aqueducts that carried the canal water over a river. Bomber Command had long considered this exposed stretch of the canal a high-priority target but had neither a bomb large enough nor a delivery system powerful enough to strike it. With the success of 617's dams raid four months earlier, and a new weapon three times the size of a normal 4,000-pound Lancaster "cookie," S/L Holden thought he now had the tools. He expected that at low altitude his experienced Lanc crews could drop the heavier bombs into the soft earthen walls of the aqueducts and, with delayed fuses giving the bombers sufficient time to climb out of harm's way, breach the canal walls. Military intelligence told Holden the canal was heavily defended, so the Lancasters, using the existing twenty-two-foot-long bomb bay for transport and delivery of the bomb, carried three gunners on this operation: a full-time front gunner, a mid-upper gunner, and a rear gunner.

The plan also called for RAF Nos. 418 and 605 Squadrons to provide Mosquito fighters to minimize the impact of enemy searchlights, flak batteries, and night fighters, and to lead the bombers to the target. With the bomber force divided in two, each section of four Lancasters and three Mosquitos would take a different route east, crossing the English coast at 1,500 feet and then descending to one hundred feet over the North Sea. When the Lancasters arrived over the canal, they would home in on marking beacons, fly about 150 feet off the ground to the target at a speed of 180 miles per hour, and drop their bombs within forty feet of the western bank of the canal. The Blockbuster fuses would delay each explosion from twenty-six to ninety seconds, enough time for the aircraft to fly clear of the blast.[16] If they breached the Dortmund-Ems Canal and caused the canal's water to drain away, the Ruhr munitions plants would not receive vital coal fuel, making it impossible to deliver prefabricated U-boats to the sea. The attack would again take place at night and it would repeat the dams raid's low-level flying tactics. But the operation would undoubtedly face tougher flak-battery opposition along the perimeter of the canal.

As skipper of Gibson's former crew, S/L Holden would lead the first section of four Lancasters in tandem with veteran pilot Les Knight, who had breached the Eder Dam on May 17, and newcomer pilots Ralf Allsebrook and Harold Wilson in the other three aircraft. David Maltby, who had successfully attacked the Möhne Dam on May 17, would lead two other veteran pilots of the dams raid, David Shannon and Geoff Rice, along with newly arrived Bill Divall, in the second section of four Lancs. Maltby had the additional responsibility of dropping the parachute beacons marking the target. Operation Garlic was scheduled for the night of September 14, 1943.

The weather was iffy that evening, and when a weather Mosquito crew discovered the canal target shrouded in fog, it contacted group headquarters, which radioed both waves of the strike force to return to Coningsby. S/L Maltby's Lancaster was low over the North Sea when the recall came. He turned for home but quickly got into trouble. One account reported that the wingtip of Maltby's bomber clipped the surface of the water; another suggested that a Mosquito on a completely different sortie (from which it never returned) collided with the Lancaster.[17] Whatever the cause of the crash, the aircraft plunged into the sea and disappeared. Shannon's crew circled the spot and directed rescue operations, but no survivors were found, just one body, that of S/L David Maltby DSO DFC, veteran of thirty-two combat operations and, at twenty-one, a hero of the dams raid. The remaining seven Lancasters and six Mosquitos returned safely to Coningsby, and S/L Holden paid a requisite visit to Maltby's widow, Nina. "It was quick," Holden explained to her. "He wouldn't have known a thing."[18]

Operation Garlic went from bad to worse. The next night, September 15, the weather appeared favourable. Skies were clear and moonlit, very much like the night of the dams raid. With the addition of the third gunner in the restored mid-upper gun position on all the Lancasters for the Dortmund-Ems op, each of the 617 crews had to get acquainted with a new crewman. Front gunner Fred Sutherland said that he and the rest of Les Knight's crew first met their new mid-upper gunner, F/Sgt. Les Woollard, when he was assigned to the canal raid that week.

"He obviously had some experience because one of the

first things he did for good luck was to go and have a pee on the tail wheel. We rushed to stop him," said Doc Sutherland, whose crewmates had previously decided to omit such a ritual, since they each had their own routines. "I always ate my chocolate bar when we were charging down the runway, and I always wore the same socks that my girlfriend [Margaret] had knitted for me."[19] But Woollard's urinating on the tailwheel was clearly a departure, and maybe an omen.

As darkness descended on the airfield, the new flight of eight Operation Garlic Lancasters, each carrying its Blockbuster bomb, rose from the runways at Coningsby. The two flights formed up in boxes of four and crossed the North Sea just fifty feet above the water to evade radar and shore batteries as they entered Dutch airspace. S/L Holden was again in the leading Lancaster as skipper to Guy Gibson's crew, which included dams raid veterans navigator Harlo Taerum, wireless operator Robert Hutchison, bomb aimer Fred Spafford, and gunner George Deering. As Holden's group of four Lancs approached the town of Nordhoorn, just inside the German border, the squadron leader chose to climb to clear a church steeple rather than veer around it at the same altitude. The others followed— Mick Martin to the right (joining the op in place of Maltby), Les Knight to the left, and Harold Wilson following. Those precious feet of sky above the steeple revealed the bombers in the moonlight, and a light battery immediately opened fire. From the front-gunner's blister in Knight's Lancaster, Fred Sutherland watched Holden's gunner fire back, but the damage was already done; German anti-aircraft shells had penetrated Holden's starboard wing tank and flames quickly shot back as far as the tailplane.

"Flames were coming up between [Holden's] ailerons," Sutherland said, and he watched in horror as the stricken Lancaster crashed and was engulfed in the explosion of the Blockbuster bomb aboard. Sutherland had little time to think of his lost dams raid comrades—Robert Hutchison, Fred Spafford, and fellow Canadians Harlo Taerum and George Deering—because shortly afterward a new enemy entered the field. "Suddenly we were in heavy ground fog."[20]

In the gathering mist, none of the aircrews could actually see the canal wall they were supposed to bomb until they were right over it, and by then it was too late to drop the Blockbuster accurately. Still, the more manoeuvrable Mosquitos began darting back and forth over the canal, trying to draw fire and silence the German anti-aircraft batteries. Meanwhile, the remaining seven Lancasters moved into a circuit about 150 feet above the canal; that altitude gave them a fighting chance to spot the canal walls, but it also made them more vulnerable to the flak batteries. Each of the Lancasters tried repeatedly to find an accurate bombing run to the target. But one by one the big bombers either disappeared into the fog or were lost to ground fire.

As F/L Wilson flew low over the target, his Lancaster was hit by flak; he managed a belly landing, but in the resulting crash all eight aircrew were killed. F/L Allsebrook dropped his bomb and then tried to direct the others to the target, but he too was shot down with all lost. P/O Divall tried to complete the operation but also went down with the loss of all crew. P/O Rice's crew searched for the target for an hour and took plenty of flak but eventually jettisoned their bomb wide of the target and flew home. F/L Shannon's crew spent seventy minutes doing the same before finally dropping the explosive; it missed the canal wall. F/L Martin's crew hit the canal at its midpoint, but the canal walls withstood the shock.

In their passes over the canal, Fred Sutherland and the rest of Les Knight's seasoned crew sat tight as their pilot edged lower and lower through the fog, trying to find a visible and accurate path to the target.

"I was about to say, 'I think we should be down a little lower,'" Sutherland said, "and we hit some treetops along the banks of the canal."[21] From his front-turret position, he could see that the radiators had been sheared off the two port Merlin engines and coolant was pouring out. Then, as Knight shut down the damaged motors, Sutherland recognized that the propeller blades were bent and useless. With the remaining starboard engines straining and Knight trying with all his strength to keep the bomber straight and level, Sutherland calmly opened up his radio microphone to communicate with his superior officer. "Two engines gone," he reported to his flight leader, Mick Martin. "Permission to jettison bomb, sir?"[22]

"For God's sake, Les," Martin called. "Yes!"

Releasing the Blockbuster helped. With the 12,000 pounds gone, the stricken Lancaster slowly ascended. Knight called on his rear gunner, Harry O'Brien (the biggest and strongest member of the crew), to come forward to the bomb-aimer's compartment below the cockpit to help Knight put pressure on the rudder pedals on the floor from below. P/O Knight turned his crippled bomber toward Holland and, he hoped, a run for an emergency landing in England. By this time, most of the bomber's aircrew had recognized that its only salvation would be gaining altitude. Knight called on two of his three gunners,

Sutherland and Woollard, to leave their stations, go aft, and start jettisoning equipment. The two men began hauling guns, ammunition, and anything that wasn't secured toward the crew door to be thrown from the bomber as quickly as possible. But their pilot knew, even when he managed to coax his aircraft above a thousand feet, that the Lancaster's starboard engines were overheating dangerously. Getting home seemed pretty much out of the question.

"We can't get back," Knight told his crew over the bomber's intercom. "We'll have to bail out."[23]

One by one, Knight's aircrew strapped on their parachutes and prepared to exit the plane—navigator Sidney Hobday, wireless operator Robert Kellow, and bomb aimer Edward "Johnny" Johnson. Then the rear gunner, Harry O'Brien, jumped. Left beside the skipper was flight engineer Ray Grayston. Because Fred Sutherland and Les Woollard had taken off their headsets to pitch the excess weight from the bomber, they hadn't heard their skipper's "bail out" order. When Sutherland had thrown as much as he could out the crew door, he put on a nearby intercom headset.

"Les, are we going to ditch?" asked Sutherland, thinking they were over water.

"Yeah, get ready," Knight answered.

By this time Sutherland had come forward in the fuselage to a blackout curtain over a blister; he ripped it away and saw that the bomber was still over land. "Les, what's going on?"

"Get ready," Knight called again to his gunner, then, "Jump!"

Doc didn't waste a moment. He and Woollard donned their parachutes and bailed out. Sutherland exited through the rear door of the aircraft. He knew there wasn't much room between the exit and the tailplane and was afraid he'd hit it or get his parachute tangled in it when he jumped. He skinned his knees going through the door but missed the tailplane. The seventh man of eight to jump was flight engineer Ray Grayston.[24] That left Knight alone in the bomber, desperately hanging on to the controls to keep the aircraft level. Because of the difficulty that Knight had experienced manoeuvring the aircraft on two engines and with a damaged airframe, Sutherland sensed that the second Knight released the stick, the bomber would flip uncontrollably into a dive and the pilot would have little chance of escaping. Ultimately, as Sutherland's parachute opened and he focused on the bomber a quarter of a mile ahead of him in the night, he watched Knight attempt to crash-land the bomber in an open pasture.

"Everybody got out except Les," Sutherland said, noting his pilot's extraordinary skill and disregard for his own safety. "He tried to land it and hit this ditch. Broke his neck."[25]

DAVE SHANNON'S LANCASTER WAS THE FIRST TO LAND back at Coningsby. He reported the losses of Allsebrook's, Wilson's, and Divall's aircraft and crews. Then Rice's bomber showed up. And two hours later, Martin's bomber—the third of eight on the raid—landed safely. By that time, AVM Ralph Cochrane knew Martin's would be the last one home. F/L Martin apologized to his commanding officer that none of the operation's crews had succeeded in breaching the canal wall, and he offered to lead those who remained from the original dams raid squadron against the canal yet again the next night.

When Cochrane asked how many members of the squadron remained, Martin said three crews from his flight and three from Dave Shannon's flight. "Six out of your original twenty-one," Cochrane said.[26]

Martin again indicated his regret that the squadron had missed the target; his superiors told Martin to get some rest. There was some discussion about promoting Martin to wing commander to lead the remaining 617 aircrew, but as the Group commanders debated the notion and decided that Martin should become interim squadron leader, Martin mused aloud about the fate of his once glorious Dam Buster squadron. "Two real ops, and six crews left," Martin said. "Maybe this is the end. They'll make us an ordinary line squadron . . . or disband us altogether."[27]

It didn't take a CO to recognize that the Dortmund-Ems Canal raid had been not only a failure but also a devastating loss for one of Bomber Command's most celebrated squadrons. With the crash of David Maltby's Lancaster and the loss of his entire crew on September 14, and the loss of five of eight Lancaster crews on September 15—including most of Guy Gibson's decorated dams raid crew—the casualty list had decimated 617 Squadron. In two nights, Operation Garlic had killed forty-one of the squadron's aircrew, made two others prisoners of war, and left five more on the run in occupied Europe. Ultimately, the failure to breach the Dortmund-Ems Canal illustrated to Bomber Command very clearly that low-altitude bombing by Lancasters had become far too costly an enterprise.

Throughout the Second World War thus far, the RAF had attempted only two such risky operations—the dams raid and the canal raid; only one had succeeded. Even though two targets on the Ruhr River had been breached and another damaged on May 16–17, eight of nineteen bombers had not returned. And without any damage inflicted during the September 14–15 raids on the Dortmund-Ems Canal, the squadron, including replacement crews, had lost six of nine aircraft and most of their crews. Over only two ops, then, 617 Squadron had lost fourteen of twenty-eight aircraft—an attrition rate of exactly 50 percent.[28]

The dismal statistics that his commanders considered back at Coningsby were of little concern to Fred Sutherland, however. In the middle of the night on September 15, the front gunner from Lancaster AJ-N had parachuted down into a Dutch pasture, not far from where his bomber and his beloved pilot had met their end. Sutherland knew he'd had the opportunity to bail out, land safely, and perhaps get away only because Les Knight had flown his last sortie so skilfully. And though he felt scared like never before in his life, Doc Sutherland was determined to make a go of it. He hid in a forest until he could confirm that he was in Holland, and then approached a woman on a farm and called out to her. When she'd recovered from the shock of encountering a downed airman, she found a schoolboy who knew enough English to connect Sutherland with the Dutch Underground. Their operatives eventually led Fred and his navigator, Sid Hobday, to an Underground contact, Henk Lindeman, who forged travel papers and fitted them with clothing that would convince German guards the two airmen were labourers on their way from Rotterdam to Paris.[29]

To get them there, they chose a train that was so crowded that the disguised airmen and their Dutch guide would disappear among the other passengers aboard. The imposters sat on the floor near the entrance to a toilet and faked an inability to hear or speak.

"Anybody in there?" people approaching the facility would point and ask.

Sutherland would nod when it was occupied or shake his head when it was vacant. He seemed to blend into the routine aboard the coach. The Dutch Underground had supplied him with identification papers that indicated he was travelling across France to the Cherbourg area to work on German coastal fortifications. At one point, a guard took his papers and held them up against the light. "It was all I could do to keep from running," Sutherland said.[30]

It occurred to him later that if the German authorities had bothered to check his hands—which didn't feature any of the cuts, bruises, or calluses typical of a labourer's hands—they would have recognized right away that he was masquerading. Instead, he and about fifteen other British and American airmen on the run managed to make their way to Toulouse and eventually to the edge of the Pyrenees Mountains and the Chemin de la Liberté (Freedom Trail). Crossing the mountain range into Spain, Sutherland gave the only good pair of shoes he had to Bill Woods, an American B-17 airman. Doc paid for the sacrifice by getting blisters on his own feet, barely managing to get himself through the mountain trails. At long last he made it to Gibraltar and completed his "home run" aboard a Liberator back to Britain. On his arrival, Sutherland sent a cable to his family and his fiancée, Margaret, back in Peace River, Alberta, to let them know he was "safe and sound." He'd successfully evaded capture for nearly three months.

* * *

ON SEPTEMBER 25, 1943—JUST TEN DAYS AFTER FRED Sutherland's Lancaster was shot down over the Dortmund-Ems Canal—Organisation Todt completed repair of the breach in the Möhne Dam caused by 617 Squadron's attack. It had taken OT seventy-nine days to complete the work (repairs began July 9), and it was done just in time for autumn rains to begin refilling the Möhne reservoir with runoff. About ten days later, on October 3, the breach in the Eder Dam—the one caused by the Upkeep bomb from Sutherland's Lancaster on May 17—was also sealed. Albert Speer, the Nazi armaments minister and head of OT, addressed part of the assembled workforce to commend it for its "exemplary work." For propaganda purposes, he also hastened to point out that "the work has been achieved with but a few German workers [showing] the extent of the enthusiasm with which they applied themselves."[31]

Reichsminister Speer ranted that predictions the breach could not be repaired until November 11 had been wrong, and that by summoning OT from its work on the Atlantic Wall, he had ensured that the rebuild could be completed more than a month ahead of schedule. Had he known that the dams could rise from the dust of the May 16–17 attack so quickly, Fred Sutherland might have questioned the accolades he and the other surviving Dam Busters had garnered. If the attack had put the dam out of commission for only seventy-nine days, was it worth the loss of nearly half the squadron? Had the raid accomplished anything close to its objective of crippling Nazi Germany's war factories, much less hastening an Allied victory? The answer may lie in those seventy-nine days and the reconstruction logistics of which Albert Speer spoke so highly.

Before masons could set a single stone in mortar to fill the dam breaches, the buildup to the reconstruction required a city-sized maze of infrastructure. A construction firm from Dortmund took on the challenge. Adjacent to the Möhne Dam, for example, the company had to build a narrow-gauge railway to supply the rebuild. Once completed, the railway moved 2,200 tonnes of building material in a hundred goods wagons daily, for a total of 5,400 wagonloads and 98,000 tonnes of freight. The support system required the firm to either repair or build from scratch a power station, a funnelled water inlet, bomb-proofed outlet tunnels, pumps, concrete mixers, a timber storage area, and a supply yard full of sand, gravel, cement, and masonry. At the Möhne, more than 247,000 cubic feet of loose stone had to be removed before reconstruction could begin. And because the quarries that had supplied stone for the original dam construction from 1908 to 1912 had been stripped clean, new stone had to come from farther away, in the Bergisches Land region. As well, the demand for so much stone to replace the dams diverted material that was earmarked for autobahn bridges;[32] as a consequence, other Nazi infrastructure suffered delays.

The workers diverted to the rebuild illustrated both the priority the Reich gave the dams and the impact on the Nazi war effort as a whole. More than a hundred conscripted Dutch carpenters assembled the scaffolding that rose to the equivalent of an eight-storey building; erection of the wood required more time and material, since sufficient steel could not be diverted from war munitions. Initially, the clearing job required ten or twenty workers standing side by side at the base of the breach. Eventually, as the repairs advanced, the workforce grew to 320 builders. Then about 250 stonemasons and their labourers began laying almost 9,000 cubic feet of stone per day.[33] This vast conscripted labour force, which Speer claimed had reduced the burden on German workers, actually exposed the vulnerability of the construction. With thousands of forced labourers on the site, OT technicians were regularly required to check the accuracy of masonry cutting and to conduct slump tests on the quality of the mortar mix. That slowed the process and diverted manpower.

Hitler had given Speer immediate and ultimate authority, following the damage assessment, to create an Einsatzstag Ruhrgebiet (Ruhr area unit) to send 50,000 OT workers to the Ruhr to join the dams repair, including 7,000 workers immediately withdrawn from construction of coastal fortifications in France, Belgium, and the Netherlands. From the end of May to October 1943, on average, 1,855 labourers worked onsite every day in eleven-hour shifts. At the peak of activity, 2,192 workers swarmed over the dam—748 French, 441 Dutch, 340 Italian, 183 Belgian, and 460 German. Each of the German workers was assigned four or five foreign workers, who had mainly been diverted from about four hundred sites along the English Channel and North Sea, building another key piece of Nazi infrastructure—the Atlantic Wall—against any Allied incursion.

As well, once burned by what the German war press called "an act of British aerial terror," Nazi leaders would not be caught off guard again.[34] Not long after the dams raid, the Möhne bristled with new large Flak guns, as well as additional searchlights, smoke-generating equipment, and balloon barrages tethered to the site. At the Eder, to defend against low-flying aircraft, steel masts were erected on the slopes adjacent to the dam. A curtain of cables strung between the masts created a massive steel spider's web of defensive works.* On the reservoir side of both dams, huge wooden deflector rafts, weighted with concrete, provided a buffer should any other depth-charge device be deployed against them. Furthermore, the focused raid on the Möhne, Eder, and Sorpe Dams on May 16–17, and the Bomber Command offensive against the Ruhr River Valley as a whole, sparked an additional strategic diversion on the German side. From the spring of 1943 on, flak batteries, artillery crews, Luftwaffe night fighters, and a host of other air and ground defensive elements of the German war machine were marshalled to protect the Ruhr when they might otherwise have gone to the Eastern Front or the Atlantic Wall, where the German High Command knew an invasion attempt was coming.

Thus, despite Reichsminister Speer's boastful assessment of OT's "exemplary work," his strong sense of supply and demand no doubt told him that rebuilding and rearming the Ruhr had a consequence. Eventually, redirecting personnel and resources to strengthening Germany's industrial heart would weaken the Nazi war effort in some of its extremities.

Even if Fred Sutherland felt frustration over how quickly the Germans repaired the dam that his crew had breached, he might have taken some satisfaction in knowing that the

---

* One consequence of the dam raid's success came from the British prime minister himself. On the day of the attack, Churchill asked for advice about defensive measures for British dams, including the Derwent—617 Squadron's practice dam. As many as eleven dams were considered vulnerable, so anti-aircraft batteries were assigned to protect them, along with, coincidentally, searchlights, barrage balloons, smoke-generating machines, and steel towers with hanging cables.

worker his forged papers claimed he was would never arrive at the intended worksite (a labour camp at Cherbourg). Instead, he'd successfully evaded German authorities and made it all the way back to England a dozen weeks after he'd been shot down over Holland.

F/Sgt. Sutherland's war was over. Once European resistance fighters had rescued and spirited an Allied airman home, the possibility that he might be captured again and reveal the identities of those underground contacts took him out of the fighting. By December 1943 Sutherland had boarded a transatlantic ship bound for Halifax, and then a train headed west to Alberta.

"When I got to Edmonton," Sutherland said, "one of our military police stopped me and gave me heck for not having my coat buttoned up properly."[35]

Sutherland soon spotted his parents and fiancée on the train platform. They had driven over three hundred miles from Peace River to meet him at the station in the provincial capital. Margaret and Fred immediately confirmed their commitment to each other—barely twenty, they each needed their parents' formal permission—and were married on January 5, 1944. Among the first people Fred encountered back home was the preacher at his church.

"Fred, have you been going to church?" the preacher asked.

"No," Doc said politely.

"Well, you know, we prayed for you and that's why you're here," the reverend claimed.

The former Lancaster gunner, now a veteran, remembered how a lucky encounter with Punch Dickins had earned him a barnstorming flight aboard the legendary bush pilot's

Bellanca float plane. He considered the marksman's skills his father had taught him as a boy that had come in handy when he was training for war at the bombing and gunnery school in Mossbank in 1942. He reflected on the value of the low-level flight training he'd done with his Lancaster crew all over England in the seven weeks prior to the dams raid. He never stopped praising the selflessness of his pilot, Les Knight, and the resistance fighters who'd helped him evade the Germans after he was shot down in September 1943. He thought about what the preacher had said and decided his survival had little to do with spirituality. "You can pray all you want," Sutherland said, "but I don't think that would have changed the outcome. It was just luck."[36]

CHAPTER TEN

"THE OLD LAGS"

OSSES SUSTAINED BY 617 SQUADRON KEPT OFFI-
cials inside the Air Force busy between May and September 1943, and beyond. While W/C Gibson and the
casualty officers had to write personalized letters of condo-
lence to next of kin following Operations Chastise and Garlic,
it was their departments and clerks who fought the paper
wars ensuring the return of effects to loved ones, the issu-
ing of service awards, and the processing of each Certificate
of Presumption of Death. After Operation Chastise, fourteen
Canadian families received such documents. Among them was
Frank Byers, the father of Vernon Byers—killed when enemy
batteries on Texel Island shot down his *K-King* bomber just
before 11 p.m. on May 16. The pilot officer's father received
standard notification that the RAF had received no information to indicate Vernon might still be alive.

Following that dispatch, however, Arthur Harris noted
that since thirty-four surviving aircrew had received decorations for bravery, it would be appropriate for those killed in

the dams raid to receive some "notation on the records . . . [of having] paid the supreme sacrifice." Easier said than done. It was more than three years after Vernon's death en route to the Ruhr that Frank Byers received the "Operational Wings and Certificate in recognition of the gallant services rendered by your son."[1]

It took even longer for the parents of Robert Urquhart to learn that their son had received the Distinguished Flying Cross while serving in Bomber Command. Just before the navigator from Saskatchewan had transferred to 617 Squadron to train for the dams raid in March 1943, he'd completed a twenty-eight-operation tour. His former CO at 50 Squadron had even signed the papers recommending the decoration. So had AVM Cochrane, but the file was subsequently misplaced. In the meantime, Urquhart had served as navigator aboard Henry Maudslay's Z-Zebra Lancaster on May 16–17 when the crew delivered its Upkeep against the Eder Dam; he disappeared when the mine exploded on top of the dam. All seven crewmen were lost that night. As a further affront, administrative inertia delayed the awarding of Urquhart's already overdue DFC until four years after the war.

"When one is removed from the actual fighting areas," the Canadian minister for national defence rationalized in a letter to Urquhart's parents, "recollection of the most important incidents [is] deferred by the exigencies of the conflict."[2]

Robert Urquhart's gallantry medal was delivered to his parents' Moose Jaw home by mail on November 7, 1949. If waiting years for the service medal of a son killed in the dams raid was arduous, however, Mary Earnshaw's test of patience was excruciating. Her husband, Ken Earnshaw, had disappeared in the action over the Möhne Dam on May 17, 1943. Soon after, she received a telegram from W/C Gibson informing her that P/O Earnshaw's pilot, John Hopgood, would have made every conceivable effort to save his crew; it was enough to offer faint hope. Seven months later, in January 1944, the casualty officer confirmed Ken's death. Adding insult to injury, the Estates Branch of the Department of National Defence in Canada required Earnshaw's widow to complete a questionnaire that undoubtedly reopened the wounds of her loss. She had to identify all surviving relatives, indicate their ages, and recount the details of their marriage and his parents' marriage. Only then could she address the matters of Ken Earnshaw's estate.

"It is my belief he left a will in Air Force custody," she wrote in the estate questionnaire, "[although] I am not aware of the place."[3] She explained that as far as she knew her husband had been depositing his service savings somewhere, and hoped the military could help her track them down. There was also an inheritance from the English side of Ken Earnshaw's family, but the war had intervened and prevented payment. Perhaps most disconcerting for the widow of this Dam Buster was that the Air Force had overlooked something more obvious. "I wish to have all my husband's belongings returned to me," she wrote twice in the estate questionnaire.[4] The date was March 3, 1944, nearly a full year after Ken Earnshaw had been killed in action.

In the final seconds of Lancaster *M-Mother*'s flight, as Hopgood attempted to gain sufficient altitude for his crew to bail out, the Lancaster was engulfed in flames, a wing fell off, and the rest came down near the village of Ostönnen, about three and a half miles from the Möhne Dam. The Luftwaffe ordered five coffins, but the intensity of the fire had left only Hopgood's remains identifiable. An exhumation of the coffins in 1947 revealed no other details, and all five crewmen were reburied in a single grave at Rheinberg War Cemetery.[5] And so the limitations of postwar science and investigation delivered one further discourtesy to the navigator from Ohaton, Alberta: P/O Ken Earnshaw had disappeared into a collective grave.

IN SPITE OF ITS DEADLY SETBACKS AND ITS UNFAIR designation as "a one op squadron," 617 Squadron had soldiered on through the fall of 1943. Arthur Harris appeared to relegate the group to intermittent special duties by calling them "the old lags squadron," an affectionate moniker for an organization of hard-bitten aircrews who only wanted to do operations. AVM Ralph Cochrane referred to 617 as his "sniper" squadron, only calling on it when he wanted a precision attack carried out.[6] One key element, however, was permanently removed from 617's arsenal of battle tactics—Lancasters would do no more low-level bombing. Despite the respect paid to its long-standing members and its special status, however, 617's reputation as "the suicide squadron" seemed to scare off all potential new commanders. Except one.

Tall, thin, dark, and soft-spoken, Leonard Cheshire had none of the flamboyance of the squadron's originator, Guy Gibson. The accomplished officer wasn't particularly extroverted, but appeared to be sensitive to others and more approachable than Gibson.[7] He had an honours degree in law from Oxford, was married to Constance Binney, an American movie star in her forties, and at the age of twenty-five was the youngest group captain in the Royal Air Force. He had completed two full tours and had earned a DSO and bar and DFC. In contrast to Gibson, Cheshire wasn't a partygoer and seemed more methodical than superstitious. He wasn't prone to rituals such as putting flying gear on exactly the same way each trip, urinating on the tailwheel of the aircraft before take-off, or carrying talismans. Cheshire claimed that an airman needed luck, not mascots. "You either have good luck or you don't," he said.[8]

In order to get the job leading 617 Squadron, Cheshire had asked AVM Cochrane if he could take a demotion. Cochrane agreed and installed him as wing commander of the old Dam Busters. Whether by luck or good planning, Cheshire responded by leading his aircrews in a series of new sorties that rivalled the dams raid for their daring and impact on the war. One operation in particular demanded nearly as much secrecy, preparation time, specialized training, and improvisation as the dams raid had in May 1943. It also threw Canadian members of the squadron back into the limelight.

Operation Taxable began as a yet another challenge for the Dam Buster crews. At 11 a.m. on May 2, 1944, AVM Ralph Cochrane assembled Cheshire and all the members of his 617 Squadron in the flight offices at RAF Woodhall Spa, which had become the squadron's new home in Lincolnshire.

"Gentlemen," Cochrane announced to a hushed briefing room, "the next time you are airborne, it will be D-Day!"[9] That really got their attention. There were cheers and fist pumps, celebrating that the efforts of Bomber Command had turned the tide. Eventually Cochrane explained that Winston

Churchill's War Cabinet had wondered whether it was possible—using the GEE navigation system and Window (airborne tinsel)—to give a credible impression on German coastal radar screens that an invasion convoy was approaching the French coast from England. Leading up to D-Day, Allied commanders had determined that it was vital not only to hide their intention to land invasion forces in Normandy but also to give the Germans the false impression that an amphibious landing was aimed east of the River Seine. D-Day planners hoped that German commanders in turn would believe the feint and keep the bulk of their forces closer to the Pas-de-Calais and farther from Normandy.[10] Cochrane said that the question of how the Allies could accomplish this ruse and who should carry it out had gone from Cabinet to Coastal Command to Bomber Command and through Arthur Harris to his old lags.

"617 Squadron is required to simulate an eight knots convoy using Lancasters cruising at 160 knots," Cochrane said at the briefing. "There is no outside help available, absolutely none. You are on your own."[11]

For some of the dams raid veterans this was déjà vu, right down to the CO's insistence that secrecy was of the utmost importance. Then 617's wing commander invited his navigators to adjourn to their own section to mull over the problem. Among them was Station Navigation Officer S/L Revie Walker, who had served a year with his pilot, Dave Shannon, as well as F/O Don MacLean, who'd flown the same period with Joe McCarthy. All four were Dam Busters. All four were used to the demands and expectations of a top-secret assignment. What they needed was a solution to Cochrane's riddle—simulating a convoy travelling at eight knots (just over nine miles per hour) across the Channel by using a squadron of Lancasters flying at 160 knots (nearly two hundred miles per hour).

It was MacLean, known around the station as the "wizard of the GEE box," who solved the tactical problem. Then Walker explained they just needed what he called the "boffins" (the backroom technical experts) to work out some of the details of MacLean's scheme; that is, what the optimum altitude was for dropping Window strips and how long each bomber needed to circle while releasing sufficient Window to create a convincing picture on German radar. It turned out that the "boffins," electronic scientists Robert Cockburn and Joan Curran, were already experimenting with Window strips at Tantallon Castle, on the Firth of Forth in Scotland;[12] they'd proved that the tinsel could in fact produce the illusion of an invasion fleet on German radar screens. The challenge for 617 Squadron crews was sustaining the illusion for eight hours over the English Channel. By May 11, the boffins and the aircrew navigators had begun to transform the theoretical into the practical.

Each Lancaster would fly a series of spiralling elliptical circuits, making a complete orbit every seven minutes. Shown on screens aboard each aircraft, the GEE navigational system would outline the circuit to fly—along two straight, parallel tracks, linked by a turn from one track to the other. With each orbit of a Lancaster, the squadron would advance the circuit by about 2,400 yards, or the distance an invasion convoy might be expected to cover on the water traversing the Channel from England to France at eight knots. The operation would involve sixteen Lancaster crews, each with its regular seven airmen plus an extra pilot, an extra navigator, and three "Window chuckers" throwing out the tinsel. Eight crews would run the pattern for four hours; then, at perhaps the most critical moment of the operation, eight more crews would seamlessly take over the pattern and continue the circuits for another four hours.

A Lancaster would drop Window on the straight leg of the GEE track—the outbound direction of the imaginary convoy—for two and a half minutes. It would stop dropping Window as it made a gentle counter-clockwise turn for one minute to the returning leg of the GEE track, then follow the returning straight leg—parallel to the outbound direction of the convoy—Windowing again as it backtracked for two and a half minutes. It would then turn counter-clockwise without Windowing for a minute, returning to the original straight leg of the GEE track only 2,400 yards ahead of where it had started its first orbit. Then it would repeat the process. The resulting image on German radar would give the impression of a naval convoy sixteen miles long and fourteen miles wide advancing at a speed of eight knots toward the port of Fécamp, on the French coast near the Pas-de-Calais. By dawn, when the second wave of Lancasters returned to base, the ruse would be complete.

The training sessions began immediately, with all 617 crews in the air for two hours a day. Soon after the pilots and navigators had learned the orbiting patterns, a member of Britain's Telecommunications Research Establishment (TRE) arranged for the 617 Squadron crews to view their progress on a captured German coastal radar set positioned at Flamborough Head; the crews took turns flying and observing the patterns on the radar screen. It was up to the navigators to ensure that the orbiting not reflect a speed uncharacteristic of a travelling convoy, or else the Germans would become suspicious of the spoof. To ensure that the GEE sets remained reliable, 617 Squadron turned to one of its stalwarts, Hugh Munro, to design a backup system. Munro, the same RCAF radar specialist who'd worked with Guy Gibson's dams raid crews from day one a year earlier at Scampton, had a second GEE set installed inside each Lancaster. The second, independent set, dubbed the "Siamese Installation," provided a failsafe for the op.

As vital to the overall success of Operation Taxable as the work of the navigational teams and the boffins was physical dispersal of the Window from the Lancasters during the flight. It proved just as intricate and required just as much accuracy. The Window strips were six feet long, with a hundred strips to each bundle; each bundle unfurled in the air accordion style. In order to perpetuate the illusion of the convoy, the Window droppers needed to propel twelve bundles of Window per minute through the Lancaster's flare chute from an altitude of 3,000 feet. It would be sustained, strenuous, and, of necessity, the most synchronized activity aboard the aircraft. To help the droppers recognize when a Windowing sequence was beginning, a green light was installed at both the navigator's table and the flare chute. The green light on indicated the Lancaster was heading on a straight leg and a Windowing sequence was required; the green light off meant the Windowing sequence was to stop.

In late May, just days before the actual op, the TRE scheduled a dress rehearsal of Operation Taxable off Flamborough Head. Just as during the practice runs over the Derwent Reservoir prior to the dams raid, the 617 aircrews were scrutinized by their superiors and the backroom scientists. When the dry run was complete, one of the boffins was heard to say, "It's more like an invasion convoy than the real thing!"[13]

Then it was time for the real thing. At 8:30 p.m., June 5, 1944, Don MacLean, Revie Walker, and the rest of the 617 navigators assembled in the briefing room. But instead of just the Operation Taxable charts on the wall, Leonard Cheshire and the station staff had affixed the charts for all the D-Day landing beaches for the squadron to see. To the east, the charts showed the assault lines of their spoof convoy to Fécamp. To the west, the airmen could see the maps showing the real convoy routes to the Normandy beaches—Utah, Omaha, Gold, Juno, and Sword—where in less than twelve hours 155,000 Allied troops would be storming ashore to begin the liberation of northwestern Europe. If nothing else, the additional charts drove home the utter necessity of succeeding in their task.

"Gentlemen, the waiting is over," W/C Cheshire began his evening briefing. "Not just the period of the recent training through which we have all been, but also for the years we have fought our way to this day."[14]

The wing commander emphasized the importance of backing the work of the squadron's navigators, ensuring that all crews followed their directions exactly. Similarly, he encouraged the Window marshals to work to the high standard their training had set. He revealed that right behind the second wave of Window drops, the Second Tactical Air Force would be roaring in over the Seine River basin to destroy all potential crossing points between Le Havre and Paris, isolating the large German armies in northern France that Operation Taxable was designed to hold in position in the Pas-de-Calais.

"Our efforts tonight will not be of the usual destructive nature," he noted. "But our successful endeavours will undoubtedly save hundreds of Allied lives this night, and possibly thousands in the weeks to come."[15]

Just after eleven o'clock, Les Munro's crew and Leonard Cheshire's crew took off to lead the first wave. Almost two hours later, Joe McCarthy and Dave Shannon and their Dam Buster veteran crews joined the operation, leading the second wave. Unbeknownst to the 617 Squadron crews, the TRE experts had set up a radar system on the Isle of Wight to monitor Operation Taxable from the south coast of England. TRE's report on the op indicated "one very slight wobble in the mid-stage," but otherwise it went off without a hitch.[16] Meanwhile, the Royal Navy joined the spoof by broadcasting shipping sound effects to reinforce the overall impression of a naval convoy. Just before dawn broke, McCarthy and Shannon made the final orbits, dropping Window in front of Fécamp, and then turned for home.

In fact, the German armies of northern France did stay put, expecting an Allied invasion at the Pas-de-Calais. And the Second Tactical Air Force did cut the bridges leading to the landing beaches, preventing reinforcement of the German counteroffensive against the Allied invasion on June 6. Operation Taxable had contributed to the overall success of D-Day.

Remarkably, however, when the 617 aircrews landed back in Lincolnshire, their senior officers didn't bother to debrief them. Clearly the squadron's brass felt that greater attention ought to be paid to the main event—Operation Overlord, in the air, on the sea, and along the Normandy invasion beaches.

As a consequence, there was no physical entry in the 617 operations record book for June 6, 1944. Thus the record of the aircrews and the boffins who had executed Operation Taxable ended up as ghostly as the "convoy" they had fabricated on the Channel. Nor did the Air Ministry care to award any decorations of merit for the successful results of the ruse. When W/C Cheshire offered a list of potential recipients, especially the navigational crew, the higher-ups rejected the nominations. "This operation did not cross the enemy coast, or at any time come under enemy gunfire," said the powers that be. "Consequently, it is not eligible to be considered for the award of decorations."[17]

ON THE EVENING OF JUNE 6, WITH THEIR FIRST INVAsion operation a success, Cheshire and Munro noticed a line of trucks, covered in tarpaulins, arriving along the perimeter of their Woodhall Spa station. On closer inspection, under the tarps they discovered shiny, shark-shaped devices with sharp noses and tail fins. The squadron had received the latest bomb innovation from design engineer Barnes Wallis. These sleek-looking explosives, called "Tallboys," would help 617 Squadron deliver an additional deterrent to German armies attempting to push the D-Day invasion back into the sea. Two days later, the call came for Cochrane's sniper squadron to cut off a specific German counteroffensive with the new weapons. Panzer tanks were on the move by rail from Bordeaux to strike back at the Allies in Normandy; en route, the railcars carrying the tanks would have to pass through the Saumur Tunnel, in the Loire Valley of southwestern France.

On June 8, Cheshire received orders to load the 12,000-pound Tallboys aboard squadron Lancasters. Just after midnight, he dropped flares from a low-flying Mosquito, marking the entrance to the tunnel. Then, from thousands of feet above, the Lanc crews unloaded the Tallboys on the flares. The 10,000 tons of earth that the bombs displaced, causing the mountain to collapse into the tunnel, had finally illustrated the devastation that Barnes Wallis had promised with his earthquake bombs at the beginning of the war. And fittingly, the Dam Buster squadron had delivered them in one of the most timely and devastating direct hits of the war.[18]

A week later, the squadron switched its attention from moving mountains to heaving the seas. Since D-Day, German E-boats (motor torpedo boats) dispatched from Le Havre naval bases on the coast of France had been harassing Allied shipping moving back and forth across the Channel in support of the Normandy beachhead. In just the second Tallboy attack, on June 14, four hundred Lancasters, including those from 617 Squadron, followed Cheshire in his Mosquito across the channel to bomb the concrete pens that housed the enemy boats. At about 3,000 feet, the wing commander spotted the E-boats lined up outside the pens along the waterfront in Le Havre. In a dive-bombing attack, he swooped in over the harbour at seven hundred feet, dropping red markers around the moored boats. With streams of flak lashing up at his aircraft, Cheshire completed his marking and roared back out to sea, out of range of the German batteries. As the final phase of the operation, the 617 Lancasters circling out over the Channel left their holding pattern, moved over the harbour, and homed in on Cheshire's markers.

"We didn't have a formation. It was a gaggle [of Lancasters]," said Joe McCarthy, piloting his bomber at about 16,000 feet over the harbour. "We got hits right on the edge of where these E-boats were all lined up. . . . The water formed a tidal wave [that] went through the pen gates all the way, hit the back and came back out again. Completely scuttled anything that was in there."[19]

The reconnaissance photos, delivered to Barnes Wallis the next day, revealed the annihilation of the German flotilla; there wasn't an E-boat left afloat in Le Havre. The Tallboys had also smashed through the doors of the E-boat pens, and those that had penetrated the pens left them in shambles. The operation was repeated the next night against the E-boat pens in Boulogne. Two nights of Tallboy attacks had destroyed 133 enemy boats. "If the Navy had done [this]," Harris complimented, "it would have been [called] a major naval victory."[20]

The day before the Tallboy attack against the E-boats at Le Havre, the Germans unleashed yet another weapon in their arsenal against their enemy across the Channel. Launched from ski-slope-like ramps in France, these pilotless flying bombs packed with explosives were designed to fly above targets in Britain, run out of fuel, fall from the sky, and detonate on impact. Hitler's so-called V (for "Vengeance") weapons were intended to terrorize urban centres across the British Isles. The first V-1 flying bomb landed on London on June 13, 1944, and the first V-2 on September 8. The campaign reached its peak in February 1945, when 232 V-2s fell on England. In all, 1,115 were launched against southern England, with 517 landing on London. The V-2 campaign killed 2,754 people and wounded 6,500 more in Britain.[21] RAF 617 Squadron assumed an immediate and active role, attacking the storage areas and launch sites of the flying bombs aimed at British population centres.

On July 4, 1944, Joe McCarthy and his original Dam Buster crew flew their sixty-seventh combat operation, against a V-1 storage facility northeast of Paris, and returned safely. It turned out to be their final op of the war, appropriately enough for the American-born pilot. McCarthy, a former Coney Island lifeguard, had spent better than half of his twenty-five years either imagining himself a pilot or actually occupying a cockpit. With his fellow RCAF crewmates—flight engineer Bill Radcliffe, rear gunner Dave Rodger, and navigator Don MacLean—McCarthy had successfully attacked the Sorpe Dam on May 16–17, earned a DSO and a DFC and bar, and completed five times the number of operations of the average Bomber Command pilot.[22] "McCarthy [has] been going continuously for about two years," AVM Cochrane told Cheshire after his July 4 op. "It's time [he] had a rest."[23]

Bomber Command scattered the crew of Lancaster ME-559, *Queenie Chuck-Chuck*, to the wind. McCarthy went to 61 Base, the RCAF's training group at Topcliffe. His original bomb aimer, George "Johnny" Johnson, had completed his second full tour in April 1944 and was honourably discharged with his DFM and a pilot officer's commission.[24] McCarthy's second bomb aimer, Danny Daniel, transferred to Cheshire's 617 crew. Ron Batson, his mid-upper gunner, and Len Eaton, his wireless operator, went to OTUs to train other, less experienced crews. Both his navigator, Don MacLean, and flight engineer, Bill Radcliffe, were posted to 1654 Heavy Conversion Unit to do the same. And Dave Rodger,

McCarthy's rear gunner, was awarded a DFC and returned to Canada that fall.

Les Munro and his crew had accumulated an equally long service record, which Cochrane terminated in July 1944 when he forced them to retire from ops too. Despite having to abort his sortie during the dams raid, Munro continued as flight commander through nearly sixty ops in Bomber Command, earning a DFC and DSO. Like McCarthy's crew, all of Munro's aircrew, coming off operations that summer, were assigned to training duties. His flight engineer, Frank Appleby, had earned a DFM and completed fifty combat operations; his navigator, Jock Rumbles, had accumulated fifty-five ops and a DFC and bar; front gunner Bill Howarth had served twenty months with Munro; and bomb aimer James Clay had forty-six combat operations behind him, and a DFC. Meanwhile, Munro's two Canadian aircrew—wireless operator Percy Pigeon and rear gunner Harvey Weeks—had completed forty-two and sixty operations, respectively. Each had received a DFC, and they served the remainder of the war at training units in Britain before returning to Canada.

Ken Brown's crew was dispersed when its members finished their tours in March 1944. The skipper himself finished the war as an instructor, married Beryl Blackband, accompanied his war bride home to Canada, and rose to squadron leader in the RCAF before retiring in 1968. Brown's flight engineer, Harry Feneron, continued his ritual of kissing the ground after each op—for another nine sorties after the dams raid—and then was reassigned to train other engineers. Wireless operator Hewie Hewstone was sent to No. 26 Operational Training Unit. Similarly, before returning home to Canada, both bomb aimer Stefan Oancia and rear gunner Grant McDonald became instructors at operational training units in the United Kingdom. After his tour with Brown, navigator Dudley Heal transferred to RAF No. 214 Squadron, flying B-17s, was shot down, and spent the rest of the war in POW camps. Rear gunner Daniel Allatson was the only member of Brown's crew not to survive the war; he'd transferred to Bill Divall's crew and was killed in the Dortmund-Ems Canal raid.

BY 1944, THE NUMBER OF SURVIVING ORIGINAL DAM Busters was dwindling, if not by attrition in combat operations then certainly as the survivors were given the option to stand down. Nearly all of Arthur Harris's "old lags," those still on active service with 617 Squadron, had accumulated sortie totals well beyond the numbers required for standard Bomber Command tours of duty. They had defied the odds and kept themselves from becoming statistics. To emphasize that fact, the nucleus of the dams raid crews had gathered just before launching Operation Taxable. On the one-year anniversary of Operation Chastise—May 16, 1944—the Petwood Hotel's officers' mess staged a party for the surviving Dam Busters as well as the A.V. Roe and Vickers personnel connected to the raid. Guy Gibson was unable to attend, but he did speak at a 617 Squadron dance three days later. It was the last time the Dam Busters' former CO celebrated with his old aircrew comrades. Through the first few months of 1944, the Air Ministry had seconded Gibson to report on accident prevention. In truth, he spent that time in an office with access to a Dictaphone and a typing pool, writing his own account of the dams raid.

By the middle of September 1944, with revisions to his memoir, *Enemy Coast Ahead*, complete, Gibson had grown weary of flying a desk. He badgered his superiors until, on September 19–20, he was allowed to borrow a Mosquito from RAF No. 627 Squadron and, as master bomber in charge of marking the target, lead a raid on Mönchengladbach. Accounts of the return flight varied. Some suggested that the Mosquito's engines ran dry, because its crew wasn't experienced in switching from one fuel tank to another; others claim a target marker got hung up in the Mosquito's bomb bay; another theory says a Lancaster mistook the Mosquito for a Luftwaffe night fighter and shot it down. Whatever the cause, the aircraft crashed near the Dutch town of Steenbergen, killing Gibson and his navigator, S/L James Warwick.

"As great a warrior as these islands have ever bred," Arthur Harris said of his master bomber.[25] Just twenty-six, and arguably Bomber Command's most celebrated and committed pilot, Gibson had flown a trailblazing 174 operational sorties on Beaufighters, Hampdens, and Lancasters, and then had organized his 617 Squadron from scratch. Remarkable enough. Then, coping with near physical and psychological collapse in the lead-up to the dams raid—his own medical officer had recommended he take sick leave—he whipped some of the top aircrews of Bomber Command into a unique low-level attacking force. And, enduring some of the most strenuous combat flying of the war to the Ruhr and back, he'd led his new squadron to deliver a demoralizing blow to Nazi Germany's industrial heart and a morale-boosting triumph for Britain, all in one night. Then, at the behest of his political and military superiors, as the Allies' standard-bearer for air warfare, he'd fronted a relentless public relations tour of North America, only to be relegated to administration duties upon his return. Gibson, the opinionated and often arrogant commander, had achieved greatness as a heroic warrior because he quite naturally backed his combat experience with the practical application of the rules of leadership. But, clearly unable to tolerate a step back from the operational cockpit, he'd gone one combat operation too many.

Before the Germans could reach the site where Gibson's Mosquito came down on September 20 and cordon it off, a Dutch citizen got to the wreckage and retrieved Gibson's wallet, which the Dam Busters' leader shouldn't have been carrying. Maverick to the end.

"Gibson was a born leader, in the highest tradition of the services," wrote Harry Humphries, Gibson's adjutant at 617 Squadron. "He was sometimes intolerant, but he had no self-doubts as to his mission, and he had a manner that instilled positive attitudes in the minds of those under his command."[26]

It had been over a year since Gibson's goodwill tour of North America, and almost a year and a half since the dams raid. At about the time of Gibson's death, the war and its warriors were racing headlong into a fifth year. There seemed little or no time to reflect on either defeats or victories. From now on, of necessity, the view seemed focused forward—to the next battle, the next campaign, the next city liberated, the next step closer to victory in Europe. For Bomber Command—still flying 5,000 sorties a week—it was the next target, the transition from night to day bombing, more and safer fighter escorts, disabling the V-1 and V-2 flying-bomb sites, liberating the Channel ports, clearing the approaches to Antwerp, choking off Germany's oil supply, and more concentrated bombing of Germany's large and medium-sized cities. Allied bombing operations approached their climax. Nearly half of the entire tonnage of bombs dropped by Bomber Command during five and a half years of war came down on German targets in the final nine months.[27]

In July 1944, the Dam Buster squadron got a new commanding officer. Leonard Cheshire had completed nearly a hundred raids, received a Victoria Cross for his service, and passed on his leadership to Willie Tait. Under Tait's command, 617 Squadron took on numerous key assignments. Perhaps the most celebrated was twice attacking the German battleship *Tirpitz*, and finally sinking the Allies' nemesis on November 12, 1944, after delivering two direct hits with Barnes Wallis's Tallboy bombs.

In the final months of the war, Canadian airman Johnny Fauquier took a demotion to assume command of 617 Squadron. Older and with peacetime experience as a bush pilot back home, Fauquier was told to maintain 617's standard of excellence. And he did, but he also recognized the strong role that his Canadian predecessors had secured in the squadron's legacy. "I thought that it would be good for Canada . . . to have a Canadian command this exalted squadron," he explained. "It is a very difficult thing indeed to follow in the footsteps of men like Gibson, Cheshire, and Tait, but we did the best we could and, in fact, we did a considerable amount of damage on our own."[28]

As the Dam Buster veterans passed the torch to new squadrons, to newer aircraft, to younger and greener aircrews, the saga of Arthur Harris's "old lags" seemed to come to an end. Those who'd survived the raid and beyond never forgot those who had not. Ken Brown's rear gunner, Grant McDonald, remained haunted by the memory of vehicles taking away the personal effects of the aircrew lost after May 16–17, 1943. "That was not a good sight at all," he'd said.[29] Some of the dams raid vets, in their final months of service, refocused on training newer crews. Others tried to adapt to life back on civvy street. Two months after the dams raid, navigator Don MacLean had married Josephine Tear, a wireless operator at Scampton station. But their postwar life had to wait for MacLean to fly another twenty operations; in fact, Josie travelled to Canada as a war bride well before F/O MacLean completed his tour and arrived home.

Some of the Dam Busters reflected on what they'd accomplished. While they didn't get carried away by its significance, they didn't want the Herculean effort of their comrades forgotten either. Johnny Johnson, McCarthy's British bomb aimer, said the dams raid showed that "We, as a nation, had given the Nazis a bloody nose."[30] Dave Rodger, McCarthy's Canadian rear gunner, characterized the odds against their success and the miracle of the raid when he commented, "We were seven men against the Reich."[31] In the final pages of his memoir, Guy Gibson asked himself, "Had it been worth it?" Naturally, as part of his assessment of the dams raid, he weighed the cost: "Fifty-five boys [sic] who had lost their lives were some of many." He also wondered about the place of his Dam Busters legacy in Bomber Command's crucible as a whole. "The scythe of war, and a very bloody one at that, had reaped a good harvest in Bomber Command," he lamented.[32]

But in addition to expressing his fear that one day a world at peace might forget the lessons learned in war, he implicitly appeared to worry that the service and sacrifice over the Ruhr River Valley that mid-May night in 1943—the deaths of those airmen as well as the lift their sacrifice had given the entire Allied war effort—might also fade from memory or significance. He encouraged others, perhaps historians and citizens, to remember what had happened there, and begged them that "movies and radio records should remind this and future generations of what happened."[33]

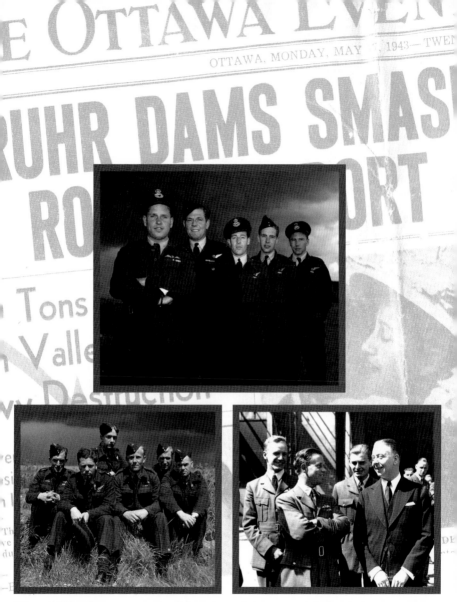

THE OTTAWA EVEN

OTTAWA, MONDAY, MAY 1943— TWEN

RUHR DAMS SMAS
RO
ORT
Tons
Valle
Destruction

When 617 Squadron crews returned from the raid, they entered the limelight in newspapers, radio, and public appearances. Photographers assembled some of the crews for glossy colour photos in the countryside. With Guy Gibson are (TOP, LEFT TO RIGHT) Fred Spafford, Robert Hutchison, and Canadians George Deering and Harlo Taerum. Another publicity photo featured (ABOVE LEFT, LEFT TO RIGHT) Johnny Johnson, Canadian Don MacLean, Ron Batson, American Joe McCarthy, Canadian Bill Radcliffe, and Len Eaton (missing for the photo was Dave Rodger). On June 22, 1943, some of the Dam Busters received military awards at Buckingham Palace. After the investiture (ABOVE RIGHT, LEFT TO RIGHT), Canadian Ken Brown, Conspicuous Gallantry Medal; Guy Gibson VC, Distinguished Serice Order and bar, Distinguished Flying Cross and bar; and Canadian Stefan Oancia, Distinguished Flying Medal, were joined by the designer of the Lancaster bomber, Roy Chadwick.

When Lancaster *E-Easy* struck an electricity pylon near Haldern-Herken, Germany, and crashed, its Upkeep bomb broke loose but did not explode. Nazi weapons experts quickly determined the dimensions, structure, and explosive potential of the *Britishe Wasserbombe* but appeared to overlook its most important secret—its backspin and ability to bounce. Despite the significant hydroelectricity loss to its war-production plants, the German Organisation Todt managed to rebuild both the Möhne (BELOW) and Eder Dams in fewer than one hundred days.

Following the dams raid, Guy Gibson was given time to write his memoirs and to appear in public, signing this enlarged aerial photo (ABOVE RIGHT) of the breached Möhne Dam. Meanwhile, a succession of new COs took over RAF No. 617 Squadron, including Leonard Cheshire (ABOVE LEFT), who led many of the original Dam Busters through Operation Taxable, another secret sortie that hastened Allied success on D-Day in Normandy.

Three months after the dams raid, in September 1943, Winston Churchill sent Guy Gibson on a publicity tour of North America so the young wing commander could press the PM's message—that Britain was on the offensive. During his stop at the BCATP training station in Calgary (BELOW), Gibson (at right) also met Hilda Taerum, the mother of his now decorated lead navigator, Harlo Taerum.

Back at UK air bases, crews such as that of Dam Buster Dave Shannon (fourth from right) and his Canadian navigator, Revie Walker (fourth from left), continued Bomber Command's campaign night and day; half the tonnage of bombs dropped between 1939 and 1945 fell on German targets in the final nine months of the war.

Based on the book by Paul Brickhill (TOP LEFT), the Associated British Picture Corporation assembled the cast and technology to recreate the famous dams raid operation as a feature film in April 1954. Three of the principals—Lancasters modified to replicate the Type 464 bombers—roared overhead (TOP RIGHT) to give onlookers a true sense of the low-level flying used to attack the dams.

The movie's producers remained true to the story on some elements, such as the Dann rangefinder (ABOVE LEFT) that bomb aimers used to calculate the precise spot to drop the bouncing bomb in front of the dam; they also replicated incidents of the low-flying bombers accidentally collecting treetop foliage in the landing gear (ABOVE RIGHT). However, the script took a few liberties, including the notion that Guy Gibson and Dave Shannon got the idea for the optical altimeter Aldis lamps while attending a dance performance where spotlights criss-crossed over the dancers onstage.

To depict the climax of the attack on the Möhne, movie producers overlaid separate "travelling matt" images of actor Richard Todd at the controls, water gushing through the broken dam, another Lanc flying below, and exploding flak outside the cockpit window. The image became *The Dam Busters* movie poster (TOP LEFT). In a poignant final scene (TOP RIGHT) actors Michael Redgrave (Wallis) and Todd (Gibson) tally the human cost of the raid.

The movie premiered in London on May 16, 1955. In the lobby of the Empire Theatre (ABOVE), members of the movie cast and actual aircrew gathered for publicity photos—white-haired Wallis with actor Todd in vest and jacket—at a model of the Möhne Dam. The next night, the Duke and Duchess of Gloucester (RIGHT) greeted (LEFT TO RIGHT) RCAF Dam Busters Joe McCarthy, Revie Walker, and Don MacLean.

When Nanton, Alberta, residents (LEFT TO RIGHT) Howie Armstrong, George White, and Fred Garratt learned the Air Force was chopping up Second World War Lancaster bombers for scrap in nearby Vulcan, they bought one for posterity. On September 26, 1960, the threesome assembled a crew to pull their prize seventeen miles—through farm fields, under hydro wires, across railway tracks and a river—arriving at Nanton two days later. Saskatchewan-born Bob Evans (LEFT) loved farming and flying from his boyhood. As a Nanton Lancaster Society volunteer, he searched for stories for the society newsletter, as well as for parts for the museum's wartime aircraft.

Since the 1980s, Nanton Lancaster Society volunteers have gathered most Tuesday nights for workshops to restore and maintain their principal Lancaster artifact. When the NLS hangar was completed in 1991, those on hand were (LEFT TO RIGHT) Lennard Hoffarth, Joe English, unknown, John Dozeman, Pat Pedersen, Jason Dozeman, Ron Jackson, Rob Pedersen, Larry Wright, Milt Magee, Bob Evans, unknown, John Green, Dan Fox, Dave Birrell, Garth Hurl, unknown. It's during the workshops that the museum's other assets—the stories of wartime aviators and aircraft—are shared and celebrated. Theirs is an organization of dreamers and doers.

Shere Fraser (TOP LEFT), daughter of Dam Buster John Fraser, spent eleven years bringing to trial a British collector who refused to return her father's flight logbook. Though the court found the man guilty, the log remains missing; in 2017, UK reporters interviewed Shere, holding a photo of her father near the Royal Albert Hall in London. In 2000, Hartley Garshowitz (BOTTOM RIGHT) visited his uncle Albert Garshowitz's gravesite at Reichswald Cemetery in Germany. In 2013, Lewis Burpee Jr. returned to Scampton to honour the memory of his father, Lewis Sr., who also died in the sortie; a 617 Squadron serviceman (TOP RIGHT) invited Lewis Jr. to sit at W/C Gibson's desk and imagine the night of May 16–17, 1943.

On April 22, 2017, during a ceremony at the Bomber Command Museum in Nanton, Shere Fraser formally returned Ken Earnshaw's stolen RCAF photo album to his nephew, Jim Heather (holding package). The historic event brought several offspring of Canadian Dam Busters together in solidarity—(ABOVE, LEFT TO RIGHT) Rob Taerum (nephew of Harlo Taerum), Fraser, Heather, and Joe McCarthy Jr.—vowing to preserve and protect the Dam Busters' legacy.

CHAPTER ELEVEN

MYTHOLOGY LOST AND FOUND

THE LONGEVITY OF THE DAM BUSTERS STORY MAY
well have begun with Guy Gibson's memoir, *Enemy
Coast Ahead*, published posthumously in 1946. Despite
some of its over-the-top depictions of 617 Squadron lore and
a few misspelled names, it seemed to capture the moment.
Gibson's own story and the tale of the Dam Busters helped
Britons identify with the young warriors who'd fought for
the values of the Commonwealth and struggled to achieve an
unexpected victory against Nazi Germany, all in spite of the
inertia of bureaucracy in high places.[1] Beyond that sympathetic reading, however, the story's appeal outside Britain in
fact originated with Gibson's goodwill tour four months after
the raid, when he addressed politicians, military leaders, the
public, and the media at personal appearances in Canada and
the United States.

In October 1943, for example, Gibson arrived in Washington, DC, where US army officials (authorized by President

Roosevelt) awarded him the Commander's Insignia to the Legion of Merit.[2] In New York, Chicago, Minneapolis, and Los Angeles, he spoke to audiences, conducted radio interviews, and answered questions at media briefings. Apparently Americans could not get enough of the story of W/C Gibson and his Dam Buster squadron. One US media syndicate, King Features, claimed, "No one accomplishment in the war appears to have generated public enthusiasm to the extent of the mining of the Möhne and Eder dams by the RAF."[3]

Gibson recognized the importance of illustrating to the Americans present that Britain and her allies had gone on the offensive against Nazi Germany. The additional subtext Winston Churchill expected Gibson to deliver, especially to American audiences, was a new call to arms—that no matter how great the US commitment to date, more was needed. By the summer of 1943, the wing commander was also keenly aware that some American airmen were arriving home having completed their US Army Air Force tours, meaning they'd flown approximately twenty-five combat missions. The contrast in tours of duty among Allied air forces was never so stark as when, during a Q-and-A session at the offices of the British Information Service (BIS) in New York, Gibson fielded questions from the American media.

"Wing Commander Gibson," one reporter piped up. "How many operations have you been on over Germany?"

"One hundred and seventy-four," Gibson said, and the room went silent.[4]

Not coincidentally, also present at Gibson's BIS press conference was RAF F/L Roald Dahl, the assistant air attaché at the British embassy in Washington. Not satisfied to write only embassy copy, Dahl moonlighted by writing contemporary stories that sparked his imagination. One of Dahl's stories had previously earned him a meeting with animator Walt Disney. In fact, in 1942, while visiting the creator of cartoon character Mickey Mouse, Dahl had also met Hollywood producer and screenwriter Howard Hawks; Dahl had pitched Hawks about one of his freelance creations, which by law he had to clear with the BIS before production. Through his embassy connections, Dahl had already written to the British Air Ministry proposing a film about the dams raid. Meanwhile, Hawks had secured a budget of $150,000 for a Hollywood production of Dahl's script.*

The next step was to meet W/C Gibson about the project; when they were introduced during Gibson's tour across the United States, Dahl had already completed a draft screenplay. All that really remained before cameras rolled was to assure the British Air Ministry that the feature film would reveal no top-secret information about the dams raid aircraft, the weapon used, or its inventor. In his script, Dahl had created a fictional scientist, named Johnstone, as the inventor of the weapon. But the project hit two fatal snags: ultimately the Air Ministry would not approve the script, and Barnes Wallis considered Dahl's Professor Johnstone to be "a caricature." The

---

* Roald Dahl's wartime flying placed him among the fighter aces of the RAF, with service in North Africa, the Battle of Athens, and Palestine. Invalided home at twenty-six, in 1942 he was posted to the British embassy in Washington to build the relationship between Winston Churchill and Franklin Delano Roosevelt. Meanwhile, Dahl's memoir of wartime service, "A Piece of Cake," was published in the *Saturday Evening Post* and earned him $1,000. That sparked his passion for creative writing, most notably children's stories such as *James and the Giant Peach* and *Charlie and the Chocolate Factory*, among many. The *Times* placed Dahl sixteenth on the list of the fifty greatest British writers since 1945. His books would eventually sell more than 250 million copies worldwide.

roadblocks at the Air Ministry and producer Hawks's eventual cooling to the whole idea left the future of the film in the hands of the Ministry of Information, which ultimately pronounced that "by now, perhaps it is rather too much past history for it to make a big hit."[5]

THERE THE SAGA OF THE DAM BUSTERS MIGHT HAVE ended. If the Ministry of Information thought the subject passé, how could anyone think otherwise? But the legacy of the dams raid had perhaps its greatest champion in the man who'd given it his blessing in the first place. Sir Ralph Cochrane, the air vice-marshal in Bomber Command who'd ordered the creation of 617 Squadron, chosen Gibson as its commander, given its aircrews their marching orders, and ultimately authorized Operation Chastise, had also conceived a plan for the story's preservation.

He'd turned to a former journalist and Second World War fighter pilot to research and write the history of the Dam Buster squadron. Paul Brickhill, who'd served in the Royal Australian Air Force, become a prisoner of war at Stalag Luft III, and published *The Great Escape* in 1950, seemed to Cochrane to be an author in search of his next bestseller. At Cochrane's insistence, and with 617's squadron leader Leonard Cheshire onside, Brickhill conducted interviews with the key surviving players, sifted through squadron records (many compiled by Harry Humphries, the founder adjutant of 617 Squadron[6]), and crafted a manuscript for publication. In his preface to *The Dam Busters*, Brickhill shared an interview excerpt with an unnamed RAF air marshal.

"What do you think 617 Squadron is worth?" Brickhill asked.

"I suppose they were worth ten other squadrons," the air marshal said. He paused and then added, "No. Ten other squadrons couldn't have done what they did, and then of course you've got to consider that inventor chap and the freak weapons he gave them."[7]

That short exchange solidified Brickhill's treatment of the Dam Busters as a story of quality, not quantity; of the exceptional ingenuity of Barnes Wallis in designing and delivering the bouncing bomb; and of a commander, Guy Gibson, driven to take a wartime flying outfit from nothing and give it the effectiveness of ten. The book was published in 1951 and became an instant success, attracting the attention of moviemakers yet again. Whereas Hollywood had dismissed the story as "too much past history," when Brickhill's book became a runaway bestseller in Britain, Robert Clark of the Associated British Picture Corporation (ABPC) quickly optioned the work for £7,500, in part because ABPC had Richard Todd on contract and somebody recognized Todd's likeness to Gibson. Before long the producers had booked actor Michael Redgrave, who relied on the wizardry of makeup artists to play a closer-to-likeness Wallis.

At the outset, producer Clark, writer R.C. Sherriff, and director Michael Anderson took great pains to present the story accurately, down to the last detail. They even corresponded with relatives of the Dam Busters, including, for example, Guy Gibson's father and Hilda Taerum, the mother of Guy Gibson's navigator Harlo Taerum, inviting her to contact them "if there is anything . . . you would wish to have altered."[8] The producers gained access to authentic locations, such as the ship tank of the National Physical Laboratory at Teddington, where Wallis and his co-workers had catapulted their model Upkeeps onto the surface of the water. Derwent Dam and Reservoir doubled as the German targets. The RAF had locked up Grantham at the end of the war but allowed ABPC producers temporary access, so the moviemakers could shoot the scenes of Harris, Cochrane, and Wallis waiting for the latest reports of the dams raid in a virtual time capsule of 5 Group headquarters.[9]

Also virtually unchanged from its wartime condition, the station at Scampton provided exterior and interior locations of hangars, offices, barracks, and crew briefing rooms with little or no additional set dressing. In fact, during the shooting, with fictional aircrew interspersed among real aircrew around the aerodrome, inevitably actors dressed in RAF officers' uniforms received salutes from real RAF personnel; rather than try to explain, the actors generally returned in kind. Director Anderson's affinity for documentary filmmaking influenced his decision to shoot the feature film in black-and-white; that, in turn, allowed him to incorporate the actual monochrome films of the Wellington bomber making test drops of the Upkeep mines along Chesil Beach in 1942–43.[10]

The most difficult characterization in the movie proved to be Upkeep, in part because the mine remained on the Air Ministry top-secret list during filming in 1954. Since the black-and-white film of the test drops showed the original spherical shape of Upkeep (before Wallis converted it to the cylindrical form), for consistency in the movie and protection of national security, the producers kept the spherical edition as the one hoisted into the Lancaster bomb bays. During the filming, someone from the government allegedly visited Scampton, saw the ABPC version of the bouncing bomb, and left the set satisfied that the moviemakers had respected the secrecy protocol.[11] All of Barnes Wallis's bombs—Upkeep, Highball, Tallboy, and Grand Slam—stayed on the top-secret list until 1962.

Authenticity came with a price tag. The Air Ministry agreed to allow ABPC to rent four Mk-VII Lancasters. In order to replicate the Lancaster Type 464 aircraft flown on the dams raid in 1943, three of the late-model bombers had their mid-upper gun turrets and bomb-bay doors removed, and the bomb bay was fitted with a facsimile receptacle for the mock-up spherical bomb (made of plywood and plaster of Paris). Props crews then painted the exteriors of the bombers: wartime camouflage on top and night black on the underside. Each Lanc had a different set of registration letters on either side, allowing three aircraft to play the parts of six different bombers. For the rental of the Lancasters, the Air Ministry charged ABPC £100 for each hour of running time, per engine! The total for three Lancs with all four engines running amounted to £1,600 per hour.[12] ABPC also hired operational RAF Cold War pilots Joe Kmiecik, Dick Lambert (replaced by Eric Quinney), Ken Souter, and Ted Szuwalski; navigator Colin Batchelor; and flight engineers Jock Cameron, Mike Cawsey, and Dennis Wheatley to do the actual flying.

Actor Richard Todd recalled the bombers' arrival at Scampton for first filming in April 1954. As the production crew and military station staff stood mesmerized, looking up, the approaching four Lancasters "in V-formation came in low over the airfield, [made] a big swing turn, then they landed in formation on the grass. There wasn't a dry eye in the house."[13]

During aerial photography, locations around England and Wales stood in for whatever the script required. Skegness in Lincolnshire doubled for Reculver, where 617 aircrews had tested the bouncing bombs. The coast of Southwold in Suffolk, and the west coast of Anglesey in North Wales, became the backdrop for crossing the enemy coast. The lowlands in Lincolnshire and Norfolk represented the Dutch polders en route to the Ruhr. And for the simulations of the attacks over the Ruhr reservoirs and against the dams, the production crew shot the Lancs flying over Lake Windermere toward the Derwent Dam in the Derbyshire Peak District.[14]

As the Lancs flew their simulated routines, a camera plane with cinematic crew dressed in flight suits captured all the dramatic aerial scenes through an open door in its fuselage. Following initial filming, when the pilots and production crews viewed the daily rushes, it became evident that the sixty-foot altitude achieved during the pre-raid training and the actual bombing runs against the dams wasn't dramatic enough on film. Erwin Hillier, the director of aerial photography, asked the pilots to fly at forty feet above the water instead. As experienced as the RAF crews flying the replica Lancasters were, low flying with permission was a thrill. "To do this in tight formation with some thirty tons of aircraft being controlled by one hand on the control column and one on the throttles," RAF pilot Eric Quinney admitted, "really does get the adrenaline flowing."[15]

Given the popularity of the Dam Busters story, the on-set conditions were powerful enough for the production crew and actors, but when the daily shooting schedule also included periodic visits from some of those who'd actually participated in Operation Chastise, the moviemaking got intense. During critical scenes in which their on-camera impersonators depicted the decision to give Upkeep the green light, the aircrew briefings before the launch of the raid, and the scenes inside the 5 Group operations room awaiting Morse-code news of the attack itself, actors Todd and Redgrave and the rest had an audience. The real Arthur Harris, Ralph Cochrane, and Charles Whitworth, as well as Dam Buster pilot Mick Martin and bomb designer Barnes Wallis, were looking on.

Early in the filming, Wallis had a chance to meet his movie self. "I'm not going to imitate you," Michael Redgrave told Wallis. "No, you must not do that," Wallis responded. "You will have to create me."[16]

Author Brickhill had gone to great lengths to illustrate not only Wallis's nature—introverted, dedicated, passionate, and undeterred—but also the relentless battle he waged with Whitehall to get his invention accepted and implemented. During a climactic scene early in the script, screenplay writer Sherriff captured what author Brickhall could only intimate: that convincing the Air Ministry of the bouncing bomb's potential impact had become truly maddening. Brickhill wrote that Wallis "got permission to build . . . prototypes of his new bomb . . . and was told he could convert a Wellington to drop them."[17] Sherriff amplified the problem in a scene where the determined scientist meets the civil servant resistant to the idea of lending Wallis a Wellington bomber for his tests.

"What possible argument could I put forward to get you a Wellington?" the bureaucrat admonishes.

"Well, if you told them that I designed it, do you think that might help?" says actor Redgrave as Wallis. Cut to the next scene, showing the Wellington taking off to conduct a test drop of the Upkeep prototype.

At Elstree Studios through the summer of 1954, the production team not only built facsimiles of office interiors and the group operations room, they also designed and built scale models of the Ruhr dams inside huge soundproof movie stages. The replica setting of the Möhne reservoir and dam was 300 feet long and 150 feet wide, complete with artificial trees, grass, and rock formations leading to the wall and towers of the dam. Lighting simulated the nighttime sky while an array of electric fans created realistic ripples on the surface of the miniature reservoir.[18] Meanwhile, a camera crane and an adjacent track for a camera mounted on a trolley gave simulated point-of-view aircrew perspectives or provided backdrops for rear-projection views behind the pilot or bomb aimer. To put the moviegoer in the cockpit, so to speak, crews replicated the complete front section of a Lancaster, mounted on a platform that was capable of pivoting like a flight simulator. In one short sequence, Gibson looks through his cockpit window to see the torrent of water rushing through the breached Möhne Dam, while another Lancaster passes beneath him and flak explodes nearby; six different pieces of film (travelling matts) were synchronized and superimposed to show mission accomplished.[19]

By unfortunate coincidence, the actual Ruhr River Valley experienced widespread flooding with catastrophic damage in 1954; Michael Anderson dispatched a film crew to Germany to shoot footage of rivers overflowing their banks as well as towns and industrial areas swamped by the natural disaster.[20] Those images, edited into the feature, became the raging waters unleashed by the breaching of the dams following the raid.

Ultimately it was R.C. Sherriff's script and Richard Todd's portrayal of Guy Gibson that gave the military side of the movie its lustre.* Initially, as he learned his lines, Todd visited Gibson's home and watched film of the man.[21] Then, during the long periods he spent in the simulated cockpit awaiting his "Action" cue, Todd took the time to learn actual flight procedure—from verbal commands and responses to the physical cockpit controls procedure—to make his portrayal of the Dam Busters' wing commander more credible. Todd personally believed the final moments of the film left the deepest impression. He as Gibson and Michael Redgrave as Wallis meet outside the briefing hall moments after the surviving crews have landed back at Scampton.

"Is it true? All those fellows lost?" Wallis asks Gibson.

The wing commander, still in some of his flying gear, offers the scientist a breakdown of the losses and his surprise that so many appear to be missing in action.

"Fifty-six men," Wallis says as he takes off his glasses, obviously distraught. "If I'd known it was going to be like this, I'd never have started it."

---

* The Second World War affected Richard Todd's life both on screen and off. By 1937, when he was eighteen, he'd already made inroads as an actor in repertory theatre in Britain. When the war broke out, he decided to enlist in the army, parachuting into Normandy at Pegasus Bridge with the British 6th Airborne Division on D-Day. Thus his active service made his performances all the more credible in other war movies such as *D-Day the Sixth of June* (1956), *The Long and the Short and the Tall* (1961), and *The Longest Day* (1962).

"If all these fellows had known from the beginning that they wouldn't be coming back, they'd have gone for it just the same," Gibson offers. "I knew them all. I know that's true." Then he recommends the inventor get some rest.

"Aren't you going to turn in, Gibby?" Wallis says finally.

No," he says haltingly. "I have to write some letters first."[22] And, yes, he does walk into the distance, up a road marked "No Entry" on its pavement, as Eric Coates's "Dam Busters March" creeps into the soundtrack for the finale. The movie's Gibson is not heroic, not even patriotic, but rather an airman fulfilling the conditions of his command while accepting its lonely responsibilities too.

THREE AND A HALF YEARS PASSED BETWEEN THE DAY that Paul Brickhill's book was optioned to the Associated British Picture Corporation, in November 1951, and *The Dam Busters* premiere in London. The blockbuster production cost ABPC about £200,000 (US$4.5 million) in 1951.[23] As the premiere approached, tickets were in such demand that the producers organized a couple of opening nights. The first, on May 16, 1955—the twelfth anniversary of the raid—was a command performance at the Empire Theatre, attended by Princess Margaret as well as some of the original Dam Busters, including Mick Martin, Sid Hobday, and Bert Foxlee. Pathé News coverage of the first premiere showed the princess welcoming relatives of those killed in action with 617 Squadron, including Florence Hatton, mother of Bill Hatton; Nellie Knight, mother of Les Knight; Dorcas Roberts, mother of Charlie Roberts; Elizabeth Nicholson, mother of Vivian Nicholson; and Guy Gibson's father and widow, Eve.

On the following night, May 17, the Duke and Duchess of Gloucester were the regal co-hosts. Present and accounted for that night were five officers still in the service of the RCAF— Ken Brown, Percy Pigeon, Don MacLean, Revie Walker, and American-born Joe McCarthy.* All veterans of the raid, the five Canadians were not featured prominently in the movie, but at the premiere they nevertheless mingled with royalty, RAF dignitaries, and the other Dam Busters present while the RAF Central Band played appropriate music in the background.

In many of the group photographs taken, especially those around the model of the Möhne Dam on display in the theatre lobby, the RCAF men appear to hang together. No doubt if McCarthy could have piloted the Trans-Canada Airlines flight to England, he'd have demanded MacLean navigate the plane. "[Revie] felt a real kinship, a real brotherhood with the guys who came through this with him," his son John Walker said later. "They were lifelong friends. They made a lot of effort to be together."[24]

The film's producers held off general release of the movie for four months, until September, so that local cinemas around Britain could ramp up public interest in the feature. ABPC encouraged local RAF associations to get involved, contacting veterans with Bomber Command connections and arranging for RAF bands to perform live when the movie came to town. The film's profits proved substantial—£400,000—and it even

---

* While he maintained ties with family and friends in the United States after the war, Joe McCarthy chose to remain in active service in the RCAF; as a result, he had to become a Canadian citizen.

registered decent box-office returns in Commonwealth countries. To no one's surprise, *The Dam Busters* was the top-grossing movie in Britain in 1955.

Just eleven years old when his aunt and uncle in Oxford drove him to a regional cinema, Charles Foster remembered "the prickle of recognition [that] ran down the back of my neck" as he watched *The Dam Busters* movie for the first time.[25] Growing up, Charles had read and reread Brickhill's book and listened to a well-worn recording of the "Dam Busters March" countless times, but perhaps most indelible of all was sitting in that movie theatre in 1961 and watching the early scene in which Richard Todd as W/C Gibson sorts through the names of potential pilots for his secret operation. With him is G/C Charles Whitworth, played by Derek Farr. Gibson selects a couple of Australians, a New Zealander, and an American. "We mustn't forget the English," Whitworth reminds Gibson as he makes his selections. "Here's Bill Astell. And David Maltby."

Choosing the pilots for the dams raid didn't really happen that way, but Maltby had indeed piloted Lancaster *J-Johnny* in the first wave of Operation Chastise, and just before 1 a.m. on May 17, 1943, had delivered the Upkeep mine that ultimately breached the Möhne Dam. Maltby, who died four months later on the Dortmund-Ems Canal raid, was Charles Foster's uncle. Both the personal connection and Foster's fascination with the mythology of the dams raid drove him to publish his own research on the story—*Breaking the Dams: The Story of Dambuster David Maltby and His Crew*—in 2008. Near the end of his account, Foster explained part of his rationale for writing it. "I have tried to tell the stories of just seven of these men, who by chance came to prominence as they took part in the most famous single operation ever undertaken by the Royal Air Force," Foster wrote.[26]

Britons who had survived the war recognized the significance of the dams raid. The event had signalled a shift from defensive tactics to offensive ones. It had given wartime British leaders and the public tangible evidence that the enemy was vulnerable. It had shown the ingenuity, courage, and resolve of the country's armed forces to accomplish what was considered nearly impossible. Consequently, for Britons the Dam Buster attack had become a touchstone of the Second World War. It had joined the mythology of such iconic wartime moments as Dunkirk, the Battle of Britain, the Blitz, El Alamein, and D-Day.

In contrast to the longevity of the books, the movie, and the music that celebrated the dams raid, the workhorse aircraft that had carried 617 aircrews into history—perhaps the most tangible part of the Operation Chastise mythology—disappeared unceremoniously. In the fall of 1954, when the Associated British Picture Corporation completed principal cinematography on *The Dam Busters*, the four Lancasters on loan from the RAF were flown back to their home station, No. 20 Maintenance Unit at Aston Down. There the four mechanical members of the supporting cast of the movie languished for two years, until they were eventually cut into pieces, sold to an aluminum company, and melted down as scrap.[27]

WHAT ONE DECISION TERMINATED IN THE UNITED Kingdom, an opposite decision made in western Canada, nearly 4,500 miles away, preserved. On February 12, 1959, a recently retired Lancaster that had done some flying in Britain at the end of the war—in fact, for a time it had been stored at the same No. 20 Maintenance Unit at Aston Down that had supplied the four Lancasters for *The Dam Busters* movie—touched down for the last time at Vulcan, Alberta.[28] Formerly a British Commonwealth Air Training Plan station teaching pilots on twin-engine Avro Ansons, the base in southern Alberta suddenly became a storage facility where unwanted warbirds went to die. Among them was Lancaster FM159, built in the spring of 1945 by Victory Aircraft in Malton, Ontario, to serve in Bomber Command. After fourteen years' peacetime service in search and rescue, Atlantic and Pacific maritime reconnaissance, Arctic ice patrols, and NORAD radar exercises, this Lanc's lifespan seemed at an end.

"I wonder what they're going to do with them?" mused a farmer from Nanton, Alberta.[29] George White had put the question to a couple of close Nanton friends—hardware store owner Fred Garratt and menswear store owner Howie Armstrong.

White learned that the Canadian Crown Assets authorities were selling some of the military aircraft at Vulcan as water bombers to firefighting operations in British Columbia. But the vast majority of the surplus Lancasters were destined to be melted down to become pots and pans. Throughout the war, farming just west of Nanton, White remembered training aircraft from Vulcan's No. 19 Service Flying Training School and High River's No. 5 Elementary Flying Training School constantly flying overhead. They had been a nonstop reminder of Canada's wartime contribution—qualified aircrews for active service. And the thought of those historic Lancs disappearing without a trace bothered him.

"What'll we offer them for one?" White asked his two coffee buddies.

"Well, it's got to be an amount we can divide by three,"[30] said Armstrong, who had worked at the family-named menswear store his father opened in Nanton in 1904. In the 1950s, frustrated by passersby who rarely pulled off the northbound highway to shop, Howie Armstrong got permission from the town's Economic and Industrial Committee to run a pipe from the source of Nanton's renowned spring water to a tap by the highway, and then posted a sign that read "Stop and Visit. Help yourself to Canada's finest drinking water!" Based on the success of his tap campaign, Armstrong suggested to his two friends that maybe a wartime Lancaster might provide a solid tourist draw, in addition to serving as an important memorial to Canadian aircrews.

The $513 offer to purchase that the three Nanton entrepreneurs put forward was accepted in August 1960. Though impulsive and rather unfocused as a vision for potential future tourism and wartime remembrance, their initiative seemed the right thing to do. The Lancaster was a piece of history. It symbolized a bygone era, not to mention the service and sacrifice of thousands of Canadian aircrews in Bomber Command from 1939 to 1945. Whatever the airplane's future, three Nanton citizens had just purchased FM159 for their town. All they needed now was a viable plan for transporting it to Nanton, seventeen miles away, without expecting to fly it there. They turned to trucker Archie Clark, who provided a vehicle into which the Lancaster's tailwheel was firmly secured, to tow the aircraft backwards overland. The journey to Nanton began on September 26. With appropriate permission, volunteers lifted power lines, tore down and restored the fences of twenty different farm properties, and navigated FM159 across the Little Bow River. The next day, the entourage reached the Canadian Pacific Railway tracks and had to wait for the crossing permit to kick in.[31] Finally, at four o'clock in the morning of September 28, police allowed the towing team to drag FM159 up onto Highway 2 for the final few miles into Nanton.

"The looks on people's faces, seeing a plane coming down the highway," Howie Armstrong said, "it was priceless!"[32]

Since stopping and looking was all Howie Armstrong had wanted road travellers to consider initially, the arrival of the Lancaster at an empty lot on the north side of Nanton had already paid its first dividend. But it would take another twenty-five years before the town officially adopted the salvaged bomber. During the intervening years, birds tried to make it their permanent home; vandals stripped it of its functioning instruments and broke all the Plexiglas covering the cockpit, gun turrets, and bomb-aimer's position; collectors enticed the town to rid itself of a deteriorating eyesore; and the Air Force even offered to take it off Nanton's hands. But a small band of local volunteers, including two of the Nanton threesome who'd saved it from the scrapyard in the first place, insisted that FM159 had value and should stay put.

Meanwhile, it was Howie Armstrong's stepdaughter who helped the town and its boosters understand why they needed to preserve the Lancaster and, even more important, its story. Around about 1973, Howie and Shirley Armstrong asked Susan Bellamy what she wanted for her birthday. It turned out to be a simple request. "All I want is to go up into the tail of the airplane, where my dad was during the war," Susan told them.[33]

By 1943, several years into the war, Susan's father, Jack Bellamy, had worked in construction, taken some accounting courses at the University of Saskatchewan, and apprenticed as a welder in the oil fields near Turner Valley, Alberta. But when all his friends began enlisting, he felt he too should do his part; he joined the Air Force. A lifelong hunter, Bellamy was a good marksman, so the BCATP streamed him into gunnery and he crewed up as a rear gunner, eventually serving with RCAF No. 428 Squadron on Lancasters. That's why his daughter Susan felt so strongly about climbing that ladder and squeezing into FM159's rear turret—to feel closer to her dad's wartime experience.

On March 22, 1945, on a bombing operation to Dessau, Bellamy's Lancaster was shot down and its crew captured near the Rhine River. F/Sgt. Bellamy had just observed his twenty-fourth birthday. When Susan climbed into the rear turret of the Nanton bomber, she had just turned twenty-one. "Susan was thrilled," Shirley Armstrong said. "Very emotional."[34]

While meaningful on a personal level, Susan Bellamy's visit to Lancaster FM159's rear turret did little to ensure the bomber's longevity. The aircraft continued to suffer from general neglect for another dozen years. Then, recognizing that the project he, Howie Armstrong, and Fred Garratt had initiated in 1960 was hanging by a thread, George White asked the *Nanton News* to help rally the town around the aging Lancaster, as a diamond in the rough. "Battered by the elements and suffering the effects of vandalism," editor Herb Johnson wrote in the fall of 1985, "the old girl won't last too much longer without some help."[35]

The Nanton Lancaster Society (NLS) convened its inaugural meeting in March 1986, and then took stock of the bomber that had sat, pretty much ignored, behind a fence at the north end of town for a quarter-century. Only one of the cockpit's instruments remained in place, and vandals had smashed it; the pilot's control yoke was gone and the throttle and mixture levers bent or broken. Much the same state of gear greeted the volunteers at the flight engineer's, navigator's, bomb-aimer's, and radio operator's positions. No matter to the motivated NLS. Within a year its volunteers had published a newsletter for its six hundred members and compiled an archive of photos, books, and historical documents. It had also placed Lancaster artifacts in the town's tourist information building and inaugurated "Open Bomber Days," allowing the public—seven hundred that first summer—to climb a ladder, the way Susan Bellamy had, for a walk through the bomber from cockpit to crew door. In a year, the little group that could had also raised $28,000, in a town of 2,000 citizens, and announced that the Lancaster would be restored to its wartime condition and would one day become the focal point of a Nanton Lancaster Society museum.

Before the NLS could consider anything close to a museum, however, it had to address the sad state of FM159's interior. Area rancher Dan Fox served as a founding NLS director and volunteered at workshop gatherings every Tuesday night, when everybody pitched in, using what they called "the farmer method" of getting things done.[36] One NLS member retrieved some cockpit instruments. Others repaired elements as basic as the pilot's seat, the flight engineer's instrument panel, the navigator's table, and the cockpit Perspex, guided by another vital acquisition—a Lancaster maintenance manual. Whether it was deciphering the aeronautics of the Lanc or just counting coins in the donation box, no job was beneath anybody.

"We had ambitious dreams of a big hangar and having the Lanc able to taxi around on a tarmac. We weren't afraid to try different things [such as] well, we can't afford to build that, but let's do it anyways," Fox said. "We had people who were dreamers."[37]

Proof that the NLS's long-term aspirations had merit appeared in the sky over Nanton in the spring of 1989. Lancaster FM213, like Nanton bomber FM159, had rolled off the Victory Aircraft assembly line at Malton, Ontario, in 1945; it had logged nearly twenty years of postwar service across Canada and had been retired in 1963. In 1977, volunteers with the then five-year-old Canadian Warplane Heritage Museum (CWHM) purchased FM213 and moved the derelict bomber to the museum's hangars in Hamilton, Ontario. It took eleven years and thousands of volunteer hours to restore the aircraft to airworthy condition. But FM213's maiden flight, on September 24, 1988, attracted an unexpected 20,000 visitors to the CWHM.[38]

To assist the Nanton Lancaster Society's first tentative steps toward restoring its salvaged Lancaster, the equally fledgling CWHM had offered support and guidance. Indeed, the two groups negotiated a trade when Nanton shipped spare Lancaster ailerons and flaps to Hamilton and received main landing gear wheels and tires in exchange.[39] Then, following its maiden flight in the fall of 1988, the CWHM Lancaster flew west as part of a goodwill tour across Canada. And on June 26, 1989, the eastern Lanc, newly minted as Andrew

Mynarski Memorial Lancaster VR-A, performed a figure-eight salute over its sister bomber in Nanton. The population of the Alberta town nearly doubled to watch the flypast. "Never in Nanton's history has any community event, that lasted less than fifteen minutes, brought such large numbers of people into town," a longtime Nanton resident commented.[40]

The excitement of witnessing the flypast enthused the Nanton group, as did the CWHM's decision to commemorate a Royal Canadian Air Force VC winner with its restored and relaunched Lancaster. On June 12, 1944, while serving as an air gunner with RCAF No. 419 Squadron, Andrew Mynarski's bomber was attacked by a night fighter over France; in desperation to escape the doomed aircraft, P/O Mynarski tried in vain to free crewmate Pat Brophy, who was trapped in his rear turret; miraculously Brophy survived the crash, but Mynarski died of burns and in 1946 was posthumously awarded the VC. The CWHM decided to display Mynarski's "VR-A" registration on the exterior of its restored Lancaster.

"We visited the CWHM and learned about their dedication . . . and thought it was a good idea," said Dave Birrell, another founding director of the NLS.[41] Then Birrell found a reference to S/L Ian Bazalgette VC in a book of Canadian war heroes at the Nanton Public Library. Although born in Calgary, Bazalgette was educated in Britain and completed his wartime service in the Royal Air Force. Birrell suggested that this was perhaps the reason his story seemed lost on Canadians and absent from the country's military history. Bazalgette had nearly completed a second full tour with RAF No. 635 Squadron's Pathfinder Force. But on his fifty-sixth op, as master bomber of a V-1 target, his Lancaster was hit by flak and—with two engines out of service—fell into a violent dive. When his third engine failed, "Baz," as he was known, ordered his crew to bail out and then crash-landed the Lanc with two other injured crewmen still aboard; the three died when the aircraft exploded.[42] Despite receiving a posthumous VC, being revered by his surviving crew, and being commemorated in Britain and France, S/L Bazalgette seemed absent from Canadian consciousness. "Obviously, here was the perfect man to associate with the Society's objectives—building a museum and preserving and restoring the Nanton Lancaster bomber," Birrell wrote.[43]

Easier said than done. After months of research, correspondence, and public announcements to search out those associated with Bazalgette's story, the Nanton group had discovered Chuck Godfrey and George Turner, Baz's wireless operator and flight engineer, respectively, and received audio recollections from Doug Cameron, the rear gunner. Then, at the last minute, Baz's sister Ethel Broderick suddenly surfaced in the United States. The NLS brought all key survivors from the airman's story together, along with another capacity audience at the museum, and on July 27, 1990, christened Lanc FM159 as the Ian Bazalgette Memorial Lancaster.

"You really did start something," Ethel Broderick said at the dedication to her brother, "something wonderful, right here in Nanton."[44]

INDEED, THE DEDICATION MARKED A TURNING POINT in the history of the museum and its emerging mission. Just as Barnes Wallis had defied the inertia of the British Air Ministry and Bomber Command to get his bouncing-bomb concept accepted, just as Guy Gibson and his aircrews had defied the odds to accomplish the dams raid, and just as Ralph Cochrane had defied the short-term memory of historians to help record the Dam Busters story in a book and movie, so the pipe dreamers of the Nanton Lancaster Society had defied the naysayers and vandals and saved a Lancaster from the scrap heap. What's more, the moment they dedicated the Ian Bazalgette Memorial Lancaster, the members of the NLS breathed life into a nearly lost legend. They were restoring an artifact to authenticity. They were raising the profile of the often-taken-for-granted Commonwealth aircrews. And most distinctive of all, they were retrieving the stories of its nearly extinct war heroes. The Nanton Lancaster had stopped being just a potential tourist attraction. Thanks to a dedicated band of volunteers, the Bazalgette Lancaster was evolving from a collection of instruments, engines, and airframe parts into a piece of living history.

In November 1990, the NLS turned first sod on that museum they'd promised to build in order to get its prized Lancaster inside and away from the elements. By the following year, the Bazalgette Lanc had enjoyed further restoration, and in July 1992 it became the primary attraction at the grand opening of the Nanton Lancaster Society Air Museum. Nearly missed amid the excitement over the new bricks and mortar and aircraft restoration bustle, however, was a gesture from two of the museum's thousands of visitors that helped plant the story of the dams raid permanently in Nanton. Sometime after the grand opening, a couple from Milo, Alberta, signed the museum register; they were so impressed by the experience of seeing the Lancaster and the accompanying displays about the aircrew who'd served in them that they decided to contribute. Society director and newsletter editor Bob Evans noted their gift in the spring edition.

"Helen Robertson, a second cousin of P/O Torger [Harlo] Taerum . . . spent considerable time and effort finding [his] memorabilia," Evans wrote. "She told members of the society that after visiting the museum and seeing what was being done to preserve Bomber Command . . . she was convinced this was the right place for Torger Taerum's medals."[45]

So, on April 16, 1993, the Robertsons came back to Nanton from the Milo area of Alberta, and in front of a handful of NLS directors and some visitors who happened to be touring the museum that day, quietly presented two big shopping bags to then museum president Dan Fox. The bags contained Taerum's logbook, other papers, photographs, and his military awards, including the dams raid DFC. "Here," she said simply to Fox. "Go to it!"[46]

Dave Birrell seized the moment. That summer, to coincide with a planned fiftieth-anniversary recognition of the dams raid, museum volunteers mounted Taerum's medals for display and dedicated a section of the museum's exhibition area to diagrams, maps, correspondence, and photographs about Operation Chastise and the Canadian airmen who'd served in the raid. To enhance the exhibit, Valour Canada, originally the Calgary Military Museums Society, crafted a short video incorporating Barnes Wallis's black-and-white film of the test drops over Chesil Beach and excerpts from *The Dam*

Busters 1954 movie feature. The producers ensured that P/O Harlo Taerum's war service remained prominent; the video recounted the story of the Alberta farm boy who'd chafed over the 1940 German invasion of Norway, who'd enlisted in the RCAF that very summer, who'd excelled in operational training in Canada and the United Kingdom, who was spotted by his commanders as having the right stuff for the dams raid, and who'd served as lead navigator in Guy Gibson's Lancaster on the Dam Buster operation.

"We started basically with an empty field here and an old beat-up Lancaster at the side of the highway," Dan Fox said. He added that what set the Nanton museum apart was "instead of just collecting stuff . . . we learned we should be telling the stories of this plane too." [47]

On Dam Busters Commemoration Day, that summer of 1993, visitors to the museum had a chance to touch the Bazalgette Lancaster and see the step-by-step story of the dams raid among the exhibits. But many at the banquet in the Nanton Community Centre that weekend also had an opportunity to meet the Canadian pilot who had successfully piloted his *F-Freddie* crew and its Upkeep mine to the Sorpe Dam fifty years before. Retired S/L Ken Brown was everything a museum eager to showcase the Dam Busters story could want—an RCAF airman with thousands of hours in the service of his country (from 1941 to 1968), a veteran with the greatest of respect and admiration for the Lancaster, and, best of all, a raconteur who could stand in front of an audience and deliver tales of the Dam Busters as if the raid had happened yesterday. Brown also had plenty of credibility;

among his many gongs he wore the Conspicuous Gallantry Medal, presented to him by Queen Elizabeth following the dams raid in June 1943.

During his address to the banquet, and with a twinkle in his eye, Brown referred to the rocky relationship he'd had with W/C Guy Gibson prior to the dams raid. He reminded his audience about Gibson punishing him for being last man through the briefing-room door and the unique way he had conducted extreme low-flying training. Then Brown recounted his attempts, just after the dams raid, to bag a rabbit on a farmer's field adjacent to the Scampton aerodrome and his confrontation with a constable who was summoned to arrest Brown for poaching.

"Do you know you're trespassing?" the British constable said to Brown when he challenged him on the farmer's land.[48]

"Go on," Brown said. "I'm waiting for a rabbit."

"It's on private property."

"Well, the rabbit was over on our property and he ran over to this side of the road. And I'm claiming him."

When Brown couldn't provide proper identification to the constable, the officer told him he'd have to come down to the station for interrogation.

"Well, I'll have to decline your invitation," said Brown defiantly.

"I demand to know why," the constable came back.

"Because I've got a loaded shotgun in my hand, and you've got nothing."

When the dust settled some days later, Brown learned that his wing commander had taken the arrest warrant, gone to court on his pilot's behalf, and resolved the incident without further action; Gibson had probably also paid the fine. Brown interpreted his CO's actions as a way of rewarding his allegiance to him and the squadron with loyalty in return. And Brown admired such loyalty. He'd expected it from his Bomber Command superiors and from every other airman at 617 Squadron. He'd expected it from all six of his *F-Freddie* Lancaster aircrew during Operation Chastise. And he'd expected it from himself.

Ken Brown's fourth son, Brock, acknowledged that his father demanded a lot from those around him, including his children. Growing up in postwar Comox, British Columbia, Brock remembered that his father, a squadron leader on the base at the time, had a commanding presence at home too; for a number of years father and son did not see eye to eye. But when museums and broadcasters came calling for his father's war stories, Brock suddenly saw his father through the prism of his wartime loyalties, responsibilities, and trauma.

In particular, when Brock watched a CBC television documentary called *The Valour and the Horror*, he saw another side to his father. When the doc producers arranged to have two German civilians who'd survived the Hamburg fire bombings of July 1943 confront veteran Ken Brown during the filming, the former bomber pilot was clearly moved by the civilians' trauma. "For the first time in my life," Brock Brown said, "I heard my dad talk about the pain of war and the feeling of the emptiness it brought."[49]

The documentary episode "Death by Moonlight: Bomber Command" also openly criticized Bomber Command for exaggerating the impact of its campaign against Germany's Ruhr

Valley war production. It painted an exaggerated picture of a bloodthirsty Arthur Harris boasting about German civilian deaths in the bombings. And it claimed that Commonwealth aircrews were duped into believing their targets every night were military, not civilian. The initial broadcast of "Death by Moonlight," in January 1992, sparked nationwide controversy. Historians, journalists, social activists, and particularly Air Force veterans offered differing perspectives; the veterans sued the CBC and the filmmakers for slander, but their class action suit was dismissed by both the Ontario Court of Appeal and the Supreme Court of Canada. The Canadian Senate, however, conducted an inquiry in 1993 and concluded that "although the filmmakers have a right to their point of view, they have failed to present that point of view with any degree of accuracy or fairness."[50]

Nevertheless, in the documentary Ken Brown appeared to agree with the premise of the producers, suggesting that Bomber Command had misled crews to believe that they were bombing only German factory sites, not population centres. "Making those statements caused my dad to lose many so-called friends," Brock Brown said. "But my dad had done his homework before making those statements, and I felt proud he stood up for what he believed was the truth."[51]

At the Dambusters Commemorative banquet, S/L Brown reflected on the overall Bomber Command statistics he'd also gathered: that during the war Canadians comprised 25 percent of all aircrew in Britain; that, per capita, Canada had more aircrew in operational squadrons than England had; and that Canadian casualties in the Second World War proved highest among aircrew—of more than 58,000 airmen lost in

Bomber Command, more than 10,000 were Canadians.[*] In other words, Canada's total commitment to the air war effort could never be questioned. Not afraid to be provocative, Brown praised the Nanton Lancaster Society Air Museum volunteers for providing a face and a voice "for those who are not here to speak on their own behalf," but he also challenged his hosts to show a younger generation what young Canadians had accomplished fifty years before. "The young fellows [then] were so concerned that we might lose our way of life . . . that this Canada of ours might suffer. I think we can give that serious thought today," Ken Brown said.[52]

It's a consciousness that ultimately the Air Force veteran instilled in his son. Brock Brown's working home office proudly displays the artifacts and images of his father's wartime service, with particular focus on the dams raid—including the red, green, and white scarf F/Sgt. Brown wore on every bombing operation, including Operation Chastise; a photo of Guy Gibson inscribed by his former 617 Squadron wing commander to Ken Brown's mother; and a portrait sketch of Ken after he'd received his Conspicuous Gallantry Medal in June 1943. As well, in the eulogy written for his father's funeral and later passed along to the Nanton museum, son Brock applauded his father's capacity as a leader "to not only ask men to risk their lives for a cause, but to actually get them to do it!"[53]

The night the Nanton Lancaster Society Air Museum marked the fiftieth anniversary of the dams raid, the rela-

---

[*] The Bomber Command Museum of Canada archives indicate that as many as 10,500 Canadian aircrew died in the service of Bomber Command, a number that does not include hundreds of Americans in the RCAF or the hundreds of Canadians who served in the RAF.

tives of Harlo Taerum's family were recognized for the gift of his records and medals. Members of Ken Brown's family watched as he delivered his anniversary keynote and was thanked by the museum volunteers "for giving everyone a better sense of who we are, what we were, and where we should be headed."[54]

Then a representative of the Canadian branch of the Bomber Command Association offered his congratulations to the museum members present. "You have an air museum that is the envy of towns and cities everywhere. . . . Your Lancaster is famous around the world," Keith Shepherd said. "Just think of the fame that has come to Nanton because of a purchase by a group of farsighted citizens, numerous dedicated volunteers, and a supportive community. . . . You have created living history."[55]

JOHN WALKER LEARNED HOW DEEPLY THE DAM BUS-ters' story resonated with his family in the late 1990s. It was Christmastime. The family had gathered at his sister's cottage on Lake Huron, near Grand Bend, Ontario. They had unwrapped all the gifts and done all the Christmas dinner dishes when Tom Phillips, John's brother-in-law, suggested that the family ought to unwind by watching a movie. How about *The Dam Busters*? Everybody in the family knew that John's father, Revie Walker, had served aboard Dave Shannon's *L-Leather* Lancaster in the dams raid, but, as was often the case with veterans, the former RCAF navigator rarely volunteered to share the experiences with his family. But that Christmas evening when the family put on the movie, something unusual happened: John Walker spent as much time watching his father as watching the movie.

Specifically, as the film depicts the attack on the Eder Dam, Richard Todd, playing Guy Gibson, instructs the Dave Shannon character to be careful getting around all the surrounding hills. The camera point of view shifts to the cockpit of *L-Leather*, with the actor playing Dave Shannon banking to port to line up his Lancaster for a bombing run over the Eder Reservoir.

"OK, Leader," says Shannon. "Going in now."

The sequence next cuts to a view from over the shoulders of the cockpit crew, looking through the cockpit Perspex toward the dam. The pilot is seated off to the left, the flight engineer to the right, and standing right behind him is the navigator.

"That's me," said the real Revie Walker, watching the movie with his family on Christmas more than half a century after the raid. "That's me."[56]

The room went quiet as the scene continued, and John Walker sensed that his dad had actually relived the experience for a few moments. The circumstances seemed to hit home, and Revie Walker teared up at thoughts of the raid. "I don't think Dad meant his feelings to be broadcast so the whole room could hear it," John Walker said. "But I could see the emotion on his face."[57]

Over time, because of moments like the one shared that Christmas day, Revie Walker's son drew closer and closer to his father's story. It wasn't easy at first, since understanding often required an adult's perspective. The breadth and depth of the dams raid came to John Walker—like the family viewing of the movie—only in bits and pieces and later in life. He often wondered why his father was so frugal, why he always shared and would do anything for a neighbour. When John discovered how close-knit the dams raid crews had become in the lead-up to Operation Chastise, he understood the principles that had governed his father's life.

"We had a small group of people," Revie told his son once. "We trained together. Became family."[58]

"Weren't you scared?" John remembered asking his father.

"I was," Revie said. "It was incredibly high-risk. We knew it. But it was worth it."

John Walker learned a little more about the Dam Busters brotherhood in 1972, when the international reunion came to Toronto. That year, as many as forty Canadian members of the former 617 Squadron attended the gathering; eleven original Dam Buster veterans showed up, including pilot Ken Brown, gunner Dave Rodger, and navigators Don MacLean and Revie Walker.[59] Still in his boyhood and allowed to tag along with his father to the reunion, John Walker was struck by the aura of the veterans, decked out in their blazers, medals, and distinctive burgundy-coloured ties with the Dam Buster logo—three bolts of lightning breaking a dam—emblazoned on them. The young John Walker was impressed and inquisitive.

"There's only one honourary Dam Buster," one of the vets told him.[60]

"Who's that?"

"[Former] prime minister John Diefenbaker," the man said. Then, recognizing that John was Revie Walker's son, the veteran carefully removed his tie and gave it to the boy as he said, "Now there's two."

It may well have been that moment, which John Walker recalled after a few visits to the Nanton Lancaster Society Air Museum, that persuaded him to get involved. He'd seen the Bazalgette Lancaster and the Dam Buster exhibits and artifacts and, after his dad's death in 2001, he'd taken his mother, Doreen, to see the displays at Nanton. The family had kept Revie's uniform and officer's hat, but all of John's siblings agreed it made more sense to donate them to the museum's Dam Buster collection. So, that summer, he drove from his home in Calgary to Nanton and joined a small ceremony during which he made the donation and a short speech reflecting on his father's experiences and the museum that cared enough to preserve them. "Dad would be proud to have [these] here," he said. "I appreciate the blood, sweat, and tears that go into this museum . . . and the remembering and the caring."[61]

On August 20, 2005, the Nanton Lancaster Society Air Museum (renamed the Bomber Command Museum of Canada [BCMC] in 2010) unveiled yet another of its landmark tributes, the Bomber Command Memorial. The wall, consisting of five panels of polished granite, displays almost 10,700 engraved names of Canadians killed in the Second World War while serving in Bomber Command. Among those names etched into the stone were the fourteen Canadians lost among seven crews on the dams raid. From the first wave of Dam Busters: on Lancaster AJ-A, bomb aimer Vincent MacCausland; aboard AJ-B, navigator Floyd Wile, front gunner Frank Garbas, and wireless operator Albert Garshowitz; aboard AJ-M, flight engineer Charles Brennan and navigator

Ken Earnshaw; and from AJ-Z, navigator Robert Urquhart and wireless operator Alden Cottam. Those in the second wave: aboard AJ-E, front gunner Harvey Glinz; from AJ-K, pilot Vernon Byers and rear gunner James McDowell. And among the third-wave crews: aboard AJ-S, pilot Lewis Burpee, rear gunner Gordon Brady, and bomb aimer Jimmy Arthur. As well, those Dam Busters lost following the dams raid were listed: navigator Harlo Taerum, front gunner George Deering, wireless operator Chester Gowrie, and bomb aimer John Thrasher.

Again the event drew almost as many spectators to the museum as the population of Nanton, including politicians, civil servants, military personnel, police, an honour guard, and veterans. Amid the tributes, ceremonial music, moments of silence, and wreath laying, there was plenty of time for those attending to move along the memorial wall and touch the names carved into the stone. Then, that afternoon, the museum reached another milestone. Following two years of painstaking work, the museum's engine crew publicly fired up one of the Bazalgette Lancaster's engines. It had been forty-six years since that engine had run. A huge puff of exhaust smoke followed by the unmistakable roar of a Merlin engine triggered cheers and applause among volunteers and spectators alike. It was the first time any of the bomber's four Rolls-Royce Merlin V-12s had actually run since FM159 went out of service and was sold to Nanton visionaries George White, Fred Garratt, and Howie Armstrong in 1960. Newsletter editor Bob Evans noted, "Our Lancaster is gradually coming to life again!"[62]

As powerful as those four engines sounded, however, none of the volunteers long associated with the BCMC let the smoke and rumble of their technical achievement obscure what president Rob Pedersen often defined as the museum's ultimate mission. "An airplane's an airplane," he said. "But if you can use it to tell a story of the people who lived in them, ran them, worked on them, then that keeps their memory alive. It keeps their contribution from being minimalized to a dot in history, instead of surviving as an expansive, living story."[63]

CHAPTER TWELVE

"FOR ALL THE GOOD IT DID . . ."

H E DOESN'T REMEMBER IT, BUT JIM MACLEAN came to Canada from Britain aboard a transatlantic ship. His father, Don MacLean, the navigator aboard *T-Tommy* in the dams raid, and his mother, Josie Tear, a radio operator with the Women's Auxiliary Air Force, had been married at Lincoln Cathedral in late 1944. When she emigrated as a war bride, she was pregnant. So Jim, born in 1945, always felt a connection to Britain. His brother Bill, born in 1947, acquired the same connection, because his dad stayed in the RCAF after the war and took the opportunity of a posting back to the United Kingdom from 1957 to 1961.

That's when the MacLean sons learned how famous their father was. They attended a British boys' public school, they believe, largely because the school discovered Don MacLean was a Dam Buster and that seemed to trump any other required entry criteria. Every May 16 they attended Dam Buster commemorations with their parents, so the boys quickly learned why the anniversary held such significance for Britons who'd gone through the war. And every year that the MacLeans lived in London, their dad was invited to the Queen's garden party at Buckingham Palace. "Because the [617] Squadron had been so extremely polite and friendly with the King [George] when they visited Scampton after the raid, the Queen never forgot," Jim MacLean said.[1]

Elizabeth, the Queen Mother, could vividly recall the darkest times of the war—the Battle of Britain, Dunkirk—and in particular the Blitz. On September 13, 1940, 181 German bombers had dropped 224 tons of high explosive and 279 incendiary canisters on London, including the inner quadrangle and Royal Chapel at Buckingham Palace.[2] Later, she and the King walked some of the streets of London's East End. "I felt as if I was walking in a dead city," the Queen Mother wrote. "All the houses evacuated [with] possessions, photographs, beds, just as they were left."[3]

Three years later, when the King and Queen visited Scampton after the dams raid, they offered the aircrews their congratulations, but also their thanks for inspiring some hope in their subjects and themselves. Yes, their Air Force bomber crews deserved the country's praise for such a daring accomplishment, but the royals also felt the Dam Busters deserved their gratitude for physically taking the war to the industrial heart of Nazi Germany, for giving the British public a victory to shout about, and for helping to lead a country, its people, and its monarchs out of their darkest days. And because the airmen had been so kind to her husband that day at 617 Squadron station, the Queen would be forever grateful. And she always showed it.

"The Dam Busters and their wives would be there [at the

Palace] together," Jim MacLean added, "but then the Queen would boot all the wives out of the room, just to be with the squadron, her boys. And they were quite happy to sit and drink with the Queen Mum."[4]

In time, too, the MacLean sons came to understand the fatalistic side of their father. Initially when they learned from him how deathly afraid of flying he'd been through the war, they considered it a logical reaction to the daily danger he faced. But there was more than fear to the mantra he recited before each op—"I'm not going to live 'til the end of the day." It was about knowing what he was up against. Because *T-Tommy* had survived Operation Chastise, the crew, particularly Don MacLean and Joe McCarthy, began to rationalize their survival this way: if McCarthy were in the cockpit, MacLean knew he could rely on his pilot. It was one less variable. It was the same for McCarthy. He would fly nowhere, in no airplane, without MacLean at the navigator's table behind him. For months on end the pair attended briefings to learn what target Bomber Command had chosen for them next, what bomb load they would carry, how heavy the flak and night-fighter opposition might be. Each man could deal with the possibility he might not get back, as long as he knew the other man was there doing his job in the aircraft with him. The rest was calculated risk. "I think they had a different kind of bond than the rest of the crew," Bill MacLean said.[5]

A bond of trust, but also a means of coping with the fear. The dams raid wasn't called a suicide mission for nothing: eight of nineteen bombers lost and fifty-three of 133 killed in action—all of Vernon Byers's crew, Norman Barlow's crew, Bill Astell's crew, Henry Maudslay's crew, Lewis Burpee's crew,

Dinghy Young's crew, all but one of Bill Ottley's crew, and all but two of John Hopgood's crew. Coping with survival may have been as difficult as dealing with the deaths. For those who came back the morning of May 17 it was tough enough. But for gunner Fred Tees the guilt of surviving proved debilitating. Although he was often positioned in the front turret, on the dams raid Sgt. Tees swapped with Harry Strange and served that one night in the rear turret; when Ottley's *C-Charlie* went down, the tail blew clear of the main crash site and Tees survived, became a POW, and then came home to Chichester, in Sussex. In March 1982, six months after he visited the crash site near Hamm, Germany, to honour the memory of his aircrew comrades, Tees died by suicide.[6]

DON MACLEAN RECEIVED HIS DISTINGUISHED FLYING Medal from Queen Elizabeth on June 21, 1943, while during that same awards ceremony at Buckingham Palace, Joe McCarthy received his Distinguished Service Order; the American received a bar to his Distinguished Flying Cross from the King in September 1944. Meanwhile, Dave Rodger, McCarthy's long-serving rear gunner, eventually got his DFC for service over an entire tour of duty at the end of the war, but did not receive it from either the King or the Queen. "They just mailed it," Nell Rodger explained. "He didn't go for any of that."[7] Although when the DFC award was announced in the local newspapers, the family got a kick out of seeing the accompanying photograph of F/L Rodger in his trademark Algoma Steel hockey sweater.

Nell (then Barbet) had met Dave on the job at the Algoma

Steel plant in their hometown, Sault Ste. Marie, Ontario, when they were teenagers in the 1930s. He worked as a test boy at the plant and she was a summer telephone operator. At the time, she wasn't interested in serious relationships, just serious dancing, skating, and party-going. That changed when Dave came home on leave from RCAF gunnery school in the fall of 1942. He sent Nell a cedar chest for Christmas, clearly illustrating his intention to marry her on his return from overseas. In September 1944, when Nell learned that Dave was en route home, she surprised him by taking the train from the Sault to Sudbury. They were married a few weeks later. Dave surprised Nell with his improved dancing skills; he'd taken lessons in England just before embarkation home.

"Well, it was cute," Nell said. "One of Dave's friends in England was married to a girl who knew how to dance. And she pushed him around the floor until he came home and attempted to jive."[8]

"Later, they would part the floor," daughter Andrea said, "and people would watch them dance."[9]

In addition to music and dancing, the Rodger household hummed with nine children. At home in Sault Ste. Marie and at their cottage on Lake Superior, the Rodger family seemed constantly in motion—skiing, hiking, swimming, and playing musical instruments. Meanwhile, Dave also became a lay minister and returned to his job at Algoma Steel, eventually retiring after nearly forty-one years of service. Despite immersing himself back in civilian life, he maintained a connection to his military family, selling poppies each November and organizing Legion funerals for community veterans when they died. Perhaps at such times of loss, Dave Rodger took it more personally. Nell remembered a period of months when he got depressed. "I didn't know what was going on," Nell said. "I thought he was angry about something that had happened. But it must have been his thinking about the past . . . losing his buddies."[10]

The Air Force had trained its airmen, and F/O Rodger was no exception, to cope—to cope with orders, challenging flight conditions, catastrophic destruction, the loss of comrades—and when they came home to stow away their traumatic memories the same way they did their uniforms, medals, and flight logs, like so much baggage. Eldest daughter Sheila said she wasn't aware of her father's role in the dams raid until she was ten years old. "Dad never mentioned the war until . . . the release of the Dam Buster movie. It might have been the first movie I saw in a theatre," she said.[11] But he still didn't talk about it except around the Dam Buster anniversaries, when, his daughter Andrea said, "Dad seemed happy to accommodate . . . historians, authors, and a few scammers wanting information or to have him sign pictures."[12]

IT WAS THEN, IN THOSE APPARENTLY INNOCENT MO-ments of exchange—at Air Force commemorations, around veterans' reunions, or sometimes just in private correspondence between Dam Buster families and their admirers—that perhaps the greatest threat to their legacy emerged, one that required the generation of dams raid sons and daughters to meet and challenge.

Shere Fraser knew she was the daughter of a Dam Buster from her childhood, but it took half a lifetime and a co-worker to help her realize the importance of this fact. Employed as a flight attendant—first for the iconic Wardair Canada passenger service in the mid-1970s, and then with WestJet, starting in 2001—Shere regularly wore an RAF pin on her lapel in honour of her father, John Fraser, bomb aimer with 617 Squadron. When members of her flight crews inquired further and learned that P/O Fraser had served aboard one of the Lancasters shot down during the dams raid, Shere was a little surprised at the fuss. Then a fellow flight attendant with roots in the United Kingdom gave her John Sweetman's book about the famous combat operation, *The Dambusters Raid*; he even highlighted paragraphs.[13] Things began falling into place for this Dam Buster's daughter—the raid, the results, the significance, and her connection.

John Fraser and his crew aboard *M-Mother* had run the gauntlet on May 16–17, 1943; they'd flown at treetop level almost all the way to the Ruhr but were hit by anti-aircraft fire en route and during the attack over the Möhne Dam. Pilot John Hopgood had managed to keep the bomber airborne long enough for some of the crew, including Fraser, to bail out. He had parachuted to safety, evaded the Germans for approximately ten days, been captured just short of the German-Dutch border, and spent the duration of the war in POW camps, finally at Stalag Luft III in Poland.

Following the long march by POWs in the winter and spring of 1945, P/O Fraser was liberated by Allied troops, then returned to England and reunited with his wife, Doris— they'd been married for only two weeks when he was shot down. Eventually in that year, Dam Buster and POW veteran Fraser came home to Canada, followed shortly after by his war bride, and the couple settled down to postwar life in British Columbia. Their three children bore names associated with the dams raid—sons John and Guy (named after Hopgood and Gibson) and daughter Shere (for the village in England where Hopgood grew up).[14] Shere knew her father only a short time, however; he was killed in 1962 when his Piper float plane struck an unmarked guide wire over log booms and crashed near Saltery Bay, BC. In the aftermath, Shere's mother needed to carry on raising her family; she dealt with the grief by tucking away all of her husband's effects, including his letters, newspaper clippings, and his wartime records. So for his daughter, at least, Dam Buster John Fraser's story lay dormant until a colleague sparked her curiosity in 2002.

With a newfound passion for her father's war story, Shere Fraser soon began to recognize something else, something uncomfortable, even sinister, about the process of remembrance and tribute for the men who'd carried out the raid. Not only had the descendants of the dams raid airmen developed a greater appreciation and fascination for the Dam Busters' story, but so too—over those years—had a growing group of war buffs, documentarians, museums, historians, and collectors. Particularly in 1993, as the fiftieth anniversary loomed in public and military consciousness, and then again in 2003, on the sixtieth—by which time the number of surviving Operation Chastise veterans had dwindled significantly—stories and memorabilia associated with Guy Gibson's dams raid squadron seemed to grow in importance . . . and value. And that's when the line between those wishing to preserve and share the Dam Busters' history for posterity and those seeking to hoard and profit by it became blurred. Initially the intersection of public good and private gain was subtle, inconsequential. But all at once the collecting overtook the sharing.

One signal of that trend appeared in Canadian newspapers in the form of a blanket request from a British researcher for information about the dams raid. In one publication, the letter to the editor invited "the relatives of any of the men who flew on the Dambuster raid" to respond.[15] Alex Bateman, of Middlesex, England, wanted to hear from the next of kin of 617 Squadron airmen in his efforts to research the story and presumably publish his findings. Whenever Bateman received responses, he began approaching the families of the Dam Busters directly, asking for records, artifacts, and personal documents that he suggested would enrich his study of the raid and its participants.

In 2002, in the process of her own research, Shere Fraser discovered the website of the Nanton Lancaster Society Air Museum and left a request for more information in the museum's digital guest book. The museum directed her to other Dam Buster families and historians.* Such contacts innocently led Shere to Alex Bateman. Hungry for as much background on her father as she could find, Shere emailed him asking what information the British collector might have in his archives. Bateman obliged by sending her P/O John Fraser's Canadian service records. Shere began to wonder how someone unrelated and unknown to the family could know so much about her father's wartime career.

---

* Shere credits Paul Morley, a teacher and writer in Hamilton, Ontario, for helping her to make contact with war historians and discover her father's dams raid experience. Like Shere Fraser, Morley has dedicated much time, travel, and research to tracking down the story of another Dam Buster airman—F/Sgt. Frank Garbas, front gunner aboard *B-Baker*.

"Did you give him Dad's service records?" Shere asked her mother.[16]

"No. I sent him a few pictures," Doris said. "Then I sent him his [RCAF] logbook because he said he was writing a book."

Shere learned that her mother had some years previously shipped the photos and logbook to Bateman. Doris sent the items to someone she sensed was genuinely interested, and trusted that the artifacts on loan would one day be returned. Indeed, in some of his earliest contacts with Shere, Bateman claimed Doris believed that none of her children had any interest in their father's story. When Shere suggested otherwise to Bateman, "That's when it all started to go wrong," she said. Undaunted, she began building a file of her research, her discoveries, and her correspondence with Bateman himself. And she launched a concerted campaign of letter writing, sending emails, making phone calls, and seeking interviews with the media to draw attention to her family's demands for action. Along the way, in 2010, Shere Fraser met and married Joe McCarthy Jr., the son of the American-born Dam Buster pilot. They became a team in life and in the pursuit of Shere's quest.

As well as raising the profile of the case to have her father's logbook returned, Shere Fraser also gained strong allies among members of the Nanton Lancaster Society Air Museum, and she was invited to join events planned for August 2003. In honour of the sixtieth anniversary of the dams raid, three generations of the extended Fraser family travelled to Nanton to participate in the festivities. They toured the Dam Buster exhibits at the museum. John Lowe, P/O Fraser's grandson, delivered a tribute to a man he never knew, but one who "epitomized the man I wanted to become." Lowe was just seventeen at the time but had already become a corporal in an air cadet squadron and was later deployed for a tour of duty in Afghanistan with Princess Patricia's Canadian Light Infantry. "The harrowing adventures he had as a young man helped shape my own passion to explore the world."[17]

Since she is also an accomplished musician, Shere offered her own unique touch to the commemoration at Nanton that day, playing a solo version of the theme from *The Dam Busters* on her flute. Meanwhile, Doris Fraser, P/O Fraser's widow, contributed a photograph of members of 50 Squadron, from which her husband and other aircrew had been selected for the dams raid; she was then escorted up a ladder into the Bazalgette Memorial Lancaster to sit in its cockpit. Shere also climbed aboard to visit the bomb-aimer's position, repeating a practice inaugurated back in 1973 when Susan Bellamy asked to see where her father had served in Bomber Command during the war. "Once I was able to climb inside," Shere Fraser said, "I could see how he managed to escape."[18]

Repeatedly, as she looked for new ways to get the missing logbook returned, she would urge Bateman to comply; once he posted a parcel to the Fraser family with a note saying, "It's a pleasure to return the logbook to the rightful owners."[19] The package arrived empty. When Shere threatened legal action, Bateman claimed that Doris had given the logbook to him as a gift and said he had evidence to prove it. Finally, in April 2015, after what Shere called "eleven years of silence," her appearances and pleas found a sympathetic ear in the United Kingdom. Several people who'd heard her story and sensed similar concerns about the disappearing Dam Busters legacy offered to help. Eventually Shere's extensive dossier against Bateman was handed to British law enforcement authorities. Shortly after, the phone rang at her home in British Columbia. It was early in the morning, and Detective Sergeant Henry Childe, with the London Metropolitan Police, was on the line asking about the latest in her case.

"Are you saying that you want to investigate this?" Shere said. "I can't believe this is happening."

"Well, this file is on my desk," Childe said, "and I need to ask you a few questions."

Within days of her contact with the London police, they had entered Alex Bateman's home and made several pertinent discoveries . . . discoveries that affected the families of several other Dam Busters.

To cope with the tension of combat operations in Bomber Command, Canadian navigator Ken Earnshaw had often turned to one of his most personal and prized possessions—an album of photographs he'd compiled from his earliest days in Air Force training in 1942, right up to the rigorous seven-week regimen preceding the dams raid in the spring of 1943. There were snaps of his parents, his sister Nora, and the farm back in Alberta to help him combat any homesickness. But most morale-boosting of all were pictures of Mary Heather, whom he'd married a few months before embarkation overseas. In fact, in the album was perhaps the last image of him from home—a picture of Ken and Mary at the train station in Bashaw, Alberta, just before he boarded for the cross-country trip to Halifax and then troopship passage overseas. Earnshaw clearly missed his loved ones and waited with great anticipation for their correspondence and more personal snapshots to add to his photo collection.

"I'm really on a letter writing spree, so, about two or three months from now I should be getting some answers," he wrote his parents in January 1943. "Mary's [last] letter was written on the 20th of December. . . . I do hope for her sake, I get back sometime soon."[20]

He did not get back. Four months later, he too went missing when John Hopgood's Lancaster was brought down by enemy fire over the Möhne Dam. While bomb aimer Fraser and rear gunner Tony Burcher bailed out safely, the Red Cross subsequently learned that the rest of *M-Mother*'s aircrew, including F/O Earnshaw, had been killed in the crash. And when the Air Force finally released Ken Earnshaw's belongings to his wife, in 1946, Mary received the photo album he'd carried with him overseas. But time and the war proved hard on Mary Earnshaw; she remarried, and eventually the photo album and F/O Earnshaw's flight log were passed to Heather Harvey, Mary's daughter, who felt little or no connection to her deceased stepfather's war history.

Around the year 2000, Heather Harvey was approached by Alex Bateman, seeking data on individual Canadian members of the Dam Buster squadron. Recently retired from the US Air Force, Harvey considered the historian's request legitimate and, as confirmed in a Bateman letter to another Earnshaw relative, she sent the British collector Ken Earnshaw's logbook and a "photo album, which contains . . . photographs of Mary and his sister Nora and family [and] some of the photographs relating to Ken's time in the RCAF."[21] The letter went on to suggest the researcher planned to incorporate what he'd received into a manuscript. In 2003, when Heather Harvey's attempts to retrieve the war artifacts yielded nothing, Ken Earnshaw's nephew, Jim Heather, got involved.

Because the Heather family farmed near Milo, in the same part of Alberta as the Taerum family, Jim had grown up hearing about one of the heroes of the dams raid—Harlo Taerum, Guy Gibson's navigator. Jim had learned the lore of Harlo's athleticism, his studiousness, his propensity for numbers that made him a natural as an observer, and how highly W/C Gibson had regarded him as lead navigator on Operation Chastise. Like so many in southern Alberta, Jim Heather had also become a supporter of the original Nanton Lancaster Society and its drive to keep the stories of Harlo Taerum, and Jim's uncle Ken Earnshaw, at the forefront of the museum's exhibits and display cases, and to acquire as many Bomber Command aircrew stories as physical artifacts. "Ken and Terry [Taerum] would have known each other well," Jim said, "both being Canadians and both being navigators."[22]

And there were all those dams raid stories that Jim Heather had come to know as well—how Gibson had relied on the advice of friend and pilot Mick Martin to choose Harlo Taerum for his navigator, and how Ken Earnshaw had accurately predicted the number of bombers that wouldn't likely return from Operation Chastise, including his own. Jim concluded that his uncle's fatalism could only have come as a result of the relentless pace of Bomber Command's campaign in the air over Germany. The odds might well catch up with him. "It was a matter of, 'Suck it up, young man, for King and country,' and muster up the guts to get on that bomber night after night flying missions over Germany," Jim said. "He could see people and planes dropping all around him . . . and it could just as easily have been Ken shot down."

Informed by such stories each time he visited the Nanton air museum, and with fewer living veterans or relatives of the Dam Busters around to speak on their own behalf, Jim Heather felt he had no choice but to pick up where other family members had left off; he would try to retrieve the war artifacts for his Earnshaw relatives, and eventually also make copies for the Nanton museum archives. By that time, he'd also learned about Shere Fraser's attempts to retrieve her father's logbook from Bateman, and he began his own steady stream of emails to the British collector, requesting that Ken Earnshaw's photo album be returned to Canada. He wrote and he waited and wrote and waited, but received no replies.

"If I didn't keep Ken's memory alive," Jim Heather said, "then there probably wouldn't be anyone else who would do it."[23]

THE ONGOING EFFORT TO RETRIEVE WAR HEIRLOOMS found yet a third Dam Buster relative as an ally. Unlike Shere Fraser, Hartley Garshowitz discovered his connection to the dams raid when he was a child, but just like Jim Heather, his uncle died in the combat operation. Just past midnight on May 17, 1943, Bill Astell's *B-Baker* Lancaster collided with a hydroelectric pylon near Marbeck, Germany, and crashed, killing all on board. Among the seven aircrew lost were three Canadians—navigator Floyd Wile, front gunner Frank Garbas, and wireless operator Albert Garshowitz; the latter two had been football and rugby competitors at school in the Hamilton, Ontario, area. Not just an athlete, Al Garshowitz had also been a prolific letter writer—corresponding with his brothers, sisters, and parents from overseas almost daily— as well as a sometime graffiti artist; just before Operation Chastise, he'd chalked onto the Upkeep mine in the belly of their Lancaster, "Never has so much been expected of so few." Garshowitz also loved taking, printing, and collecting photographs, even if protocol prohibited it. "Have I told you that I'm keeping a picture album of the snaps that I don't think will pass the censor?" Garshowitz wrote his family. "It's half full now. Lovely pictures."[24]

Garshowitz might well have argued that his photo-taking was all in the line of duty. In late March 1943, right after Guy Gibson had organized his mystery squadron to prepare for a lot of low-level flight training, he'd dispatched Bill Astell's Lanc crew to fly over and photograph every sizable lake in the British Isles as prospective training sites, and to have the shots developed and delivered to him within thirty-six hours. With all that photography of what was below and around their bomber, why would anyone care that along the way shutterbug Garshowitz also offered to take a few shots of his aircrew mates at work inside their bomber?

"Many pictures that I took from home and also that were sent to me, I'm going to start to send home," he said in the same letter. "The ones I don't need, OK. I just want to keep a skeleton amount. I'm enclosing ten. Standing by . . . Albert."[25]

Born in 1956, eleven years after the war, Hartley Garshowitz tripped over part of his uncle's story while searching for additions to his stamp collection. As a boy, Hartley discovered letters that his uncle had sent to his father, David Garshowitz, from Britain during the war. Hartley certainly recognized the significance of the letters and knew that his uncle had died while serving in Bomber Command—indeed, Hartley's middle name is Albert, after his uncle—but the censor's tape and UK stamps affixed to the letters looked intriguing and colourful. He couldn't resist adding them to his collection. By the time his father, David, eventually passed the wartime letters to him, Hartley realized that what was inside the envelopes had greater value than the postage stamps affixed outside; he began exploring the stories of his uncle Albert Garshowitz, killed in action on the Dam Buster raid. The hobby became a part-time occupation and eventually a journey of discovery. There were more than a hundred letters, all chronologically numbered.

When one of Hartley's cousins pointed out the Alex Bateman letter published in a Toronto newspaper, appealing for relatives of Dam Busters to come forward with their stories and artifacts, Hartley Garshowitz, now an adult, contacted Bateman and explained that he was Albert Garshowitz's nephew. Through the 1990s, he copied some of the clippings, letters, and photos in his uncle's collection and offered them to Bateman for his research.

Then, during a battlefield tour of Europe in 2000, the two men met. That summer, Hartley Garshowitz had joined his parents and two aunts, as well as family members related to Floyd Wile and Frank Garbas—two of his uncle's crewmates also killed in action—and together they travelled to a number of sites related to the dams raid, including the graveyard where Guy Gibson is buried, the crash site of his uncle's *B-Baker* Lancaster, and the Möhne Dam. But even before the tour began, Bateman met Hartley Garshowitz's family members in London and helped them on their way at the start of their tour. "So I had a very good relationship with Alex," Garshowitz said.[26]

Several years later, after he'd communicated with the Nanton Lancaster Society Air Museum and learned of Shere Fraser's attempts to reach Bateman for the return of her father's flight log, Garshowitz offered to assist Shere in whatever way he could, using his already established friendships and acquaintances among Dam Buster aficionados.

As for Hartley's uncle, W/O Abram "Albert" Garshowitz's body was buried initially in Borken, near the crash site, and after the war relocated to the Reichswald Forest Cemetery, where his tombstone shows his rank and name, his age, twenty-two, and the Star of David. But like Shere Fraser's pursuit of her father's logbook and Jim Heather's wish to restore the memory of his uncle Ken Earnshaw with that photo album, Hartley Garshowitz found perhaps the richest part of his uncle's legacy in that box of letters he had tripped over while looking for exotic stamps in the basement back in 1994. The box contained a letter mailed to Albert Garshowitz's mother in Hamilton a month after the dams raid took her son. In the handwritten note, Sgt. R.R. Land at first offered sympathy for Sarah Garshowitz's loss and a hope that the pain would soon pass. "Your son is the bravest," Land wrote. "He used to teach me some wireless work for a job I was doing at the time I met him."[27]

Clearly Sgt. Land treasured the wartime friendship with Sgt. Albert Garshowitz (promoted to warrant officer by the time of the dams raid). Inside the envelope with the letter,

Land had enclosed photographs—another interest shared by the two sergeants—taken when Albert enjoyed a forty-eight-hour leave away from bombing operations with 57 Squadron, and between the training flights with 617 Squadron leading to Operation Chastise. Perhaps to reassure Garshowitz's mother, Land explained that Albert had always spoken about her, to the point that Land felt a real connection with her.

"Could you let me have a photograph of you, Mrs. Garshowitz?" Land asked finally. "Somehow, I feel I know you very well . . . as one Jewish girl to a much wiser Jewish lady. Well, I've said enough." And she signed off exactly the way Albert always did. "*Standing by* . . . Rosaline."[28]

SHERE FRASER HADN'T SLEPT WELL IN DAYS. LEADING up to January 9, 2017, she spent her waking hours preparing her notes, organizing her thoughts, and bolstering her courage for the ordeal ahead—testifying in the trial of Alexander Bateman for the theft of John Fraser's logbook. Among her many thoughts while waiting for the satellite connection from Britain to her laptop computer camera, Shere kept repeating to herself, "I'm a Dam Buster's daughter. I'm fearless, like my dad." When the pre-dawn call came through from Wood Green Crown Court in London, Judge John Dodd QC first asked Shere where she was located. She explained that she was seated in her kitchen. There in front of her, on her kitchen island, she had placed all the pertinent research to buttress her case against Bateman—133 pages of documents—coincidentally equal to the number of aircrew who'd served on Operation Chastise in 1943.

During cross-examination, the counsel defending Bateman criticized Shere Fraser's actions in bringing the case to trial. "And all of your harassing of Alex Bateman," she pointed out. "And all your phone calls . . ."

"May I have a moment, Your Honour?" Shere responded, and with his permission, she quickly dug out a relevant document—the telephone bill listing all her long-distance phone calls from Canada attempting to reach the defendant in Britain. She asked if the judge would permit its submission and held the sheet of paper up to her computer camera. "Do two phone calls that lasted no more than sixty seconds each constitute harassment?" she asked.

Defence counsel, clearly nonplussed, moved on.

On the third day of the trial, after insisting all along that he did not have John Fraser's logbook, claiming it had been stolen from his home, Bateman was asked by the judge if he had it in his possession. The next day Bateman revealed that, yes, he had a copy of it. At another point in the trial, a London police officer who'd searched Bateman's home indicated that investigators had found other property that Bateman had solicited from Canada; the officer held an exhibit bag that contained Ken Earnshaw's missing album and hundreds of his photographs, torn from their pages. Eventually, after five days of testimony and summation, the jury returned a guilty verdict. While the police had never actually retrieved John Fraser's logbook from Bateman's home, he was sentenced to two years in prison for the theft. A few weeks later, at the sentencing, which Shere Fraser and her husband Joe McCarthy Jr. attended in London, Judge Dodd spoke to Bateman in the courtroom.

"The jury plainly did not believe you. And neither do I," Shere said, quoting the judge. "You lied repeatedly to conceal the truth as to what happened to the logbook. It remains a mystery as to what you actually did with it."

Following Bateman's sentencing, on the steps outside the courthouse in London, Shere Fraser responded to questions from media and announced she was offering a reward of £5,000 for information leading to the safe return of her father's flight log. It was a poignant moment—a bittersweet victory in the case, but still no logbook.

"This is not a document. It's not a piece of paper. It's a piece of my father's legacy of courage," she said to the media present, with emotion in her voice. "Instead of looking at it like it's a commodity . . . please help us bring a piece of Dad home."

As she spoke in front of cameras and microphones that day, she felt some redemption. Shere held in her hands the other piece of history she believed had nearly suffered the same fate as her father's log—Ken Earnshaw's photo album, still in the police evidence bag. Authorities had delivered the bag to her on the promise that she would return it to its rightful owners back in Alberta. At a ceremony in the Bomber Command Museum of Canada at Nanton, on April 22, 2017, Shere Fraser presented the evidence bag to Jim Heather, representing the Earnshaw family. The plastic sack still contained the recovered photo album and the 290 loose snapshots waiting to be put back in place.

"I was a justice of the peace in Nunavut and the Northwest Territories, so I know how hard it is to get any kind of satisfaction," Jim Heather said. "It's remarkable to have [the album] returned. Things like this just don't happen."[29]

To date, the logbooks belonging to John Fraser and Ken Earnshaw are still considered missing.

AS WAR INEVITABLY DOES, THE DAM BUSTER RAID LEFT some unexplained loose ends. Operation Chastise had that kind of impact on Lewis Burpee and the crew of *S-Sugar*. For whatever reason, at midnight just before the third wave of the operation took off from Scampton, P/O Burpee turned to fellow Canadian pilot Ken Brown and said goodbye—and Brown knew he meant it. Then Burpee climbed aboard his Lancaster, with full crew and armed bouncing bomb, and took off eastbound for the Ruhr dams. Less than two hours later, just before 2 a.m., Burpee was nearly blinded by searchlights at the Gilze-Rijen Luftwaffe aerodrome; he tried to evade possible anti-aircraft fire, but his Lancaster crashed in the manoeuver. The resulting aircraft fire and explosion of its Upkeep killed the crew, incinerated nearby buildings, and knocked people down a couple of miles away. "A shooting down by searchlight," a Luftwaffe airman said.[30]

The inferno left four of *S-Sugar*'s seven aircrew unidentifiable: flight engineer Guy Pegler, navigator Tom Jaye, front gunner William "Ginger" Long, and bomb aimer Jimmy Arthur were all burned beyond recognition. W/O Arthur had been the last to join Burpee's crew at 106 Squadron, during the opening week of the Battle of the Ruhr in March 1943. For that first op, he'd sensed a bit of security knowing two others aboard *S-Sugar* were fellow Canadians; they'd all been trained at places back home with familiar names—Burpee at Centralia, Ontario, Brady at Mossbank, Saskatchewan, and

Arthur at Jarvis, Ontario. But as was so often the case in Bomber Command, Jimmy Arthur's friendship with his fellow Canadians and the rest of the Lancaster crew was short-lived, perhaps eight weeks at most, ending with Operation Chastise.

The vagaries of the *S-Sugar* crash dislodged rear gunner Gordon Brady's turret from the rest of the aircraft; his body, showing few signs of injury, remained intact. The former ambulance corporal from Ponoka, Alberta, had served his entire operational Air Force career with his fellow Canadian skipper and had died with him. Just before the raid, he and Burpee had celebrated their birthdays—Brady's twenty-seventh and Burpee's twenty-fifth. But they'd had to do it away from Scampton, with its strict RAF adherence to isolating the officers' mess from the sergeants' mess. Not known to either man was that W/C Guy Gibson had recommended Brady for a commission, but G/C Charles Whitworth had temporarily questioned it. Air Force administration eventually approved the commission on May 10, 1943, but when Burpee's entire crew was killed a week later, bureaucrats simply filed Brady's case with the notation "Recommendation Cancelled."[31]

For expediency, after the crash on May 17, 1943, the crew of *S-Sugar* was buried at Zuylen Cemetery, Princenhage, in Holland. Then, in 1948, when the Commonwealth War Graves Commission assumed responsibility, Burpee's crew members were exhumed and reburied at Bergen-op-Zoom Cemetery on the north shore of the Scheldt Estuary. Ironically, P/O Lewis Burpee, who'd chafed at the rigid RAF protocol that kept him separated from his NCO crew at Scampton, suffered much the same fate in death. At Bergen-op-Zoom, his comrades' unidentifiable remains were buried in a communal grave in

Plot 24, while Burpee was buried beneath a single headstone in a completely different plot.

What Air Force clerks and graves administrators appeared to miss—a need for human kindness—the chaplaincy did not. In June 1943, Lewis Burpee's parents in Ottawa and his wife, Lillian, heard from S/L H.F. Davidson, who was with the RCAF chaplain services overseas. The chaplain wrote that he had met P/O Burpee on his rounds and called him one of the squadron's "old timers in this business," saying in addition that Lewis "was very highly regarded by his comrades and the senior officers of the squadron."[32] It was at least some comfort for a grieving and pregnant wife in Newark, England, and Lewis's parents in far-off Canada.

"Lillian says that she is waiting for an exit permit so that she can go out to you in Ottawa," Davidson continued. "Rest assured that we are ready to do anything we can for your son's wife if she needs our help."

Later that spring, the International Red Cross confirmed that Lillian Burpee's husband had been killed in action. The RAF and the King and Queen also sent requisite condolences. And arrangements were expedited by Lillian Burpee's in-laws in Ottawa for her transatlantic passage to Canada. On Christmas Eve 1943, Lillian Burpee gave birth to the son her husband would never know. She named him Lewis Burpee Jr. And beyond a note she received from Guy Gibson, in which he signed off, "Best of luck. Always your friend," Lillian had little or no further contact with the dams raid or its participants. To reflect on it proved too painful. "It was a wound that would never heal," her son said. "She could never look back on it with any dispassion. It was just too raw."[33]

As a consequence, for much of his life, all that Lewis Burpee Jr. knew of his father's wartime service came from the copy of Gibson's *Enemy Coast Ahead* that had sat in his bedroom from the age of two. In time, he learned that his mother's family had lived in Greenwich, near the docks in London's East End, and as a result spent many nights during the Blitz in a backyard air-raid shelter. As a woman of twenty-one early in the war, Lillian had done home service working in a plant. Lewis Jr. also learned about his father—that he'd wanted to become an architect but on the family's recommendation had worked in retail at Ogilvy's department store in Ottawa instead, then joined the RCAF in 1940 and been posted overseas as a pilot the following year. One night in 1942, Lillian and Lewis met in a pub, fell in love, and were married; seven months later P/O Burpee was killed in action in the Dam Buster raid.

"For all the good it did," Lewis Burpee Jr. said, "I know it caused [my mother] misery just to remember. She felt all her subsequent life that she was cheated out of the life she would have had with my father."[34]

In 2013, during the seventieth anniversary of the dams raid, Lewis Burpee Jr. travelled to the United Kingdom to participate in ceremonies and observances in Lincolnshire. At a pub specially decorated with Dam Buster memorabilia, Lewis was photographed in front of a wall of portraits of dams raid aircrewmen, including his dad. He attended ceremonies, watched flypasts, and travelled to the Scampton airfield where his father's last op had begun. He toured the field, explored the wartime hangars, and visited the halls and briefing rooms inside the main station building, left very much the way they were when 617 Squadron resided there. A commemoration volunteer, whose daytime job was with ground crew at the base, took Burpee Jr. to Guy Gibson's office and invited him to sit at the wing commander's desk. It overlooked the airfield. He tried to imagine his father's state of mind that night seventy years before.

"What must it have been like?" he wondered. "They know this raid is going to be a big one. They know when they go out that they're going to lose somebody. Nineteen aircraft went out. Only eleven came back. It took a lot of guts."[35]

Before the Canadian visitor left Gibson's office that day in 2013, his volunteer guide had returned to see him out. The man was so moved by the presence of a Dam Buster's son that he presented Burpee with a coat hanger he'd unscrewed from a wall inside the Scampton station briefing room. He told Burpee not to say anything but to tuck it into his pocket as a keepsake. It's now affixed to his office door in Ottawa.

Lewis Burpee Jr. considers his father skilled and courageous and the raid significant as "a glorious poke in the eye for the German leadership." More than that, he's proud that memorials, museums, and, most important of all, Britons and Canadians have prevented his father's anonymity and perpetuated knowledge of his wartime deeds. "It wasn't a D-Day," Burpee said finally. "It wasn't a victory at Tobruk. It was a single raid on an important target. But seventy years later, they're keeping the memory alive."[36]

OF THE 133 AIRMEN WHO FLEW OPERATION CHASTISE on May 16–17, 1943, twenty-nine were Canadians. Fourteen died in the raid. Fred Sutherland, front gunner in Les Knight's

N-Nuts Lancaster, remains at this writing the sole surviving Canadian Dam Buster. Doc Sutherland admitted he's lived an extraordinary life. Smitten by flying after that childhood barnstorming flight with Punch Dickins over Peace River, Alberta, in the 1930s; acknowledged for his gunnery marksmanship in the British Commonwealth Air Training Plan when he enlisted in 1941; and crewed up with fellow Canadian gunner Harry O'Brien, F/Sgt. Sutherland found a wartime home aboard Lancasters with his Australian pilot, Les Knight.

Then, in March 1943, told by his commanders that he could abbreviate his tour of duty in Bomber Command by volunteering for a secret operation, Sutherland and the aircrew of *N-Nuts* helped breach the Eder Dam, the second target attacked on the Ruhr River during Operation Chastise in May 1943. Dodging the bullet that night, he went on to survive after being shot down in the disastrous Dortmund-Ems Canal raid in September 1943. Finally, evading capture in occupied Europe for weeks with the help of the Dutch and French Underground, and ultimately escaping over the Pyrenees to a flight back to England, Fred Sutherland returned home to Canada at the end of an incredibly eventful year.

As if those weren't enough deadly escapes for one lifetime, in the 1970s, during a fire patrol in the Rocky Mountains, the twin-engine Cessna in which he was a fire observer crashed into a mountainside; he was quickly rescued by helicopter.[37] But that was his last working flight. Despite all his close calls, he considers his survival through the war simply a run of good luck. And as far as the dams raid? "I rarely talk about it to anybody," he said in an interview in June 2017. "But I never forget it. It's the most important thing that ever happened to me."[38]

* * *

NOT SO MUCH AT THE TIME, BUT IN THE YEARS THAT followed the war, members of the Dam Buster aircrews faced questions about the merits of the dams raid. Had Operation Chastise delivered a crippling blow to German industrial production or just temporarily boosted morale on the home front? Was the damage it inflicted worth the cost in lives? Had the operation been like a latter-day Charge of the Light Brigade—magnificent, but not war? Or, in more modern terms, a marvellous motion picture that made no military sense at all?

Historians have argued about the impact of the raid on Nazi war production and the war itself from the very moment Sir Archibald Sinclair, the secretary of state for air in Britain, announced at the Royal Albert Hall that the Allies had delivered "a trenchant blow for the victory of the Allies,"[39] the same afternoon the Operation Chastise crews returned. Analysis of Jerry Fray's high-altitude reconnaissance photographs, taken just hours after the raid, showed widespread devastation. Indeed, nearly 10.5 billion cubic feet of unleashed reservoir water had ripped away hydroelectric equipment, flattened towns, submerged Luftwaffe airfields, decimated foundries, factories, and infrastructure, and strewn wreckage for ninety-three miles downstream. The torrent had killed 1,400 people inside enemy territory. Some interpret the speed with which the Möhne and Eder Dams were repaired—seventy-nine days—as evidence of the ultimate failure of Operation Chastise. Others take the view that the operation boosted Allied morale at a critical moment in the war and forced the Reich to redirect supplies, manpower, and attention to defending industrial sites closer to home, sucking away valuable resources from the building of the Atlantic Wall and support of German armies on the Eastern Front in the Soviet Union.

Seventy-five years of hindsight provides additional perspective. The dams raid remains just one of thousands of Bomber Command operations. It cost fifty-three lives—a devastating loss when measured against the 133 aircrew who flew on the raid that night. But by comparison, the Battle of Berlin cost 2,690 Allied airmen, almost three hundred killed on the first night of the siege alone. And Operation Chastise was consistent with the Allies' peripheral strategy, a strategy of taking the war against totalitarian regimes to the enemy. Even in the winter of 1943, three and a half years into the war, an Allied land campaign remained only in the planning stages; Operation Husky into Sicily and Italy was two months away, and any attempt at liberating northwestern Europe was more than a year into the future. Consequently, the British Air Ministry's best stopgap would remain the bomber offensive, delivering repeated body blows to the enemy's industrial infrastructure.

But Bomber Command may have achieved more than was immediately realized. On the surface, Arthur Harris's offensive against the Ruhr forced the Reich to channel vast numbers of German military and industrial personnel to industrial sites to protect production and meet the Allied threat. The domino effect, some argue, forced the Nazis to resort to a sensational, but less effective, retaliation in the form of their V-1 and V-2 programs, while at the same time delaying potentially more deadly programs such as the development of a jet fighter and their experiments in nuclear, biological, and chemical warfare.

Had the campaign against the Ruhr, and in particular the dams raid, not distracted the German High Command the way it did, it's likely that Britain would have much sooner felt the consequences of Nazi propaganda minister Joseph Goebbels's plans for total war and armament minister Albert Speer's augmenting of war production. David Bashow, a former Canadian Air Force fighter pilot and military academic, contends that had Bomber Command's strategic offensive not diverted the Third Reich, "Germany would have had no scruples about bombing Britain to dust, had the means been available to it."[40]

Pilot Joe McCarthy saw some of the impact of their night's work at closer range and had perhaps a better sense of the raid's physical impact than any of the other Dam Buster pilots. He and his crew had released their Upkeep on the Sorpe earthen dam about 12:45 a.m. on May 17; then, en route home, they flew northwest, arriving over the Möhne about fifteen minutes after it had been breached by the first-wave bombers, which by then had moved on to the Eder. McCarthy noted that Möhne reservoir water was still pouring through the dam and down the valley with shocking force. He lamented the deaths of the forced labourers below the dams, but lauded the overall damage inflicted.

"Industry that had been making steel was flooded. Seventy-five to eighty bridges were wiped out. An airport had water up to the tops of its hangars," McCarthy said. "The loss of water to both civilian and commercial outlets was tremendous. They rebuilt the dams, but they never got the water levels up to [those before the raid] for two years. . . . It was definitely minimum force providing maximum effect."[41]

His navigator, Don MacLean, recognized the impact of all-out war on the combatants at the time and characterized the rationale for the dams raid not in terms of practicality but, in his view, something greater. "We were convinced . . . we were fighting for the survival of certain principles that were more valuable than life itself," he said. "And because of those principles we welcomed the challenge. It's as simple as that."[42]

Sources

UNPUBLISHED SOURCES

Author Interviews

Shirley Armstrong, Nanton, AB, June 23, 2017
Brock and Terry Brown, Red Deer, AB, June 19, 2017
Lewis Burpee Jr., Ottawa, ON, October 27, 2017; January 11, 2018
Bob Evans, Nanton, AB, June 23, 2018
Dan Fox, Nanton, AB, June 23, 2017
Shere Fraser, Blaine, WA, January 28–29, 2018
Hartley Garshowitz, Toronto, ON, November 26, 2017
Jim Heather, Nanton, ON, June 21, 2017
Bill and Jim MacLean, Burlington, ON, July 24, 2017
Bill McBride, Hamilton, ON, June 30, 2017
Joe McCarthy Jr., Blaine, WA, January 28–29, 2018
Rob Pedersen, Nanton, AB, June 20, 2017
Fred Sutherland, Rocky Mountain House, AB, June 18–19, 2017
Elinor Taerum Stensland, Nanton, AB, June 20, 2017
Melvin Taerum, Nanton, AB, June 20, 2017
Doreen Walker, London, ON, June 24, 2017
John Walker, Calgary, AB, June 24, 2017

Other Interviews

John Fraser, Bob Kellow, Don MacLean, Mick Martin, Harry O'Brien, Dave
    Rodger, Dave Shannon, Revie Walker, Barnes Wallis—interviews by Harry J.
    Boyle, 1961, for CBC Radio, "The Dams Raid," *Venture*.

SOURCES

Joe McCarthy—National Air Force Museum, Trenton, ON, c. 1990s.

Nell Rodger, Carolyn Rodger—interview by J'Lyn Nye, Sault Ste. Marie, ON, August 18, 2018.

Unpublished Works

Brown, Brock. "Who Is Ken Brown? A Tribute by Brock Brown." Written after Ken Brown's death on December 23, 2003.

Matich, M.A.J. Fred. "Some Engineering Aspects of the Dams Raid." Prepared for the May 1994 meeting of 122 (St. Gregory's) Squadron, Islington, ON.

Institutional Sources

Bomber Command Museum of Canada archives, Nanton, AB

Canadian War Museum, Ottawa, ON

Canadian Warplane Heritage Museum, Hamilton, ON

Imperial War Museum, London, UK

Library and Archives Canada, Ottawa, ON

National Air Force Museum, Trenton, ON

National Archives, Kew, London, UK

Science Museum Archive, Wroughton, Wiltshire, UK

PUBLISHED SOURCES

Books

Arthur, Max. *Dambusters: A Landmark Oral History*. London: Virgin Books, 2009.

Barris, Ted. *Behind the Glory: The Plan That Won the Allied Air War*. Toronto: Macmillan Canada, 1992.

———. *Juno: Canadians on D-Day, June 6, 1944*. Toronto: Thomas Allen, 2004.

Bashow, David L. *No Prouder Place: Canadians and the Bomber Command Experience, 1939–1945*. St. Catharines, ON: Vanwell Publishing, 2005.

Bessner, Ellin. *Double Threat: Canadian Jews, the Military, and World War II*. Toronto: New Jewish Press, 2018.

Birrell, Dave. *Big Joe McCarthy: The RCAF's American Dambuster*. Nanton, AB: Nanton Lancaster Society, 2012

———. *Baz: The Biography of Ian Bazalgette VC*. Nanton, AB: Bomber Command Museum of Canada, 2014.

———. *FM159: The Lucky Lancaster*. Nanton, AB: Bomber Command Museum of Canada, 2015.

Bishop, Arthur. *Billy Bishop: The Courage of the Early Morning; A Biography of the Great Ace of World War I*. Toronto: McClelland and Stewart, 1965.

Bowyer, Chaz. *Bomber Barons*. Barnsley, UK: Leo Cooper, 2001.

Boyle, Andrew. *Trenchard: Man of Vision*. London: Collins, 1962.

Braddon, Russell. *Leonard Cheshire VC*. London: Evans Brothers, 1954.

Brickhill, Paul. *The Dam Busters*. London: Evans Brothers, 1951.

Campbell, J.A. *The Airborne Years: A Personal Account of Wartime Flying in the Royal Canadian Air Force*. Uxbridge, ON: self-published, 1984.

Churchill, Winston S. *The Second World War: The Hinge of Fate*. Boston: Houghton Mifflin, 1950.

Conrad, Peter C. *Training for Victory: The British Commonwealth Air Training Plan in the West*. Saskatoon, SK: Western Producer Prairie Books, 1989.

Cooper, Alan W. *The Men Who Breached the Dams*. London: William Kimber & Co., 1982.

Countryman, Barry. *R100 in Canada*. Erin, ON: Boston Mills Press, 1982.

Dallek, Robert. *Franklin D. Roosevelt and American Foreign Policy, 1932–1945*. New York: Oxford University Press, 1979.

Douglas, Gen. Sir Howard. *A Treatise on Naval Gunnery*. London: John Murray, 1855.

Douglas, Sholto. *Combat and Command: The Story of an Airman in Two World Wars*. New York: Simon and Schuster, 1963.

Douglas, W.A.B. *The Creation of a National Air Force: The Official History of the Royal Canadian Air Force*, vol. 2. Ottawa: University of Toronto Press, Minister of Supply and Services Canada, 1986.

Dunmore, Spenser, and William Carter. *Reap the Whirlwind: The Untold Story of 6 Group, Canada's Bomber Force of World War II*. Toronto: McClelland & Stewart, 1991.

Elmes, Jenny. *M-Mother: Dambuster Flight Lieutenant John "Hoppy" Hopgood*. London: History Press, 2015.

Euler, Helmuth. *The Dams Raid Through the Lens*. London: Battle of Britain International, 2001.

Falconer, Jonathan. *The Dam Busters: Breaking the Great Dams of Western Germany, 16–17 May 1943*. Thrupp, Stroud, Gloucestershire, UK: Sutton Publishing, 2003.

———. *Filming the Dam Busters*. Thrupp, Stroud, Gloucestershire, UK: Sutton Publishing, 2005.

Filey, Mike. *Toronto Sketches 3: The Way We Were*. Toronto: Dundurn Press, 1994.

Flower, Stephen. *Barnes Wallis' Bombs*. Chalford, Stroud, Gloucestershire, UK: Amberley Publishing, 2002.

Foster, Charles. *Breaking the Dams: The Story of Dambuster David Maltby and His Crew*. Barnsley, South Yorkshire, UK: Pen and Sword Aviation, 2008.

Gibson, Guy. *Enemy Coast Ahead*. London: Michael Joseph, 1946.

————. *Enemy Coast Ahead—Uncensored*. Manchester, UK: Crécy Publishing, 2003.

Greenhous, Brereton, Stephen J. Harris, William C. Johnston, and William G.P. Rawling. *The Crucible of War, 1939–1945: The Official History of the Royal Canadian Air Force*, vol. 3. Ottawa: University of Toronto Press, Minister of Supply and Services Canada, 1994.

Hallam, Vic. *Lest We Forget: The Dambusters in the Derwent Valley*. Chesterfield, UK: Ladas Printers, 1993.

Harris, Sir Arthur. *Bomber Offensive*. London: Collins, 1947.

Harrison, Irene. "The Earnshaws." In *Lure of the Homestead*. Edmonton, AB: Ohaton Community Book Club, 1977.

Hartley, Michael. *The Challenge of the Skies*. Edmonton, AB: Puckrin's Production, 1981.

Hatch, F.J. *Aerodrome of Democracy: Canada and the British Commonwealth Air Training Plan, 1939–1945*. Ottawa: Directorate of History, Department of National Defence, 1983.

Hawton, Hector. *Night Bombing*. London: Thomas Nelson, 1944.

Holland, James. *Dam Busters: The Race to Smash the Dams, 1943*. London: Bantam Press, 2012.

Humphries, Harry. *Living with Heroes: The Dam Busters*. Banham, Norwich, Norfolk, UK: Erskine Press, 2003.

Johnson, George "Johnny." *The Last British Dambuster: One Man's Extraordinary Life and the Raid That Changed History*. London: Ebury Press, Random House, 2014.

Jones, R.V. *Most Secret War: British Scientific Intelligence, 1939–1945*. London: Hamish Hamilton, 1978.

Kellow, Bob. *Paths to Freedom: A True Experience Which Took Place Between September and December 1943*. Winnipeg, MB: self-published, 1992.

King, W.L. Mackenzie. *The British Commonwealth Air Training Plan: Broadcast by Right Honourable W.L. Mackenzie King, M.P., Sunday, December 17, 1939*. Ottawa: King's Printer, 1939.

Lancaster, Stan, ed. *Critical Moments: Profiles of Members of the Greater Vancouver Branch of the Aircrew Association*. Vancouver, BC: Aircrew Association, 1989.

Lawrence, W.J. *No. 5 Bomber Group RAF, 1939–1945*. London: Faber & Faber, 1951.

Lynn, Vera. *We'll Meet Again: A Personal & Social History of World War Two*. London: Sidgwick & Jackson, 1989.

Middlebrook, Martin. *The Nuremberg Raid, 30–31 March 1944*. London: Penguin, 1973.

————. *The Berlin Raids: RAF Bomber Command Winter, 1943–44*. London: Viking, 1988.

Middlebrook, Martin, and Chris Everitt. *The Bomber Command War Diaries: An Operational Reference Book, 1939–1945*. New York: Penguin, 1985.

Molson, K.M. *Pioneering in Canadian Air Transport*. Winnipeg, MB: James Richardson & Sons, 1986.

Morris, Richard. *Guy Gibson*. London: Viking Penguin Group, 1994.

———. *The Biography of Leonard Cheshire, VC, OM*. London: Viking, 2000.

———. *16/17 May 1943 Operation Chastise: The Raid on the German Dams*. Oxford: Archaeopress Publishing, 2009.

Naiman, Arnold. *Flashbacks: Stories from a WWII Hero*. Edited by Sandy Naiman and Martin Lager. Toronto: Mosquito Press, 2011.

Owen, Robert, Steve Darlow, Sean Fest, and Arthur Thorning. *Dam Busters: Failed to Return*. Stotfold, Hitchin, Herts, UK: Fighting High Publishing, 2013.

Peden, Murray. *A Thousand Shall Fall: The True Story of a Canadian Bomber Pilot in World War Two*. Toronto: Stoddart, 1988.

Pyves, Richard R. *Night Madness: A Rear Gunner's Story of Love, Courage, and Hope in World War II*. Markham, ON: Red Deer Press, 2012.

Reader's Digest Association. *The Canadians at War 1939/45*. vol. 1, *The Night They Broke the Dams in Happy Valley*. Toronto: Reader's Digest, 1969.

Richards, Denis. *The Fight at Odds*. vol. 1 of *Royal Air Force 1939–1945*. London: HMSO, 1953.

———. *Portal of Hungerford: The Life of Marshal of the Royal Air Force, Viscount Portal of Hungerford*. London, UK: William Heinemann, 1977.

Roberts, Leslie. *Canada's War in the Air*. Montreal, QC: Alvah M. Beatty, 1942.

Rowley, Clive. *Dambusters: The Most Daring Raid in the RAF's History*. Lincolnshire, UK: Mortons Media Group, 2013.

Saward, Dudley. *Bomber Harris: The Authorised Biography*. London: Buchan & Enright, 1984.

Schweyer, Robert. *Sights on Jarvis: No. 1 Bombing and Gunnery School, 1940–1945*. Nanticoke, ON: Heronwood Enterprises, 2003.

Smith, Albert, and Ian Smith. *Mosquito Pathfinder*. Manchester, UK: Crécy, 2003.

Speer, Albert. *Spandau: The Secret Diaries*. London: Macmillan, 1976.

Sutherland, Alice Gibson. *Canada's Aviation Pioneers: 50 Years of McKee Trophy Winners*. Toronto: McGraw-Hill Ryerson, 1978.

Sweetman, John. *The Dambusters Raid*. London: Arms and Armour, 1990.

Tedder, Lord. *With Prejudice: The War Memoirs of Marshal of the Royal Air Force Lord Tedder*. Boston: Little, Brown and Company, 1966.

Thompson, Sir Robert. *Make for the Hills: Memories of Far Eastern Wars*. Barnsley, UK: Pen & Sword, 1989.

Thorning, Arthur G. *The Dambuster Who Cracked the Dam: The Story of Melvin "Dinghy" Young*. Barnsley, UK: Pen & Sword, 2008.

Vance, Jonathan. *High Flight: Aviation and the Canadian Imagination.* Toronto: Penguin, 2002.

Ward, Chris, and Andreas Wachtel. *Dambuster Crash Sites: 617 Dambuster Squadron Crash Sites in Holland and Germany.* Barnsley, UK: Pen & Sword, 2007.

Williams, James N. *The Plan: Memories of the British Commonwealth Air Training Plan.* Luskville, QC: Canada's Wings, 1984.

Woods, Laurie. *Halfway to Hell: Aussie Sky Heroes in Bomber Command.* Moorooka, AU: Boolarong Press, 2011.

PERIODICALS, NEWS FEATURES, BROADCASTS, JOURNALS, PAMPHLETS, VIDEOS, AND WEBLOGS

Anderson, Michael, dir. *The Dam Busters.* Associated British Picture Corporation, 1955. DVD, StudioCanal, 2006.

Bennett, T. "Operation Taxable." *FlyPast*, November 1984, 58–62.

Birrell, Dave. "Dambuster Navigator." *Airforce* 27, no. 1 (Spring 2003): 37–41.

Brown, Ken. "Remember the Dambusters." Keynote address presented at the 50th anniversary commemoration of the dams raid, Bomber Command Museum of Canada, July 17, 1993, Nanton, AB.

Calgary Herald. "Flier Gets D.F.C. after Dam Raid." May 26, 1943.

———. "Terry Got Dam Busters to the Job: WC Gibson Tells His Mother Here." September 13, 1943.

Campbell, William R. "An Epic of Aerial Progress." *Canadian Aviation* 3, no. 9 (September 1930).

Canadian Press. "Great Ruhr Dams Smashed, Berlin Hit and Rome Seaport Levelled in Raids." *Ottawa Evening Journal*, May 17, 1943.

———. "Dam Buster Gibson Pays Tribute to Lost Navigator Taerum." September 21, 1943.

CBC Radio. "The Dams Raid," prod. Harry J. Boyle. *Venture*, 1961.

Collins, A.R. "Dam Busting: The Uncivil Engineering Behind the Famous Wartime Raid." *New Civil Engineering,* May 1972.

Coward, Noël, and David Lean, dirs. *In Which We Serve.* London: Two Cities Films, 1942.

Daily Colonist. "R.C.A.F. Bombardier Took Part in Möhne Dam Raid." February 1945.

Davies, Caroline. "How the Luftwaffe Bombed the Palace, in the Queen Mother's Own Words." *The Guardian*, September 13, 2009.

Davies, Russell. "The Dam Busters: The Book, the Film and Now the Lager Ad," *Telegraph Magazine*, April 17, 1993, 44–48.

Dodds, Ron. "The Dambusters: Après moi le deluge." *The Legionary,* May 1968.

Florence, Elinor. "The Last Canadian Dambuster." *Elinor Florence* (blog). http://elinorflorence.com/blog/dambuster-fred-sutherland.

Foster, Charles. *Dambustersblog*. www.dambustersblog.com.

Hallam, Vic. "The Dambusters 50th Anniversary Commemoration." 1993.

Hastings, Max. "The Dam Busters: The Men and the Hour." *Telegraph Magazine*, April 17, 1993.

Hawthorn, Tom. "The Last of the Dambusters." *Globe and Mail*, January 15, 2003.

Hillier, S/L Steve. "The History of 617 Squadron, The Dambusters, 1943–1993." Forces & Corporate Publishing, 1993.

Hulbert, Vi. *Reflections of a Parson's Wife*. Pamphlet, 1943.

Hutchison, George. "War Made the Difference!" *London Free Press*, July 24, 1972.

Jacobs, Peter. "The Dambusters: A Tribute to 617 Squadron Royal Air Force." *Lincolnshire Echo*, 1993.

———. "The Dambusters at 60: Exploding the Myths Behind the Men Who Breached the Ruhr Dams, 16/17 May 1943." *Lincolnshire Echo*, 2003.

Johnson, Herb. "Bomber Needs Community Support." *Nanton News*, September 26, 1985.

Johnson, Ian, "Hamilton's Bomber Marks 25 Years Back in the Sky." CBC News, September 24, 2013.

Kilduff, Peter. "Clayton Knight, A Yank in the RFC/RAF." *Cross & Cockade International*, Autumn 2010.

Kirman, Joseph M. "Excerpts from the January 1993 Senate Report: The Valour and the Horror." *Canadian Social Studies*, Winter 1994.

König, Hans Werner. "A Picture I Will Never Forget." *The Dambusters 50th Anniversary Commemoration*, 1993.

May, Joan. "Modest 'Dam Buster' Hero Gets Enthusiastic Welcome." *Calgary Herald*, September 13, 1943.

McKenna, Terence, and Brian McKenna. *The Valour and the Horror. Death by Moonlight: Bomber Command*. National Film Board, CBC, Galafilm, 1992.

Meadows, Jack. "A Decisive Factor." *Aeroplane Monthly* (February 1989): 97–100.

Morley, Paul. "Searching for a Missing Dam Buster." *Hamilton Spectator Magazine*, May 17, 2013.

Nanton Lancaster Society. *On the Wings of a Lancaster* (video), 1996.

Ottawa Evening Citizen. "Lewis J. Burpee, Winner of D.F.M Is Now Missing." *Ottawa Evening Citizen*, May 18, 1943.

Paul, David. "Widow Fights for the Return of Dambuster Husband's Log Book." *International Express*, July 15, 2003.

Pigeon, Greg. "Dambuster Percy Pigeon Helped Save Democracy." *Williams Lake Tribune*, November 10, 1992.

Saunders, Wayne. "A Forgotten Ottawa Dambuster." *Airforce* 35, no. 3 (January 2012), 13–17.

Shortland, Jim. "The Dambusters Raid—In Perspective." *Despatches*, April 2003.

Stecyk, Tamara. "The Dambusters Raid." *WestJet* magazine, July 2003, 34–37.

Stopes-Roe, Jonathan. "Barnes Wallis: A Portrait by His Grandson." *Royal Air Force Benevolent Fund*, June 24, 2003. www.rafbf.org/news-and-blogs/barnes-wallis.

The Telegraph. "Harry Humphries: The Shortage of Time Gave Him a Formidable Task to be Ready to Attach the Ruhr Dams." February 21, 2008.

Tooth, Helen. "Milo School Prints Fine Year Book." *Calgary Herald*, July 24, 1943.

US Office of War Information. "American Talks to Australia and New Zealand." Recorded in Washington, DC; broadcast November 4, 1943.

Walsh, Tom, "Big Joe, the American Dambuster." *Airforce* 32, no. 3 (Fall 2008): 53–57.

Wilkins, Tony. "30 Minutes over Berlin with Guy Gibson." *Defence of the Realm: British Military News, Technology and History* (blog). https://defenceoftherealm.wordpress.com/2016/07/16/30-minutes-over-berlin-with-guy-gibson/.

Williams, Frank C. "The Raid on the Dams. Part One: Preparation, The Attack." *Airforce* 9, no. 2 (July–August–September 1985): 27–29.

———. "The Raid on the Dams. Part Two: The Attack." *Airforce* 9, no. 3 (October–November–December 1985): 16–20.

———. "The Raid on the Dams. Part Three: Back Home." *Airforce* 9, no. 4 (January–February–March 1986): 7–10 and 36–38.

NOTES

CHAPTER ONE

1. Murray Peden, *A Thousand Shall Fall: The True Story of a Canadian Bomber Pilot in World War Two* (Toronto: Stoddart, 1988), 389.
2. Guy Gibson, *Enemy Coast Ahead* (London: Michael Joseph, 1946), 225.
3. Hector Hawton, *Night Bombing* (London: Thomas Nelson, 1944), 112.
4. Gibson, *Enemy Coast Ahead*, 226.
5. Gibson, *Enemy Coast Ahead*, 226.
6. Hawton, *Night Bombing*, 110.
7. Quoted in Dudley Saward, *Bomber Harris: The Authorised Biography* (London: Buchan & Enright, 1984), 193.
8. John Sweetman, *The Dambusters Raid* (London: Arms and Armour, 1990), 98.
9. Peden, *A Thousand Shall Fall*, 389.
10. Sir Archibald Sinclair, quoted in Hawton, *Night Bombing*, 109.
11. Albert Smith and Ian Smith, *Mosquito Pathfinder* (Manchester, UK: Crécy, 2003), 269.
12. Lewis Burpee to Lillian Burpee, September 1942, courtesy Lewis Burpee Jr.
13. Lewis Burpee Jr., telephone interview with author, October 27, 2017, Ottawa, ON.
14. Burpee to Lillian Burpee, September and October 1942, courtesy Lewis Burpee Jr.
15. J.A. Campbell, *The Airborne Years: A Personal Account of Wartime Flying in the Royal Canadian Air Force* (Uxbridge, ON: self-published, 1984).

16. Jonathan Falconer to Malcolm Kelly, email correspondence, January 17–27, 2018; author's collection, with permission.

17. Gibson, *Enemy Coast Ahead*, 228.

18. Quoted in Charles Foster, "James Arthur," *Dambustersblog*, June 5, 2015, https://dambustersblog.com/category/james-arthur/.

19. Peden, *A Thousand Shall Fall*, 390.

20. Smith and Smith, *Mosquito Pathfinder*, 270.

21. Hawton, *Night Bombing*, 113–116.

22. Gibson, *Enemy Coast Ahead*, 234.

23. Quoted in US Office of War Information, "American Talks to Australia and New Zealand," recorded and broadcast November 4, 1943, from Washington, DC.

24. Quoted in Tony Wilkins, "30 Minutes over Berlin with Guy Gibson," *Defence of the Realm: British Military News, Technology and History*, July 16, 2016, https://defenceoftherealm.wordpress.com/2016/07/16/30-minutes-over-berlin-with-guy-gibson.

25. Quoted in Richard Morris, *Guy Gibson* (London: Viking Penguin Group, 1994).

26. Gibson, *Enemy Coast Ahead*, 237.

27. Quoted in Gibson, *Enemy Coast Ahead*, 238.

28. Quoted in Gibson, *Enemy Coast Ahead*, 238.

CHAPTER TWO

1. Quoted in Gibson, *Enemy Coast Ahead*, 249.

2. Gibson, *Enemy Coast Ahead*, 250.

3. Gibson, *Enemy Coast Ahead*, 251.

4. Jonathan Stopes Roe, "Barnes Wallis: A Portrait by His Grandson," *Royal Air Force Benevolent Fund*, June 24, 2003, https://www.rafbf.org/news-and-blogs/barnes-wallis-%E2%80%93-portrait-his-grandson.

5. David L. Bashow, *No Prouder Place: Canadians and the Bomber Command Experience 1939–1945* (St. Catharines, ON: Vanwell Publishing, 2005), 152.

6. Clive Rowley, *Dambusters: The Most Daring Raid in the RAF's History* (Lincolnshire, UK: Mortons Media Group, 2013), 37.

7. Quoted in Andrew Boyle, *Trenchard: Man of Vision* (London: Collins, 1962).

8. Sweetman, *The Dambusters Raid*, 1.

9. Sweetman, *The Dambusters Raid*, 1.

10. Sweetman, *The Dambusters Raid*, 3.

11. Sweetman, *The Dambusters Raid*, 5.

12. Sweetman, *The Dambusters Raid*, 4.

13. Sweetman, *The Dambusters Raid*, 6.

14. Denis Richards, *Portal of Hungerford: The Life of Marshal of the Royal Air Force, Viscount Portal of Hungerford* (London: William Heinemann, 1977).

15. James Holland, *Dam Busters: The Race to Smash the Dams, 1943* (London: Bantam Press, 2012), 37.

16. CBC Radio, "The Dams Raid," *Venture*, produced by Harry J. Boyle, 1961.

17. Barnes Wallis Papers, Science Museum Library & Archives, Wroughton, UK.

18. A.R. Collins, "Dam Busting: The Uncivil Engineering Behind the Famous Wartime Raid," *New Civil Engineering*, May 1972.

19. Paul Brickhill, *The Dam Busters* (London: Evans Brothers, 1951), 19.

20. Quoted in Brickhill, *The Dam Busters*, 24–25.

21. Quoted in Sweetman, *The Dambusters Raid*, 18.

22. *A Note on a Method of Attacking the Axis Powers*, Wallis Papers.

23. Quoted in Sweetman, *The Dambusters Raid*, 19.

24. Wallis Papers.

25. Gen. Sir Howard Douglas, *A Treatise on Naval Gunnery* (London: John Murray, 1855), 107–8.

26. CBC Radio, "The Dams Raid."

27. Collins, "Dam Busting."

28. CBC Radio, "The Dams Raid."

29. Sweetman, *The Dambusters Raid*, 36.

30. Quoted in Holland, *Dam Busters*, 73.

31. Quoted in Sweetman, *The Dambusters Raid*, 42.

32. Quoted in Sweetman, *The Dambusters Raid*, 45.

33. Quoted in Sweetman, *The Dambusters Raid*, 44.

34. Quoted in Holland, *Dam Busters*, 74.

35. Quoted in Sweetman, *The Dambusters Raid*, 46.

CHAPTER THREE

1. Quoted in Jonathan F. Vance, *High Flight: Aviation and the Canadian Imagination* (Toronto: Penguin, 2002), 196.

2. *Ottawa Morning Journal*, August 11, 1930.

3. Quoted in Vance, *High Flight*, 197.

4. Quoted in Barry Countryman, *R100 in Canada* (Erin, ON: Boston Mills Press, 1982), 87–92.

5. William R. Campbell, "An Epic of Aerial Progress," *Canadian Aviation* 3, no. 9 (September 1930): 17.

6.   Vance, *High Flight*, 190.

7.   Quoted in Vance, *High Flight*, 199.

8.   F.J. Hatch, *Aerodrome of Democracy: Canada and the British Commonwealth Air Training Plan, 1939–1945* (Ottawa, ON: Directorate of History, Department of National Defence, 1983), 7.

9.   W.L. Mackenzie King, *The British Commonwealth Air Training Plan: Broadcast by Right Honourable W.L. Mackenzie King, M.P.*, Sunday, December 17, 1939 (Ottawa, ON: King's Printer, 1939).

10. Ted Barris, *Behind the Glory: The Plan That Won the Allied Air War* (Toronto: Macmillan Canada, 1992), 7.

11. Martin Middlebrook and Chris Everitt, *The Bomber Command War Diaries: An Operational Reference Book, 1939–1945* (New York: Penguin, 1985), 11.

12. Quoted in Jack Meadows, "A Decisive Factor," *Aeroplane Monthly* (February 1989): 98.

13. Quoted in Leslie Roberts, *Canada's War in the Air* (Montreal, QC: Alvah M. Beatty, 1942), 29.

14. King, *The British Commonwealth Air Training Plan*.

15. Vance, *High Flight*, 195.

16. Mike Filey, *Toronto Sketches 3: The Way We Were* (Toronto: Dundurn Press, 1994), 15.

17. Bill MacLean, interview with author, July 24, 2017, Burlington, ON.

18. Jim MacLean, interview with author, July 24, 2017, Burlington, ON.

19. Quoted by Jim MacLean, interview.

20. Quoted in George Hutchison, "War Made the Difference!" *London Free Press*, June 24, 1972.

21. Hatch, *Aerodrome of Democracy*, 125.

22. United Kingdom, Air Ministry Pamphlet 133, "Aircrew Training: Abridged Report of the Conference Held in the United Kingdom, January/February 1942," May 1942, 13; "The British Commonwealth Air Training Plan," HQ 927-1-1, VI, DHist 80/408.

23. Hatch, *Aerodrome of Democracy*, 166.

24. Hatch, *Aerodrome of Democracy*, 167–168.

25. Don MacLean, observer's flight log, April 27, 1942, courtesy MacLean family.

26. Jim and Bill MacLean, interviews.

27. Peter Kilduff, "Clayton Knight, A Yank in the RFC/RAF," inaugural Leaman Lecture at the 41st Cross & Cockade International Annual General Meeting, April 17, 2010; *Cross & Cockade International*, Autumn 2010.

28. Quoted in Robert Dallek, *Franklin D. Roosevelt and American Foreign Policy, 1932–1945* (New York: Oxford University Press, 1979), 199.

29. Quoted in Arthur Bishop, *Billy Bishop: The Courage of the Early Morning; A Biography of the Great Ace of World War I* (Toronto: McClelland and Stewart, 1965), 232.

30. Clayton Knight to Bogart Rogers at the Los Angeles Clayton Knight Committee office, June 30, 1942, DHist 80/68, File 47.

31. W.A.B. Douglas, *The Creation of a National Air Force: The Official History of the Royal Canadian Air Force,* vol. 2 (Ottawa, ON: University of Toronto Press, Minister of Supply and Services Canada, 1986), 633.

32. Quoted in Tom Walsh, "Big Joe, the American Dambuster," *Airforce* 32, no. 3 (Fall 2008): 54.

33. Quoted in Walsh, "Big Joe," 54.

34. Douglas, *The Creation of a National Air Force,* 242.

35. Douglas, *The Creation of a National Air Force,* 243.

36. Dave Birrell, *Big Joe McCarthy: The RCAF's American Dambuster* (Nanton, AB: Nanton Lancaster Society, 2012), 32.

37. Douglas, *The Creation of a National Air Force,* 640.

38. Douglas, *The Creation of a National Air Force,* 640.

39. Denis Richards, *Royal Air Force 1939–1945,* vol. 1, *The Fight at Odds* (London: HMSO, 1953), 180–181.

40. Middlebrook and Everitt, *The Bomber Command War Diaries,* 239.

41. Quoted in Birrell, *Big Joe McCarthy,* 46.

42. Dorothy Bailey, *A Collection of Wartime Letters by Bill Radcliffe,* quoted in Dave Birrell, *Big Joe McCarthy,* 58.

43. Bailey, *A Collection of Wartime Letters,* quoted in Birrell, *Big Joe McCarthy,* 59.

44. Bailey, *A Collection of Wartime Letters,* quoted in Birrell, *Big Joe McCarthy,* 59.

45. Nell Rodger, interview with J'Lyn Nye, with permission, August 18, 2017, Sault Ste. Marie, ON.

46. Walsh, "Big Joe," 54.

47. Hatch, *Aerodrome of Democracy,* 109.

48. Sir Arthur Harris, *Bomber Offensive* (London: Collins, 1947), 96–97.

49. John Fraser, RCAF Record of Service, 1941–1942, courtesy Shere Fraser.

50. Quoted in "R.C.A.F. Bombardier Took Part in Mohne Dam Raid," *Daily Colonist,* February 1945.

51. Quoted in "R.C.A.F. Bombardier Took Part in Mohne Dam Raid."

52. Quoted in "R.C.A.F. Bombardier Took Part in Mohne Dam Raid."

53. Quoted in "R.C.A.F. Bombardier Took Part in Mohne Dam Raid."

54. Quoted in Gibson, *Enemy Coast Ahead,* 238.

55. Hatch, *Aerodrome of Democracy,* 175–176.

56. Fred Sutherland, interview with author, June 18–19, 2017, Rocky Mountain House, AB.

57. Sutherland, interview.
58. Sutherland, interview.
59. Hatch, *Aerodrome of Democracy*, 36.
60. Sutherland, interview.
61. Sutherland, interview.
62. Sutherland, interview.
63. Sutherland, interview.
64. Sutherland, interview.
65. Sutherland, interview.

CHAPTER FOUR

1. Ken Brown, "Remember the Dambusters," keynote address, 50th Anniversary Commemoration of the Dams Raid, July 24, 1993, Nanton, AB, courtesy Bomber Command Museum of Canada archives.
2. Martin Middlebrook, *The Berlin Raids: RAF Bomber Command Winter 1943–44* (London: Viking, 1988), 25.
3. Brown, "Remember the Dambusters."
4. Brown, "Remember the Dambusters."
5. Quoted in Birrell, *Big Joe McCarthy*, 93.
6. Brown, "Remember the Dambusters."
7. Brown, "Remember the Dambusters."
8. Gibson, *Enemy Coast Ahead*, 243.
9. Sutherland, interview.
10. Gibson, *Enemy Coast Ahead*, 243.
11. George "Johnny" Johnson, *The Last British Dambuster: One Man's Extraordinary Life and the Raid That Changed History* (London: Ebury Press, Random House, 2014), 138.
12. Brown, "Remember the Dambusters."
13. Quoted in Johnson, *The Last British Dambuster*, 132.
14. Quoted in Johnson, *The Last British Dambuster*, 133–34.
15. Quoted in Charles Foster, "Vernon Byers," *Dambustersblog*, October 4, 2014, https://dambustersblog.com/category/vernon-byers/.
16. Dave Birrell, "Dambuster Navigator," *Airforce* 27, no. 1 (Spring 2003): 37–41.
17. Helen Tooth, "Milo School Prints Fine Year Book," *Calgary Herald*, July 24, 1943.
18. Quoted in Birrell, "Dambuster Navigator," 37.
19. Harlo Taerum to Hilda Taerum (telegram), July 26, 1941, Bomber Command Museum of Canada archives.
20. Harlo Taerum, flight log entries, January 22, 26, and February 12, 1942, Bomber Command Museum of Canada archives.

21. Sydney J. King letter to Bomber Command Museum of Canada, December 5, 2002, Bomber Command Museum of Canada archives.

22. Laurie Woods, *Halfway to Hell: Aussie Sky Heroes in Bomber Command* (Brisbaine, AU: Boolarong Press, 2011), 59.

23. Woods, *Halfway to Hell*, 60.

24. King to Bomber Command Museum, December 5, 2002.

25. Gibson, *Enemy Coast Ahead*, 244.

26. Quoted in Sweetman, *The Dambusters Raid*, 62.

27. Harold Roddis, quoted in Vic Hallam, *Lest We Forget: The Dambusters in the Derwent Valley* (Chesterfield, UK: Ladas Printers, 1993), 23.

28. Noël Coward and David Lean, dirs., *In Which We Serve* (London: Two Cities Films, 1942).

29. Sweetman, *The Dambusters Raid*, 62.

30. Sweetman, *The Dambusters Raid*, 53.

31. Albert Garshowitz, letter to family, Hamilton, ON, October 20, 1942, courtesy Hartley Garshowitz.

32. Floyd Wile, RCAF Joint Air Training Plan (BCATP) training record, courtesy Don Lightbody.

33. Albert Garshowitz, letter to family, Hamilton, ON, September 24, 1942, courtesy Hartley Garshowitz.

34. Quoted in Robert Owen, Steve Darlow, Sean Fest, and Arthur Thorning, *Dam Busters: Failed to Return* (Stotfold, UK: Fighting High Publishing, 2013), 32.

35. Quoted in Owen et al., *Dam Busters*, 35.

36. Albert Garshowitz, flight log entry, February 13, 1943, courtesy Hartley Garshowitz.

37. Albert Garshowitz, letter to family, Hamilton, Ontario, April 19, 1943, courtesy Hartley Garshowitz.

38. Gibson, *Enemy Coast Ahead*, 244.

39. Gibson, *Enemy Coast Ahead*, 253.

40. Sweetman, *The Dambusters Raid*, 97.

41. Quoted in Gibson, *Enemy Coast Ahead*, 257.

42. Gibson, *Enemy Coast Ahead*, 259.

43. Foster, Charles, "Alastair Taylor," *Dambustersblog*, October 29, 2014, https://dambustersblog.com/category/alastair-taylor/.

44. Richard Trevor-Roper, quoted in Gibson, *Enemy Coast Ahead*, 259.

45. Sweetman, *The Dambusters Raid*, 66.

46. Gibson, *Enemy Coast Ahead*, 260.

47. Gibson, *Enemy Coast Ahead*, 260.

48. Gibson, *Enemy Coast Ahead*, 267.

49. Harrison, Irene, "The Earnshaws," in *Lure of the Homestead* (Edmonton, AB: Ohaton Community Book Club, 1977), 333.

50. Ken Earnshaw, attestation papers, June 2, 1941, Bomber Command Museum of Canada archives.

51. Ken Earnshaw, letter, May 13, 1942, Bomber Command Museum of Canada archives.

52. Ken Earnshaw, letter, February 9, 1943, Bomber Command Museum of Canada archives.

53. Ken Earnshaw, letter, April 7 and 12, 1943, Bomber Command Museum of Canada archives.

54. Holland, *Dam Busters*, 233.

55. Ken Brown, flight log entry, April 1943, courtesy Brock Brown.

56. Brown, "Remember the Dambusters."

57. Quoted in Charles Foster, "Dams Raid Medical Officer Dies, Aged 97," *Dambustersblog*, January 28, 2016, https://dambustersblog.com/2016/01/28/dams-raid-medical-officer-dies-aged-97/.

CHAPTER FIVE

1. Quoted in CBC Radio, "The Dams Raid."

2. Quoted in Birrell, "Dambuster Navigator," 38.

3. Vincent MacCausland, letter to Mrs. Burns MacCausland, April 17, 1943, Canadian Letters & Images Project, Vancouver Island University, Nanaimo, BC.

4. Charles Foster, "Harvey Glinz," *Dambustersblog*, April 30, 2014, https://dambustersblog.com/?s=glinz.

5. Quoted in Foster, "Harvey Glinz."

6. Quoted in Foster, "Harvey Glinz."

7. *London Gazette*, May 14, 1943.

8. Gibson, *Enemy Coast Ahead*, 270.

9. Hallam, *Lest We Forget*, 24.

10. Gibson, *Enemy Coast Ahead*, 270.

11. Quoted in Hallam, *Lest We Forget*, 24.

12. John Walker, interview with author, June 24, 2017, Calgary, AB.

13. DFC citation of Daniel Revie Walker, February 12, 1942, courtesy Bomber Command Museum of Canada.

14. Quoted in CBC Radio, "The Dams Raid."

15. Quoted in CBC Radio, "The Dams Raid."

16. Quoted in Birrell, *Big Joe McCarthy*, 101.

17. Quoted in Gibson, *Enemy Coast Ahead*, 247.

18. Quoted in W.J. Lawrence, *No. 5 Bomber Group RAF 1939–1945* (London: Faber & Faber, 1951).

19. Quoted in CBC Radio, "The Dams Raid."

20. Quoted in Birrell, *Big Joe McCarthy*, 106.
21. Quoted in Birrell, *Big Joe McCarthy*, 106.
22. "Lewis J. Burpee, Winner of D.F.M. Is Now Missing," *Ottawa Evening Citizen*, May 18, 1943.
23. Charles Foster, "Lewis Burpee," *Dambustersblog*, May 25, 2015, https://dambustersblog.com/2015/05/25/dambuster-of-the-day-no-106-lewis-burpee/.
24. Lewis Burpee, flight log entry, courtesy Lewis J. Burpee Jr.
25. Lillian Burpee to Lewis and Lilian Burpee (parents), February 2, 1943, courtesy Lewis Burpee Jr.
26. Gibson, *Enemy Coast Ahead*, 275.
27. Gibson, *Enemy Coast Ahead*, 271.
28. Quoted in CBC Radio, "The Dams Raid."
29. Quoted in Holland, *Dam Busters*, 261.
30. Foster, "Dams Raid Medical Officer Dies."
31. Quoted in Birrell, *Big Joe McCarthy*, 106–107.
32. Quoted in Birrell, *Big Joe McCarthy*, 107.
33. Gibson, *Enemy Coast Ahead*, 276.
34. John Fraser to Doris Fraser, April 1943, courtesy Shere Fraser.
35. Quoted in Sweetman, *The Dambusters Raid*, 69.

CHAPTER SIX

1. Quoted in "Harry Humphries: The Shortage of Time Gave Him a Formidable Task to Be Ready to Attack the Ruhr Dams," *Telegraph*, February 21, 2008.
2. Quoted in Holland, *Dam Busters*, 282.
3. Quoted in Sweetman, *The Dambusters Raid*, 103.
4. Stephen Flower, *Barnes Wallis' Bombs* (Chalford, UK: Amberley Publishing, 2002), 49.
5. Quoted in CBC Radio, "The Dams Raid."
6. Charles Foster, "Neville Whitaker," *Dambustersblog*, November 22, 2014, https://dambustersblog.com/2014/11/22/dambuster-of-the-day-no-82-neville-whitaker/.
7. Quoted in CBC Radio, "The Dams Raid."
8. Quoted in Flower, *Barnes Wallis' Bombs*, 46.
9. Quoted in Sweetman, *The Dambusters Raid*, 100.
10. Quoted in Flower, *Barnes Wallis' Bombs*, 50.
11. Sutherland, interview.
12. Quoted in Birrell, *Big Joe McCarthy*, 108.
13. Quoted in Flower, *Barnes Wallis' Bombs*, 50.

14. Quoted in Sweetman, *The Dambusters Raid*, 102.

15. Max Arthur, *Dambusters: A Landmark Oral History* (London: Virgin Books, 2009), 154–155.

16. Johnson, *The Last British Dambuster*, 161.

17. Quoted in Charles Foster, "Francis Garbas," *Dambustersblog*, November 20, 2013, https://dambustersblog.com/2013/11/20/dambuster-of-the-day-no-55-francis-garbas/.

18. Ellin Bessner, *Double Threat: Canadian Jews, the Military, and World War II* (Toronto: New Jewish Press, 2018), 82.

19. Quoted in Gibson, *Enemy Coast Ahead*, 280.

20. Gibson, *Enemy Coast Ahead*, 279.

21. Quoted in CBC Radio, "The Dams Raid."

22. Quoted in Johnson, *The Last British Dambuster*, 162.

23. Grant McDonald, in Stan Lancaster, ed., *Critical Moments: Profiles of Members of the Greater Vancouver Branch of the Aircrew Association* (Vancouver, BC: Aircrew Association, 1989), 318.

24. Brown, "Remember the Dambusters."

CHAPTER SEVEN

1. Holland, *Dam Busters*, 297.

2. Sweetman, *The Dambusters Raid*, 98.

3. Quoted in Sweetman, *The Dambusters Raid*, 125.

4. Quoted in Sweetman, *The Dambusters Raid*, 125.

5. Helmuth Euler, *The Dams Raid Through the Lens* (London: Battle of Britain International, 2001), 92.

6. Quoted in Charles Foster, "Les Munro" *Dambustersblog*, August 4, 2015, https://dambustersblog.com/2015/08/04/sqn-ldr-les-munro-dso-dfc/.

7. Quoted in Foster, "Les Munro."

8. Sweetman, *The Dambusters Raid*, 126.

9. Quoted in Sweetman, *The Dambusters Raid*, 127.

10. Quoted in Charles Foster, "Norman Barlow," *Dambustersblog*, February 21, 2014, https://dambustersblog.com/2014/02/21/dambuster-of-the-day-no-64-norman-barlow/.

11. Quoted in Birrell, "Dambuster Navigator," 38.

12. Quoted in Gibson, *Enemy Coast Ahead*, 283.

13. Quoted in Flower, *Barnes Wallis' Bombs*, 54.

14. Holland, *Dam Busters*, 308.

15. Quoted in Charles Foster, *Breaking the Dams: The Story of Dambuster David Maltby and His Crew* (Barnsley, UK: Pen and Sword Aviation, 2008), 138.

16. Foster, *Breaking the Dams*, 109.
17. Sutherland, interview.
18. Quoted in Euler, *The Dams Raid Through the Lens*, 55.
19. Alan W. Cooper, *The Men Who Breached the Dams* (London: William Kimber & Co., 1982), 86–87.
20. Brown, "Remember the Dambusters."
21. Holland, *Dam Busters*, 200.
22. Sweetman, *The Dambusters Raid*, 108.
23. Brown, "Remember the Dambusters."
24. Quoted in Euler, *The Dams Raid Through the Lens*, 106.
25. Quoted in Euler, *The Dams Raid Through the Lens*, 106.
26. Brown, "Remember the Dambusters."
27. Gibson, *Enemy Coast Ahead*, 286.
28. Quoted in CBC Radio, "The Dams Raid."
29. Gibson, *Enemy Coast Ahead*, 287.
30. Gibson, *Enemy Coast Ahead*, 287.
31. Quoted in Euler, *The Dams Raid Through the Lens*, 67.
32. Quoted in Gibson, *Enemy Coast Ahead*, 289.
33. Quoted in Euler, *The Dams Raid Through the Lens*, 67.
34. Quoted in CBC Radio, "The Dams Raid."
35. Flower, *Barnes Wallis' Bombs*, 55.
36. Flower, *Barnes Wallis' Bombs*, 55.
37. Quoted in CBC Radio, "The Dams Raid."
38. Quoted in Gibson, *Enemy Coast Ahead*, 291.
39. Quoted in CBC Radio, "The Dams Raid."
40. Quoted in Birrell, *Big Joe McCarthy*, 122.
41. Quoted in Birrell, *Big Joe McCarthy*, 122.
42. Quoted in Birrell, *Big Joe McCarthy*, 122–123.
43. Johnson, *The Last British Dambuster*, 170–171.
44. Johnson, *The Last British Dambuster*, 171.
45. Quoted in Birrell, *Big Joe McCarthy*, 124–125.
46. Brown, "Remember the Dambusters."
47. Euler, *The Dams Raid Through the Lens*, 68.
48. Quoted in Foster, *Breaking the Dams*, 145.
49. Foster, *Breaking the Dams*, 145.
50. Quoted in Euler, *The Dams Raid Through the Lens*, 68.
51. Quoted in CBC Radio, "The Dams Raid."
52. Quoted in Sweetman, *The Dambusters Raid*, 42, 116.
53. Quoted in Gibson, *Enemy Coast Ahead*, 294.
54. Quoted in CBC Radio, "The Dams Raid."
55. Gibson, *Enemy Coast Ahead*, 295.
56. Sutherland, interview.

57. Fred Sutherland, email correspondence with author, January 23, 2018.

58. Sutherland, email correspondence.

59. Quoted in CBC Radio, "The Dams Raid."

60. Quoted in Sweetman, *The Dambusters Raid*, 119.

61. Quoted in CBC Radio, "The Dams Raid."

CHAPTER EIGHT

1. Don MacLean, flight log entry, May 16–17, 1943, courtesy MacLean family.

2. Quoted in Birrell, *Big Joe McCarthy*, 126.

3. Johnson, *The Last British Dambusters*, 168.

4. Quoted in CBC Radio, "The Dams Raid."

5. Quoted in CBC Radio, "The Dams Raid."

6. Quoted in CBC Radio, "The Dams Raid."

7. Quoted in Birrell, *Big Joe McCarthy*, 128-129.

8. Quoted in CBC Radio, "The Dams Raid."

9. Quoted in Birrell, *Big Joe McCarthy*, 132.

10. MacLean flight log entry, May 16–17, 1943.

11. Jim and Bill MacLean, interviews.

12. Brown, "Remember the Dambusters."

13. Quoted in Brown, "Remember the Dambusters."

14. Brown, "Remember the Dambusters."

15. Sweetman, *The Dambusters Raid*, 168.

16. Brickhill, *The Dam Busters*, 103.

17. Rowley, *Dambusters*, 38.

18. Quoted in Sweetman, *The Dambusters Raid*, 169.

19. Quoted in Sweetman, *The Dambusters Raid*, 171.

20. Quoted in Johnson, *The Last British Dambuster*, 188–89.

21. Quoted in Frank C. Williams, "The Raid on the Dams. Part Three: Back Home," *Airforce Magazine* 9, no. 3 (October-November-December 1985): 37.

22. Quoted in Holland, *Dam Busters*, 358.

23. Quoted in Williams, "The Raid on the Dams," 37.

24. Quoted in Williams, "The Raid on the Dams," 37.

25. CBC Radio, "The Dams Raid."

26. Quoted in CBC Radio, "The Dams Raid."

27. Quoted in Birrell, "Dambuster Navigator," 39.

28. Quoted in Sweetman, *The Dambusters Raid*, 168.

29. Quoted in Sweetman, *The Dambusters Raid*, 168.

30. Quoted in Euler, *The Dams Raid Through the Lens*, 115.

31. Quoted in Euler, *The Dams Raid Through the Lens*, 115.

32. Canadian Press, "Great Ruhr Dams Smashed, Berlin Hit and Rome Seaport Levelled in Raids," *Ottawa Evening Journal*, May 17, 1943.
33. Quoted in Holland, *Dam Busters*, 356.
34. Sweetman, *The Dambusters Raid*, 151.
35. Sweetman, *The Dambusters Raid*, 152.
36. Sweetman, *The Dambusters Raid*, 166.
37. Euler, *The Dams Raid Through the Lens*, 174.
38. L.J.H. Hoesen, quoted in Sweetman, *The Dambusters Raid*, 152.
39. Darja Michajlowna, quoted in Euler, *The Dams Raid Through the Lens*, 128.
40. Karl-Heinz Dohle quoted in Euler, *The Dams Raid Through the Lens*, 119.
41. Sweetman, *The Dambusters Raid*, 156.
42. Brickhill, *The Dam Busters*, 105.
43. Sweetman, *The Dambusters Raid*, 157.
44. Dohle, quoted in Euler, *The Dams Raid Through the Lens*, 119.
45. Albert Speer, *Spandau: The Secret Diaries* (London: Macmillan, 1976).
46. Barnes Wallis, "A Note on a Method of Attacking the Axis Powers," Barnes Wallis Papers.
47. Wallis, "A Note on a Method of Attacking the Axis Powers."
48. Quoted in Euler, *The Dams Raid Through the Lens*, 193.
49. General Sir Harold Alexander, quoted in Winston S. Churchill, *The Second World War: The Hinge of Fate* (Boston: Houghton Mifflin, 1950), 780.
50. Winston Churchill, BBC broadcast, May 19, 1943.
51. Johnson, *The Last British Dambuster*, 189.
52. Guy Gibson to Mary Earnshaw, May 17, 1943, courtesy Bomber Command Museum of Canada.
53. Harlo Taerum to family, May 1943, courtesy Bomber Command Museum of Canada.
54. Vi Hulbert, *Reflections of a Parson's Wife* (pamphlet, 1943), 14.
55. Quoted in Brickhill, *The Dam Busters*, 107.
56. Quoted in Barnes Wallis Papers.
57. Harlo Taerum to family, May 1943, courtesy Bomber Command Museum of Canada.
58. Barnes Wallis Papers.
59. Quoted in CBC Radio, "The Dams Raid."
60. Marilyn McDowell, interview with author, May 24, 2018, Burlington, ON.

CHAPTER NINE

1. Quoted in Joan May, "Modest 'Dam Buster' Hero Gets Enthusiastic Welcome," *Calgary Herald*, September 13, 1943.
2. Quoted in May, "Modest 'Dam Buster.'"

3. Quoted in May, "Modest 'Dam Buster.'"

4. Quoted in interview with John Burton, published by US Office of War Information, Washington, DC, November 4, 1943.

5. Quoted in May, "Modest 'Dam Buster.'"

6. "Terry Got Dam Busters to the Job: WC Gibson Tells His Mother Here," *Calgary Herald*, September 13, 1943.

7. Hilda Taerum, greetings to Gibson during visit to No. 3 Service Flying Training School, Calgary, September 11, 1943, courtesy Bomber Command Museum of Canada.

8. Hilda Taerum, greetings.

9. Birrell, "Dambuster Navigator," 39.

10. Canadian Pacific telegraph to Hilda Taerum from RCAF casualties officer, September 17, 1943.

11. Birrell, "Dambuster Navigator," 41.

12. Quoted in "Dam Buster Gibson Pays Tribute to Lost Navigator Taerum," Canadian Press, September 21, 1943.

13. Middlebrook and Everitt, *The Bomber Command War Diaries,* 409.

14. Middlebrook and Everitt, *The Bomber Command War Diaries*, 408–409.

15. Jimmy Watson, quoted in Brickhill, *The Dam Busters*, 111.

16. Foster, *Breaking the Dams*, 150.

17. RAF Coltishall Operations Record Book, AIR 28/168.

18. Quoted in Brickhill, *The Dam Busters*, 118.

19. Quoted in Rowley, *Dambusters*, 82.

20. Sutherland, interview.

21. Sutherland, interview.

22. Quoted in Brickhill, *The Dam Busters*, 121.

23. Quoted in Sutherland, interview.

24. Rowley, *Dambusters,* 82.

25. Sutherland, interview.

26. Quoted in Brickhill, *The Dam Busters*, 123.

27. Quoted in Brickhill, *The Dam Busters*, 124.

28. Foster, *Breaking the Dams*, 170.

29. Rowley, *Dambusters,* 83.

30. Sutherland, interview.

31. Quoted in Euler, *The Dams Raid Through the Lens*, 194.

32. Euler, *The Dams Raid Through the Lens*, 184.

33. Euler, *The Dams Raid Through the Lens*, 184.

34. *Westfälische Landeszeitung—Rote Erde*, official press release, May 19, 1943.

35. Quoted in Elinor Florence, "The Last Canadian Dambuster," *Elinor Florence*, July 29, 2015, with permission, http://elinorflorence.com/blog/topic/12317.

36. Sutherland, interview.

CHAPTER TEN

1. Steve Darlow, "On the Altar of Freedom," in Owen et al., *Dam Busters: Failed to Return*, 29.

2. Quoted in Robert Owen, "I think so, stand by," in Owen et al., *Dam Busters: Failed to Return*, 75.

3. Quoted in Department of National Defence, Estates Branch questionnaire, March 3, 1944, 3, courtesy Bomber Command Museum of Canada archives.

4. Department of National Defence questionnaire, 4.

5. Grave Confirmation Unit No. 39 report, 1947, Bomber Command Museum of Canada archives.

6. Quoted in Brickhill, *The Dam Busters*, 130.

7. Johnson, *The Last British Dambuster*, 213.

8. Russell Braddon, *Leonard Cheshire VC* (London: Evans Brothers, 1954), 115.

9. Quoted in T. Bennett, "Operation Taxable," *FlyPast* (November 1984): 58.

10. R.V. Jones, *Most Secret War: British Scientific Intelligence 1939–1945* (London: Hamish Hamilton, 1978), 513.

11. Quoted in Bennett, "Operation Taxable," 58.

12. Bennett, "Operation Taxable," 59.

13. Quoted in Bennett, "Operation Taxable," 61.

14. Quoted in Bennett, "Operation Taxable," 62.

15. Quoted in Bennett, "Operation Taxable," 62.

16. Quoted in Bennett, "Operation Taxable," 62.

17. Quoted in Bennett, "Operation Taxable," 62.

18. Brickhill, *The Dam Busters*, 198.

19. Quoted in Birrell, *Big Joe McCarthy*, 214.

20. Quoted in Brickhill, *The Dam Busters*, 201.

21. Vera Lynn, *We'll Meet Again: A Personal & Social History of World War Two* (London: Sidgwick & Jackson, 1989), 178.

22. Birrell, *Big Joe McCarthy*, 231.

23. Quoted in Brickhill, *The Dam Busters*, 210.

24. Johnson, *The Last British Dambuster*, 218.

25. Quoted in Chaz Bowyer, *Bomber Barons* (Barnsley, UK: Leo Cooper, 2001), 159.

26. Harry Humphries, *Living with Heroes: The Dam Busters* (Banham, UK: Erskine Press, 2003), 91.

27. Middlebrook and Everitt, *The Bomber Command War Diaries*, 568.

28. Johnny Fauquier interview, National Air Force Museum of Canada archives, Trenton, ON.

29. Quoted in Holland, *Dam Busters*, 359.
30. Johnson, *The Last British Dambuster*, 193.
31. Quoted in Sweetman, *The Dambusters Raid*, 69.
32. Gibson, *Enemy Coast Ahead*, 300.
33. Gibson, *Enemy Coast Ahead*, 300.

CHAPTER ELEVEN

1. Foster, *Breaking the Dams*, 185.
2. *The London Gazette* (3rd supplement), November 30, 1943, 5284.
3. AIR files 20/4821, National Archives, Kew, London.
4. Quoted in Sir Robert Thompson, *Make for the Hills: Memories of Far Eastern Wars* (Barnsley, UK: Pen & Sword Aviation, 1989), 36.
5. Dr. D.R. Pye (Provost of University College, Press and Censorship Bureau of the Ministry of Information), quoted in Euler, *The Dams Raid Through the Lens*, 210.
6. Jonathan Falconer, *Filming the Dam Busters* (Thrupp, UK: Sutton Publishing, 2005), 41.
7. Brickhill, *The Dam Busters*, 11.
8. W.A. Whittaker (ABPC) to Hilda Taerum, January 13, 1954, courtesy Bomber Command Museum of Canada
9. Jonathan Falconer, *The Dam Busters: Breaking the Great Dams of Western Germany, 16–17 May 1943* (Thrupp, UK: Sutton Publishing, 2003), 211.
10. Falconer, *Filming the Dam Busters*, 42.
11. Flower, *Barnes Wallis' Bombs*, 340.
12. Falconer, *Filming the Dam Busters*, 70–71.
13. Quoted in Falconer, *Filming the Dam Busters*, 93.
14. Falconer, *Filming the Dam Busters*, 117.
15. Quoted in Falconer, *Filming the Dam Busters*, 99–100.
16. Quoted in Flower, *Barnes Wallis' Bombs*, 339.
17. Brickhill, *The Dam Busters*, 37.
18. Falconer, *Filming the Dam Busters*, 128.
19. Falconer, *Filming the Dam Busters*, 135.
20. Falconer, *Filming the Dam Busters*, 117.
21. Falconer, *Filming the Dam Busters*, 339.
22. Michael Anderson, dir., *The Dam Busters*, Associated British Picture Corporation, 1955, StudioCanal, 2006), DVD.
23. Falconer, *Filming the Dam Busters*, 41.
24. John Walker, interview with author, June 24, 2017, Calgary, AB.
25. Foster, *Breaking the Dams*, 10.

26. Foster, *Breaking the Dams*, 198.

27. Falconer, *Filming the Dam Busters*, 82.

28. Birrell, *FM159, The Lucky Lancaster* (Nanton, AB: Bomber Command Museum of Canada, 2015), 51.

29. Quoted by Shirley Armstrong, interview with author, June 23, 2017, Nanton, AB.

30. Quoted in *On the Wings of a Lancaster* (Nanton Lancaster Society, 1966), video.

31. Birrell, *FM159*, 57.

32. Quoted in Armstrong, interview.

33. Quoted in Armstrong, interview.

34. Armstrong, interview.

35. Herb Johnson, "Bomber Needs Community Support," *Nanton News*, September 26, 1985.

36. Dan Fox, interview with author, June 23, 2017, Nanton, AB.

37. Fox, interview.

38. Ian Johnson, "Hamilton's Bomber Marks 25 Years Back in the Sky," CBC News, September 24, 2013.

39. Birrell, *FM159*, 88.

40. "Mynarski Lancaster over Nanton," Nanton Lancaster Society newsletter (Fall/Winter 1989).

41. Dave Birrell, correspondence with author, December 24, 2017, Nanton, AB.

42. Dave Birrell, *Baz: The Biography of Ian Bazalgette VC* (Nanton, AB: Bomber Command Museum of Canada, 2014), 141.

43. Birrell, correspondence with author.

44. Quoted in Birrell, *Baz*, 192.

45. "P/O Torger Taerum's DFC Now in NLS Air Museum," Nanton Lancaster Society newsletter (Spring/Summer 1993).

46. Quoted in "Remembering the Dambusters," video of 50th anniversary commemoration of the dams raid, July 17, 1993, Nanton, AB.

47. Fox, interview.

48. Brown, "Remember the Dambusters."

49. Brock Brown, "Who is Ken Brown? A Tribute by Brock Brown," December 23, 2003, with permission.

50. Joseph M. Kirman, "Excerpts from the January 1993 Senate Report: The Valour and the Horror," *Canadian Social Studies* (Winter 1994): 62–63.

51. Brock Brown, interview with author, June 19, 2017, Red Deer, AB.

52. Brown, "Remember the Dambusters."

53. Brock Brown, interview.

54. Dan Fox, quoted in "Remembering the Dambusters."

55. Quoted in "Remembering the Dambusters."

56. Quoted by John Walker, interview.

57. Walker, interview.
58. Walker, interview.
59. Cooper, *The Men Who Breached the Dams*, 155.
60. Walker, interview.
61. Walker, interview.
62. "Lancaster FM159, Merlin Engine Runs First Time in Forty-five Years," Nanton Lancaster Society newsletter (Fall/Winter 2005).
63. Rob Pedersen, interview with author, June 20, 2017, Nanton, AB.

CHAPTER TWELVE

1. Jim MacLean, interview.
2. Lynn, *We'll Meet Again*, 74.
3. Caroline Davies, "How the Luftwaffe Bombed the Palace, in the Queen Mother's Own Words," *Guardian*, September 13, 2009.
4. Jim MacLean, interview.
5. Bill MacLean, interview.
6. Euler, *The Dams Raid Through the Lens*, 103.
7. Nell Rodger and Carolyn Rodger, interview with J'Lyn Nye, August 18, 2017, Sault Ste. Marie, ON.
8. Nell Rodger, interview.
9. Andrea Rodger, correspondence with author, August 14, 2017, Whitehorse, YT.
10. Nell Rodger, interview.
11. Sheila Rodger, quoted in author correspondence with Andrea Rodger, August 14, 2017, Whitehorse, YT.
12. Andrea Rodger, correspondence.
13. Tamara Stecyk, "The Dambusters Raid," *WestJet* magazine, July 2003, 34.
14. Sean Feast, "Mother's Love—Tony Burcher, DFM and John Fraser," in Owen et al., *Dam Busters: Failed to Return*, 61.
15. Alex Bateman, letters to the editor, *Toronto Sun*, December 5, 1993.
16. Shere Fraser, interview with author, January 28, 2018, Blaine, WA.
17. John Lowe, correspondence with author, February 22, 2018, Vancouver, BC.
18. Quoted in Stecyk, "The Dambusters Raid."
19. David Paul, "Widow Fights for the Return of Dambuster Husband's Log Book," *International Express*, July 15, 2003.
20. Ken Earnshaw to Joseph and Janet Earnshaw, January 22, 1943, courtesy Jim Heather.
21. Alex Bateman to Lillian Heather, January 23, 2001, courtesy Jim Heather.
22. Jim Heather, interview with author, June 21, 2017, Nanton, AB.

23. Heather interview.
24. Albert Garshowitz, letter to Samuel and Sarah Garshowitz, May 12, 1943, courtesy Hartley Garshowitz.
25. Garshowitz to Garshowitz.
26. Hartley Garshowitz, interview with author, November 26, 2017, Toronto, ON.
27. Rosaline Land to Sarah Garshowitz, June 21, 1943, courtesy Hartley Garshowitz.
28. Land to Garshowitz.
29. Heather, interview.
30. Herbert Scholl, quoted in Euler, *The Dams Raid Through the Lens,* 106.
31. Gordon Brady, recommendation for commission, Library and Archives Canada.
32. H.F. Davidson, RCAF Chaplain Services, letter to Lewis and Lilian Burpee, June 12, 1943, courtesy Lewis Burpee Jr.
33. Lewis Burpee Jr., interview with author, January 11, 2018, Ottawa, ON.
34. Burpee Jr., interview.
35. Burpee Jr., interview.
36. Burpee Jr., interview.
37. Rowley, *Dambusters,* 83.
38. Sutherland, interview.
39. Quoted in Euler, *The Dams Raid Through the Lens,* 115.
40. David Bashow, "Bomber Command: A Blunt Instrument of War," speech presented to 20th anniversary event at Bomber Command Museum of Canada, August 2006, Nanton, AB.
41. Joe McCarthy, interview, conducted by National Air Force Museum of Canada, Trenton, ON, c. 1990s.
42. Quoted in Hutchison, "War Made the Difference!"

PHOTOGRAPH CREDITS

PAGE 5

Frank Garbas and Albert Garshowitz: courtesy Hartley Garshowitz; Ken and Mary Earnshaw: courtesy Jim Heather; Vincent MacCausland: courtesy Charles Foster, dambustersblog.com; Gibson crew © Imperial War Museum, CH 018005; Robert Urquhart: RAF Benevolent Fund.

PAGE 6

Canadian survivors © Imperial War Museum, CH 9935; Debrief group © Imperial War Museum, CH 009683; Les Knight with King: ww2images.com, A12047Q.

PAGE 7

Canadian survivors © Imperial War Museum, CH 9935; Joe McCarthy with Queen: courtesy Joe McCarthy Jr.; Crash site: ww2images.com, Astell Crash 1; Floyd Wile: courtesy Don Lightbody.

PAGE 8

Möhne Dam before raid: ww2images.com, Möhne Dam 11; Eder Dam before raid: ww2images.com, Eder Dam 3; Möhne breached © Imperial War Museum, HU 004594; Möhne aerial: ww2images.com, A12061Q; Flood damage to railway and houses: L.T. Wright file, courtesy Bomber Command Museum of Canada.

SECOND PHOTO SECTION

PAGE 1

Newspaper background: courtesy Lewis Burpee Jr.; Gibson crew © Imperial War Museum, TR 1127; McCarthy crew © Imperial War Museum, TR 1128; Award recipients at Buckingham Palace: ww2images.com.

PAGE 2

Unexploded Upkeep © Imperial War Museum; Möhne Dam reconstruction: ww2images.com; Leonard Cheshire © Imperial War Museum, CH 12667; Gibson autographs dam photo: ww2images.com, A02884B.

PAGE 3

Gibson at Calgary training station: courtesy Bomber Command Museum of Canada; Shannon crew © Imperial War Museum, CH 017504.

PAGE 4
Paul Brickhill: ww2images.com; Low-flying Lancasters: courtesy Clive
Rowley; Bomb-aiming device: StudioCanal; Foliage in landing gear:
StudioCanal; Dancers backstage: StudioCanal.

PAGE 5
Dam Busters poster: StudioCanal; Redgrave and Todd: StudioCanal; Movie
premier photos: courtesy Jim and Bill MacLean.

PAGE 6
Howie Armstrong, George White, and Fred Garratt; Bob Evans in Lanc nose;
transporting Lancaster across tracks: courtesy Bomber Command Museum of
Canada.

PAGE 7
Lancaster maintenance crew; transporting Lancaster across river: courtesy
Bomber Command Museum of Canada.

PAGE 8
Shere Fraser with photo: PA-Sally Wardle/Canadian Press; Hartley
Garshowitz: courtesy Hartley Garshowitz; Lewis Burpee Jr.: courtesy Burpee
family; Dam Buster relatives with Lancaster: courtesy Bomber Command
Museum of Canada.

INDEX

Page numbers in italic followed by *n* refer to footnotes.